NEW STUDIES IN BIBLICAL THEOLOGY 51

CANON, COVENANT AND CHRISTOLOGY

T0334822

NEW STUDIES IN BIBLICAL THEOLOGY 51

Series editor: D. A. Carson

CANON, COVENANT AND CHRISTOLOGY

Rethinking Jesus and the Scriptures of Israel

Matthew Barrett

APOLLOS

Academic
An imprint of InterVarsity Press
Downers Grove, Illinois

APOLLOS (an imprint of Inter-Varsity Press, England)
36 Causton Street, London SW1P 4ST, England
Website: www.ivpbooks.com
Email: ivp@ivpbooks.com

InterVarsity Press, USA
P.O. Box 1400, Downers Grove, IL 60515, USA
Website: www.ivpress.com
Email: email@ivpress.com

Inter-Varsity Press, England, publishes Christian books that are true to the Bible and
that communicate the gospel, develop discipleship and strengthen the church for its
mission in the world.

IVP originated within the Inter-Varsity Fellowship, now the Universities and Colleges
Christian Fellowship, a student movement connecting Christian Unions in universities and
colleges throughout Great Britain, and a member movement of the International Fellowship
of Evangelical Students. That historic association is maintained, and all senior IVP staff and
committee members subscribe to the UCCF Basis of Faith. Website: www.uccf.org.uk.

InterVarsity Press®, USA, is the book-publishing division of InterVarsity Christian Fellowship/
USA® and a member movement of the International Fellowship of Evangelical Students.
Website: www.intervarsity.org.

For copyright acknowledgments, see p. xviii.

First published 2020

Set in 9.85/13.75pt Minion Pro and Gill Sans Nova (OTF)
Typeset in Great Britain by CRB Associates, Potterhanworth, Lincolnshire
Printed and bound in Great Britain by Ashford Colour Press Ltd, Gosport, Hampshire

UK ISBN: 978-1-78359-544-0 (print)
UK ISBN: 978-1-78359-545-7 (digital)

US ISBN: 978-0-8308-2929-3 (print)
US ISBN: 978-0-8308-3187-6 (digital)

British Library Cataloguing-in-Publication Data
A catalogue record for this book is available from the British Library.

Library of Congress Cataloging-in-Publication Data
A catalog record for this book is available from the Library of Congress.

To Lorelei
Look to Jesus. In him all God's promises come true.
'Of this man's offspring God has brought to Israel
a Saviour, Jesus, as he promised.'
(Acts 13:23)

Contents

Series preface

New Studies in Biblical Theology is a series of monographs that address key issues in the discipline of biblical theology. Contributions to the series focus on one or more of three areas: (1) the nature and status of biblical theology, including its relations with other disciplines (e.g. historical theology, exegesis, systematic theology, historical criticism, narrative theology); (2) the articulation and exposition of the structure of thought of a particular biblical writer or corpus; and (3) the delineation of a biblical theme across all or part of the biblical corpora.

Above all, these monographs are creative attempts to help thinking Christians understand their Bibles better. The series aims simultaneously to instruct and to edify, to interact with the current literature and to point the way ahead. In God's universe, mind and heart should not be divorced: in this series we will try not to separate what God has joined together. While the notes interact with the best of scholarly literature, the text is uncluttered with untransliterated Greek and Hebrew, and tries to avoid too much technical jargon. The volumes are written within the framework of confessional evangelicalism, but there is always an attempt at thoughtful engagement with the sweep of the relevant literature.

'Biblical theology' is not an expression with a widely agreed meaning. Among evangelicals it presupposes that God himself stands behind all of Scripture (however diverse the style and content of the individual human authors), making it possible to trace the trajectories and developments within the canon. That is why theologians of a more liberal persuasion are convinced that 'biblical theology' in that sense is impossible: one may usefully speak of 'biblical theology' only to refer to descriptive analysis of biblical books and corpora that are too disparate to allow for canonical trajectories and canonical theology. In a wide-ranging discussion Matthew Barrett explores this field from the perspective of the Gospels, deploying interesting and stimulating insight that will certainly be picked up and developed by many pastors and theologians. Jesus himself ties together the old and new covenants. He *fulfils* the Scriptures, but effectively does so only by being obedient to them. The dynamic casts fresh light not only on Christ, but on the Scriptures themselves.

D. A. Carson
Trinity Evangelical Divinity School

Author's preface

For many years now I have benefited from the scholarship of Don Carson. One thing I appreciate about him is his commitment to integrate biblical theology and systematic theology. Rather than divorcing these two disciplines from each other, Don has demonstrated how integral they are to each other. What God has joined together, let no one separate. The church and academy need both, and Don has left an example to younger scholars like me by writing on both and showing how mutually dependent they are on each other. So I am grateful to Don for his invitation to contribute to the NSBT series. There are also few as experienced as him in the continuing defence of an evangelical doctrine of Scripture. While this book is a positive presentation rather than a polemical one, I do hope it will fortify evangelicals and remind them that their doctrine of Scripture depends not on a few proof texts but is far more organic, grounded as it is in the character of God, his covenantal speech and Christological fulfilment. Biblical theology is crucial to a right understanding of Scripture's inspiration and unity.

I am also grateful to the leadership at Midwestern Baptist Theological Seminary, Jason Allen, Jason Duesing and Charles Smith, for their continuing support of my scholarship. It is a joy to teach at a seminary that values theology in the classroom but also ensures its professors have time to write theology. This too serves the church. I have also had inspiring conversations with many other colleagues as we have marvelled at the divine author's intent across redemptive history to give us a unified canon. I must thank Samuel Bierg for his initial digging into sources for the bibliography and excitement on the topic itself, and I am so grateful for Joseph Lanier, who hunted down countless journal articles for the bibliography. Joseph, Timothy Gatewood, Ronni Kurtz and Jenn Foster all pitched in to arrest pesty typos and create the indices. Thank you.

I am also thankful to the team at IVP who worked so hard to make sure this book looks its best. Philip Duce applied a fine editorial eye to the flow and logic of my argument, making sure it was sound and persuasive. Eldo Barkhuizen did a superb job editing the manuscript, catching the most minute mistakes.

As always, I am indebted to my wife, Elizabeth, who has the hardest job of all: homeschooling our four children. I do not know how she does it, but I do know our kids will be in her debt for the time and love she puts into her craft. Alongside her responsibilities, she picked me up from time to time. This book was a difficult one to write, an intense labour. Yet she was patient, at times encouraging me not to give up but to press on because too few Christians know what their Saviour thinks about the Old Testament.

May this book be an exercise in *credo ut intelligam* (I believe in order to understand).

Matthew Barrett

Abbreviations

JTC	*Journal for Theology and the Church*
JTI	*Journal of Theological Interpretation*
JTS	*Journal of Theological Studies*
km	kilometres
LCC	Library of Christian Classics
m.	Mishnah
NAC	New American Commentary
NASB	New American Standard Bible
NDBT	*New Dictionary of Biblical Theology*, ed. T. Desmond Alexander and Brian S. Rosner, Downers Grove: InterVarsity Press, 2000
Ned.	*Nedarim*
NICNT	New International Commentary on the New Testament
NICOT	New International Commentary on the Old Testament
NIGTC	New International Greek Testament Commentary
NIV	New International Version
NIVAC	New International Version Application Commentary
NovT	*Novum Testamentum*
n.p.	no publisher
NSBT	New Studies in Biblical Theology
NSD	New Studies in Dogmatics
NT	New Testament
NTS	*New Testament Studies*
OT	Old Testament
PNTC	Pillar New Testament Commentary
Presb	*Presbyterion*
ProEccl	*Pro Ecclesia*
SBJT	*Southern Baptist Journal of Theology*
SJT	*Scottish Journal of Theology*
SPB	Studia post-biblica
SPT	Studies in Philosophical Theology
STI	Studies in Theological Interpretation
Them	*Themelios*
ThTo	*Theology Today*
TNTC	Tyndale New Testament Commentaries
TynBul	*Tyndale Bulletin*
VT	*Vetus Testamentum*
WBC	Word Biblical Commentary

Abbreviations

WTJ	*Westminster Theological Journal*
WUNT	Wissenschaftliche Untersuchungen zum Neuen Testament
ZAW	*Zeitschrift für die alttestamentliche Wissenschaft*
ZECNT	Zondervan Exegetical Commentary on the New Testament

Copyright acknowledgments

Introduction: reorienting the hermeneutical approach to Jesus and the Scriptures of Israel

Evangelicals are those who base their identity, at least in part, on the inspiration of Scripture.[1] Central to an evangelical confession is the belief that Scripture, not in part but in whole, is breathed out by God.[2] Its God-breathed nature does not merely apply to Scripture's main message but characterizes its very words, and not just some words but all words; for the evangelical inspiration is *verbal* and *plenary*. That is a remarkable affirmation since Scripture consists not of one, but sixty-six books written over the course of two testaments (covenants) and thousands of years; the plural *Scriptures* may be more appropriate in that sense.

Nevertheless, although there are a variety of human authors, each of whom makes a unique contribution to the whole canon, Scripture has one divine author. While it is fitting to discuss what Moses, David, John or Paul said, in the final analysis the evangelical believes he or she can refer to what God himself has said in and through any author or book of the Bible. In short, what the human author says, God says. That is because the Scriptures originate from God, are breathed out by God and are his saving speech to a world under sin's curse. On the basis of inspiration, the evangelical concludes that the text of Scripture is authoritative, inerrant and sufficient for faith and practice.

The implications of scriptural inspiration for the discipline of biblical theology are legion.[3] To begin with, if all Scripture is breathed out by God, then Scripture cannot be an anthology of human literature, nor can it be a

---

[1] I say 'in part' because the belief in inspiration is necessary but not sufficient to qualify one as an evangelical. Other key doctrinal commitments (e.g. the cross as an atonement) are necessary as well. Nevertheless, a commitment to the inspiration and authority of Scripture is fundamental to being an evangelical; some might even say it is one of evangelicalism's most important qualities.

[2] See 2 Tim. 3:16–17. All Scripture is from the ESVUK (sometimes ESV, US version, retained) unless otherwise noted.

[3] See chapter 1.

1

mere collection of human religious experience about God. Rather, the whole of Scripture stands united by a single and primary author: God. Rather than a collection of man's highest thoughts about God, the Christian Scripture is God's self-communication to humanity about who he is and what he has done to redeem a lost race in Adam. Inspiration guarantees that the canon's *many* stories tell *one* story; there is a single story to be told because there is a single divine author, who has declared himself to be its architect and creator. He is not only the main actor in the drama of redemption but the drama's scriptwriter.

Presupposed is a striking reality: it is because the story of Scripture has one divine author that his *divine authorial intent* is embedded throughout Scripture's storyline. Mysterious as it may be, the evangelical believes the Spirit carried along the biblical authors so that everything the human authors said is exactly what God himself intended.[4] That concursive operation between God and the human authors also entails that God's intention is conveyed throughout the final product of Scripture.

What makes this providential and miraculous accomplishment far more extraordinary is the fact that the Old and New Testaments were not handed to humanity all at once but progressively over long periods of time, and often through ordinary and difficult human circumstances. God did not breathe out his word *in toto* at any one moment in redemptive history, but did so in a diachronic fashion.[5] The point is, not only is a human authorial intention present in any book of the canon but in and through that human author is imbued a divine authorial intention as well, and one that builds with each new revelation in God's unfolding story.

The structure of this unfolding story and the historical development of this divine revelation is *redemptive* in nature.[6] In the context of God's manifestation of himself to Israel, revelation comes through redemption and redemption through revelation. God speaks, then acts on that speech, only to speak again to interpret his mighty acts and what they mean for his people. The main medium through which this revelatory and redemptive

---

[4] See e.g. 2 Peter 1:21.

[5] This point will be stressed in chapter 2. Presupposed in such a statement is the important and foundational belief that we have no access to what the human author intends other than the words of the biblical text itself. As Vanhoozer (2000: 58) says, 'our only access to the events to which the Bible bears witness is *in* and *through* the literary form, not apart from it. If the literary form of the Bible is essential to its theological and historical content, then biblical theology ignores the diverse literary genres of the Bible at its peril'. Emphases original.

[6] See chapter 3.

tapestry occurs is the *covenant*. Yahweh cuts a covenant with his people, making certain covenant promises he intends to fulfil. After making those covenant promises, he performs mighty acts to fulfil his covenant word (if not in full at least in part), only to return and interpret what his mighty acts mean and how they serve to fulfil his original covenantal word. In short, God not only speaks but is his own interpreter. We can label this a *word–act–word* revelation, and it is one that takes on inscripturated form as Israel's history develops.[7]

Yet here is something marvellous: the scriptural story in which this covenantal word is revealed in a diachronic fashion takes on a *Christological* focus, either through predictive prophecy or, more often than not, through types and patterns (whether they be persons, events, objects or institutions). The presence of typology leads the biblical theologian to go so far as to say that Christ is not only the centre but the *telos* of redemptive history: all previous revelation points to him and finds fulfilment in him. Every type, in other words, has its antitype.

To elaborate, this simple, but profound, characteristic of divine revelation, and Scripture in particular, makes biblical theology all the more complex and rewarding. If there is divine authorial intent throughout the canon that increases in its visibility with each new canonical revelation from God and is manifested through each new epoch of his divinely orchestrated story, then both predictive prophecy and typology are legitimate revelatory media. Inspiration and its close cousin, divine authorial intent, turn hermeneutics into a rich discipline. For if God can reveal his redemptive intentions across history so that one revelation builds upon what was revealed beforehand, then it is possible for God to plant typological seeds in initial revelations that will then blossom in later revelation, only to reach full bloom in *the* definitive revelation of God: the Word Christ Jesus.[8] Christ is not merely another revelation from God but is divine revelation personified and embodied – he is the archetype.

Again, *covenant* is often the medium. Through his covenant(s) God promises to redeem Adam's race, but will do so through Eve's own offspring, sending a Messiah, a Christ, who will be God's definitive covenant word to his people, providing the redemption he first promised to Adam and Abraham. In the meantime, God embeds his drama with

---

[7] See chapter 2.
[8] See John 1:1. In the next chapter this point will be expanded via a discussion of *sensus plenior*.

countless types that serve to foreshadow Christ, the antitype, who is to come. For the Israelite, these types are designed to cultivate faith that God's word is true: he is a God who comes through on his covenant word, a word that is not only spoken by the prophets but put into writing as a permanent covenant witness to God's faithfulness and mercy. The Scriptures, then, are the treaty, the book and the constitution of the covenant, written with God's own finger, sufficient for God's own people.

It is here, however, that the evangelical encounters a strange hermeneutical dilemma, one that has led some biblical scholars to question whether an evangelical view of Scripture, and with it biblical theology itself, is the right path to take.[9] When one engages with Scripture, and the New Testament in particular, where is one to look to understand the *nature* of this God-given text? Naturally, one turns to the apostle Paul. After all, few define what Scripture is with such precision and clarity so that the church understands how God has communicated and what authority they are to live by as followers of Christ. As Paul says to Timothy, and by extension to the Christian church, 'All Scripture is breathed out by God and profitable for teaching, for reproof, for correction, and for training in righteousness, that the man of God may be complete, equipped for *every* good work' (2 Tim. 3:16–17). On the basis of Paul's words, it is lucid what Scripture is and what it is designed to accomplish. From Paul's epistles one is able to put forward inspiration itself with confidence, as well as Scripture's corollary attributes.

The problem is, when one encounters Jesus and the Gospels, one is hard pressed to find such an explicit approach as Paul's to Timothy. The evangelical turns to the person at the core of the Christian faith, Jesus Christ, whose authority as the incarnate God-man is rivalled by none, and searches for a comparable proof text to 2 Timothy 3:16–17 (or, if one were to consider Peter, 2 Peter 1:21). In doing so, one walks away disappointed and perplexed that Jesus could be so silent on the *nature* of Scripture. Here is the Son of God himself, the Messiah, the Christ, the one who establishes the new covenant, on whom all the Scriptures of Israel depend, and no statement equivalent to Paul's (or Peter's) can be found on his lips, at least one that is as theologically specific as Scripture's own ontology.

In the history of modern academia, this disparity has led some (at times, many) biblical scholars to believe there is a divide between the Jewish

---

[9] See chapter 2.

mindset of Jesus and the later, ecclesiastical, mindset of Paul and other New Testament writers. In its most extreme form, Paul becomes the creator of Christianity and its doctrinal commitments, but that (Hellenistic?) paradigm is foreign to Jesus of Nazareth.[10] While inspiration, then, may be foundational to the church, it is anachronistic to push such a doctrinal agenda back on Jesus and first-century Judaism.

The implications of such a dichotomy are not insignificant for biblical theology and hermeneutics. If inspiration is a product of the Christian church and alien to the person whose name it bears, then canonical unity is improbable at best and impossible at worst. In this scheme the incongruity between Jesus and apostles like Paul and Peter becomes but a small paradigm for the larger disconnect between the testaments. The canon is not unified by one divine author but is the result of divergent theologies. Hence one can describe the theology of Deuteronomy and Isaiah, or Matthew and Paul, not as distinct contributions that form a single canonical message, but as dissimilar religious outlooks that lack a unified centre. God is no longer the ultimate author and scriptwriter; as a consequence, there is no primary agent whose authorial intent gives birth to a single story (or theology) in history. Pushed far enough, history itself is no longer *redemptive*, for that label assumes types have antitypes and promises have fulfilments. Biblical theology is either jettisoned or redefined as a result.

Such an orientation to biblical theology, and inspiration too, has a recent past that stems from the Enlightenment and still tempts evangelical scholars today.[11] Evangelicals pay lip service to inspiration, but when we turn to the text itself the divine author may have little functional imprint across the canon. Our hermeneutic betrays a deistic God, one who has inspired the text but thereafter has no role in how the whole text (and its story) comes together over the course of history. With an overemphasis on *human* authorial intent, the formative role of *divine* authorial intent across the canon remains ambiguous. That has no small effect on biblical theology.

It is into this hermeneutical darkness that the present project hopes to shed light borrowed from biblical theology itself. It is true that if the evangelical reads Jesus and the Gospels with the same linguistic expectations as one would read Paul or Peter, then the temptation described above to

---

[10] Chapter 2 will address this approach.

[11] Granted, it may not always be in this extreme form I have articulated for the purpose of making a point; nevertheless, at times its more subtle forms can be just as or even more dangerous to the evangelical doctrine of Scripture. See chapter 2.

despair of canonical unity and scriptural inspiration will be a difficult hurdle to overcome. Christ and the Gospel writers do not speak to the nature of Scripture *in the same way* as the epistles.[12] One is hard pressed to find Jesus and the Evangelists conveying Scripture's metaphysical identity in a didactic manner.

The relative (though not absolute) absence of direct reflection on Scripture's ontology by Jesus and the Gospel writers, however, need not tempt the evangelical to despair or retreat into canonical discontinuity. For this study will argue that *Jesus and the apostles have just as convictional a doctrine of Scripture, but it will be discovered only if one reads the Gospels within their own canonical horizon and covenantal context. The nature of Scripture that Jesus and the Gospel writers presuppose may not be addressed directly, but manifests itself powerfully when one reads the words of Jesus and the Gospel writers within the Old Testament's promise–fulfilment pattern and typological tapestry.*

That means the interpreter must look not for extended didactic sermons or parables from Jesus on the inspiration of Scripture. Instead, the Gospel writers intend the interpreter to pay attention to the way Jesus sees his own life, death and resurrection – indeed, his own filial and messianic identity – as the *fulfilment* of the covenant promises and typological patterns foreshadowed in the Old Testament.[13] The Gospel writers want

---

[12] This is *not* to deny that a powerful case can be made for Scripture by looking at what Jesus assumes in his quotations or allusions to Scripture. I agree with Blomberg (2016: 696–701) and Wenham (1994), e.g., when they look to the many ways Jesus assumes the historicity of the OT and its reliability as verbal, plenary inspired Scripture. I too utilize such an approach in Barrett 2016, and it will be one I marshal at strategic points in this study (see e.g. chapters 3–5). Nevertheless, what I am arguing here is that there may be a deeper, more organic, way to ground Jesus' view of the Scriptures; i.e. by means of his own Christological reading of Scripture and its promise–fulfilment pattern. In short, these two approaches should not be set over against one another but complement each other.

[13] The approach I am describing is not without parallel. In fact, it is another way of saying that the interpreter should be mindful of genre, distinguishing Gospel from Epistle. The same dilemma I have described is present e.g. in discussions of justification. One could claim, after comparing Paul and Jesus, that justification by faith alone is a doctrine pervasive in Paul but entirely absent from the teachings of Jesus (perhaps with the exception of Luke 18:9–14). One might go so far, granting certain law-oriented teachings of Jesus (e.g. Sermon on the Mount), to say that Jesus' teaching is in conflict with Paul's theology. But this is not necessary. The entire life of Christ is meant to be a recapitulation of Adam's and Israel's history. As the obedient son, the true Israel, the last Adam, Christ is tempted but resists, fulfils all righteousness and goes to the cross as the sinless sacrifice. In other words, when the life (and teachings) of Jesus are considered within the broader scope of his redemptive mission, suddenly justification shines through and can no longer be set over against Paul. See chapter 5. In similar fashion, one should approach the topic of Scripture in the NT with the same hermeneutical care and sensitivity, differentiating how Jesus and Paul approach the subject by recognizing that their conclusions are in continuity with one another.

their readers to witness who Christ is and what he does so that their eyes may be opened to the grand scheme of the divine author who planned this redemptive story from start to finish.

Through the eyes of the Evangelists, the reader learns that the covenant promises Yahweh made through the Law and the Prophets have been fulfilled in the person and work of Christ, and that is a claim not imposed on Jesus by the Gospel writers but a claim Jesus himself heralds.[14] For that reason, nothing demonstrates Scripture's divine origin and trustworthy nature more than the *gospel* of Jesus Christ.[15] In the advent of the Son of God, the Word has become flesh (John 1:14), announcing to Jew and Gentile alike that God has come through on his inscripturated, covenant word. For that reason, the canon is eschatological by design; the Scriptures are not adopted by Jesus and the church, but the Scriptures give birth to Jesus and the church, the swaddling clothes in which Christ is born, says Luther.[16]

Moreover, the argument above will be further substantiated not merely by turning to the fulfilment theme throughout the Gospels, but by examining the way Jesus fulfils the Scriptures in his redemptive mission. To be more specific, it is the *redemptive, covenant obedience* of Christ that secures a righteousness for all those who trust in Christ. But an obedience to what exactly? Answer: an obedience to the Scriptures. For they are the covenant treaty of the new covenant Mediator. *By looking to the manner in which Jesus accomplishes redemption – that is, his self-conscious covenant obedience to the Scriptures – one also discovers Jesus' own attitude towards the Scriptures.*[17] What that means for the interpreter of the Gospels is key: one need not pedal through the Gospels looking for a proof text about Scripture's ontology. Rather, one should primarily look to the *mission* of the Son to discover the *attitude* of the Son towards the Scriptures of Israel. It is in Jesus' humble trust in and obedience to the Scriptures for the sake of securing eternal life for the believer that the interpreter's eyes are opened to just what Jesus believes these Scriptures to be: the word of God.

Last, this study will conclude by establishing *who* Christ is.[18] For if he is who he says he is – the eternal Son of God – then what he says about the

---

[14] See chapter 3.

[15] See chapters 3 and 4. Theology proper grounds Scripture; the gospel confirms it. Barrett (2022).

[16] See p. 197ff. of chapter 4.

[17] See chapter 5. I reject eternal subordination (EFS). I refer only to the Son's temporal mission.

[18] See chapter 6.

Scriptures cannot be dismissed. If he appears to speak with authority concerning the Scriptures, it is because he is their original, divine author as the pre-existent Son of God. His divine identity, then, is of no little significance. Establishing his divinity is instrumental to a faith that submits itself to the Bible Jesus read, a faith that seeks understanding from none other than the authority of Jesus Christ, the Word made flesh.[19]

With that trajectory in place, we now turn to preliminary issues in hermeneutics and biblical theology that must be settled to establish the presuppositions of this study's argument.

---

[19] To clarify, the emphasis in this study, in a variety of ways, on the Word made flesh, on God's revelation personified in Christ, is not a disguised back door into Barthian hermeneutics. Actually, evangelicals – though they may not always realize it – have a stronger claim to a Christological understanding of Scripture than the Barthian view. Not only can evangelicals declare that Christ is the Word of God, but they can also say that this same Christ had no hesitancy affirming Scripture itself to be the Word of God. In other words, it is the Word *made flesh* that reveals the Word *inscripturated* to be the Father's divinely inspired speech to his covenant people. Furthermore, when the Son manifests the revelation of the Father through his incarnation, he solidifies and confirms that the inscripturated word of the triune God is as reliable and true as its divine author. Ironically, evangelicals have a more legitimate claim to Christology precisely because they seek to hold the same view of Scripture as Christ himself. See chapter 7. One other matter: Although this book stresses Christ as the culmination and fulfilment of God's revelation, readers should not assume Christ is where revelation begins, or that Christ exhausts revelation, or that Christology is the grounding for our doctrine of God. Duby (2019: 132) exposes this mistaken assumption: 'But the fact that supernatural revelation culminates in the coming of Jesus Christ is taken by some to mean that the incarnation itself is the starting point or even the exclusive basis on which the doctrine of God must stand.' By contrast, 'the incarnation should be understood within the broader context of the supernatural revelation given by God in Holy Scripture. The incarnation must inform our doctrine of God without being its first or only epistemological principle.' I presuppose the latter throughout this book. My purpose here is not to address the doctrine of God, but see Barrett 2022.

1

Divine authorial intent, canonical unity and the Christological presuppositions of biblical theology

By the twenty-first century it is well recognized, both among theologians and biblical scholars, that the naturalistic presuppositions that structured historical-critical methods from the Enlightenment to Protestant liberalism had devastating consequences for the doctrine of Scripture and hermeneutics. For example, Brevard Childs observes how traditional doctrinal tenates such as biblical authority and divine inspiration were fundamental to biblical scholarship for the first sixteen hundred years of the church's existence, rarely being challenged, but in the modern era biblical authority and inspiration were questioned and discarded.[1]

One must be careful not to oversimplify the Enlightenment or neglect to recognize its variegated representatives. Not everyone was given over to rationalism or methodological naturalism.[2] Nevertheless, doubtless a major wing was. Tracing the reception of the Bible from Baruch Spinoza to the twentieth century in their study *The Bible in Modern Culture*, Roy A. Harrisville and Walter Sundberg have shown that major segments of modernity gave birth to what they label 'rationalist biblical criticism' (RBC).[3] In particular, the hermeneutical methods of RBC had serious consequences for the Gospels and Christology. 'Historical criticism sought to measure the meaning of Jesus' message according to the standards of

---

[1] Childs 2004: 300–301.
[2] See Woodbridge 1986: 237–270; 2016: 137–170.
[3] Harrisville and Sundberg 2002.

9

Enlightenment morality and rationality. Biblical critics eventually retreated from the claim that an historically pristine portrait of Jesus could be disclosed by scholarly investigation.[4]

It should be added that such a 'retreat' was not due to an evaluation of the person of Jesus alone. Evaluating Jesus' use of the Old Testament, RBC judged the New Testament's Christocentric reading of the Old Testament fanciful. This evaluation was an innovation to be sure. 'Before the modern period,' say Douglas Moo and Andy Naselli,

> Christian interpreters were quite happy to explain that the OT is compatible with the NT; their recourse was various forms of what we might call the 'figural' sense. They extensively employed allegory and typology to show how the NT appropriates the OT to uncover the OT's true, 'spiritual' meaning.[5]

That all changed when a 'hermeneutics of consent' was replaced by a 'hermeneutics of suspicion' due to the rise of higher criticism in the modern era. How the New Testament authors interpreted the Old Testament (i.e. in a figural, typological and Christological way) was now considered problematic in the light of the 'modern insistence that the "historical" sense is a text's only legitimate meaning'. Indeed, the 'death knell for the traditional approach to the OT was insisting that the "grammatical-historical" meaning is the text's only legitimate meaning'.[6]

This is not, however, an assessment voiced by evangelicals alone. Consider Hans Frei for example: pre-critical interpretation assumed 'one cumulative story' so that 'figuration or typology was a natural extension of literal interpretation'. One of figuration's 'chief uses had been as a means for unifying the canon'. Then 'historical-critical eyes' peered over the hermeneutical horizon only to set the literal and figural over against each other, judging the latter a 'preposterous historical argument'. With all the attention on the human author's 'grammatical and lexical exactness', historical critics redefined the literal to be 'concerned with specific texts and specific historical circumstances', so that the 'unity of the Bible across millennia of differing cultural levels and conditions . . .

---

4 Ibid. 2.
5 Moo and Naselli 2016: 704–705.
6 Ibid.; cf. Stuhlmacher 1979: 124; Lampe and Woolcombe 1957: 15; McCartney 1988: 102–103; Vanhoozer 2000: 58.

seemed a tenuous, indeed dubious hypothesis to them'.[7] The divine author, and his intent across the canon, was eclipsed by the priority of the human author(s), all in the name of proper grammatical-historical exegesis.[8]

The Christological and typological interpretation of the Old Testament by Jesus and the New Testament authors was rejected because RBC precluded *divine authorial intent*, either in part or in whole.[9] In other words, presupposed was the belief that God does *not* act in such miraculous and providential ways, either to breathe out Scripture (1 Tim. 3:16–17) and carry along the biblical authors by his Spirit (2 Peter 1:21), or to infuse Scripture's promise–fulfilment tapestry with a meaning that could go beyond the human author's immediate understanding (1 Peter 1:10–12).[10] There is no single, divine author who intervenes and guides the canon and its narrative from start to finish because there is no divine–human concursus intrinsic to the inspiration event itself. Instead, the canon consists of disparate human contributions that have no single theological and textual cohesion.

Can biblical theology survive after the Enlightenment?

What have been the consequences of such an approach for the discipline of biblical theology? In short, such an approach precludes canonical

---

[7] Frei 1974: 2, 7–8.

[8] It would be mistaken to assume that an Enlightenment methodology was strictly a hermeneutical issue, removed from its doctrine of God. As biblical scholars, theologians and historians look back and evaluate the hermeneutic of modernity, a hermeneutic that is still alive today, it has become ostensible that such a naturalistic methodology was backed by a naturalistic metaphysic, an ontology of God that betrayed Scripture's own testimony concerning his attributes and mighty acts. The classical view of God from the Fathers to the Reformers was substituted for theistic personalism, making verbal, plenary inspiration, divine authorial intent and canonical unity implausible, even inconceivable. To see this in detail, consult Carter 2018: 31–91. Grenz and Olson (1992) are persuaded that divine transcendence was substituted for divine immanence. While that may not be the only trend, it is a major one.

[9] E.g. J. D. Semler wrote about typology, 'He who assumes no types . . . is deprived of nothing whatever; and even he who is most fond of typology cannot, for all that, place it among the fundamentals of Christianity.' Quoted in Sykes 1979: 86; cf. Von Rad (1979: 22), who concludes that typology 'came to a sudden end in rationalism'. Typology, then, can be a fitting test case, determining where one stands on inspiration and divine authorial intent across the canon. In contrast to Semler, e.g., 'To read the Bible typologically or intertextually is to let Christian theology transform the presuppositions one brings to the text.' Vanhoozer 2000: 60.

[10] Davidson 1981: 2.

unity: a unified narrative is an impossibility.[11] Graeme Goldsworthy explains:

> The idea that God himself has a purpose that is accurately revealed in the redemptive–historical narrative of the Bible as a whole has been under attack since the seventeenth century. Biblical theology comes to be regarded by many as a futile exercise on the basis that there is no discernible theological unity to the canon.[12]

Goldsworthy believes the consequences are devastating not only for biblical theology but for the biblical text itself:

> Historical criticism in its extreme form rejected the dogma that God both set in train the events of history and also acted within them. It rejected the notion of divine revelation within space and time, and thus ultimately made biblical theology impossible. In its place it put the study of the history of religious ideas.[13]

The importance of Goldsworthy's insight cannot be overemphasized. While some modern thinkers were direct, announcing their abandonment of scriptural inspiration, others were subtle, allowing their neglect of divine authorial intent to eat away at canonical unity, until no unity was left at all. There was, says Craig Carter, an 'undermining of the unity of the Bible as a single narrative, which was done by ignoring divine authorship and concentrating on human authorship alone'.[14] As is often the case in biblical scholarship, emphasis is everything. To emphasize human authorial intent at the expense of divine authorial intent is to undermine the Scriptures as a singular drama with a concentrated plotline; it is not surprising that divine inspiration and authority were soon dismissed in the process.

---

[11] It is not the purpose of this chapter to provide a survey. However, see the following for an in-depth analysis of the variegated ways unity is understood in biblical studies: Baker 2010; Dohmen and Söding 1995; Carson 2000. Carson, e.g., examines (1) Davies 1994 and the issue of confessionalism, (2) Olson 1998 and postmodern epistemology, (3) four different trajectories within canonical unity (e.g. Sanders 1972; Childs 1970; etc.), and (4) Morgan's (1995) post-biblical confessional approach.

[12] Goldsworthy 2012: 34. Goldsworthy lays the blame, in part, at the feet of Johann Philipp Gabler. On the history of biblical theology, see Childs 1992: 30–51; Bray 1996: 193–208; Mead 2007: 13–59; Scobie 2003: 3–102.

[13] Goldsworthy 2012: 43.

[14] Carter 2018: 98.

Although it is tempting to think that more recent scholarship has moved past such an approach, remnants can still be found; its influence is powerful and should not be underestimated. German and Lutheran New Testament scholar Ernst Käsemann, for example, makes the following provocative claim: 'The one biblical theology, going from a single root and maintaining itself in unbroken continuity, is wish-fulfilment and fantasy.'[15] In more recent years German New Testament scholar Udo Schnelle, author of *Theology of the New Testament*, has argued that the person of Jesus Christ is what makes biblical theology so intolerable: 'A "biblical theology" is not possible because: (1) the Old Testament is *silent* about Jesus Christ, [and] (2) the resurrection from the dead *of one who was crucified* cannot be integrated into any ancient system of meaning formation.'[16]

Or consider James Barr, who writes, 'An exegesis which would work strictly within the confines of the canon is certainly a possibility that could be added to other forms of exegesis, but it is doubtful how it could be the basic theological form of exegesis.' Barr then pushes back against Childs:

> And Childs' argument in favor of the final text, while an important consideration for the interpretation of individual books, like Genesis, or even the Pentateuch, or Matthew, does not thereby validate an extension to the point where the canon of the entire Scripture would define it as if it was a single text.[17]

What does this mean for Scripture as a whole and the New Testament in particular?

> The NT as we have it is a fragmentary collection of documents from the earliest period, while the bulk of the material has vanished forever. By and large there is no internal coherence. The tensions everywhere evident amount to contradictions.[18]

---

[15] Käsemann 1969: 18.

[16] Schnelle 2009: 52. In German, 'Eine Biblische Theologie is nicht möglich, weil 1) das Alte Testament von Jesus Christus *schweigt*, 2) die Auferstehung *eines Gekreuzigten* von den Toten als kontingentes Geschehen sich in keine antike Sinnbildung integrierten lässt.' Schnelle 2007: 40. Emphases original. Cf. Hays 2014: 3.

[17] Barr 1976: 110–111.

[18] Ibid. 109. Given Barr's statement, no wonder Vanhoozer (2000: 56) concludes, 'Modern biblical criticism, while professing to study the text scientifically, in fact approached the text with the anti-theological presuppositions of secular reason and hence with a bias against the unity of the text and an anti-narrative hermeneutic. Perhaps nothing is so typical of the historical-critical method than its tendency to fragment the text.'

In this scheme the Bible is fragmentary and atomized.

R. E. Murphy draws a similar conclusion for the discipline of biblical theology but from a literary perspective: 'It is neither possible nor desirable to find a unity in the literary witness. The proof of that is the fact that no one has succeeded in capturing the alleged unity.' Murphy says:

> The great variety of the literature, which practically everyone admits, prevents any unity worthy of the name. One cannot expect a unity from a literature that was composed of oral and written traditions over a period of a thousand years.[19]

Given assessments from twentieth-century biblical scholars like Käsemann, Schnelle, Barr and Murphy, D. A. Carson is on target to observe how

> many scholars find that such a notion of the canon is precisely the problem. They are convinced that the NT documents themselves betray divergent and mutually contradictory theologies. To speak of a canonical wholeness or a canonical authority is to speak of a chimera.[20]

From *Heilsgeschichte* to *Endgeschichte*

Whether canonical wholeness and authority is a 'chimera' is decided in large part by one's view of history. Since the Enlightenment, many biblical scholars approached Scripture as merely another chapter in *secular history*, one in which the biblical authors reported about an event with redemptive significance that occurred within their own religious experience.[21] They did not allow for the assumption that what Scripture says God says, because they had no pre-commitment to a biblical *Heilsgeschichte* (salvation history) framework.[22]

By contrast, pre-modern, pre-critical exegetes approached the Scriptures as the revelation of *salvation history*, one in which God spoke

---

19 Murphy 2000: 82–83.

20 Carson 2000: 92. Carson also notices how many such scholars have been influenced by Walter Bauer's 1934 work *Rechtgläubigkeit und Ketzerei im ältesten Christentum*, where he 'argued that heresy preceded orthodoxy, that earliest Christianity was far more diverse than its later forms, and that to read unified theology into the earliest decades is sheer anachronism'. For a response, see Köstenberger and Kruger 2010; Kruger 2018.

21 For a case study, see Legaspi 2010.

22 O'Collins 1971: 89; cf. Goldsworthy 2012: 60–61.

through the biblical authors not only to give but interpret his redemptive word–act revelation.[23] Those who follow this pre-modern, pre-critical approach to history will agree with Ehlen, who says, 'Basic to the witness of both the Old and the New Testament' is the 'conviction that God has taken a direct hand in earthly, human affairs, particularly in a specific chain of events by which the total welfare of mankind, its salvation (German: *Heil*), is being prepared for and revealed to the world.'[24] Ehlen concludes:

> The history of this step-by-step process is now seen to constitute the very core of the Scriptures. It may be called the *historia sacra* or, referring to its actual subject matter, the *Heilsgeschichte*: the story of the many successive words and works of God toward restoration of total well-being to his people.[25]

Gerald O'Collins defines *Heilsgeschichte* by placing emphasis on its revelational and Christological nature (contra Schnelle). *Heilsgeschichte* 'commits us to the view that God acts and reveals himself in history', and Jesus is at the 'heart of salvation history', not just as a 'model of human faith' but as the Son of God, incarnated for the purpose of bringing salvation history to its appointed fulfilment.[26] According to O'Collins, therefore, a *Heilsgeschichte* theology is a 'theology of salvation history' that 'makes a positive assessment of the Old Testament's function for Christian faith'.[27] Salvation history is eschatological by nature because the divine author of the Old Testament is at work to fulfil his word through his Son, who not only has been resurrected but has ascended to the right hand of the Father and will one day return to judge the living and the dead. 'A salvation-historical view stands committed to a genuinely futurist eschatology,' meaning '*Heilsgeschichte* theology implies an *Endgeschichte* (final history) still to come.'[28]

Persuaded by *historia sacra*, an increasing number of biblical scholars today have turned critical towards presuppositions and methods indebted

---

[23] See George 2011: 17–43; Steinmetz 1980: 27–38.

[24] Ehlen 1964: 517.

[25] Ibid. For a treatment of history and its historians, see Sailhamer 2001: 8–11.

[26] O'Collins 1971: 89; cf. Goldsworthy 2012: 61.

[27] Ibid.

[28] Ibid.

to Enlightenment hermeneutics wherever they are seen.[29] For example, Richard Hays has responded to Schnelle by observing Schnelle's incongruity with the biblical authors themselves. As mentioned, Schnelle listed two reasons 'for the impossibility of a biblical theology': (1) 'the Old Testament is *silent* about Jesus Christ', and (2) 'the resurrection from the dead *of one who was crucified* cannot be integrated into any ancient system of meaning formation'.[30] But Hays counters by pointing out the obvious: these reasons

> directly contradict the explicit testimony of the NT writers them-
> selves! They emphatically do not think the OT is silent about Jesus
> Christ, and they assert that the resurrection of Jesus from the dead
> actually provides the hermeneutical clue that decisively integrates
> Israel's entire system of meaning formation.[31]

There is a certain irony to Schnelle, given the context in which he criticizes biblical theology on Christological grounds: 'Schnelle holds the chair as Professor of New Testament at the University of Halle-Wittenberg: the geographical proximity of Professor Schnelle to Luther's home base accentuates the hermeneutical distance travelled by biblical scholarship since the sixteenth century.'[32] Schnelle is a far cry from Luther, who believed the Old Testament was the 'swaddling cloths and the manner in which Christ lies'.[33] Childs's thesis, which started this chapter, finds its verification in someone like Schnelle: after the Reformation there was a major shift, a change in attitude towards the Scriptures, as seen in the way they were, and still are, interpreted.

In sum, attacks on scriptural authority in the form of undermining canonical unity not only have a long history stretching back to modernity

---

[29] The evaluation of Craig Carter is one that resonates: 'the Enlightenment movement of "higher criticism" is a dead end, a sideshow, a deviation from orthodoxy, and a movement that is now in the late stages of self-destruction'. Carter 2018: xviii. As a result, they are turning to pre-critical exegetes instead. E.g. Daley (2003: 69–70) comments, 'a significant number of Christian theologians and biblical scholars are turning with interest and even respect to the exegetical efforts of the patristic era in the hope of finding there modes for new ways of reading the Bible with both scholarly sophistication and a reverent, orthodox faith'.

[30] Schnelle 2009: 52. Emphases original. In German, 'Eine Biblische Theologie ist nicht möglich, weil 1) das Alte Testament von Jesus Christus *schweigt*, 2) die Auferstenhung *eines Gekreuzigten* von den Toten als kontingentes Geschehen sich in keine antike Sinnbildung integrierten lässt.' Schnelle 2007: 40.

[31] Hays 2014: 3–4.

[32] Ibid.

[33] Luther 1960: 236; cf. Hays 2014: 1.

but demonstrate precisely *how* biblical authority slips away in the name of modern, enlightened exegesis. In an attempt to major on human authorial intent, divine authorial intent and, with it, divine authorship, was (and still is) relegated to an inferior position or, worse, abandoned. With its demise, divine inspiration was also thrown into question. A failure to read the Scripture as a single narrative with canonical unity, it turns out, was a hermeneutic that spelled the death of divine inspiration and *Christian* interpretation.

Perhaps that is why Karl Barth, who rejoiced at his liberation from the presuppositions of liberalism, felt that if he had to choose between the historical-critical method and inspiration, he would not hesitate in his decision. 'I should without hesitation adopt the latter, which has a broader, deeper, more important justification. The doctrine of inspiration is concerned with the labour of apprehending, without which no technical equipment, however complete, is of any use whatever.'[34] While scholars may debate whether Barth shed all the presuppositions of the historical-critical method on which he was bred, his default instinct towards inspiration is what distinguishes him from Rudolph Bultmann and company.[35] Barth may be neo-orthodox, but his default instinct is what distinguishes, or at least should distinguish, evangelical biblical theologians as well.

The task of biblical theology: Gabler versus Vos

If Barth is right, then any hermeneutic or biblical theology that denies divine authorship and seeks to eliminate divine authorial intent in the Scriptures cannot stand. Yet more can be said, and this is where it is necessary to part ways with Barth: any hermeneutic or biblical theology that affirms inspiration but then insists that it is the role of the biblical scholar to decipher *what* parts of Scripture are inspired and what parts are not is also illegitimate. Though debatable, this may be the more dangerous threat to biblical theology and scriptural inspiration since it often goes undetected due to its subtle methodology.

Such an approach, or something close to it, can be seen in Johann Gabler, whom some have called the father of biblical theology due to his

---

[34] Barth 1933: 1.
[35] Harrisville and Sundberg 2002: 13.

1787 lecture at the University of Altdorf *De justo discrimine theologiae biblicae et dogmaticae regundisque recte utriusque finibus*.[36] 'We must investigate what in the sayings of the Apostle is truly divine, and what perchance merely human.' The biblical theologian is to decide 'whether all the opinions of the Apostles, of every type and sort altogether, are truly divine, or rather whether some of them, which have no bearing on salvation, were left to their own ingenuity'.[37] For Gabler, only those parts of the biblical story and message in accord with universal religious principles can be labelled revelatory because only they were acquired by rational, enlightened logic and are therefore truly divine in origin.[38]

In a recent survey on the origins of biblical theology, J. V. Fesko concludes that Gabler was indebted to the Enlightenment presuppositions of Johann Semler (1721–91), who wrote *A Free Investigation of the Canon* (1771), drawing these same conclusions a decade earlier.[39] Fesko also notices that there is a strange and telling absence of Christ in Gabler's hermeneutic. 'Gabler's commitment to rationalism is therefore evident not only in his stated methodology, but especially in the absence of any mention of Christ, whether for his understanding of dogmatic or biblical theology.'[40]

The absence of Christ in Gabler's proposal for biblical theology is problematic first and foremost because it fails to heed the way Jesus himself read the Scriptures; as a result, Gabler has failed to read the text as *Christian* Scripture. The empty tomb confirms that the Scriptures, from start to finish, in their totality, are inspired by God and therefore true: God has in fact come through on his word by sending his Word as promised of old through the Law, the Prophets and the Psalms. As much as the books of the Bible may have many different human authors, the gospel of Jesus Christ leads one to conclude that in the final analysis the Bible is one book with one divine author.[41]

There is, therefore, an organic unity to biblical theology that cannot be reached via Gabler's Christless methodology. Old Princetonian Geerhardus Vos presents a far better paradigm when he positions biblical theology's

---

[36] 'On the Proper Distinction Between Biblical and Dogmatic Theology and the Specific Objections of Each.' Gabler 1980; 1992. Scobie contests the claim that Gabler is the father of biblical theology. Scobie 1991: 34.

[37] Gabler 1980; 1992: 500–501. Similarly, see 497.

[38] Ibid. 501. For a fuller treatment of this point, see Fesko 2008: 447–448; McGrath 1994: 20.

[39] Fesko 2008: 448; also cf. McGrath 1994: 20; Dennison 2008: 350.

[40] Fesko 2008: 448.

[41] Swain 2011: 91.

starting point within the sphere of divine revelation itself and from there submits to Scripture's own terms of interpretation.[42] 'Biblical Theology, rightly defined, is nothing else than *the exhibition of the organic progress of supernatural revelation in its historic continuity and multiformity.*'[43]

The difference between Gabler and Vos may seem miniscule, but it is critical.[44] Gabler took biblical theology's commitment to history to an extreme, so that revelation itself was paralysed by the biblical theologian's historical investigation and findings.[45] Vos believed such an approach to be rationalistic, thus eliminating and neutralizing (his choice of words) the 'revelation-principle'.[46] Vos, by contrast, saw the revelatory character of Scripture as primary, the interpretative authority to biblical theology's use of history. As Fesko says, '*Vos always saw the historical nature of biblical theology subordinated to the principle of its revealed character.*'[47] While some biblical theologians of the Enlightenment period concluded that the 'word is merely reflective of human ideas or symbols, not actual divine acts in history', Vos, on the other hand, 'believed recognizing the inspired and authoritative character of special revelation was destructive to the critical Enlightenment-influenced biblical theology such as that of Gabler'.[48]

That difference is most conspicuous in the way Christ and covenant are the *telos* of biblical theology in Vos's paradigm but glaringly absent from Gabler. Whereas Gabler saw the Old Testament as lacking Christian identity in comparison with the New Testament, Vos avoids that testamental (covenantal) bifurcation by always holding out Christ as the goal of the old covenant. 'Unlike Gabler, who saw the Old Testament as sub-Christian and the New Testament as the Christian testament,' says Fesko,

Vos argues that the various stages of the historic, gradual, progressive unfolding of God's revelation in Christ are manifested through the

---

[42] E.g. Vos 1948: 13.

[43] Vos 1980: 15. Emphasis original.

[44] For a contrast between Gabler and Vos, see Fesko 2008: 445–453. What follows is indebted to Fesko's insight.

[45] This has led Dennison (2008: 343) to conclude that 'the discipline formulated by Gabler was *not* biblical theology at all. Rather, Gabler's conception of biblical theology was merely a critical hybrid of the grammatical-historical hermeneutical method. He adapted his exegetical method to the spirit of the Enlightenment while attempting to sustain stability for less than orthodox Christian beliefs in an era of transition and confusion.' Emphasis original.

[46] Vos 1980: 15.

[47] Fesko 2008: 450–451. Emphasis original.

[48] Ibid. 451.

various covenants where the theologian sees the Savior designated as the seed of the woman, the seed of Abraham, the seed of Judah, and the seed of David.[49]

For example, Vos writes, 'From the beginning all redeeming acts of God aim at the creation and introduction of this new organic principle which is none other than Christ.' What does that mean for the Old Testament? 'All Old Testament redemption is but the saving activity of God working toward the realization of this goal, the great supernatural prelude to the Incarnation and the Atonement.'[50]

Fesko concludes his study of biblical theology by identifying three essential characteristics, all of which must be present to qualify one's theology as biblical:

1 'the divine origin of special revelation'
2 'the organic unity of the whole'
3 'the typological relationship between foundational revelation and the coming eschatological revelation of God in Christ and covenant'.[51]

Already, points 1 and 2 have been stressed; attention must be given to point 3 to see its indispensability to biblical theology.

Christ the centre:
the Christological clamp

If history has a sacred, redemptive character to it, then Christ must be the centre of biblical theology as well as its *telos*. More to the point of the present study, the canonical unity that supports the enterprise of biblical theology and presupposes the inspiration of the canon itself hinges on Christ, the one on whom the entire narrative depends. As Goldsworthy has said:

If we allow that such Christ-centredness is indeed a key attribute of the entire biblical canon, the unity of the canon must also be asserted.

---

[49] Ibid.
[50] Vos 1980: 12.
[51] Fesko 2008: 455.

That God has spoken to us, first by the prophets and then by his Son
(Heb. 1:1–2), is the centre of the quest for biblical theology.[52]

Rather than attempting to arrive at such a unity by empirical investigation,
warns Goldsworthy, which will only result in hermeneutical scepticism,
'we must allow the *person of Jesus* to establish the basis of unity in
Scripture'.[53]

What Goldsworthy calls the 'key attribute of the entire biblical canon'
Peter Stuhlmacher calls the 'Christological clamp'. This 'clamp' means one
cannot bifurcate the Old Testament from the New (contra Gabler, Schnelle).
To do so is to pretend Christ has not come to fulfil the Scriptures that spoke
of him. 'There are many places where the New Testament relates to the Old
with regard to its contents. *The reigning center of these points of reference is
the New Testament testimony to Christ.*'[54] Taking his cue from Jesus' own
testimony in the Gospels, Stuhlmacher concludes:

> The center of the New Testament, the gospel of Jesus Christ, is thor-
> oughly formulated in Old Testament language and bears witness to
> the eschatological salvation provided by God for Jews and Gentiles.
> This testimony connects the New Testament inextricably with the
> Old. Because of this Christological clamp, the Old Testament belongs
> to Jews and Christians alike . . .[55]

With Christ the centre, salvation history – and the gospel in particular – is
the intended context within which the canon not only unfolds but finds its
justification and purpose.[56]

If there is a 'Christological clamp', then there are certain presuppositions
that must be in place for biblical theology to work. These presuppositions
are never so visible as they are when one studies the way the New Testament
interprets the Old Testament. G. K. Beale provides five theological presuppositions he believes underlie the New Testament's interpretation of the
Old Testament:

---

[52] Goldsworthy 2012: 45

[53] Ibid. (cf. 52). Emphasis added.

[54] Stuhlmacher 1995: 9. Emphasis original.

[55] Ibid. 11. Emphasis removed.

[56] 'It seems to me impossible to justify the canon apart from salvation history and it is not
by accident that its justification is inevitably questioned whenever salvation history is rejected.'
Cullmann 1967: 294.

1 Corporate solidarity or representation is assumed.

2 On the basis of point 1 above, Christ is viewed as representing the *true Israel* of the OT *and* the true Israel – the church – in the NT.

3 *History is unified* by a wise and sovereign plan so that the earlier parts are designed to correspond and point to the later parts (cf. Matt. 11:13–14).

4 The age of *eschatological fulfillment* has come but has not been fully consummated in Christ.

5 As a consequence of point 4, it may be deduced that the later parts of biblical history function as the broader context to interpret earlier parts *because they all have the same, ultimate divine author, who inspires the various human authors.* One deduction from this premise is that *Christ and his glory as the end-time center and goal of redemptive history are the key to interpreting the earlier portions of the OT and its promises* [Matt. 5:17; 13:11, 16–17; Luke 24:25–27, 32, 44–45; John 5:39; 20:9; Rom. 10:4; 2 Cor. 1:20].[57]

While each of these will be explored in this study, points 3 and 5 have particular relevance. Point 3 explains why the biblical theologian cannot be satisfied with a *secular* reading of history, but instead must insist on *redemptive* or *salvation* history.[58] Earlier parts 'correspond and point to the later parts' because the text has a divine author and its story is governed by a divine actor, one who is in full control, bringing his plan of redemption

---

[57] Beale 2012a: 53. First emphasis added; second emphasis original. Similar points are stressed by Goldsworthy (2012). Elsewhere Beale, focusing on the nature of typology, will emphasize this fifth point by saying that the 'broad redemptive-historical perspective was the dominant framework within which Jesus and the New Testament writers thought, serving as an ever-present heuristic guide to the Old Testament. In fact, it is this framework which should be seen as the wider literary context within which the New Testament authors interpreted Old Testament passages.' Beale 1994: 394.

[58] Carson, building on the categories of Balla (1997), makes a similar point by differentiating between a narrow and wider view of history. A narrow view 'excludes even the possibility of accepting as true any biblical affirmation of God acting in history. It operates, in fact, on naturalistic assumptions. In other words, it does not deny the possibility of the existence of God, but denies that history can find any evidence of him. History is a closed continuum.' Such a view is held by Räisänen (1990). On the other hand, a wide view 'allows that God may well have operated in the domain of what "really happened" in space and time, observable to human witnesses (*e.g.* the resurrection). Adherents to the former definition call for a "purely historical" approach to the study of the NT documents; the latter definition is prepared to blend history and theology.' Carson 2000: 93.

to fulfilment in history. To assert a cohesive canon, therefore, is to assume history itself is united by the redemptive purposes of its divine architect and monarch.

Hence Beale can then say, in point 4, that redemptive history is *eschatological* in nature, finding its fulfilment in Christ, a point I have already emphasized. To be avoided, then, is any approach to biblical theology that would sever eschatology from hermeneutics.

> The NT writers' selection of OT texts was not random or capricious or out of line with the original OT meaning but determined by this wider, overriding perspective, which views redemptive history as unified by an omnipotent and wise design.[59]

Point 5 is relevant as well. Jesus and the New Testament authors assume history is unified in their interpretation of the Old Testament, and on that basis are likewise justified to presuppose the presence of the divine author across *both* Testaments. In other words, not only is *history* unified because its architect is working out his plan of redemption in history, but the *canon* is unified because its divine scriptwriter has breathed out his redemptive, covenantal word through his human authors. Diverse as those authors may be, variegated as their historical contexts may be, they have one divine author who has spoken in and through them and their contexts to deliver a unified word to the people of God that is, in one sense, timeless, for all people and at all times.

With point 5 in place, Beale can identify the 'one grand assumption of all':

> Jesus and the apostles believed that the OT Scriptures were 'sacred' and were the Word of God. Therefore all authoritative theological discussion had to be based on and proceed from this sacred body of literature. For Jesus and his followers, what the OT said, God said; and what God said, the OT said.[60]

There is an organic connection between God's *authority* and God's *words*. If they are God's *words*, then when any book or text in Scripture

---

[59] Beale 2012a: 98.
[60] Beale (ibid. 53), who is in debt to Green (2010: 130).

is approached it is imperative to determine what God himself means.[61] His divine authorial intent matters: biblical theology depends on it.

Unity of substance, *sensus plenior* and typology

Unity of substance

To review, divine authorial intent ensures that the diversity of human authorship across the canon is not chaotic, arbitrary and without progression. It is because there is a single divine author that there is a single narrative that builds in anticipation until its divine promises reach their fulfilment in Christ.[62] Put otherwise, to read Scripture as *Christian Scripture* – with the gospel at its centre – means approaching the text knowing the triune God has spoken in every epoch whether by providence or miracle to bring to fruition his redemptive plan communicated since the beginning.

The implications for hermeneutics are significant. 'The interpretative consequence of the canon reflecting the triunity of its divine author', says Richard Lints,

> is that knowing the meaning of any text is a function of knowing the meaning of every text. As we read the canon, the historical conditions under which the multiple authors and editors produced the books of Scripture are not to be privileged above the triunity of its divine authorization.[63]

Though always preserving the integrity of the many human authors, privileging the triunity of the divine author is essential because apart from such a privilege the canon's unity is driven by *pragmatics*. Instead, it should

---

[61] Poythress 1994: 90.

[62] Throughout this study I will use the phrase 'predictive prophecy and typology' because it seems the best way to keep both of these categories under the prophetic umbrella. Although typology will be touched on in the next chapter, it should be noted here that there is a prophetic element to typology; direct prediction is not the only type of prophecy. Beale explains, 'If typology is classified as partially prophetic, then it can be viewed as an exegetical method since the New Testament correspondence would be drawing out retrospectively the fuller prophetic meaning of the Old Testament type which was originally included by the divine author.' Beale 1994: 401.

[63] Lints 2015: 25.

stem from a unity of *substance*. As Carson explains, 'those with a high view of Scripture insist that what gives the canonical documents their unity is that, for all their enormous diversity, one Mind, one Actor, stands behind them; they constitute a truly revelatory base'. For that reason, Carson elaborates, 'the unity here envisaged is a *unity of substance* in the source documents themselves'.[64]

The implications for how one approaches biblical theology are not insignificant:

> The efforts of 'whole-Bible' biblical theology may sometimes be thwarted by the complexities of the task, and sometimes mocked by inadequate work, but they are not intrinsically doomed to frustration; there is an intrinsic unity that is to be pursued and explored.[65]

Carson concludes, 'In the final analysis, those who cannot agree to some kind of intrinsic unity in the Scriptures will always find their attempts at "whole-Bible" biblical theology, however admirable, to be the fruit of either accident or pragmatism.'[66] To be blunt, biblical theology is a fool's errand if the biblical scholar rids himself or herself of a commitment to the canon's intrinsic, conceptual unity.

There are few places where a unity of substance is seen with such vivid clarity as in the Gospels, where Jesus reads the Scriptures as divinely inspired texts that, in some fashion, speak of him. To borrow the vocabulary of Hays, Jesus reads *backwards*; following his example, and having seen the resurrected Lord for themselves, the disciples are taught to read backwards as well.[67] Jesus is fully convinced that Israel's fathers and prophets spoke of his day and the salvation he would secure.

Yet whether or not Jesus can interpret the whole of the Old Testament as a unified, canonical narrative loaded with Christological import depends on whether that canon is embedded with divine authorial intent throughout, and one that progresses, develops and reveals such intent the closer it approaches the advent of Christ. Everything hinges on whether the triune God himself has not only breathed out the Scriptures through the human authors but whether this progressive revelation of

---

[64] Carson 2000: 97. Emphasis added.
[65] Ibid.
[66] Ibid.
[67] Hays 2014: 2.

himself from Adam to the last Adam carries his tone of voice, that is, his intended meaning.

For that reason, *sensus plenior* is of great importance.

Sensus plenior

At the heart of *sensus plenior* is the conviction that the interpreter should not treat the text as if the human author is sufficient. There is also a fuller meaning intended by God to go beyond what even the human author understands in the moment.[68] As Robert Brown contends, there is an

> additional, deeper meaning, intended by God but not clearly intended by the human author, which is seen to exist in the words of a biblical text (or group of texts, or even a whole book) when they are studied in the light of further revelation or development in the understanding of revelation.[69]

Although a text is situated at a particular point in history, nevertheless it reaches beyond that historical parameter due to the progressive nature of revelation. As the canon builds and God's redemptive story unfolds, what was before dim now shines bright. This fuller meaning blossoms into

---

[68] To see how *sensus plenior* fits into the hermeneutical spectrum, Pennington (2012: 111–112) deciphers the differences between three hermeneutical categories: (1) 'Behind the Text', which is *historical* in nature, occurs when the interpreter uses redaction, form, source, social-scientific and historical criticism, as well as grammatical-historical exegesis, or engages with quest(s) for a historical Jesus. (2) 'In the Text', which concerns *literary* features, includes literary, narrative and composition criticism, genre analysis and intratextuality. What is crucial to observe at this point is this: human authorial *and* divine authorial intent pervade both of these categories (Behind the Text and In the Text). However, there is a third category where divine authorial intent supersedes the human author: (3) 'In Front of the Text', which concerns canonical and theological qualities. Here one finds the history of interpretation, reception history and *Wirkungsgeschichte*. Pennington also identifies disciplines and approaches to reading that are to be associated with this third category, including biblical theology, redemptive history, theological reading, *regula fidei*, figural reading and intertextuality. One need not agree with Pennington on every detail of these categorizations to see that divine authorial intent involves, but ultimately cannot be constrained to, the historical ('Behind the Text') and literary ('In the Text') features. As important as redaction criticism or genre analysis, e.g., may be for understanding the human author's intent, they are insufficient if one is to take that next step to understand the canonical features ('In Front of the Text'), the latter of which cannot be explained merely by a human author.

[69] Brown 1955: 92. Also see Brown 1953: 141–162; 1955: 92; 1963: 262–285; LaSor 1978b: 260–277; Moo 1986: 179–211. But to see how a Protestant view differs from a Roman Catholic view, see Poythress 1994: 108, n. 25.

maturity with the long-anticipated arrival of Israel's Messiah.[70] That which was foreshadowed through the human author's words is *amplified* as it progresses and reaches its fulfilment in Christ, just as the divine author envisioned. The meaning of a prophetic passage, especially if typological in nature, can be *enlarged* and *expanded*, escalating beyond the human author's immediate understanding due to the divine author's knowledge, understanding and eschatological intent.

To clarify, *sensus plenior* is not to advocate (as some fear) for a secret knowledge or some mystical extra meaning that is uprooted from the text itself or from history.[71] As God breathes out his words in and through the human author(s), his divine authorial intent is not circumscribed to what the human author understands in his immediate context.[72] God, as the divine author, can convey a fuller meaning that will become clearer as his progressive revelation builds and is in his timing fulfilled in redemptive history.[73] 'We may therefore legitimately speak of a "fuller meaning" than any one text provides,' says Carson.

> But the appeal should be made, not to some hidden divine knowledge,
> but to the pattern of revelation up to that time – a pattern not yet

---

[70] The literature on *sensus plenior* is vast and so is the controversy over its legitimacy. For an entryway to the literature, see Compton 2008: 23–33. It should also be qualified that *sensus plenior* is not antithetical to an evangelical affirmation of inspiration. To the contrary, says Moo, inspiration is thrown into question only if 'the meaning of Old Testament texts *must* be confined to what we can prove their human authors intended'. Moo 1986: 201. Emphasis original. For a response to some of the most common objections to *sensus plenior*, see Moo and Naselli 2016: 730–734.

[71] See Poythress 1994: 110. This is what some evangelicals fear *sensus plenior* will lead to, ultimately undermining inerrancy. Moo and Naselli (contra Kaiser) respond to that fear (and objection) with insight: 'Sometimes the NT attributes to OT texts more meaning than the OT author could have possibly known. That is fatal to inerrancy only if the meaning of the OT texts must be confined to what we can prove their human authors intended.' Moo and Naselli 2016: 722. Brown (via Manuel de Tuya) is also insightful: 'From the fact that God is using an instrument which is capable of knowledge, it does not follow that God can use this intelligent instrument only in as much as he actually knows all that God wanted to express.' Brown 1955: 133.

[72] While I am suspicious of Christological analogies, there could be a correlation between *sensus plenior* and the *extra Calvinisticum*. The person of Christ cannot be circumscribed to the human nature of Christ due to the divine nature. Meaning and intention cannot be circumscribed to the human author due to the divine author. The analogy fails, however, because the hypostatic union deals with one person but with Scripture there is dual authorship or persons. Nevertheless, there is commonality in this: in both cases it is the divine side that justifies something 'extra', something beyond the human.

[73] Moo qualifies, 'To be sure, God knows, as He inspires the human authors to write, what the ultimate meaning of their words will be; but it is not as if he has deliberately created a *double entendre* or hidden a meaning in the words that can only be uncovered through a special revelation.' Moo 1986: 206. To see this point played out via a test case (Ps. 22), see Poythress 1994: 108.

adequately discerned. The new revelation may therefore be truly new, yet at the same time capable of being checked against the old.[74]

Carson's careful nuance is worth repeating, lest one think *sensus plenior* gives a licence to the worst forms of postmodern exegesis. When the fuller meaning comes to light in redemptive history, it does not go *against* the original text in which it was conveyed but is 'capable of being *checked against* the old' and is consistent with the wider 'pattern of revelation'. It is necessary, then, to avoid thinking of dual authorship as if the two authors 'simply stand side by side', Poythress qualifies. Instead, there is an inherent unity so that 'each points to the other and affirms the presence and operation of the other'.[75] Concursive operation is key to canonical unity.

As was hinted at before, *sensus plenior* is to be expected if Scripture is duly authored and inspired by God: meaning is not limited to the human author but originates from the divine author himself, who governs history and sees his divine purpose through until its full maturity.[76] 'This grows out of the belief that God has a unified plan and that plan is known to him, even if he reveals it to his creatures progressively.'[77] God, therefore, is not only the main actor in the drama of redemption but the primary author

---

[74] Carson 1984: 93. The refusal to detach typology from history is a distinctive of an evangelical biblical theology and, ultimately, an evangelical view of Scripture. Although Carson has in mind 1 Cor. 10:1–11, his conclusion is applicable across the canon: 'we cannot avoid the implications of Paul's insistence that Christ was the rock that followed the Israelites, and that these things "were written down *as warnings for us*, on whom the culmination of the ages has come." The language suggests purpose, ultimately *divine purpose*.' Carson 2004: 400. Emphases added.

[75] Poythress 1994: 96. Hays does not use the language of *sensus plenior* but seems to have something similar in mind when he speaks of multiple senses in reference to a figural reading of the OT by the NT authors. For the 'Evangelists the "meaning" of the Old Testament texts was not confined to the human author's original historical setting or to the meaning that could have been grasped by the original readers. Rather, the Evangelists received Scripture as a complex body of texts given to the community by God, who had scripted the whole biblical drama in such a way that it had multiple senses. Some of these senses are hidden, so that they come into focus only *retrospectively*.' Hays 2016: 358. Emphasis original.

[76] '[F]or God to mean all that the human author means does not imply that the human author means all that the divine author means. The doctrines of revelation and inspiration do not demand such an equal sharing of understanding. God's meaning can be more than the human author's, but it can never be less than that of the human author.' Glenny 1995: 485. Kaiser (1994: 55–69) is aggressive in his attack of *sensus plenior*, arguing that it undermines biblical authority. But that is to miss Glenny's precise nuance: all Scripture is inspired but that does not mean the divine author and his meaning are limited to a single human author's cognitive comprehension at the moment he pens the text. Inspiration and understanding overlap but should not be confused as synonymous. God's understanding goes beyond the human author's, which should not surprise us since he is the Creator not the creature.

[77] Feinberg 1988: 128.

and scriptwriter.[78] If he really is the divine author, says Beale, 'then we are not only concerned with discerning the intention of the human author but also the ultimate divine intent of what was written in the Old Testament, which could well transcend that of the immediate consciousness of the writer'.[79]

Likewise, says Pennington, the 'divine authorship of Scripture means that the meaning of a text is not and cannot be limited to its human author's intent'. In other words:

Asserting a meaning of the text beyond the historical one is a necessary result of understanding the Bible not just as a mere record of religious beliefs and events but also as the Word or speech of the living God, who continues to speak through and from the Word.[80]

Quoting Vanhoozer, Pennington concludes:

Thus, when we confess the Bible to be God's Word, another stratum of divine discourse emerges at a higher, canonical, level of complexity. What God is doing at this level *depends* on the human discourse, but it cannot be *reduced* to human discourse.[81]

Whenever a text is interpreted one must not only consider the human author and his historical background, but must also consider what God is saying through the human author, taking into account the rest of redemptive history, some of which the human author may or may not understand in its eschatological entirety.[82]

Take for example prophetic fulfilment in the Gospels from the book of Isaiah, which chapters 3 and 4 will focus on at length. 'Isaiah's intention', says Poythress, 'was that we should understand whatever God intended by

---

[78] Caneday 2019: 144.

[79] 'If we assume the legitimacy of an inspired canon, then we should seek to interpret any part of the canon within its overall canonical context (given that one divine mind stands behind it all and expresses its thoughts in logical fashion).' Beale 1994: 401. On the relationship between inspiration and typology, see Parker 2011.

[80] Pennington 2012: 117.

[81] Pennington (ibid.), quoting Vanhoozer 2006: 69–70. Emphases original.

[82] Poythress 1994: 96. Also consider Bock 1999: 94–95: 'Progressive hermeneutics argues for stability of meaning,' explains Bock, 'while also honoring the dimensions that dual authorship brings to the gradual unfolding of promise. The literary-theological argument is that God reveals the outworking of His promise gradually as Scripture unfolds its meaning and introduces new promises and connections.'

his words. Hence there *is* a unity of meaning . . . We do not have two diverse meanings, Isaiah's and God's simply placed side by side with no relation to one another.'[83] Or as Ben Meyer writes, 'In prophecy what the symbol intends is identical with what God, for whom the prophet speaks, intends.' However, this 'may enter the prophet's own horizon only partially and imperfectly'.[84]

This much is assumed by Peter when he refers to the inner mindset and deliberation of the prophets through whom God spoke:

> Concerning this salvation, the prophets who prophesied about the grace that was to be yours searched and enquired carefully, enquiring what person or time the Spirit of Christ in them was indicating when he predicted the sufferings of Christ and the subsequent glories. It was revealed to them that they were serving not themselves but you, in the things that have now been announced to you through those who preached the good news to you by the Holy Spirit sent from heaven, things into which angels long to look. (1 Peter 1:10–12)[85]

'The Holy Spirit knew beforehand the course of history with its consummation in Christ, and so in guiding the writers he intended a deeper meaning than they understood,' comments Wenham.[86] Hence Paul can refer to the 'revelation of the mystery that was kept secret for long ages but has now been disclosed and through the prophetic writings has been made known' (Rom. 16:25–26).

Such a principle, it should be qualified, applies not merely to Isaiah but to those during and after the time of Christ. For instance, it is not necessary for Luke to comprehend every future implication intended by Jesus' parables, nor is it required for someone like John to have exhaustive knowledge of what will take place in the eschaton according to his vision in Revelation.[87]

---

[83] Poythress 1994: 97. Emphasis original.

[84] Meyer 1979: 246.

[85] Contra Kaiser 1994: 55–69. For a response to Kaiser, see Poythress 1994: 85–88; Moo and Naselli 2016: 721–722.

[86] Wenham 1994: 107–108.

[87] Poythress 1994: 97. A similar point may be insinuated by Vos (1948: 355). Poythress puts no limits on the depths of *sensus plenior* since we are dealing with a divine author who is infinite in wisdom. Using Paul as an example, Poythress explains, 'We are not dealing with "bare" human nature . . . We are already dealing with the divine, namely the Holy Spirit. Paul as a human being may not be immediately, analytically self-conscious of all the implications of what he is saying. But people always know more and imply more than what they are perfectly self-conscious of. How far does this "more" extend? We are dealing with a person restored in

Typology as revelatory and prospective

If Peter is right, then not only direct predictive prophecy (e.g. Isa. 9:6–7; 11:1–5; Mic. 5:2; Zech. 9:9) but *typology*, which pervades Scripture from start to finish (and may be more prevalent than direct prediction), proves to be instrumental.[88] Typology is one of the central ways – some say it is *the* central way – Jesus and the New Testament authors see the Old Testament fulfilled in the New Testament (e.g. 1 Cor. 10:6, 11; Rom. 5:14; 1 Peter 3:21; Heb. 8:5; 9:24).[89] Through typology the divine purpose is communicated not only in the initial type but most of all as that type approaches its fulfilment in the antitype itself – *antitype* being 'the reality that corresponds to the type'.[90] Nevertheless, for the biblical authors such typology, in which this deeper meaning was deposited so often, was never meant to be detached from history. Paul grounds the last Adam in the first Adam (Rom. 5), and Jesus (and John) roots the crucifixion in the serpent Moses lifted up in the wilderness (John 3:14), and so forth. 'The biblical revelation is an organism – the essential elements of the whole are to be found in every part.'[91]

In that light, Brown's definition of *sensus plenior*, though a good one, deserves one slight tweak: *sensus plenior* does not merely apply to *words* but to *types* as well (types being persons, institutions, events, etc.).[92] The reason for this is that typology is not just a hermeneutical method that later Old Testament or New Testament writers apply to earlier Old Testament

---

the image of Christ, filled with the Holy Spirit, having the mind of Christ. There are incalculable depths here. We cannot calculate the limits of the Holy Spirit and the wisdom of Christ. Neither can we perform a perfect analytical separation of our knowledge from our union with Christ through the Holy Spirit.' Poythress 1994: 98–99.

[88] Davidson (1981: 405–406) defines typology as a 'hermeneutical endeavor on the part of the biblical writers [that] may be viewed as the study of certain OT salvation-historical realities (persons, events, or institutions) which God has specifically designed to correspond to, and be prospective/predictive prefigurations of, their ineluctable (devoir-être) and absolutely escalated eschatological fulfillment aspects (Christological/ecclesiological/apocalyptic) in NT salvation history'. Poythress (2016: 242) is far more succinct: 'A *type* is a symbol that points forward to a greater or climactic realization.' Emphasis original.

[89] Davidson 1981: 1; Goppelt 1982: 196.

[90] Poythress 2016: 242.

[91] Wenham 1994: 107–108.

[92] I am not saying that *sensus plenior* and typology are synonymous. The former is a broader category than the latter, so that *sensus plenior* may be characteristic of other forms of revelation. My point here, rather, is to guard against distinguishing them so much that they are unrelated. Moo distinguishes between *sensus plenior* and typology, but says the former has to do with words and the latter with things. I agree with Glenny (1995: 500) that if 'words represent things', Moo's 'distinction is difficult to maintain'. Yes, there is a distinction but also much overlap.

texts; rather, typology is a form of *revelation itself,* one (significant) way God *reveals* what is and what is to come in Christ.[93]

This qualification avoids subjectivity, as if the New Testament authors are inventing types that are foreign to the Old Testament.[94] Instead, typology is organic and intrinsic to the Old Testament itself, infused and imbued therein by the divine author, but only progressively unveiled as the divine author reveals such types for what they are with further revelatory clarity. In short, there is a historical correspondence between the antitype and the Old Testament type, but also a transcendence as the type is brought to fulfilment in the antitype just as intended by the divine author.[95]

This unveiling of types centres on Christ, the antitype. The New Testament authors count it their privilege to identify some of these types to show their fulfilment in Christ.

> The NT writers' recognizing of OT types that are embedded within Scripture is due to Messiah's revelatory act that both exposes the types with sharper clarity and illumines eyes to see what was concealed within plain sight in Scripture's text.[96]

That is why Warfield describes the Old Testament as furniture in a room dimly lit, yet with the arrival of Christ and the canon of the New Testament the lights come on so that one sees God's furnishings with greater clarity.[97] The furnishings were always there, but only in Christ's light do we see light.[98] Or, as Augustine said, 'The New Testament is in the Old concealed, and the Old is in the New revealed.'[99]

---

[93] To 'identify typology as a hermeneutical term or key locates the discussion within interpretation of Scripture rather than principally within the nature of revelation where it belongs. To categorize typology as the NT writers' "hermeneutical endeavor" and to identify biblical typology with nomenclature such as "typological interpretation" or "exegetical method" seems to subvert the claim that biblical types are prophetic foreshadowings or prefiguring clues of things to come which are recognizable within the OT before they reach fulfillment in their NT antitypes.' Caneday 2019: 141. Also see Seitz 2001: 10.

[94] This is why Caneday, quoting Parker, says, 'biblical types do not call for *typological interpretation.* Rather, our role is to identify types, symbols, and allegories that are in Scripture and not creatively invent them as the phrase "typological interpretation" suggests.' Caneday 2019: 142. Emphasis original. Cf. Parker 2017: 67.

[95] Davidson 1981: 403.

[96] Caneday 2019: 141, 150.

[97] Warfield 1932: 141–142.

[98] Here I am playing on Ps. 36:9.

[99] Augustine, *Quaestionum in Heptateuchum* 2.73, as quoted in Waltke 2007: 560.

Typology, then, is key to this concealing and revealing across the canon. As will be seen in chapters 2–4, *persons* (Adam, Moses, Elijah, David), *objects* (tabernacle, temple, lamb, rock), *events* (exodus, sacrifices, exile) and *institutions* (priesthood/priest, kingdom/king) are all types that have a fuller meaning that goes beyond what the human author might have understood at the time, thanks to the divine author's intention.[100] As Poythress explains, the

> significance of a type is not *fully* discernible until the time of fulfillment. The type means a good deal at the time, but it is open-ended. One can anticipate in a vague, general way how fulfillment might come, but the details remain in obscurity. When the fulfillment does come, it throws additional light on the significance of the original symbolism.[101]

That means, then, that *sensus plenior* is intrinsic to the progressive nature of revelation itself, typology included. When a type is first revealed in Scripture, it is at this point – its conception – that the human author's purview is the most limited, not knowing all the intentions the divine author has in mind. But as revelation progresses, and that type is elaborated by later Old Testament and New Testament authors, the distance between

---

[100] In part, what distinguishes typology from allegory is the *historical* nature of these types. As Thiselton explains, 'The major difference between *type* and *allegory* is that the former is grounded in *history* and presupposes corresponding *events*; the latter is grounded in a linguistic system of signs or *semiotic codes* and presupposes resonances or parallels between *ideas* or *semiotic meanings*.' Thiselton 2000: 730. Emphases original. Beale captures the difference with his definition of typology: 'Typological interpretation involves an extended reference to the original meaning of an Old Testament text which develops it but does not contradict it. Put another way, it does not *read into* the text a different or higher sense, but *draws out* from it a different or higher application of the same sense.' Beale 1994: 395. Emphases original. Cf. as well Von Rad 1979: 21. With these differences in mind, *sensus plenior* is not an excuse for unjustified allegory, the type that is divorced from history, dependent on 'semiotic codes' (Thiselton 2000: 730). The Fathers are a model of theological interpretation because they refuse to divorce theology from the text itself. The Reformers retrieve the patristic emphasis on theological interpretation, but with a notable suspicion towards allegory that segregates exegesis from history. See Carson 2011: 198; Dennison 2008: 357–358; George 2011: 17–73. The second half of this chapter and especially chapter 6 will build on this 'Great Tradition', drawing on Augustine, Hilary of Poitiers, Thomas Aquinas and John Calvin, for example. In doing so, *sensus plenior* will assist our understanding of typology but always in a way that is faithful to how the divine author has embedded his divine authorial intent textually and canonically across redemptive history. This project cannot explore the depths of Theological Interpretation of Scripture and debates over patristic and medieval methods, but consult Billings 2010; Carson 2011: 187–207; Vanhoozer 2005a; Wright 2019.

[101] Poythress 1987: 115–116. Emphasis original.

human authorial intent and divine authorial intent narrows. It narrows because the human authors more and more understand what the divine author intends and how he will bring this type to fulfilment. Put otherwise, prior to a type maturing within the canon, the human author has limited understanding as to what the divine author will do with the type.[102]

To our benefit, the reader who has the advantage of seeing the type in view of its antitype can look back on how an Old Testament text escalates and conclude that God added and did not add meaning at the same time. In our experience we see meaning increase with the progression of redemptive history. What the original readers could not have seen in their limited purview is later seen as the type blossoms more and more. Yet, at the same time, the meaning never changes because God is the original scriptwriter and what he intended that type to foreshadow in the end was present all along, even if veiled to human eyes.[103] 'Even earlier readers could appreciate that there was more meaning than what they could presently grasp, because they could know, from what they grasped even then, that the climax was still in the future.'[104]

---

[102] Carson puts it this way: 'The one dramatic differential between what the human author means and what God the inspirer of Scripture means is found *toward the beginning* of a typological trajectory – i.e., before it has been established *within the canonical Scriptures themselves* as a typology in the making. I suspect that later OT writers begin to discern the shape of at least some typologies to which their own writings contribute; when the seed of that typology first appears, it is hard to justify the thesis that the human author has any clue.' Personal correspondence, 8 March 2019. Emphases original.

[103] I owe this point to Poythress (2016: 227). This point has led Glenny (1995: 499) to say that it may be better to speak of multiple 'dimensions or aspects of meaning'. 'A later-revealed fuller divine meaning is not a new meaning of a text. It is a legitimate extension of the concept affirmed in the text in its original context, which is a part of the total divine meaning of that text.'

[104] Poythress 2016: 227. Kaiser and company will object by appealing to the difference between meaning and significance, as if the NT's typological reading of the OT is mere application. But as others have responded, this sharp divide between meaning and significance is artificial and quite narrow, foreign to how language works. 'Meaning has many aspects,' syas Glenny. 'It includes referents, concepts, implications, goals and attitudes, among other things.' Therefore, while there is a 'difference between the original signification and a later significance', nevertheless we 'cannot say a Biblical statement only had a referential aspect of meaning in its original context, nor can we say the conceptual meaning found in the original statement cannot be applied to referents other than those to whom it was originally addressed'. Glenny quotes Oss (1988: 125) to point out also that a 'strict separation between "meaning" and "significance" "results in a loss of normativeness for the message of the Bible"', the very thing someone like Kaiser is so concerned to preserve. This is ironic since a 'strict separation' resembles neo-orthodoxy's 'dichotomy between the propositional context of a text and one's personal encounter (application) with the text'. Glenny 1995: 496–497. It was Poythress, however, who first pointed out similarities with neo-orthodoxy (1986: 17–19). For other critiques of the meaning–significance–application divide, see Pennington 2012: 132–134; Frame 1987: 82–98; Oss 1988: 105–127.

Sensus plenior is helpful if for no other reason than it moves the interpreter beyond the grammar and historical background of the human author to the divine author's intention not just in one text but across the canon as it progressively and typologically unfolds in God's own timing and according to his own plan.[105] More to the point, it is because *sensus plenior* is grounded in the intention of the divine author that typology is *eschatologically* oriented, not merely being *retrospective*, but *prospective* as well.[106] That is because there is a predictive and prophetic nature or component, one the New Testament authors recognize (rather than invent).[107] That prophetic component is intended by the divine author himself.[108] As Carson explains, when a New Testament author

claims that something or other connected with the gospel is the (typological) fulfillment of some old covenant pattern, he may not necessarily be claiming that everyone connected with the old covenant type understood the pattern to be pointing forward, but he is certainly claiming that *God himself designed it to be pointing forward.*[109]

As insightful as Hays is to stress reading backwards, *sensus plenior* and typology, if revelatory, demand the interpreter to read forwards as well. In fact, we read backwards *in order to* read forwards.[110] Typology, says

---

[105] Therefore, I think Blomberg's warning is justified and needed today: 'Jesus' *hermeneutic* hardly matches what some Christian college or seminary professors have taught as the only proper way for believers to handle the Scriptures. There is a pervasive typological, and occasionally Christological, interpretation of the Bible in the Gospels' portrait of Jesus' approach to the Old Testament that is hard to relegate solely to later redaction. If the conservative religious leaders in Jesus' day were (wrongly) outraged by some of his applications of Scripture, especially to himself, then their successors among today's evangelical instructors had best beware of ever insisting that all forms of typological or Christological interpretations of the Bible that do not reflect the human authors' original intentions are misguided.' Blomberg 2016: 699. Emphasis original.

[106] France 1971: 39–42; Baker 1991: 198; Von Rad 1965: 2.363–366, 384. On the disparate views, see Carson 2004: 406.

[107] See Davidson 1981: 94, 402.

[108] With typology 'there is revealed a divine design, in which the OT realities were superintended by God so as to be advance-presentations of the NT realities'. Ibid. 402.

[109] Carson 2004: 406. Emphasis added. Carson adds, 'In other words, *when* the type was *discovered* to be a type (at some point along the trajectory of its repeated pattern. Only after its culmination?) – i.e. when it was discovered to be a pattern that pointed to the future – is not determinative for its classification as a type.' Ibid. Emphasis original.

[110] As much as I appreciate Hays (2014), he gives the impression that the NT authors *create* types or echoes by reading backwards; hence his stress on retrospective as opposed to prospective. But this is misguided: types in the OT are revelatory, which means God himself has embedded them in the OT. They are not read back into the OT by the NT authors; instead, the

Davidson, is 'not merely the recognition of a recurring rhythm or structural analogy within God's revelation in history but consists of divinely designed, predictive (devoir-être) prefigurations'.[111]

If that is not the case, then the reader of Scripture is invited to interpret an individual passage or the whole story of Scripture in a way that risks subjectivity, seeing allusions, echoes or types where there are none. If there is no divine intention and *sensus plenior*, then 'we are simply "overhearing" a human voice from long ago, a voice to which we may respond in whatever way suits our own value system'. On the one hand, warns Poythress, 'equating divine and human meaning in the Bible' does guard the interpreter from 'the arbitrariness of an allegorical system'. On the other hand, it can succumb to its own arbitrariness. For 'when we use this idea in order simply to stick to human meaning, arbitrariness can still exist in the area of application'.[112]

Yet if there is a divine authorial intention that not only is tied to the human author but anticipates a fuller meaning through the human author, one that is progressively revealed and interpreted as the divine author brings to fulfilment his plan of redemption in Christ, then arbitrariness is discouraged from entering the hermeneutical process, at least if one takes into consideration not only the original human author but the entire canon

---

(note 110 *cont.*) NT authors are identifying types that already exist, presupposing that God himself intended them to be progressively unveiled. In other words, Hays is right to observe the *retrospective* nature of intertextual interpretation. However, at times he goes too far, as if the NT authors are inventing types where they otherwise do not exist, or as if the OT authors could never have known their words were participating in what would eventually lead to a figural fulfilment. Pushing the retrospective nature too far, so as to exclude production altogether, cannot fully explain how there is intertextuality within the OT itself, before one ever enters the NT. Nor can it explain passages like John 3 and Luke 24 where Jesus issues a rebuke to Nicodemus and then to the two disciples on the road to Emmaus (even calling them foolish!) for not understanding the many places where the OT spoke of what Christ accomplished at the cross and in the resurrection. In other words, the NT authors are not inventing types where there are none; rather, they are recognizing types where God has placed them. That assumes typology is revelatory in nature, and that typology has a prospective orientation that lends future authors to recognize its presence. All that to say, as long as the retrospective quality is not pushed to an absolute degree, the concept is fruitful, explaining how intertextuality works.

[111] Davidson 1981: 407; cf. DeRouchie 2018: 164.

[112] Poythress 1994: 87. Poythress compares a single intention/interpretation approach to a *sensus plenior* approach by means of the Christological metaphor: 'The human instrument is taken up into the divine message, rather than the divine message being "trimmed down" to suit the human instrument. If we were willing to use the analogy of the person and natures of Christ, we could say that Deuteronomy 5:22–33 is analogous to the Chalcedonian view (human nature taken up into the divine person), whereas the "single interpretation" approach is analogous to a kenotic view (divine person "losing" some attributes for the sake of assuming human nature).' Ibid. 94–95.

of Scripture.[113] Hence the importance of a *redemptive–historical, canonical approach* that pays attention not only to the textual and epochal horizons, but to the canonical horizon. 'Since meaning is a holistic concept, and God is the author of the Scriptures,' says Lints, 'a faithful interpreter must take the whole of God's horizon (the canonical horizon) and the reality of the progressive nature of that horizon (its epochal significance) into account.'[114] The text's dual authorship invites the interpreter to discern its meaning by also searching out the divine author's intention with the entire canon in view.[115]

From fruit to flower: Augustine and Christological progression

Discerning meaning, however, is not as easy as it sounds. As already hinted at, the canon, after all, did not drop down from heaven but developed over time. It follows the projection of redemptive history, which develops gradually. With every stage in its story, its *telos*, Christ Jesus, is unveiled a little more. Even when Christ encourages his listeners to search the Scriptures, for 'it is they that bear witness to me' (John 5:39), he assumes there has been development; the Jews in the audience familiar with the story of the Torah would have assumed the same. Jesus intends his audience to read the Scriptures as a unity that centres around himself; Christ is the centre, the intertextual glue, so to speak. Nevertheless, the Scriptures do not reveal the fullness of Christ all at once. If they did, then Christological intertextuality from Old Testament to New Testament would be unnecessary and Jesus' own Christological reading of the Old Testament, one imitated by his disciples, would be emptied of its type–antitype structure.

Turning to an agricultural illustration, yet one innate to Scripture itself (e.g. Isa. 11; Jer. 23), Augustine captures the sort of progressive Christological revelation present throughout the Scriptures. In his *Expositions of the Psalms* Augustine writes:

---

[113] Perhaps this is why Poythress (ibid. 90), adds that the reader must not only consider what is said directly but what God implies: both are embedded with his divine authority.

[114] Lints 1993: 294–295.

[115] 'The attempt to draw out the divine intention of a text is certainly part of the exegetical task. And above all, if we assume the legitimacy of an inspired canon, then we should seek to interpret any part of that canon within its overall canonical context (given that one divine mind stands behind it all and expresses its thoughts in logical fashion).' To do so does not mean, as some suppose, that we are leaving exegesis behind. Rather, exegesis is broadened not only to consider the immediate context of a text but its canonical context as well. Beale 1994: 401.

At that time the New Testament was hidden within the Old, as fruit is in the root. If you look for fruit in a root you will not find it; yet you will not find any fruit on the branches either, unless it has sprung from the root.

Augustine then comes to his point:

Christ himself, inasmuch as he was to be born according to the flesh, was hidden in the root, that is to say, in the bloodline of the patriarchs. At the appointed time he was to be revealed, like fruit forming from the flower, and so Scripture says, *A shoot has sprung from Jesse's stock, and a flower has opened.* (Isa. 11:1)[116]

Independent of Augustine, LaSor uses the same illustration but draws out its implications for *sensus plenior*:

An ordinary seed contains in itself everything that will develop in the plant or tree to which it is organically related: every branch, every leaf, every flower. Yet no amount of examination by available scientific methods will disclose to us what is in that seed. However, once the seed has developed to its fullness, we can see how the seed has been fulfilled ... [and] we have sufficient revelation in the Scriptures to keep our interpretations of *sensus plenior* from becoming totally subjective.[117]

With this illustration of a seed and tree in mind, LaSor strives for balance when he concludes that *sensus plenior* 'lies outside and beyond the historical situation of the prophet, and therefore cannot be derived by grammatico-historical exegesis', and yet *sensus plenior* is also 'part of the history of redemption, and therefore it can be controlled by the study of Scripture taken in its entirety'.[118]

---

[116] Augustine 2001b: 470–471. Carter (2018: 159) believes Augustine's point should even lead us to think of Christ in the OT in *sacramental* terms: 'Augustine uses this image of root and fruit to stress that Christ really is present in the Old Testament, which functions sacramentally to bring us to him.' However, apart from divine authorial intent in this progressive unveiling of the fruit (Christ), no intertextual unity exists; far from a sacramental presence there would be a real absence.

[117] LaSor 1978a: 55–56.

[118] Ibid.; cf. Beale (1994: 393), who agrees and reiterates LaSor's point.

Capturing both these aspects or senses is no easy accomplishment, but doing so is imperative if one is to preserve not only the immediate historical meaning of a text but also the wider, canonical framework that serves to outline, expand and amplify that text's ultimate purpose and fulfilment. As G. K. Beale notes, 'Consideration of the immediate literary context of Old Testament verses, which is what most exegetes affirm as an essential part of the historical-grammatical method, should therefore be *supplemented* with the canonical literary context.'[119]

From the process of revelation in history to revelation incarnated in history

The main focus of this project is not the nature of typology per se, nor is it an exploration of the countless ways *sensus plenior* may show itself across the canon. Rather, these are means to a much larger end: establishing Scripture's inspired character not in part but in whole. Demonstrating the canon's unity across redemptive history in the person that binds the covenants and testaments together is critical to achieving that end. Showing Jesus to be the 'Christological clamp' is paramount to confirming canonical unity and the canon's divine origin.

Incarnational accommodation, therefore, is living proof that the Scriptures from Moses to the prophets are not segregated human records but a unified divine communication. When the Son of God becomes incarnate and secures redemption on behalf of the ungodly, any residual canonical ambiguity disappears; it is now clear that types which preceded the incarnation were intended by God himself to testify to his Son. The fulfilment of such prefigurement provides the interpreter with deep hermeneutical assurance: *in the gospel of Jesus Christ the reader of Christian Scripture receives firm validation that the Scriptures are from God and carry his divine voice from beginning to end.*

That fundamental belief characterized Jesus' ministry from start to finish. Jesus assumed the entire scriptural witness was from his Father and therefore every part of it was infused by his divine authorial intent, permitting Jesus to look to it not only in its parts but in its whole. That led Jesus to conclude that from 'Moses and all the Prophets' the Scriptures spoke 'things concerning himself' (Luke 24:27). More remarkable still,

---

[119] Beale 1994: 394. Emphasis added.

Jesus not only (1) observed a canonical unity to the Scriptures that he attributed to the divine author, and he not only (2) assumed divine authorial intent was communicated in and through the many human authors, but Jesus believed (3) his own teaching, actions and mission were the fulfilment, culmination and consummation of that which the divine author promised in the Hebrew Scriptures.

Yet the advent of Christ not only involved Christ's presupposing and confirming the Old Testament as his Father's Spirit-inspired, canonical and covenantal revelation, and announcing, as the new and final Prophet of God, that he had come to reveal his Father and his Father's new covenant word to his people; it also meant (4) Christ himself *is* the Word from the Father, revelation incarnate, the one and only one who brings to fulfilment God's covenant word in ages past. As Vos explains, 'the process of revelation is not only concomitant with history, but it becomes incarnate in history'.[120]

It is to that process of revelation within history that we now turn in an effort to understand the supreme revelation that becomes incarnate in history for us and our salvation.

---

[120] Vos 1948: 6.

2

The book of the covenant and canon consciousness

If Jesus' own understanding of the Scriptures is to be explored, it is necessary to answer that central question at the start: What is the historical milieu that defines Jesus' own reception of Israel's Scriptures? The answer is found in the question itself. The Scriptures Jesus read and inherited within his own Jewish context were the Scriptures *of Israel*. That sounds obvious, but it cannot be taken for granted when one considers the many quests for the historical Jesus that dislocate Jesus from the history of Israel.

Nor should one miss how such an assertion situates the Scriptures of Jesus' day within a Hebrew paradigm that assumes at every turn Yahweh's supernatural presence and vocal governance throughout his people's journey from Egypt to Canaan. In one sense, there was nothing radical about Jesus' presuppositions concerning the *nature* of the Hebrew Scriptures. The Jews of Jesus' day, including Jews who opposed him, agreed that the Scriptures on which their religious beliefs were grounded were God given and God breathed. What was controversial about Jesus was the way he interpreted those Scriptures, believing they were fulfilled in himself. Yet there was no debate between Jesus and the Jews over whether the Scriptures were divinely inspired, inerrant and sufficient for Jewish faith and practice. As Vos has said, Jesus' witness to the truthfulness of the Scriptures was not a belief in which 'Jesus stood alone'. 'Every orthodox person, Jewish or Christian, shared that with Him. In His treatment of the Bible Jesus was the most orthodox of the orthodox.' Those who would try to attribute to Jesus a 'laxer or freer attitude' towards the Scriptures rest their case 'on a lack of discrimination'.[1]

---

[1] Vos 2014: 358.

This much can be seen in the way Jesus and the Jews insinuated dual authorship: on numerous occasions they referred to what Moses or David or Isaiah had said (see chapters 3 and 4). Nevertheless, they also understood that through their forefathers God himself had spoken, so that what their forefathers said, God said. This divine–human concursus may have been oral in its expression (at least in some cases) but it was literary as well. What God said through Moses or David or Isaiah to Israel took the form of inscripturation as well as declaration.

Moreover, by the first century Jesus and the Jews had a definitive canon of Scripture and it was this canon that became the centrepiece to their hermeneutical, Christological and eschatological debates with one another. Jesus could claim the words of Isaiah, quote from the psalms of David, and allude to the writings of prophets like Ezekiel, Jeremiah and Zechariah only because his Jewish listeners, which included scribes and Pharisees, assumed the writings of such Hebrew forefathers originated from the mouth of God and carried divine authority.

The manner in which such Scriptures came to Jesus deserves further articulation if Jesus' own presuppositions concerning the Scriptures of Israel are to be understood. In this chapter several main contours that define God's covenantal speech to Israel will be explored. To begin, consider three overarching developments in Israel's reception of Yahweh's word.

Yahweh's covenantal word

First, there is no question in Israel's mind that it is *God's* word that explains their existence, and the *covenantal* nature of that word is what defines them as a called-out, redeemed people of Yahweh. From the efficacy of God's speech-act at creation to the initial covenant promises made to Abraham to the delivery of God's written word at Sinai to the prophetic word before, during and after exile, the people of Israel are to understand the word of God, communicated orally and in writing, as nothing other than the divine discourse that brought them into existence and instructed them in the way of covenant blessing.

Whether it was Moses, Samuel, David, Jeremiah or Isaiah, each carried a message from God, though communicated to them in diverse ways, a message not to be heard only once but written down and revisited. Yet that message was not arbitrary in its timing nor was the divinely chosen medium irrelevant to its success. God spoke a saving word in and through the cutting of covenants with his people, covenants that not only explained Israel's genesis but maintained their relationship with Yahweh as his chosen people. Within the context of these covenants, God's word took on permanent literary form, as seen for example with the Law of Moses, the psalms of David and the writings of the Prophets, not because God merely approved their message but rather because the message itself originated from the mouth and finger of God.

Through God's covenants, God's word proved instrumental for several reasons.

1. To say that God's word throughout Israel's history is wrapped within the context of his covenantal relationship with his people is to accentuate that for Israel revelation comes through *redemption*, and redemption through God's *revelation*. God's word is covenantal because it is a saving word to his people. As redemptive history progresses, therefore, so too does God's covenantal word.[2] God's speech inscripturated defines Israel because his discourse is a covenantal discourse, one with saving efficacy, even if it is diachronic in its delivery. This point will be returned to below.

2. The word communicated through God's covenants is meant to structure the covenant Israel is to live by without compromise. At Sinai, for example, the word of Yahweh is so closely tied to the covenant Yahweh cuts that the word becomes the *constitution* of the covenant, instructing Israel as to what covenant life with Yahweh is to look like and what curses or blessings await them should they disobey or obey that covenant word. Even the location of this covenant treaty in the ark of the covenant is meant to serve as an ever-present witness for and against Israel. At points the law at Sinai will even be referred to as the *book of the covenant*, the authoritative and sufficient word from God to his people, Israel.

3. The covenantal nature of the word is intended by God to be *prophetic* and *eschatological* due to its *Christological* orientation. This last point depends on the first; that is, revelation comes through redemption and redemption through revelation. God's covenantal word promises the redemption of God's covenant people will be brought to fulfilment in God's Messiah. As will be seen in chapters 3 and 4, Christ sees himself as the fulfilment of the covenant promises God made to Israel's forefathers, as do the apostles after the resurrection and ascension. Christ ushers in the

---

[2] I say this within the context of Israel's history, or more broadly within redemptive history. It is not meant to be taken absolutely, as if to preclude general revelation.

kingdom of God ('Repent, the kingdom of God is at hand') and with it a new covenant, one he will ratify by means of his own sacrificial blood.

The covenant God made with Abraham, and the promises God spoke to Abraham, escalate across redemptive history, and are solidified in God's inspired, written word, until they find their fulfilment in him who is their *telos*, Christ Jesus. Therefore, there is a covenantal nature to God's spoken and written word because the word of God is redemptive in its power. Yet that covenant word develops in its revelation of God's plan of redemption until it is clear that God will send a final, definitive covenantal Word, namely his own Son, to reveal the Father, inaugurate God's kingdom and establish a new covenant that brings prior covenants to their appointed fulfilment.

Progressive and diachronic

Second, the revelatory nature of the word that God communicates to his people is *progressive* in nature because the covenantal medium through which it is born is diachronic. As already hinted at, God's revelation of himself to Israel is itself redemptive in nature, but since the redemption of the people of God is progressive, building across the biblical story-line until the arrival of the Messiah, so too is the revelation of God to his people. 'Revelation is the interpretation of redemption.' Therefore, says Vos, it must 'unfold itself in instalments as redemption does'.[3] Vos does qualify, however, that revelation and redemption are not absolutely coextensive, 'for revelation comes to a close at a point where redemption still continues'.[4]

The progressive, diachronic nature of the covenant word God speaks to his people also assumes that the unity present in revelation across redemptive history is amalgamated by its goal. Within the context of his covenant promises, God's revelation to his people builds with anticipation towards its own culmination. As becomes apparent the closer the reader gets to the advent of Yahweh's Messiah, the unity present throughout progressive revelation is built on the expectation of his arrival. God's word may be progressive in its delivery, but Christ is always the centre throughout. Yahweh's covenant promises made and reiterated from Adam

---

[3] Vos 1948: 6.
[4] Ibid.

to the Prophets take on fuller form the nearer history itself approaches the redemption this Christ will consummate.

Therefore, to say that God's covenantal word is progressive is also to say that such a progression is focused on and driven by Christology. The phrase 'redemptive history' can be used in biblical theology because God's covenantal word has been fulfilled in him whom John calls the Word, the one who not only was with God but was God (John 1:1). The unity present in the canon, a unity of substance (see chapter 1), is one Jesus inherited and is due to its divine author, who not only communicated to his people his plan of redemption but then, at the proper time, fulfilled that promissory word by sending his own Son (Heb. 1:1–2). Canonical wholeness is dependent on divine authorship: it is whole only if God comes through on his covenant promises by means of his own Son, which leads to the next point.

Word–act–word revelation in the economy of the gospel

Third, the covenantal and redemptive revelation of God to his people is a *word–act–word revelation*, one that proves its credibility in the economy of the gospel. While he may not have been the first to conceive such a pattern, Vos capitalizes on a word–act revelation in his own presentation of biblical theology. While Vos uses the labels of 'act revelation' and 'word revelation', I will use 'word–act–word revelation' instead because it captures the final, or third, step in the revelatory process, namely *interpretation*.

If, as the second point above has stressed, revelation comes through redemption progressively, then the covenantal pattern of that redemptive revelation has a threefold tapestry.

1. As stated already, God is not silent but reveals himself for the purpose of redemption and often does so in redemptive history itself through certain covenant promises he makes to his people (though not exclusively through the medium of covenant promises). As will be seen, this initial word revelation is habitual, as is evident in the redemptive-covenantal promises God makes to Adam in Genesis 3:15, Abraham in Genesis 15 and 17, Moses in Exodus 20 and following, David in 2 Samuel 7, and so on.

2. Generally, that covenantal word of promise is then followed by divine *actions* that demonstrate the credibility of God's word. Yahweh does not

merely promise Moses he will liberate his people as the next step in the fulfilment of his promises to Abraham, but God then reveals himself as the mighty Lord in his defeat of the Egyptians and liberation of his people through the Red Sea to the mountain of Sinai. Yahweh's mighty acts vindicate his covenantal promises. As we will see in chapters 3–5, nowhere is this point more visible than with Christ, whose life, death and resurrection bring the Law and the Prophets to fulfilment.

3. God not only acts on his covenantal word of promise (word–*act* revelation), but he then provides the official, authoritative interpretation of his actions, leaving no hermeneutical ambiguity (word–act–*word* revelation). 'Such act-revelations', says Vos, 'are never entirely left to speak for themselves; they are preceded and followed by word-revelation.'[5] In short, God is his own interpreter. Those who are the recipients of his covenantal word–act revelation are not left to themselves to decipher or speculate what his mighty acts mean: God himself speaks to interpret his mighty acts so that there is no doubt as to the fulfilment of his covenantal word. His authoritative interpretation is the hermeneutical key to understanding how his mighty acts fulfil his covenant promises. Apart from that interpretative word, God's people have no authoritative interpretation of the supernatural and providential events they have experienced.

Nevertheless, it would be a mistake to think that the word–act–word pattern is not a process. Biblical theology assists the reader, helping him or her to see how this pattern develops across redemptive history. God may reveal his covenantal promises in one epoch, only to wait until another epoch to act on that covenantal word, and yet wait until yet another epoch to provide the full, authoritative interpretation of what he has done across the span of redemptive history.[6] That is not always the case: sometimes the word–act–word process is condensed within a short period of time (e.g. Israel's exodus from Egypt to Sinai; the Son's incarnation from cradle to ascension). Even then, however, subsequent revelation from God follows in which he further clarifies and expands upon what took place in order to explain its meaning both then and in the light of present and future fulfilment (e.g. the latter prophets; the book of Acts).

---

[5] Ibid. 7.

[6] It is a struggle for contemporary readers to see this because they read with a complete canon in hand; the undiscerning reader may forget that large periods of silence sometimes separate the word–act–word occurrences.

With the whole narrative of the Scriptures in view, the word–act–word tapestry is what structures the entire storyline and the entire canon. While word–act–word revelation may occur repeatedly at various intervals within redemptive history, it also, in the broadest sense, is the structure of redemptive history *as a whole*. As Vos observes, 'The usual order is: first word, then the act, then again the interpretive word. The Old Testament brings the predictive preparatory word, the Gospels record the redemptive-revelatory fact, and the Epistles supply the subsequent, final interpretation.'[7] What Vos is describing is biblical theology, but his description observes how the skeleton of biblical theology, its very structure, depends on the fulfilment of the 'predictive preparatory word' *in the Gospels*. As will be seen in future chapters, Jesus assumes that the history of Israel and their Scriptures is defined by this word–act–word revelation. What the prophets foretold and foreshadowed is brought to fulfilment in Jesus, and Jesus and his apostles provide the authoritative, divinely inspired and canonical interpretation of that word–act fulfilment.

This word–act–word revelation also manifests the credibility of God's word. Not only is God his own interpreter (i.e. word–act–*word* revelation) but he confirms the reliability of his word in his own fulfilment of that word. The trustworthiness of the word is never more visible than in the economy of the gospel of Jesus Christ. Nowhere does the truthfulness of the Scriptures of Israel shine brighter than in the objective, historical person and work of Jesus Christ. The incarnation is proof that God has come through on his word. The fulfilment of his covenantal promises in his own Son demonstrates the truthfulness of his word. Canonical reliability is confirmed by Christological revelation.

An expansive biblical theology that exhibits these three marks (covenantal, progressive, word–act–word revelation) cannot be provided here; nevertheless, what follows seeks to demonstrate in brief the presence of these three defining characteristics with the purpose of establishing the presuppositions present in Jesus' own reception of the Scriptures of Israel. As those three show themselves, it will also become clear that the product for Israel is a written word from Yahweh, one that serves as the constitution of their covenant, yet one that looks for its fulfilment in the Word, Christ Jesus.

---

[7] Vos 1948: 7.

God's word creates God's covenant people

Word, creation and covenant

From the start of the Hebrew Scriptures it is God's word that creates. In the opening chapters of Genesis it is through divine speech-acts that the cosmos is created *ex nihilo* (Gen. 1:3):

> By the word of the LORD the heavens were made,
>> and by the breath of his mouth all their host . . .
> For he spoke, and it came to be;
>> he commanded, and it stood firm.
> (Ps. 33:6, 9)

The authors of the New Testament underscore the verbal efficacy of this word at creation as well: 'By faith we understand that the universe was created by the word of God' (Heb. 11:3).

The creative power of God's word not only brings the cosmos into existence by divine, verbal fiat, but it is the word of God that establishes a covenant at creation with Adam, who is made in the image of his Creator. By his word God declares, 'Let us make man in our image, after our likeness. And let them have dominion . . . over all the earth' (Gen. 1:26). The garden becomes a type of Edenic temple, one whose beauty will later be artistically pictured on the temple walls.[8] It is a temple first and foremost because it is there that the presence of the Lord dwells, as Adam and Eve commune not only with one another but with their Creator. So far has the Creator accommodated himself to the creature that it is safe to assume the couple could hear the 'sound of the LORD God walking in the garden in the cool of the day' even before their catastrophic fall into sin (Gen. 3:8).

But the garden is also a kingdom of sorts. This much is plain in the way Adam is meant to image his Creator. Already typology and types manifest themselves in this creation story. The *imago Dei* itself is a type of its Creator, even a *metatype* because it will set the trajectory of every other type yet to come in Israel's history.[9] The image of God is created as a vicegerent, one

---

[8] Beale 2004: 29–80.
[9] Wellum 2016: 117.

meant to live in covenant with the Lord of the covenant and in his name exercise dominion over the creation (Gen. 1:28). Adam is but a little king in the kingdom of the great King, the lord of the covenant.

The presence of a covenant at creation may not be labelled as such but it is present throughout the Genesis narrative.[10] The covenant of creation is further warranted by certain covenant stipulations that are set in place by the Lord, much like a suzerain Lord in his pact with his vassals. Besides the many trees 'the LORD God made to spring up' from the ground, trees 'pleasant to the sight and good for food' (Gen. 2:9), two other trees were planted as well: the tree of life and the tree of the knowledge of good and evil (Gen. 2:9b). Put to the test, Adam is commanded by his covenant Lord, 'You may surely eat of every tree of the garden, but of the tree of the knowledge of good and evil you shall not eat, for in the day that you eat of it you shall surely die' (Gen. 2:17). Should Adam obey, the period of testing and probation will end, and he will eat of the tree of life for ever. Disobedience, however, will bring on his head the curses of the covenant agreement: exile and death.

The story that ensues is tragic, as Adam listens to the word of the woman and the word of the serpent rather than to the word of his Creator. In Adam all humanity is plunged into death and condemnation, corrupted by the nature Adam ruined. And later biblical authors, like the Prophets, read Israel's identity and corruption through the covenant of creation. Describing Israel, Hosea says, 'But like Adam they transgressed the covenant' (6:7). Ultimately, Christ himself will be set in contrast to Adam as a second Adam, whose covenant headship recapitulates Adam's trial but with different results.[11]

Polluted as they may be, God does not remain silent, but his word is heard once more, promising that from the woman will come an offspring to bruise the head of the serpent (3:15). The word of God not only creates the cosmos and the covenant at creation but that same word creates redemption, rescuing Adam's fallen race from the condemnation they deserve. This first word or gospel – this *protoevangelium* – will bring about the restoration of humanity and creation through a seed of the woman.

With such a redemptive word in place, the story of Israel will eventually climax with a son born to one of Eve's daughters, born so that Adam's

---

[10] A full defence cannot be provided here of the covenant of creation, but see Gentry and Wellum 2012: 177–222; Dumbrell 2013: 1–58.

[11] See chapter 5.

children will be reborn. Adam's image is but a type of the *true image* of God. What is astonishing to discover, however, is that this true image is not just a greater Adam and a greater son of God than Adam, but he is the Son of God himself, the true image of God, the one through whom creation was made and continues to be sustained.[12] Echoing Genesis, Paul writes of Christ that

> He is the image of the invisible God, the firstborn of all creation. For by him all things were created, in heaven and on earth, visible and invisible, whether thrones or dominions or rulers or authorities – all things were created through him and for him.
> (Col. 1:15–16)

The author of Hebrews says something similar: Christ 'is the radiance of the glory of God and the exact imprint of his nature, and he upholds the universe by the word of his power' (Heb. 1:3).

As the true image of God, this Son of God becomes incarnate to fulfil his mission of redemption as the last Adam. Like the first son of God, the first Adam, the last Adam represents his fellow man by becoming a man; yet, unlike Adam, he is the Son of God (Luke 3:38), who listens to the word of the covenant and remains obedient to his Father (John 5:19; 8:28), securing a new covenant by which Adam's race will be redeemed through his righteousness (Rom. 5:14; 1 Cor. 15:45). As a Son, he is the perfect image and representation of God; all those adopted into the family of God are privileged to participate in his sonship (Eph. 1:3–7) so that by the Spirit they are conformed more and more into his image (Rom. 6:4; 8:29; Eph. 4:24; Col. 3:10).[13]

Adam failed to rule, to have dominion over the Edenic kingdom, and to cast out the serpent as an intruder (Gen. 3:1–7). But the last Adam announces at the start of his ministry that in him the 'kingdom of heaven' – a phrase that conveys the universal extent of Christ's royal reign – is at hand (Matt. 4:12–17; cf. Mark 1:15, which uses 'kingdom of God').[14] The proof of that claim is seen when he casts out demons (Matt. 4:24) and binds the strong man, the devil (Matt. 12:29; cf. Col. 2:15; Rev. 12:7–12; 20:10). After he accomplished his mission of redemption, he

---

[12] For a full treatment of the *imago Dei* across the canon, see Beale 2011: 357–468.

[13] Wellum 2016: 130.

[14] Pennington 2017: 67–76.

ascended to his throne in heaven to reign over creation (Luke 24:51; Acts 1:9; Eph. 1:20–22) until his second return, when he will judge the living and the dead (Matt. 24:29–31; 25:31–46; Mark 9:1).[15] The last Adam's victory over the evil powers of this world inaugurates a new creation, which is both individual (2 Cor. 5:17; Gal. 6:15) and corporate (Rev. 21:1–8). He is the King of kings and Lord of lords (Rev. 17:16; 19:14), the righteous Davidic king who will restore God's kingdom rule over the whole earth (Eph. 1:7; Rev. 5:9–10).[16] Genesis 3:15 is but the beginning of this eschatological hope.[17]

Called into covenant: Abraham

Like Noah, Abraham is another Adam, though not the last Adam. God's covenant with Abraham carries and renews God's covenant word of promise to both Adam and Noah, but with fuller implications detailed.

Abraham is a pagan when God first speaks to him, calling him out of the land he knows to inherit a foreign land that he has never seen, promising to make a great nation out of the loins of the patriarch (Gen. 12:1–3). In time the divine call will be formulated within the context of a covenant. The 'word of the LORD' once again came to Abraham in Genesis 15, but this time Abraham boldly asks how the word of the Lord will come true when he has no offspring (15:2–3). Again, the 'word of the LORD came to him' (15:4), promising Abraham he will have a son of his own, an heir to the promise (15:4). If Abraham can count the stars of the heavens, then he can number his offspring (15:5). In that decisive moment Abraham believes the word of the Lord and is counted righteous (15:6), and his example will set the pattern for all who will be saved by faith after him (Gal. 4).

Still, Abraham seeks verification, asking, 'O LORD God, how am I to know that I shall possess it?' (15:8). Verification is given when the Lord cuts and seals a covenant with Abraham. The covenant is portrayed when the presence of God, as manifested through a smoking firepot and a flaming torch, pass between the carcasses of animals butchered in half for the ritual (Gen. 15:9–21). The bloody graveyard is the most serious way God can ensure his word will not falter. By passing through the carcasses, God

---

[15] On the already-not-yet nature of this kingdom reign of Christ, see Wellum 2016: 125; Carson 1996: 254; Gentry and Wellum 2012: 591–602; Schreiner 2008: 41–116; Ridderbos 1975: 44–90.

[16] On the seed and dominion restored, see Dempster 2003: 59–69.

[17] Due to limitations in space, the Noahic covenant will be bypassed. However, see Gentry and Wellum 2012: 147–176.

makes a self-declaration: should he break his covenant word to Abraham, so too will God be torn in two.[18] These curses of the covenant will fall on God's own head.

Since it was typically the lesser party that would have to pass between the carcasses and swear the oath, the Lord himself passing through indicates that he has initiated the covenant and has established this covenant through his own word.[19] The initiative is his: the covenant is his making. This covenant will not end with Abraham but will continue with his offspring in the land God promised, demonstrating that the 'word of the LORD' is intent on distributing divine grace to Abraham and the offspring he will father. 'I will establish my covenant between me and you and your offspring after you throughout their generations for an everlasting covenant, to be God to you and to your offspring after you' (Gen. 17:7). Here is a covenantal word that is for ever binding: Abraham's offspring will be called out by that same word as the specially chosen people of God (17:8–14).

The covenant with Abraham is foundational to the rest of the storyline and the coming of the promised One. On the one hand, the seed narrows, for God selects Abraham out of all the people on earth. On the other hand, the promise widens, for it is through Abraham's offspring that not only his immediate descendants, the nation of Israel, are yet to come, but all the nations of the earth will one day be blessed (Gen. 17:4–6). Also, it is clear from the slicing of animals and the suzerain's self-binding pact that this is a covenant that is God-initiated, unilateral and unconditional. At the same time, it is not surprising to discover conditional factors at play as well. Although it is God's word that establishes the covenant, obedience on Abraham's part, and the part of his offspring, is required (Gen. 17:1; 18:19), and that obedience is tested when God tells Abraham to sacrifice the heir of the promise, Isaac (22:16–18).

The faith and obedience of Abraham are remarkable. Still, it is not long before his imperfection shows, revealing to the reader that Abraham, like Adam and Noah before him, is not the obedient son, the promised heir of Genesis 3:15. It is a sobering indication that if Adam, Noah and Abraham cannot obey, humanity will not be able to produce one who can. God remains a faithful covenant partner, fulfilling his promises. But a faithful

---

[18] Ibid. 251.
[19] Hamilton 2010: 430–433.

covenant partner from humanity is not to be found; God himself must provide a man who will obey without wavering and meet God's perfect standard of righteousness.[20] As the story progresses, the reader is led to wonder, 'When, O Lord, will you provide a son of Adam who is a faithful, obedient covenant partner?' That is a question the New Testament authors are prepared to answer (Acts 3:25; Gal. 3:13–14, 26–29; Eph. 2:11–22; Heb. 2:16): they believe Abraham's true heir has arrived and with his covenant fidelity blessing for the nations.

The constitution of the covenant

The word inscripturated by the finger of God

The creative agency of the word takes the form of a promise for Abraham but that promise begins to mature when the word of the Lord calls Moses to liberate Abraham's offspring, Israel, whom God calls his firstborn son (Exod. 4:22–23; Ps. 89:27). Except this time the word of the Lord is inscripturated, taking on written form.

When Yahweh speaks to Moses from the burning bush, he introduces himself as the same God who spoke to his father, Abraham. 'I am the God of your father, the God of Abraham, the God of Isaac, and the God of Jacob' (Exod. 3:6). Moses is commissioned as a type of prophet; through Aaron he will be the voice of God to Pharaoh (4:10–12), commanding the king of Egypt to let God's people go each time with 'Thus says the LORD' (e.g. 4:22). Resistant as Pharaoh is, hard as his heart may be, his magicians and their gods are impotent before the God of Israel (Exod. 7 – 15), the one whose name is 'I AM WHO I AM' (Exod. 3:14). Under the unbearable weight of Yahweh's plagues, Pharaoh reluctantly bows to Yahweh's command, and Israel is liberated from bondage, freed to worship the God of her fathers.

Released from the hand of her oppressor, Israel is led by Moses to the base of Mount Sinai. The context of Sinai is covenantal to its core. Having seen the redemptive hand of the Lord (Exod. 19:4), Israel is now to live in covenant obedience with her God:

Now therefore, if you will indeed obey my voice and keep my covenant, you shall be my treasured possession among all peoples,

for all the earth is mine; and you shall be to me a kingdom of priests and a holy nation. These are the words that you shall speak to the people of Israel.
(19:5–6)

When Israel agrees to these words (19:8), God descends in a thick cloud 'that the people may hear when I speak with you, and may also believe you for ever' (19:9). God's speech is the focal point of the covenant, always to be feared, yet gracious in the salvation it promises.

At Sinai the people of Israel are to consecrate themselves before their holy God (19:10–15) and stand before the foot of the shaking mountain as Moses mediates on their behalf, climbing the mountain to enter the presence of the Holy One (19:16–20). The purpose is for Moses to hear God speak and to receive divine words that will instruct Israel how they are to live in covenant with their Saviour. The ten words (or commands; cf. 20:1–17) Moses receives are written on two tablets that are called 'the testimony' (31:18).[21] They testify to the covenant made between God and Israel at Sinai; indeed, they act as the *constitution* of the covenant. It is for good reason, then, that Exodus 24:7 labels the ten words of Yahweh the 'Book of the Covenant'.[22]

'Canon is inherent in covenant': the treaty document in the ancient Near East

Does the ANE background shed any light on the covenantal nature of the tablets at Sinai? Meredith Kline makes a compelling case in the affirmative. Examining a variety of ANE texts, Kline points to the treaty document and discerns striking similarities.

ANE treaties involved at least two parties: an overlord and vassals. The prerogative belonged to the overlord. He was the sovereign and therefore he would determine, stipulate and regulate the conditions and promises of the agreement. Yet such a covenant was not merely verbal: it was inscripturated, resulting in the production of some type of treaty document. The treaty document or tablet was not an afterthought to the covenant but the covenant itself centred on the document:

---

[21] Scholars speculate whether the commands are spread across both tablets or written twice as a copy for the covenant recipient. See Kline 1989: 113–130.

[22] Exod. 24:7 comes after not only the ten words or commandments but a whole litany of laws, so the book of the covenant may be more expansive than just the Ten Commandments.

The central role played by the treaty tablet in which the covenant was customarily inscripturated is attested by the fact that the preservation of these tablets was at times made the subject of a special document clause in the text of the treaties.[23]

In addition, these special documents were public in nature, possessed by both sides, read for all to hear. The 'clause' Kline identifies stipulated that copies of the covenant document or tablet were to be manufactured. Once these copies were made, they were given to both representatives. It was a sacred, holy moment, a religious ceremony even, because the reception of one's copy was accompanied by the presence of one's god.[24] The god bore witness to the affirmations and denials of each party involved. Furthermore, the covenant was kept by a consistent return to its inscripturated stipulations. Not only was the covenant tablet to be 'carefully guarded' but it was to be 'periodically read publicly in the vassal kingdom'.[25]

The tablet was not irrelevant to the covenant itself; it was no mere archival record of what had taken place, but was a *living document*. For this reason, the document was referenced at strategic points in the treatise. Looking to examples like the 'tablet of silver' Hattusilis III produced for Ramses II, the 'iron tablet' Tudhaliyas IV 'inscribed' for Ulmi-Teshub, and the tablet Mursilis II delivered to a vassal on behalf of his father, Kline observes:

> It is recorded that a treaty was written at such and such a place and in the presence of named witnesses. It is stated by a suzerain that he wrote the tablet and gave it to a vassal, just as, in the case of God's covenant at Sinai, Israel's heavenly Sovereign inscribed for them the tablets of stone.[26]

The written document was so directly connected to the covenant that a 'canonical sanction' was issued, threatening a curse should the inscripturated document be illegitimately changed, violated or manipulated. Consider the 'inscriptional imprecation' of the treaty between Tudhaliyas IV and Ulmi-Teshub: 'Whoever . . . changes but one word of this tablet . . .

---

[23] Kline 1989: 27.
[24] Ibid. 28.
[25] Ibid.
[26] Ibid.

may the thousand gods of this tablet root that man's descendants out of the land of Hatti.'[27] The covenant at Sinai issued similar curses should the treatise document be added to or subtracted from, or should Israel fail to keep its stipulations. 'You shall not add to the word that I command you, nor take from it, that you may keep the commandments of the LORD your God that I command you' (Deut. 4:2).[28]

One should not miss how such imprecations followed if the document itself was altered or if it was left unfulfilled. In many cases the wrath of the gods was threatened should one party not carry out its end of the covenant. *The point is, there was a close, even direct, correlation between the covenant and the document itself so that the authority of the covenant was enclosed within the authority of the tablets.*

> The way in which the content of the treaties and the treaty tablet itself merge in the charge to guard it and in the conjoined curses against offenders reveals how closely identified with the idea of suzerainty covenant was its inscripturated form.[29]

Therefore, Kline is warranted to speak of a *canon*. 'And the inviolable authority of these written tablets, vividly attested to by the document clause and, especially, the documentary curse, sufficiently justifies our speaking of the canonicity of these treatises.'[30]

The ANE background need not determine how one interprets the story of Israel at Sinai in every way, as if one must be a slave to such background over against the biblical witness itself. Nevertheless, the background buttresses the type of *authority* inherent in the Sinai covenant and its tablets of stone, as well as the type of authority that characterizes all Scripture in Sinai's trail. If the covenant and tablets at Sinai are at all similar to the suzerain covenant and its treaty form, then Israel understood these tablets to be a type of canon, and one that was binding. Israel, in other words, believed that 'canon is inherent in covenant'.[31] Yahweh is the suzerain, Israel the vassal, as apparent not only in Yahweh's superiority but in his unique rights to enact the covenant in the first place. The tablets of

---

[27] As quoted in McCarthy 1963. Kline also gives the examples of Suppiluliuma's treaty with Niqmad of Ugarit, and Suppiluliuma's treaty with Mattiwaza. Kline 1989: 29–30.

[28] Also consult Deut. 27:2 and Josh. 8:30, and notice the similarities with Rev. 22:18.

[29] Kline 1989: 30.

[30] Ibid.

[31] Ibid. 43.

stone serve as the constitution of the covenant, bearing witness not only to the nature of the covenant itself but to the curses and blessings that follow, depending on the vassal's adherence to or deterrence from the inscripturated word of their suzerain. The two tablets do not merely serve as a memorial but are live documents, ratified by the living God himself.

Nevertheless, there are differences between the biblical account and ANE accounts. For example, in the ANE accounts, the reception of the treaty in its inscripturated form by the vassal occurs in the presence of a god or the gods. But the biblical account, and the nature of the covenant, is unilateral in nature. *The reception of the treaty document is not merely in the presence of a god but the suzerain himself is God.* He who cuts the covenant need not summon a god as his witness: the covenant-making suzerain is God himself. That is both serious and personal; serious because the suzerain himself exercises the divine prerogative in this covenant, yet personal because Israel need not find a divine witness external to the covenant. Their God has entered into the covenant as the primary party, swearing on his own name that he will fulfil the conditions of the covenant. That is something no other nation around Israel could claim. Israel truly was God's special, called out and chosen covenant people, and their possession of the two tablets was proof. Such was the blessing (and, potentially or inevitably, the curse) of their canon.

So direct and personal is the communication of the word of God to the people of God that the ten words are said to be written by the *finger* of God himself. 'And he gave to Moses, when he had finished speaking with him on Mount Sinai, the two tablets of the testimony, tablets of stone, written with the finger of God' (Exod. 31:18). Although the narrative underlines the transcendent holiness of God in the delivery of this testimony (19:12–13, 18), the fact that it is written by God himself, with his own finger, communicates that this God, who is wholly other, has descended upon the mountain to enter a covenant relationship with his chosen people in a saving way. His accommodation is their salvation.

That these words act as the living constitution or canon of the covenant is also perceptible from their location within Israel. As Israel camps in the wilderness, the tablets lie within the ark of the covenant (Deut. 31:26), which resides within the Tabernacle's Most Holy Place, with the Deutero-nomic document close by in the sanctuary. Its location in the ark and in the sanctuary conveys that the tablets were not only from God but served as his permanent testimony to the covenant he had ratified with his people.

'This disposition of them', says Kline, 'was in accord with the regular custom of enshrining treaty documents.'[32] Furthermore, the ark was the focal point because it was there that the presence of God descended on the mercy seat between the two cherubim (Exod. 25:20–22; cf. Heb. 9:3–4).[33] The location is strategic, conveying the holiness of God's presence and the sacred nature of his ten words. Should these words be broken, it is no random law that has been violated but the voice of the covenant-making God himself.

As personal as the covenant may be, Israel must never forget proper identities; their existence entirely depends on recognizing where authority originates and resides. Yahweh is the suzerain and they are the vassal. They enjoy the countless blessings of the kingdom, but he always remains their King. That truth and reality the treaty itself assumed in every way. For not only was Yahweh, the King or the Suzerain, the author of its canon (written by his own finger) but his presence ensured the treaty's fulfilment. In other words, the tablets signified both Yahweh's personal commitment and his lordship.

Such an authority did not cease when Israel pilgrimed from Sinai to the land of promise, for the tablets represented Yahweh's continuing presence with his covenant people. The tablets not only ratified but regulated the covenant on a continuing basis, and with it the kingdom within which the Israelite was a citizen. There was, then, a sufficiency to the canon that Israel experienced in their everyday life as God's kingdom people.[34] Yet the constitution of the covenant, the canon of the kingdom, also pointed forward, promising the arrival of a Messiah-King who would fulfil God's covenant promises and establish God's kingdom in all its consummated glory. '*Tanakh*', says Carson, 'carries God's authority with it, and anticipates a messianic kingdom.'[35]

For our purposes, however, what is pertinent is the way such covenantal authority stems from the nature of the covenant document or treaty itself.

---

[32] Ibid. 36.

[33] On the significance of God's presence on the ark in the Most Holy Place, see Merrill 1994: 404.

[34] 'Through Moses, his covenant mediator, the Lord God addressed to his earthly vassals the law of his kingdom. His authoritative treaty words, regulative of Israel's faith and conduct, were inscripturated on tablets of stone and in "the book." Both these deposits of covenantal revelation accorded closely in their formal structure and ceremonial treatment with the ancient treaties, not least with respect to those documentary features of the treaties that provided the justification for our describing them as canonical.' Kline 1989: 35.

[35] Carson 2004: 398.

'Yahweh adopted the legal-literary form of the suzerainty covenants for the administration of his kingdom in Israel', but he does so as a suzerain who is the divine author as well.[36] That means, then, that the tablets inscribed with the Decalogue, as well as the Deuteronomic document that shadowed such tablets, carried a divine authority due to their divine inspiration. Over against Old Testament scholarship that is epistemologically suspicious, Kline contends:

> It is necessary to insist constantly that the Scriptures, whether the Mosaic covenant documents, which constituted the nuclear Old Testament canon, or any other Scripture, are authoritative – uniquely, divinely authoritative – *simply in virtue of their origin through divine revelation and inspiration*.[37]

Kline then draws a conclusion for their sufficiency:

> Certainly, then, their authority as such is not to be accounted for by looking beyond them elsewhere. As divinely authoritative revelation, documentary in form and with unalterable content, they possess the essential components for a definition of canon properly conceived.[38]

Torah, sacrifice and the covenantal corpus

The history of Israel from Exodus 19 and 31 (and Deut. 31:26) forward oscillates on these words, these laws from the finger of God. Not only was Israel's *Sitz im Leben* defined by the covenant at Sinai, but the Scriptures that followed, in all their diversity, were as well. They were, to use Kline's vocabulary, 'covenantalized', so that 'all the inspired literature' (i.e. the entire Old Testament) 'served the covenant and inevitably bore its stamp'.[39]

It need not be law per se to bear this stamp either; whether it be history, wisdom literature or prophecy, each traces its origin to the divine suzerain and his original covenantal stipulations. In that sense, Kline is right to conclude that the diverse literatures 'employed in the Old Testament all function as *extensions* (free and creative to be sure) of some main section

---

[36] Kline 1989: 35.
[37] Ibid. 37. Emphasis added.
[38] Ibid.
[39] Ibid. 47. A similar emphasis is present in Vos 1980: 10.

or feature of the foundational treaties' at Sinai. Granted, the 'functional extension may be by way of administrative or judicial application or by way of didactic or confessional elaboration'. Nevertheless,

> in each case a special relationship can be traced between the function and a particular element of the treaty documents, and thus a literary dimension is added to the functional in our identification of the Old Testament in all its parts as a covenantal corpus.[40]

What Kline presupposes in such an assertion is that this covenantal corpus can be interpreted as an indivisible unit only because it ultimately is not the product of man, the vassal, as much as man may be essential to its production and instrumental to its unique literary contribution. In the final analysis, such canonical–covenantal unity can be explained only by the suzerain: the covenantal corpus originates from the divine author, who exercises control over its generation and dissemination.

Still, as definitive as the covenantal corpus may be, it expands, progresses and develops, so that as redemptive history climbs to its culmination it is not restricted to the Decalogue or the Deuteronomic treatise, as much as it stems from those scriptures. Through Moses, God narrates Israel's heritage, from Adam to Noah, from Abraham to Joseph (the book of Genesis). The same God who created the cosmos has created a chosen people through whom salvation will one day come to the nations. Moreover, through Moses God provides the authoritative interpretation of Israel's exodus from Egypt, leaving no ambiguity that it is the Lord himself who has redeemed his people from slavery and set them apart as his holy nation (see the book of Exodus).

Yahweh not only gives his people ten words that are to be at the centre of covenant life and community, but a whole law that is to instruct Israel how to live as a nation devoted to God in the midst of nations worshipping foreign deities (e.g. Exod. 25 – 40; the book of Leviticus). Nevertheless, there is good reason why the giving of the law is immediately accompanied by blood. In Exodus 24, for example, the 'Book of the Covenant' is read to all the people (24:7) and they, as the vassals in this covenant, all pledge allegiance. However, this covenant is between the Holy One and a sinful

---

[40] Emphasis added. That explains Kline's thesis: 'whatever the individual names of the several major literary genres of the Old Testament, as adopted in the Old Testament their common surname is Covenant'. Kline 1989: 47.

people. Therefore, after Moses read the Book of the Covenant he 'took the blood and threw it on the people and said, "Behold the blood of the covenant that the LORD has made with you in accordance with all these words"' (24:8). Though the parallel is not exact, one cannot help but remember how God's covenant with Abraham involved bloody carcasses. Here again, in Exodus 24, blood is present to confirm and seal the covenant. But this time the blood must be thrown all over the people by their mediator, Moses, if they are to remain covenant partners with Yahweh.

Despite the blood sprinkled over Israel, it is not long until they transgress the Book of the Covenant, requiring that sacrifices be made continually for Israel's forgiveness. Within that extensive law the priesthood and the tabernacle take form, and atonement is made for Israel's infractions against the Book of the Covenant by means of a sacrificial system, yet another sign of God's mercy and grace. On the Day of Atonement, for example, the high priest enters the Holy Place with a sin offering that he offers first for his own sin (Lev. 16:3, 6, 11–14). Next, the priest takes two goats, one to be 'presented alive before the LORD to make atonement over it, that it may be sent away into the wilderness' (16:10), and the other to be killed as a 'sin offering that is for the people' (16:15). Just as the blood of the bull was sprinkled on the mercy seat – on which the very presence of God descends – so too the blood of the goat (16:15). Why? The high priest must make atonement 'because of the uncleannesses of the people of Israel and because of their transgressions, all their sins' (16:16).

Notice, sacrifice and atonement are necessary because Israel proves time and again that they cannot and will not obey the law, the Book of the Covenant, though it promises covenant life to all who adhere to its commands. 'You shall therefore keep my statutes and my rules; if a person does them, he shall live by them: I am the LORD' (Lev. 18:5). David and Paul alike will attest to the law's holy and righteous character, because the law ultimately reflects the character of its divine architect (Ps. 19; Rom. 7:12). With every transgression, then, Israel's need for a righteous substitute is heightened. While God provides a way for atonement, nevertheless such offerings cannot finally take away sins, as the author of Hebrews underscores (10:4).

Needed, then, is a sacrifice to end all sacrifices; such a sacrifice will have to be unique, originating from God, yet representing man, and doing so in a way that reveals no imperfection. As will be seen soon enough, prophets like Isaiah pull back the typological curtain further to reveal that the righteous branch from David's line (Isa. 11:1–10) will also be a suffering servant, one who will be pierced for the transgressions of God's people in order to redeem them once and for all (Isa. 52:13 – 53:12). As God's obedient Son, this servant suffers the penalty of the law for Israel's sake: he is born under the law's curse to bear its curse. In doing so, this Son of God, this promised seed of the woman, wins the sonship of those in Adam. 'But when the fullness of time had come, God sent forth his Son, born of woman, born under the law, to redeem those who were under the law, so that we might receive adoption as sons' (Gal. 4:4–5). As chapter 5 will reveal, God's own Son is sent to be the new Moses, but this Mediator will spill his own blood for the forgiveness of sins (Matt. 26:28; 1 Peter 1:2; cf. Exod. 24:7–9).

Israel's covenant unfaithfulness results in devastating consequences when they approach the land God promised to their father Abraham. Her refusal to enter the land at God's command results in forty years of wandering in the wilderness. Her journey is chronicled by Moses (i.e. in the book of Numbers); and as Moses nears his own death, he preaches God's law to Israel afresh, reminding her of the faithfulness of Yahweh to his covenant promises, motivating Israel to respond in repentance and obedience (i.e. the book of Deuteronomy). Deuteronomy as a 'historical treatment is covenantal' for it is 'precisely the treaty document given by Yahweh through Moses to be the canonical foundation of Israel's life in covenant relationship to himself'.[41]

These five books of Moses, the Torah (the Pentateuch), prove to be the bedrock of Israel's Scriptures. The Pentateuch, says Moberly, is the Old Testament's Old Testament.[42] Or, as Fesko explains,

> all OT revelation subsequent to the Pentateuch is built on themes and concepts found within the first five books of the Bible. This means, then, that one finds a hermeneutical relationship between the Pentateuch and the rest of the OT, one that is exhibited in the intra-canonical interpretation within the OT.[43]

Given the Pentateuch's foundational role to all revelation that followed, there is no question that Israel believed the Torah originated from Yahweh himself, nor did Israel doubt the Torah to be authoritative and sufficient

---

[41] Ibid. 56.
[42] Moberly 1992.
[43] Fesko 2008: 453–454.

to instruct her in the way of the covenant. Yahweh spoke to Moses and through Moses to instruct his people according to his ways. When such authority is questioned by those within Israel, as in Numbers 12 by Miriam and Aaron, Yahweh interjects, declaring to all that he has indeed spoken to Moses, so that the words of Moses are the words of the Lord: to disobey the word of Moses is to disobey the word of the Lord. While God may choose to make himself known to a prophet in a vision (Num. 12:6), with Moses God speaks directly. 'With him I speak mouth to mouth, clearly, and not in riddles, and he beholds the form of the LORD' (12:8).

The faithfulness of God to his covenant word

The Law, the Prophets and the Psalms

God's word does not end with Moses and the Torah, however, but continues to progress as redemptive history itself develops until it reaches its culmination in the person and work of Christ.

The Torah is only a part of the Hebrew Scriptures Jesus inherited. He will not only point to the Law but to the Prophets and Psalms as the Scriptures of Israel, the Scriptures of God, which he has come to fulfil. As he says after his resurrection, 'everything written about me in the Law of Moses and the Prophets and the Psalms must be fulfilled' (Luke 24:44). His reference to the Law may be broad, incorporating not merely the laws at Sinai but the entire Pentateuch. Likewise, his reference to the Prophets and Psalms may be expansive, encompassing both former prophets (Joshua to Kings) and latter prophets (Jeremiah to the Twelve). Jesus could be reaching as far back as Joshua and Samuel, though he no doubt has in view the rise of David with his mention of the Psalms, as well as the voices of the prophets before and during Israel's exiles.

The reason Jesus can move from the Law to the Prophets and Psalms is because he assumes, as did his fellow first-century Jews, that the revelation of God in and through the Scriptures is redemptive in nature. God's plan of redemption continues and with it his revelation of himself to Israel. That redemptive revelation is covenantal in character, as seen already with Adam, Abraham and Moses. Yet the redemptive, covenantal framework of God's word reaches a high point with the kingship and kingdom of David, who himself serves as a type of the Messiah-King yet to come in

David's own lineage (e.g. Isa 11:1–10; Jer. 23:1–8; 33:14–26; cf. Matt. 1:1). In a variety of ways David is representative of the Prophets and the Psalms, though that is to paint with a broad brush. To see why, consider the state of Israel prior to David's ascent to the throne.

The Book of the Law

With the establishment of the covenant at Sinai, the constitution of the covenant is embraced by Israel, visibly demonstrated by its location within the ark and the tent of meeting. God promises to keep his covenantal word to Abraham, and gave his covenant people his law to instruct them in the way of covenant life under Moses. However, Israel is a hard-hearted son; like Adam in the garden, Israel rejects the word of their covenant-making Father. Yahweh's holy word is meant to lead his people in the way of holy, covenant life; instead Israel distrusts Yahweh, looking to the ways of the surrounding nations and their gods. Their covenant disloyalty becomes conspicuous when Israel refuses to enter the land God promised to their father, Abraham (Deut. 1:1–33), disbelieving God's word to defeat his enemies and establish Israel within the land of blessing. The result is devastating: that generation will never enter the land but will wander in the wilderness.

What is astounding, however, is Yahweh's gracious persistence and refusal to abandon his people, the covenant with Abraham, and the promise of his word (Gen. 34:6–7). He will not let his word return empty (Isa. 55:11); his covenant promises to Abraham will not fail. He will raise up the next generation to enter the land under the leadership of Joshua, the new Moses. Like Moses, Joshua is not to let the 'Book of the Law' leave his lips but it is to be his constant guide (Josh. 1:7–8). As God renews his covenant with Joshua, he does so by once again writing his law on stone (Josh. 8:30–35), providing his people with the constitution of his covenant once more. The Torah in written form is to be Israel's all-sufficient authority, which leads Joshua to read 'all the words of the law' before the people; there was 'not a word of all that Moses commanded that Joshua did not read before all the assembly of Israel' (8:34–35).

Like Moses before him, the time comes when Joshua joins his fathers and the leadership of Israel is passed on to his successor. Again, as with Moses, God takes this opportunity to remind his people that 'not one word [of his] has failed of all the good things that the LORD your God promised concerning you' (Josh. 23:14). Israel has not always been faithful to uphold the covenant; often they have rebelled against the covenant word of their

God. Not Yahweh: he has been faithful to his covenant, dedicated to bringing his covenantal promises to fulfilment. In Joshua 23 the message is clear – the God of Israel is faithful and therefore his word proves true; it is a reflection of his very character, just as Israel's disobedience is a reflection of her character.

The conclusion to Joshua gives away the story's ending. Israel, says Yahweh, is incapable of serving the Lord (Josh. 24:19). That prophetic word of judgment that was previously threatened in the covenant at Sinai now becomes a reality when Israel enter the era of the judges, an era of blatant and uncontrolled idolatry, summarized in that infamous indictment 'In those days there was no king in Israel. Everyone did what was right in his own eyes' (Judg. 21:25).

Torah in the hand of the king: Deuteronomy 17:18–19 and the psalter as the confession of the covenant

It is little surprise that 1 Samuel begins, the 'word of the LORD was rare in those days' (3:1). Nevertheless, the silence would be broken when God raised up Samuel (1 Sam. 1 – 2). Samuel's prophetic ministry, however, consisted of speaking the word of God to a king intent on disobeying it.

No longer wanting Yahweh to be her King, Israel instead demands to be like the nations.[44] Israels gets her king, but it is a king who reflects the hardness of her own heart. King Saul is not one who walks in the ways of Joshua, who ensured not one word of God's law was neglected by the people (Josh. 8:34–35). Time and again, Saul betrays the word of the Lord, even manipulates God's word to justify his own agenda. In the end the prophet Samuel is sent to declare Saul's demise. Saul refuses to listen to and follow the 'voice of the LORD' as spoken through the prophet (15:19). Saul 'rejected the word of the LORD' (1 Sam. 15:23); therefore, God rejects Saul as king.

With Israel rebelling against God's word for centuries, will God remain faithful to his word, fulfilling his covenant promises to Abraham? Israel deserves the curses threatened in the covenant treaty at Sinai. Nevertheless, Yahweh is full of steadfast mercy, refusing to go back on his covenant word. Despite Israel's unfaithfulness, Yahweh remains faithful to the covenant.

---

[44] To 'ask for kingship is an implicit denial of divine rule; to ask for kingship which will identify Israel more with her world is, in effect, to ask for the abrogation of the basis (Exod. 19:3b–6) on which the covenant rule over Israel had rested'. Dumbrell 2013: 206.

Given the hardness of Israel's heart, however, a new king is needed, a king who will reflect God's own heart as revealed in the Torah (1 Sam. 13:14). As Deuteronomy 17:18–19 explains, the king is to be one who copies the Torah, always keeps the Torah present among the people, and habitually reads the Torah. By doing so, he will 'learn to fear the LORD his God by keeping all the words of this law and these statutes, and doing them' (Deut. 17:19).

Unlike Saul, David proves to be that king who, like Moses and Joshua, turns Israel's attention first and foremost to the law of God. David's reign is structured according to Deuteronomy 17:18–19, as are the intentions of his heart. That much is noticeable in the decisions David makes, first manifested in his childlike trust in God's covenant promises over against a pagan threat like Goliath, a pattern that will persist as David repeatedly triumphs over the Philistines in the name of Yahweh. Yet it is not only David's actions that display what the king's allegiance to the Torah is to look like, but it is his own *words*, words that are born out of the Spirit of God (in contrast to the vacancy of the Spirit with Saul; 1 Sam. 16:14).

The blessed man, says David, is the one whose 'delight is in the law of the LORD', so that 'on his law he meditates day and night' (Ps. 1:2). The 'words of the LORD', says David with confidence, 'are pure words', as pure as 'silver refined in a furnace' and 'purified seven times' (Ps. 12:6). David believes the Lord is one who 'will keep them', guarding Israel 'from this generation for ever' (12:7). David considers the law of the Lord to be 'perfect' and capable of 'reviving the soul', 'sure' and therefore able to make 'wise the simple', 'right', leading to the 'rejoicing' of the heart, being 'pure' and able to enlighten the 'eyes', and 'true', a 'righteous' word altogether. So precious is the Torah to David that he considers it more desirable than 'fine gold' and sweeter than the 'honeycomb'. By God's word, concludes David, 'your servant' is 'warned' and it is 'in keeping them' that 'there is great reward' (Ps. 19:7–11). David himself confesses his own adherence to the Torah, echoing Deuteronomy 17:18–19, when he exclaims:

> For I have kept the ways of the LORD . . .
> For all his rules were before me
>   and his statutes I did not put away from me.
> (Ps. 18:21–22)

As David sings of his love for the Torah, his words of praise and devotion are uttered in the Spirit, so that what David says God says. For this reason, Jesus and his fellow Israelites not only believed the Law and the Prophets, but the Psalms as well, were holy Scripture (Luke 24:44; Mark 12:36).

The other psalmists will, in similar fashion to David, say the same about the word of Yahweh (cf. Pss 33:4–6; 111:7–8; 119:86, 89, 93, 105, 129, 160), even connecting his word to his covenant to demonstrate that his word is trustworthy. Psalm 105 is exemplary:

> He remembers his covenant for ever,
> the word that he commanded, for a thousand generations,
> the covenant that he made with Abraham,
> his sworn promise to Isaac,
> which he confirmed to Jacob as a statute,
> to Israel as an everlasting covenant,
> saying, 'To you I will give the land of Canaan
> as your portion for an inheritance.'
> (Ps. 105:8–11)

Psalm 105:8–11 demonstrates that the psalter as a whole is an extension of the covenant treaty these psalmists pay allegiance to in the sight of Israel. As Kline says, 'the covenant is the Psalter's sphere of existence'. Practically, this means that when the psalmist utters praise, 'whether magnifying the majesty of Yahweh's person or the wonder of his ways in creation or redemption', such psalms 'were a part of Israel's tributary obligations; they were the spiritual sacrifices of the lips offered to the Great King'.[45]

Kline's observation not only applies to the individual psalmist, but the psalter's words of adulation are applicable to all Israel, a means of confirming the people's adherence to the covenant and its treaty. 'As vehicles of private and public devotion they were a continual resounding of Israel's "Amen" of covenant ratification.' Psalms 78, 105 – 106, and 135 – 136, for example, not only 'rehearsed the course of covenant history', but

> were confessional responses of acknowledgment to the surveys of
> Yahweh's mighty acts in Israel's behalf which were contained in the
> historical prologues of the treaties, responses suitable for recitation

---

[45] Kline 1989: 62–63.

in ceremonies of covenant reaffirmation where those acts were memorialized (cf. Deut. 26:1ff; Josh. 24:16–18).[46]

In other words, the psalms served an indispensable purpose: they were the vassal's public adherence to the covenant treaty and its divine suzerain. By repenting and confessing their delight in the book of the covenant they welcomed its author and all the covenant blessings he promised.

Kline concludes:

> In the use of the psalms extolling the law of God, Israel submitted anew to the stipulations of the covenant ... The Psalter's function in covenantal confession suggests that it may be regarded as an extension of the vassal's ratification response.[47]

David, Yahweh's anointed one, exemplifies what this covenant obedience looks like in the Psalms, and his covenant fidelity proves typological of his messianic successor. The psalter (Book 1 especially: Pss 1 – 41) is designed to convey this much. In Psalm 1 we witness what a faithful Israelite is to look like, one who is righteous and vindicated by the Lord. Next Psalm 2 introduces us to the Lord's anointed, his chosen King, begotten as a Son to rule and reign over the nations. Then begin the many Davidic psalms where David's covenant obedience to the Torah – as a new Adam – is exemplified for Israel (e.g. Pss 3 – 24). David, it becomes clear, is the Lord's anointed king. Yet even he is a type of *the Anointed One*, whose Adamic–Davidic obedience as the righteous man (Ps. 1) and the Lord's begotten Son (Ps. 2) will result in the redemption of Israel and victory over God's enemies. As will be seen in chapters 3–5, this righteous man and begotten Son is none other than Jesus Christ, and his covenant obedience to the Torah (Matt. 4:1–11) is the very means to Israel's justification (Gal. 4:4–5). For this reason, a Gospel writer like John will quote from the psalter to identify for his readers who this crucified and risen Jesus is (see chapter 6).

Wisdom as the way of the covenant

Similar implications follow for wisdom literature, which has David's son Solomon as one of its primary authors. Why is it that Proverbs, for example,

---

[46] Ibid.
[47] Ibid.

begins by declaring that the 'fear of the LORD is the beginning of knowledge' (1:7)? It is because fear is entirely appropriate for a king and people accountable to a suzerain lord and his covenant treaty. In other words, it is another way of saying that the 'way of wisdom is the way of the covenant'.[48] Like each unique contribution to the Old Testament (covenant), the wisdom literature functions as an exposition of the covenant and its documents, illuminating the knowledge the covenant gives so that Israel can be the beneficiary of its blessings.

Contemporary academics and preachers often treat individual proverbs in isolation from one other and their canonical and covenantal context, as if these sayings are unrelated, insightful tidbits from a sage to the discerning. Yet they are far more if read within Israel's covenantal context. They are the real-life applications of the covenant itself. Wisdom literature, Kline says, is 'the explication of the covenant'; it explicates by 'translating the covenant stipulations into maxims and instructions regulative of conduct in the different areas of life and under its varying conditions'. Kline adds, however, that the 'wisdom books are equally concerned with the outworking of the covenant sanctions in human experience'; hence the sometimes minute and meticulous advice a book like proverbs provides.[49]

If the hearer, the covenant member, is to achieve the knowledge Proverbs 1:7 values above all else via a fear of the Lord, then the wisdom books must drive the reader into the specifics of covenant life (i.e. how to live according to the covenant treaty itself). The way of life in the covenant must be articulated with clarity and precision, and explicated broadly, particularly when its members encounter threats not only to the covenant but to its Creator. That explains why a wisdom book like Lamentations is so necessary. Lamentations 'applies the wisdom motif of theodicy to the peculiarly prophetic province of the corporate history of Israel under the Mosaic covenant'.[50]

The covenant with David and David's greater son

If we return to David, we discover that David not only writes and sings about the character of the Torah, the covenant and its divine author, but directly encounters the word of Yahweh as well. That is because he is

---

[48] Ibid. 64.
[49] Ibid. 65.
[50] Ibid. 66.

Israel's King, charged with representing Israel in her covenant with Yahweh, and likewise responsible for representing the covenant maker to the covenant people. As Wellum says, 'The king becomes the administrator and mediator of God's covenant with Israel, thus representing God's rule to the people and representing the people as a whole to God (2 Sam. 7:22–24).'[51]

If David is the representative of Israel, God's son, then sonship ties into kingship as well for David. 'The sonship that was applied to the nation of Israel (Ex. 4:22–23; cf. Hos. 11:1) is now applied to David and his sons.' Yahweh will 'relate to the Davidic kings as a father to a son (2 Sam. 7:14; 1 Chron. 17:3; cf. Psalm 2; 89:26–27)'.[52] Yet that relation will not only apply to David and Solomon, but to the righteous branch of David (Jer. 23:1–8; Isa. 11:1–10), David's greater son, the Son of God himself. And 2 Samuel 7 sets this trajectory in motion.

The context of 2 Samuel 7 is important. In 2 Samuel 5 David is anointed king of Israel, the one who will shepherd God's flock (5:2). As shepherd, David protects the flock from the threat of the Philistines (5:17–25). With victory in his hands, David enters Jerusalem, but does so with the ark of the covenant. As the ark enters the holy city, the presence of the Holy One 'sits enthroned on the cherubim' as King, the 'LORD of hosts' (6:2). The ark is the footstool of the throne on which Yahweh sits and reigns (1 Sam. 4:4; Pss 18:10; 99:5; 132:7–8; 1 Chr. 28:2).[53] As discovered already, inside the ark is the constitution of Israel's covenant. Where the covenant treaty is, there is the presence of Yahweh; where the word of the covenant travels, there the covenant mercy of Yahweh is manifested.

Since the ark is the symbol of divine presence and revelation, it makes sense, in David's mind, that such an ark should have a sanctuary. In 2 Samuel 7 David tells Nathan the prophet that he will build a house for the Lord so that the ark no longer dwells in a tent (7:2). To his surprise, God rejects David's plans. That same night God addresses David through his prophet, for David will not build a house for the Lord; the Lord will build a house for David (7:4–9). It is the Lord who first took David from the obscure pasture and raised him up as prince over Israel (7:8). It will be the Lord, then, who makes David's name great (7:9) and appoints a 'place

---

[51] Wellum 2016: 140.
[52] Ibid.
[53] For the ANE background, see Dumbrell 2013: 216–217.

70

for my people Israel' (7:10). The covenant promises made to Abraham will continue with David and his offspring.

In the end, it is the Lord who will build a house for David, but it will be David's son who will be its architect:

> When your days are fulfilled and you lie down with your fathers, I will raise up your offspring after you, who shall come from your body, and I will establish his kingdom. He shall build a house for my name, and I will establish the throne of his kingdom for ever. I will be to him a father, and he shall be to me a son.
> (7:12–14; cf. 1 Chr. 17:11–14)

As much as Yahweh speaks of David's son, Solomon, who will build the temple of the Lord, his promise goes beyond David's immediate heir. The kingdom of David, says the Lord, is a kingdom that will be established *for ever*. There will be no end to David's throne. 'And your house and your kingdom shall be made sure for ever before me. Your throne shall be established for ever' (2 Sam. 7:16). Yahweh's promise to remain faithful to David and his kingdom, to place an offspring on his throne for ever, is elaborated at great length in Psalm 89:34–36.

David himself interprets the promise in this way, incorporating the language of covenant:

> For he has made with me an everlasting covenant,
>   ordered in all things and secure.
> (2 Sam. 23:5)

David also believes this covenantal word to be certain and reliable.[54] It is a 'revelation' from God himself, says David, and the Lord's 'words are true' (7:27, 28). As with Abraham, Moses and Joshua, God's word addresses David with covenantal intentions and covenantal promises, promises as trustworthy as the God who made them. Like his covenant with Abraham, God's covenant with David is unilateral and unconditional, and brings the Abrahamic covenant one giant step further in its consummation.

---

[54] So too does Solomon: 'Blessed be the LORD who has given rest to his people Israel, according to all that he promised. Not one word has failed of all his good promise, which he spoke by Moses his servant' (1 Kgs 8:56).

As unconditional as this covenant may be, the Lord requires obedience:

If your sons keep my covenant
  and my testimonies that I shall teach them,
their sons also for ever
  shall sit on your throne.
(Ps. 132:12)[55]

'In general terms the line would not fail. Yet in particular terms, benefits might be withdrawn from individuals.'[56] Unfortunately, few kings after David and Solomon reflect such adherence to Deuteronomy 17:18–19 or the everlasting covenant God promises to David. God's unconditional promise is coupled to a covenant partner who cannot and will not be faithful and obedient as God's kingly son.

Although the Davidic line continues, those who sit on David's throne neglect the Torah and the covenant promises of God that started with Abraham, as books like 1 and 2 Kings demonstrate at great length. The situation becomes so dire that at one point it appears as though the Scriptures of Israel are lost altogether (e.g. 2 Kgs 22:8). Nevertheless, God is not silent but continues to call his chosen people back to the covenant. Prophets like Elijah (1 Kgs 17 – 19; 2 Kgs 1 – 2) and Elisha (1 Kgs 19:19–21; 2 Kgs 2 – 7) confront the people with their sin, promising the curses of the covenant if they continue to stray from their covenant maker.

So hard is the heart of Israel, so wayward is his bride in her idolatry, that Yahweh finally brings the ultimate judgment upon her: exile from the land and bondage to a foreign nation and its gods (2 Kgs 17 and 25). Israel is handed over to her enemies and walks away from her land and temple in shame, all because she 'did not obey the voice of the LORD their God but transgressed his covenant, even all that Moses the servant of the LORD commanded'. In short, she 'neither listened nor obeyed' (2 Kgs 18:12).

The failure to keep the covenant only exposes Israel's need for a Davidic son who will obey the law and remain faithful to the covenant, bringing redemption to Israel, restoring the covenant blessings the covenant promised. That messianic hope for David's greater son will finally be achieved in King Jesus (Matt. 1:1; Mark 10:47; Luke 1:32–33; Acts 2:29–30;

---

[55] A similar unconditional–conditional dynamic was seen with Abraham.
[56] Dumbrell 2013: 226.

4:23–30; 13:23; Heb. 1:5). He will not only build a temple that cannot be destroyed (Matt. 26:61; 27:40; Mark 14:58; 15:29; John 2:19–22; Heb. 3:3), but will reign over God's everlasting kingdom as a Son faithful to the covenant (Matt. 19:28–29; Luke 22:29–30; John 18:36; Heb. 1:8; Rev. 19:11–16). It is this Son of David that defines the gospel, a gospel, says Paul, that God

> promised beforehand through his prophets in the holy Scriptures, concerning his Son, who was descended from David according to the flesh and was declared to be the Son of God in power according to the Spirit of holiness by his resurrection from the dead, Jesus Christ our Lord.
> (Rom. 1:2–4)

Since this resurrected Davidic Son of God was 'promised beforehand through his prophets', it is to such prophets that we now must turn.

The Prophets as prosecutors of the covenant treaty

Taking our cue from Christ in Luke 24, the focus so far has centred on the Law and the Psalms, but little has been said about the prophets and their place in the Scriptures of Israel. As mentioned already, 'the Prophets' in Luke 24:27 may be a broad reference, including former prophets (Joshua to Kings) and latter prophets (Jeremiah to the Twelve). Even then, the prophetic office can be said to originate as far back as Moses (Deut. 18:5). Regardless, with attention given to the former prophets, the latter prophets also hold an essential role in the biblical storyline.

The historical setting for the prophets is chronologically variegated to say the least. Prophets like Isaiah, Jeremiah, Micah, Nahum, Habakkuk and Zephaniah address the people of Judah prior to the fall of Jerusalem (AD 586). Prophets like Daniel and Ezekiel address Judah just before their demise and then after as well, while a prophet like Obadiah addresses Judah after their captivity. Prophets like Haggai, Zechariah and Malachi minister within one of the three returns from exile (538–445 BC). In the north prophets like Hosea, Amos and Jonah address Israel until the fall of Samaria in 722 BC. It is not the purpose here to recount their various messages; nevertheless, what is essential to observe is *where* their message comes from and how it defines their role as *prophet* to God's covenant people.

First, the prophet is to be the representative of Yahweh to his people. To qualify, the prophet's role, typically, does not involve a mediation or representation identical to that of the priest. While the priest represents the people *to Yahweh*, the prophet usually represents Yahweh *to the people*, and not always on the best of terms.[57]

The prophetic role is cultivated within the context of the covenant and pre-existing suzerain–vassal obligations. By representing Yahweh, the prophet represents the covenant as well. 'The prophets were the representatives of Yahweh in the administration of his covenant over Israel to declare his claims and enforce his will through effective proclamation.'[58] The prophets did so in at least five different ways, though each of these is connected to the others:

1 *Judgment*: 'The documentary legacy of their mission reveals them confronting Israel with judgment.'
2 *Proclamation*: 'They proclaim the sovereign name of the covenant Lord: Yahweh, Creator, God of hosts.'
3 *Rehearsal*: 'They rehearse the gracious acts of his reign through the history of his relationship with Israel.'
4 *Reiteration*: 'They reiterate interpretively the obligations his treaty has imposed (cf. Ezra 9:11; Dan. 9:11), calling into review Israel's rebellious ways.'
5 *Confrontation*: 'They confront the sinful nation with the curses threatened in treaty text and ratificatory rite, while renewing promises of unquenchable grace.'[59]

When these five are taken as a whole, it becomes clear that the prophetic literature is an expansion of the covenant treatise at Sinai.[60]

Yet one need not read the prophetic literature long to realize that points 1 (judgment) and 5 (confrontation) take up large swaths of the prophetic witness because Israel does not keep the covenant, inviting the curses the covenant treaty originally threatened. Israel's idolatry results in the

---

[57] Young 1985: 28.
[58] Kline 1989: 58.
[59] Ibid. 59. This listing is my doing, not Kline's.
[60] Ibid. Kline calls the prophets 'extensions'.

transgression of the covenant, and consequently many of the prophets embark on a mission that will be disciplinary from the start. They are, one could say, the prosecutors in Yahweh's case against his unfaithful bride.

> The peculiarly prophetic task was the elaboration and application of the ancient covenant sanctions. In actual practice this mean that their diplomatic mission to Israel was by and large one of prosecuting Yahweh's patient covenant lawsuit with his incurably wayward vassal people.[61]

Such a prosecuting role is not foreign to the ANE context either. The suzerain might send an emissary representing him and the covenant to the vassal(s) should he fear a breach in the covenant.[62] In a similar way, the prophet acts as an ambassador and speaks with an authority that stems from Yahweh himself and his covenant treaty.

Second, the prophet is the vocal cords of Yahweh. Old Testament theologians are quick to point out that to be a prophet is to be elected by God himself, set apart to give him a voice, a voice that is then to be heard by the people of God.[63] Young maintains that although the Mosaic Law was 'the foundation upon which the theocratic kingdom was to be built' and although the 'revelation at Sinai was amply sufficient to make known the will of God', nevertheless Israel's idolatry and waywardness made further revelation necessary.[64] God must speak once again to draw his people back, and the prophets are his verbal means of summons.

In this time of transition from the wilderness to the land Yahweh promised Abraham, 'Israel needed once more to hear the voice of the living God.' 'The work of the Levites was not sufficient for that time and so God is to give to Israel His prophets, who would declare His will to the nation.'[65] It is this open line of communication that sets Israel and her relationship with Yahweh apart from the mute idols of the nations (e.g. Isa. 46:7, 10).

> The chosen nation is characterized by the fact that she possesses the Word of God . . . The people of Canaan hearken unto the divines and

---

[61] Ibid.
[62] Ibid. 63.
[63] Vos 1948: 193; Young 1985: 13; House 1998: 185, 251; Waltke 2007: 805; Shead 2012.
[64] Young 1985: 20.
[65] Ibid. 21.

the enchanters; Israel however, is to hearken unto the prophet. One nation hearkens to the word of man; the other is to give ear only to the Word of God [cf. Deut. 18:15].[66]

It is because Yahweh speaks in and through these prophets that it is appropriate to acknowledge that the prophets did not merely write for their own day but for a day to come. Contrary to Hermann Gunkel and his school of form criticism, Young argues against the assumption that the 'prophets were merely men of their own time'. It is critical to pay attention to the 'life situation' the prophets functioned within; nevertheless, to restrict their message to their immediate historical milieu is to fail to understand the prophetic institution itself. 'According to the consistent representation of the Scriptures, the prophets did not speak only to their own generation, nor were their messages called forth merely because of certain historical situations.'[67]

Rather, the historical situation itself gave birth to a prophetic message from God that not only addresses Israel's current circumstances but Israel's future hope. Instead of setting the 'life situation' or 'historical situation' of Israel over against the divine origins of the prophetic message or the divine authorial intent embedded within that message, both of which enable the prophet to address not only Israel's current situation but its future, it is far more in line with prophetic literature itself to see the historical situation as the reason why it is so necessary for Israel to hear directly from God. His voice alone can address her current situation, either in the land or exiled from the land, and his voice alone can speak to her future hope. The prophetic institution, therefore, is the God-appointed means to that end.[68]

That God speaks to these prophets and these prophets speak for God is assumed throughout their prophetic message. Jeremiah is said to be chosen by God before he was born (Jer. 1:4–5) and is told to speak whatever God commands him to speak (1:7–8). 'Behold, I have put my words in your mouth,' says the Lord to Jeremiah (1:9), and not only does this word

---

[66] Ibid. 23, 27. Prophecy, 'the gift of God, and the superstitions of Canaan, have nothing to do one with another'. Ibid. 24.

[67] Ibid. 254.

[68] Ibid. 155. As chapters 3 and 4 will demonstrate, the Evangelists view the prophets in this way as well, which explains why they can reference their writings as applicable to the ministry, mission and work of Christ (e.g. John 12:37–41). Nor are the Evangelists alone in this assessment of the prophets: Peter and Paul utilize the same Christologically oriented hermeneutic (e.g. Acts 3:24; 13:16–47; Rom. 1:2).

originate from the Lord himself but the Lord is the one who says he will watch over his word 'to perform it' (1:12). In order for Ezekiel to speak 'my words' to the people (3:4), the Lord gives Ezekiel a vision in which a scroll with the words of the Lord are placed in his mouth; Ezekiel is to eat and digest this scroll so that his words are none other than God's words (2:7 – 3:3). While these are vivid pictures describing the synonymous nature of God's word with the prophet's word, all other prophets, major and minor, exhibit this same presupposition. In the first verse of most prophetic books, it is always the 'word of the LORD that came to' the prophet, whether Hosea, Joel, Micah, Zephaniah, Haggai, Zechariah or Malachi.[69] That vocabulary is so prevalent that in a book like Isaiah it dowses the fabric of the prophet's message from start to finish.[70]

Not only are the prophets aware that God is speaking to and through them, as is manifested in their use of phrases like 'Hear the word of the LORD,' but at times it is the voice of God that is identified directly: 'Give attention to me, my people.'[71] This transition from the Prophet's to Yahweh's voice in the first person occurs in a variety of ways. Using Jeremiah as an example, Shead identifies three ways (the third originating from A. van Selms). These include the following:

1. *Embedded discourse.* The text begins with a statement like 'this word came to Jeremiah from the LORD' (Jer. 27:1) but then Jeremiah introduces God's own voice, 'Thus the LORD said to me' (Jer. 27:2). 'This habit biblical Hebrew has of constant direct speech has the effect of creating immediacy.'[72]

---

[69] The wording differs slightly: 'came to' Hosea, Joel, Jonah, Micah, Zephaniah; 'came through' Zechariah and Malachi.

[70] Cf. Isa. 1:1–2, 10, 18, 20, 24; 2:1, 15–16; 5:24; 6; 7:3, 7, 10; 8:1, 3, 11; 9:8; 10:24; 13:1; 14:22, 24, 27, 28; 15:1; 16:13; 17:1; 18:4; 19:1, 17; 20:2–3; 21:1, 10–11, 13, 17; 22:12, 14–15, 25; 23:1, 11; 24:3; 25:8; 28:16, 22, 26, 29; 29:10, 13, 22; 30:1–2, 6, 8, 12, 15; 31:4; 36:10; 37:6, 21–22, 33; 38:4–5; 39:8; 40:1, 5, 25; 41:13; 42:5; 43:1, 10, 14, 16; 44:2, 6, 24, 26, 27, 28; 45:1, 11, 13–14, 17–18, 22; 48:17, 22; 49:1, 3, 5–8, 18, 22, 25; 50:1, 5; 51:22; 52:3–5; 54:17; 56:1, 4; 57:15, 19, 21; 58:14; 59:20–21; 61:1; 63:8, 13; 66:1, 5, 9, 12, 20–22. Examining these references, Young concludes that 'the prophet believed that he had been the recipient of an objective revelation. He did not think that he was uttering words which had found their origination in his own mind, but rather that he had received a message which God had given to him.' So strong and direct was such an emphasis that at times the 'personality of the prophet even recedes completely into the background, and the speaker appears to be God Himself'. And yet, throughout the book, Isaiah continues to be an active, thinking subject in this reception of revelation, as seen in a passage like Isa. 6. Young 1985: 175; cf. 188. A discussion of the method of prophetic revelation is beyond the scope of this book but see my forthcoming work *The Trinity and the Mystery of Inspiration* (2022).

[71] For examples of the former, consult Isa. 1:10; 49:22; Jer. 2:4; Amos 1:5; Mal. 1:2. For examples of the latter, see Isa. 49:22; 51:1, 4.

[72] Shead 2012: 111.

Although one is listening to Jeremiah, it is God who is speaking and addressing his people directly.

2. *Drift of speaker.* A passage starts with Jeremiah's voice ('the word of the LORD has come to me'; 25:3) and is then transcended by Yahweh's own voice ('Therefore thus says the LORD of hosts'; 25:8), but in a subtle manner so that the reader is led to assume that what Jeremiah says is what Yahweh says. In other words, 'the prophet's voice is displaced without notice by the encroaching voice of God'.[73]

3. *Telescoping.* 'disparate voices in the text are blended together' (e.g. Jer. 45:1–4).[74]

In all three, the 'voice of the prophet is replaced by the voice of God'.[75] Whatever the method, being the voice and mouth of the Lord is what distinguishes these prophets from those prophets Israel is to identify as false prophets. The latter spoke not the word of God but their own word, a word that does not originate from the mouth of the Lord (e.g. Deut. 13:1–11; 18:22; Jer. 14:14; 23:16–32; Ezek. 13:3, 7). Israel will know a true prophet from a false prophet by the truthfulness of the word spoken (Deut. 13:1–11; Ezek. 13:7). What if Israel should wonder, 'How may we know the word that the LORD has not spoken?' Yahweh specifies the answer ahead of time:

> when a prophet speaks in the name of the LORD, if the word does not come to pass or come true, that is a word that the LORD has not spoken; the prophet has spoken it presumptuously. You need not be afraid of him.
> (Deut. 18:21, 22)

Furthermore, these prophets understand that they are operating on the foundation of the original covenant treaty and its surrounding historical narrative (i.e. the Pentateuch). For example, the historical books, says Kline, did not only serve as 'literary' background to interpret the 'prophetic messages':

> The historical documents were suitable for legal service in the administration of the covenant. They constituted the official record witnessing to Yahweh's fidelity and to the vassal people's continual

---

[73] Ibid.
[74] Selms 1976: 103, 111–112.
[75] Shead 2012: 116.

non-compliance with his commandments. In them the prophets had in hand documentary testimony substantiating their case in their mission as agents of Yahweh's covenant lawsuit against Israel.[76]

Inspiration and canon consciousness: Jeremiah and Zechariah

Old Testament scholars have long acknowledged that out of the many prophets, it is Jeremiah whose book is not only saturated with 'word' vocabulary but he is told to put into a book that which has been revealed.[77] For example, Shead claims that the 'vocabulary of word and words is used more liberally in Jeremiah than in any other major Old Testament book' and, therefore, Jeremiah 'is arguably the book above all others in the Old Testament that lends itself to systematic reflection on the word of God'.[78]

Shead organizes this word vocabulary into three categories: (1) *Messenger Formula*, 'Thus says the LORD' (used 155 times), (2) *Narrative Formula*, 'The word of the Lord came to Jeremiah, saying . . .' (used 23 times), and (3) *Disjunctive Heading* (or *Wortgeschehensformel*), 'the word that came to Jeremiah from the LORD'.[79] Out of these three, the disjunctive is found in Jeremiah alone. But more to the point, these three not only characterize word vocabulary but serve to structure the entire book of Jeremiah, so much so that they '"subsume entire discourses under the heading of YHWH speech" and ultimately convert what were once oracles, sermons and narratives addressed to a range of audiences into a single written message from the Lord'.[80]

Moreover, like Isaiah, Ezekiel, Habakkuk and others, not only is the word of the Lord revealed to Jeremiah, but Yahweh instructs Jeremiah to put it into writing (e.g. Jer. 25:13; 30:2; 51:60). Even when the scroll is burned in a fire by Jehoiakim, Jeremiah is not only instructed to do a rewrite but an expansion on what was written before, a process that involves Jeremiah's dictating to Baruch, son of Neriah (36:32).[81] These written words carry the same authority as what Jeremiah originally heard from the Lord. As much as the spoken word, the written word of Jeremiah is equally God's word. The written word is no further removed from God than the

---

[76] Kline 1989: 57.
[77] See Young 1985: 159–160.
[78] Shead 2012: 44, 46.
[79] Ibid. 45.
[80] Shead (ibid.), quoting Biddle (1996: 121–122).
[81] Shead 2012: 48.

spoken word because when Jeremiah speaks it is God who speaks to him and through him. In that sense, whenever a biblical author writes under the Spirit's superintendence, he undergoes a prophetic task, regardless if he holds the technical office of prophet.[82]

The significance of Shead's observations should not be missed: 'Clearly, it was not merely a general message that Jeremiah received. We can safely conclude that the message from God came to Jeremiah in words. To put it in theological terms, this act of revelation was *verbal*' (emphasis original). But does not its medium (i.e. *human* words via *human* persons) pose a challenge for God? Not at all.

> The notion that human language can be an adequate vehicle for the divine word is a bone of contention among theologians, and yet the remarkable implication of the book's opening paragraph is that the inescapable imprecision of human language does not prevent it from conveying the word of God.[83]

Such a point can be applied to the Old Testament at large.[84] One should not forget that it is Yahweh himself who prepared the human authors to write what they write and in the way they write it. Even the distinct and diverse personalities and training of the biblical authors are orchestrated by God as preparation for the word he will have them write. The Bible, observes Poythress,

> makes it very clear that what God says does not cease to be what God says just because a human intermediary is introduced (Deut. 5:22–33). After all, it is God who chose the human intermediary and who fashioned his personality (Ps. 139:13–16).[85]

This verbal quality is further seen in the way the word moves from singular to plural. The 'word' of the Lord (singular; e.g. Jer. 26:1–2) is heard and received by Jeremiah, who then turns to communicate the 'words' of the Lord (plural; cf. Jer. 19:2) to Israel, and not only orally but via a written

---

[82] A 'book may be recognized as prophetic, its author moved by a prophetic impulse, when the words it contains are recognized to be the words of God'. Shead 2012: 261.

[83] Ibid. 54; cf. 126, 137–138.

[84] To see the prophetic form of inspiration applied across the canon, see Blocher 2016: 497–541.

[85] Poythress 1994: 93.

word, one that originates from Yahweh himself and bears his authority over his covenant people. '*What is heard and obeyed is described in Jeremiah as the word of God, and when that word is spoken or written by the prophet the words that come out are the words of God.*'[86] We are not without warrant to conclude that the prophets spoke and wrote the *words of God.*

It should also be acknowledged that the prophets are not only aware of their own God-inspired words, but those of other prophets as well. They possess a 'canon consciousness', one readily apparent in the exilic and post-exilic eras.[87] Such canon consciousness is visible, for example, in Zechariah. There we read that the

> word of the LORD came to Zechariah, saying, 'Thus says the LORD of hosts, render true judgments, show kindness and mercy to one another, do not oppress the widow, the fatherless, the sojourner, or the poor, and let none of you devise evil against another in your heart.'
> (7:9–10)

Consistent with their fathers, the people refuse. They 'turned a stubborn shoulder and stopped their ears that they might not hear' (Zech. 7:11). In other words, they pretend to be deaf at the word of the Lord and demonstrate their defiance by refusing to meet the needs of the poor and oppressed in their midst. 'They made their hearts diamond-hard lest they should hear the law and the words that the LORD of hosts had sent by his Spirit through the former prophets' (7:12). As a result, the anger of the Lord is roused, and he returns the favour: 'As I called, and they would not hear, so they called, and I would not hear' (7:13).

Notice, Zechariah attributes the Spirit to 'former prophets' in 7:12. He is aware that the same Spirit at work in his own message was previously at work in other prophets. Zechariah recognizes a continuity between his prophetic office and message and that of prior prophets: they both speak and write according to the Spirit. However, there is a continuity in the people's reaction as well. Just as their fathers rejected the law and the prophets, so too do they reject the law and the prophets in Zechariah's day. In doing so, they reject the Spirit himself. How fitting, then, for Stephen to

---

[86] Shead 2012: 60. Emphasis original.
[87] Dempster 2003: 30; Lohfink 1965: 35; Sailhamer 2001: 13.

evaluate the hardness of heart he saw in the religious leaders of his own day and conclude, 'You stiff-necked people, uncircumcised in heart and ears, you always resist the Holy Spirit. As your fathers did, so do you. Which of the prophets did your fathers not persecute?' (Acts 7:51–52).

Stephen verifies that there is within the Prophets a *conceptual homogeneity* across redemptive history, one that even pervades the inscripturated word, due to the Spirit's inspired presence. That homogeneity explains, in part, why both Jesus and Stephen were put to death: Israel continued to grieve the Spirit by killing those who came with the word of the Lord in the name of the Lord, and, ultimately, even putting to death the Lord himself the great Prophet promised to Moses (Deut. 18:15–22; Acts 3:17–24).

Is conceptual homogeneity intrinsic to the covenant treaty?

The trajectory followed so far is meant to bring into focus the unity of the canon Israel saw develop before her very eyes as well as its divine origin. However, some have questioned canonical unity since there was not one book, materially speaking. Scrolls not only were the medium for the diverse books called 'Scriptures', but even particular books, like Isaiah or Jeremiah for example, would have required a plurality of scrolls. If the medium itself is heterogeneous, then is the claim of a unified canon not an attempt to read back into the Scriptures a homogeneity that is not intrinsically present?[88]

In response to such an objection, one would be wise to recognize the distinction between physical or material unity and conceptual unity. The lack of the former does not necessarily mean the absence of the latter. 'Theoretically,' says Dempster,

> physical division does not necessarily imply conceptual disunity, as a glance at a multi-volume work on any modern library shelf will show. Similarly, in ancient Israel, the physical separation of texts did not imply that there was not a Text of which they comprised parts. The deposit of separate volumes together in one archive was already one means to indicate their conceptual unity.[89]

---

[88] To hear this objection, see Barr 1983: 15.
[89] Dempster 2003: 21.

Dempster demonstrates that such conceptual unity is not only present in the way Israel perceives the Scriptures but neither is it foreign to other ANE narratives (e.g. the Epic of Gilgamesh). 'It is certain that the Hebrew Bible, despite being composed of many texts, is not for that reason precluded from being a Text.'[90]

Did Israel believe the Hebrew Scriptures are a conceptual unity, even if materially divided, because (1) of certain literary threads that are consistent throughout or (2) for theological reasons (i.e. the one, divine author brought unity to the many human authors)? One need not choose between the two. As seen already, Israel presupposes Yahweh to be a speaking God: his authoritative words are the words of Moses and the Prophets. Yet that should not preclude one from also acknowledging the canon's literary unity at the level of the human author.

To be precise, it is because there is a divine author who speaks in and through the human author(s) that literary unity is possible across the canon. To choose between the two is but a false dichotomy, one foreign to pre- and post-exilic Israel. Dempster explains:

> despite the literary heterogeneity, there is at the same time a remarkable structural homogeneity, for this vast variety of genres is set within books, which are placed within an extraordinary narrative outline commencing with creation and ending with the exile and return of the Jewish people.[91]

In other words, the 'amazing diversity of texts is set within a comprehensive narrative framework, which provides an overarching literary and historical context. Thus the many shorter texts together contribute to this larger textual framework and find their meaning and significance within it.'[92]

Dempster is not saying that the Bible is only to be accepted due to its literary pedigree; nevertheless, he is saying that its literary features and structure showcase its intrinsic unity, and 'ignorance of its literary features impedes understanding'.[93] For that reason, the Bible is both literature *and* sacred: it is sacred literature. It follows, then, that the history into which it

---

[90] Ibid.
[91] Ibid. 22–23.
[92] Ibid.
[93] Ibid. 24.

speaks cannot be relegated to the secular realm; it is sacred history, or redemptive history as argued in chapter 1.

If the Scriptures of Israel are neither a 'hotchpotch of old religious traditions (at worst) or an anthology of ancient literature (at best)',[94] but there is a theological as well as literary unity to them, then it will not suffice to label the canonical witness a mere *anthology*. To do so not only fails to pay attention to what the text itself claims to be but also ignores the unified story the text portrays.

> Such an 'anthology' would contain no storyline, coherence or unity – and, in the judgment of many, any unity that might exist would be strictly artificial. On such a view the Text is a literary and historical accident resulting from a 'political' decision.[95]

Many biblical scholars see the text as a literary-historical accident because as they look at its *parts* they do not see a purposeful pattern in the text *as a whole*. As mentioned in chapter 1, they reject Scripture's inspiration, the foundation of 'authorial unity', convinced such an assumption is the relic of a 'precritical era'. Yet Dempster points out that such a 'theological judgment has gone hand in hand with an enchantment with the minute details of the biblical text rather than with its more global features, which *ipso facto* cannot exist'.[96] The symptoms of such a method surface in the artificial and excessive atomism of modern biblical studies. 'The concern for studying smaller and smaller sections of the biblical text and the increasing specialization of scholars studying the minutiae of philology and morphology have resulted in a loss of perspective.'[97] In other words, they have so zoomed in on the text that they have neglected its wider unitary picture and narrative cohesion.

If Dempster is right that 'historical criticism has contributed to a fragmented understanding of the text, so that any unity is an illusion', then what is needed is a 'wide-angle-lens perspective', and that is a lens biblical theology can provide.[98] Biblical theology may prove to be the lens that helps the church and academy alike see Scripture for what it is, namely a

---

94 Ibid. 22.
95 Ibid. 27.
96 Ibid. 28.
97 Ibid. 28–29.
98 Ibid.

textual unit with embedded divine purpose rather than a patchwork invention of an accidental human feat.

To allay the fears of some, the emphasis on conceptual unity and the wide-angle-lens perspective is not meant to flatten out the covenants or the two testaments, as if diversity vanishes for the sake of conformity.[99] Instead, conceptual unity preserves literary diversity across the canon, certifying that the canonical witness continues to progress from Moses to the Prophets until it reaches its fulfilment in Christ. The beauty of conceptual unity is that it does not flatten the canonical witness but guarantees that its diverse testimony progresses with purpose.

> The fact that the Hebrew canon is structured in terms of a narrative sequence with commentary means that canonization does not 'flatten' the text into a one-dimensional uniformity; rather, it provides for evolution, diversity and growth within an overarching framework in which the various parts can be related to the literary whole.[100]

As a result, the many literary structures of the Scriptures are made to shine in all their assorted brilliance due to the conceptual unity present in the task of biblical theology. By following Scripture's grand story, biblical theology recognizes 'the profoundly historical rootedness of the biblical books', and also 'accepts their occasional nature, literary quality and powerful vitality'.[101] Biblical theology, says Rosner, 'treats such texts with a due sensitivity to the different genres and literary features represented'. Yet such 'due sensitivity' is feasible only if conceptual, canonical unity is presupposed. 'Biblical study is incomplete until biblical theology has been done.'[102]

---

[99] Although, admittedly, this 'flattening' can be a tendency. 'There is a temptation in studying the Bible's theology too quickly to read one part of it in the light of another and thus to miss the individual contours of the terrain and flatten out the whole.' Rosner 2000: 6.

[100] Dempster 2003: 43.

[101] Rosner 2003: 4.

[102] Ibid. Hence Rosner defines biblical theology as follows: 'theological interpretation of Scripture in and for the church. It proceeds with historical and literary sensitivity and seeks to analyse and synthesize the Bible's teaching about God and his relations to the world on its own terms, maintaining sight of the Bible's overarching narrative and Christocentric focus.' Rosner 2000: 10. Also compare to Vanhoozer (2000: 63), who says, 'Biblical theology is a description of the biblical texts on levels that display their theological significance. Accordingly, biblical theology is nothing less than a theological hermeneutic: an interpretive approach to the Bible informed by Christian doctrine. The biblical theologian reads for the theological message communicated by the texts taken individually and as a whole collection.' For a more elaborate definition, see Carson 2000: 100–101.

The wide-angle lens: Jesus, the canon and the new covenant

If there is such a thing as conceptual unity and a *wide-angle lens*, then one would expect, ironically perhaps, the prophets to *narrow* their focus. In other words, if the story of Israel and Yahweh's covenant promises are governed by the divine agent and scriptwriter, then at the proper time a narrowing in focus must occur. This is precisely what the reader notices the closer he or she approaches Jesus and the Gospels. The covenant promises made to Abraham are wide, universal in scope, but their fulfilment requires the story to narrow not only to an event but to a person who will bring those promises to fruition. In some respects, the people of Israel understand this, which explains their anticipation of a Messiah.

That anticipation builds with the prophets. On the one hand, the prophets paint with broad brush strokes, leading Israel to hope for an end-time renewal of covenant blessing. Consider Isaiah, for example. Pennington defines Isaiah's eschatological vision as a certain '*hope in the restoration of God's reign*'.[103] What covenant blessings does that restoration entail?

- comfort and tenderness from God (40:1–2, 11; 51:5; 52:9; 54:7–8; 55:7; 61:2–3)
- the presence of God himself (41:10; 43:5; 45:14; 52:12)
- help for the poor and needy (40:29–31; 41:17; 55:1–2)
- the renewing of all things (38:6; 42:9–10; 43:18–19; 65:17; 66:22)
- the judgment of God's enemies (42:13–17; 47:1–15; 49:22–26; 66:15–17, 24)
- the healing of blindness and deafness (42:18; 43:8–10)
- the forgiveness of sins (44:22; 53:4–6, 10–12)
- the making of a covenant (41:6; 49:8; 55:3; 59:21).[104]

That last one is central to restoration. Isaiah 40 – 66, for example, issues a call for Israel's renewal: they will be created anew as a people and this recreation will occur through a *new* covenant.

How will this take place? Through God's word. Isaiah speaks of the 're-creation of Israel through the divine word, which has as its aim the

---

[103] Pennington 2012: 15. Emphasis original.
[104] Ibid. 15–16. This is my summary but Pennington's categorization.

establishment of an everlasting covenant (55:3)'.[105] As seen so far, the word of God is powerful; through his word God creates the universe, calls Abraham, establishes a covenant people and issues an everlasting dynasty through King David. God's word is no less powerful in Isaiah (cf. 40:1–11). Now, says Isaiah, God will speak once more and this time create a new covenant; Israel will undergo a new exodus, one in which the 'glory of the Lord shall be revealed' (40:5; cf. 42:16; 43:16–19; 49:9–11; 51:10) and 'the word of our God will stand for ever' (40:8).[106] Through his word he will establish an everlasting covenant of peace, fulfilling his initial promises to David (54:10; 55:3). Isaiah has in mind not just immediate liberation from foreign powers but a new creation, one in which the nations will gather to worship Yahweh as their Lord, fulfilling his covenant promises to Abraham (e.g. 66:19, 22–23).

Prophets like Ezekiel likewise promise the hope of restoration and new creation, declaring that all God's people will receive a new heart and spirit, and will all be permanently indwelt by the Spirit. As early as Deuteronomy 30:6 Yahweh promises Israel that he 'will circumcise your heart and the heart of your offspring, so that you will love the Lord your God with all your heart and with all your soul, that you may live'. Similar imagery is adopted by Ezekiel when the Lord says he will not only gather Israel from the nations and cleanse them from all their idols (36:24, 25), but implant within them a new heart, one of animate flesh rather than lifeless stone:

> I will give you a new heart, and a new spirit I will put within you.
> And I will remove the heart of stone from your flesh and give you a
> heart of flesh. And I will put my Spirit within you, and cause you to
> walk in my statutes and be careful to obey my rules.
> (36:26–27)

The implantation of a new heart, one from the Spirit, is what will enable all God's people to walk in his ways and obey his law.

Jeremiah conveys a similar message, but appeals to *new covenant* language (31:1) and turns to imagery of the law written directly on the heart itself. The Lord promises a day yet to come when he 'will make a new

---

[105] Dumbrell 2013: 277.

[106] Dumbrell (ibid.) says these chapters mark the 're-institution of the covenant'. While there is some truth to that, this new covenant is far more than a reinstitution. The results of this covenant will be far more effective and extensive than before.

covenant with the house of Israel and the house of Judah', though this covenant will not be 'like the covenant that I made with their fathers on the day when I took them by the hand to bring them out of the land of Egypt' (31:31–32). That is a covenant that 'they broke, though I was their husband' (31:32). This covenant, by contrast, will be different because 'I will put my law within them, and I will write it on their hearts.' With the internalization of the law, the word of God, 'I will be their God, and they shall be my people' (31:33). No longer will they tell each other to know the Lord, for they will 'all know me, from the least of them to the greatest . . . For I will forgive their iniquity, and I will remember their sin no more' (31:34).

Notice, the transition from old to new covenant is also a transition from God's word written on tablets of stone to God's word written on the human heart. Jeremiah, in other words, insinuates the *telos* of the canon. 'The goal of the canon', says Dempster,

> is that the law of God, heard so powerfully at Sinai, be written in each human being's heart: that God's law be transferred from the tablets of stone, scrolls, and codices of papyrus and leather in the ancient world, or books printed on paper or distributed via digital media in the modern world, and inscribed on human hearts by the Holy Spirit (2 Cor. 3).

Dempster concludes, 'The canon is thus not written merely for information but it is written to give life.'[107]

But how will all these new covenant blessings be brought to fulfilment? How will this redemption, in all its diverse forms, be accomplished?

Who will inaugurate these last days of the Spirit?

The answer requires the prophets to *narrow* their focus to one who is a prophet, priest and king all in one.[108] Eschatological hope and the validity of God's covenant word rest on the shoulders of Yahweh's anointed One and covenant mediator, God's obedient Son who speaks a saving, prophetic word

---

[107] Dempster 2016: 146–147.

[108] Even in the OT these three offices overlap, so that the word rules over God's covenant people and the king rules through God's word, so that where the word of God is found so too is the presence of God. A similar pattern is true of the priest, who intercedes by means of the word and instructs the people according to the word. To see this further, see Poythress 2017: 270. Is one office primary? That is debatable. See e.g. Dumbrell 2013: 210–211.

to God's covenant people. This promised One will mediate God's word (as *prophet*), mediate God's presence (as *priest*) and mediate God's rule (as *king*).[109] 'All this will be accomplished through God's anointed, humble Servant (42:1–4; 45:4; 49:3–5; 52:13 – 53:12) and witnesses (43:10; 44:8).'[110]

What will be shocking, though not without prefigurement from the Old Testament, is that this prophet, priest and king will intercede by becoming a *servant*, suffering in order to mediate reconciliation through his own blood.[111] Hence the book of Hebrews opens describing the person and work of Christ through all three offices: 'Long ago . . . God spoke to our fathers by the prophets, but in these last days he has spoken to us by his Son', *the Prophet* (1:1–2); 'After making purification for sins,' as *the Priest*, 'he sat down at the right hand of the Majesty on high,' as *the King* (1:3).

It is no wonder, then, why the book of Hebrews appeals to Psalm 110, for it not only speaks of a second *kingly 'Lord'* whom the Lord places at the right hand of his throne until his enemies are made his footstool (110:1; cf. 1:13), but also a *for-ever priest* after the order of Melchizedek (110:4; cf. Heb. 5:6). Through this 'priestly kingship', says Dumbrell, 'the demand contemplated for all Israel in Exodus 19:3b–6 has been embodied' in the 'person of the king'.[112] Typologically fulfilled in Christ, the author of Hebrews can conclude that although Jesus 'was a son, he learned obedience through what he suffered', 'being designated by God a high priest after the order of Melchizedek' (5:8, 10). Consequently, he is the 'source of eternal salvation' (5:9).

But what about the prophets? Like the Psalms, they too introduce and foreshadow this anointed One in variegated ways, sometimes by direct prophecy but often by means of typology (as with sacrifices). Consider the threefold office once more.

1. *King.* Isaiah speaks in royal terminology at times, promising a 'shoot from the stump of Jesse', a righteous branch, on whom the Spirit will rest (Isa. 11:1–2). Likewise, Jeremiah:

> Behold, the days are coming, declares the Lord, when I will raise up
> for David a righteous Branch, and he shall reign as king and deal

---

[109] Poythress 2016: 269–271.
[110] Pennington 2012: 15–16.
[111] Hence there is an overlap between prophet, priest and king. This overlap is seen with Moses, who is all three, but not seen in its fullness until Christ.
[112] Dumbrell 2013: 228.

wisely, and shall execute justice and righteousness in the land . . .
And this is the name by which he will be called: 'The LORD is our
righteousness.'
(23:5–6)

This righteous Branch will be a *king*, but one far greater than David
(Rom. 1:3–4).

To combine metaphors, this king will also be Israel's true *shepherd-king*.
As God announces through his prophets, he will establish his 'servant
David' as a shepherd to his people: 'And I will set up over them one
shepherd, my servant David, and he shall feed them . . . And I, the LORD,
will be their God, and my servant David shall be prince among them'
(Ezek. 34:23–24; cf. Zech. 13:7; Matt. 26:31; Mark 14:27; John 10:1–18).

2. *Priest*. But again, what Jesus' disciples will find so surprising is that
this righteous branch, this Davidic king and shepherd, is also a servant who
suffers. He is not only a king, but a *priest*, and one who will lay his own life
down to mediate atonement. Yet they should have been familiar with such
a motif in the Prophets. Isaiah, for example, refers to the servant as one
who suffers, being pierced for the transgressions of the people, one who is
crushed for their iniquities (53:5). Nevertheless, his sufferings will not have
the last word. For

> when his soul makes an offering for guilt,
>   he shall see his offspring; he shall prolong his days;
> the will of the LORD shall prosper in his hand.
> (53:10)

After his sufferings and resurrection, Jesus' disciples, with eyes now open,
did not hesitate to teach others that Isaiah 53 has Christ as its ultimate
fulfilment (Acts 8:26–35). 'Servant Israel', says Dumbrell,

> is swept up into an idealized presentation of a single Servant figure
> (cf. 49:3) who, in dying for Israel and its world (42:6; 49:6; ch. 53) by
> his being highly exalted, brought the restored Israel to servanthood
> (54:17; 56:6; 65:9; 65:13–15). Jesus will be this ideal Israelite and thus
> representative Israel.[113]

---

[113] Ibid. 281.

Furthermore, as hinted at already, it is this same servant that Isaiah says is the righteous Davidic branch, the one on whom the Spirit rests (11:1–5), and the one who will one day bring God's people out of exile to establish a new, eternal, 'everlasting covenant' due to God's 'steadfast, sure love for David' (55:3).[114] Unlike Israel's priests, who profaned the covenant (see Mal. 2:1–16), a high priest will come and in great humility sprinkle his own blood on the mercy seat to ensure a better covenant (Heb. 4:14 – 8:13). The life and peace God envisioned in his covenant with Levi (Mal. 2:4–5) will finally stand by means of a priest from a different order. For this reason Christ is 'the mediator of a new covenant, that those who are called may receive the promised eternal inheritance' – now that he has died as a ransom to set them free from the sins 'committed under the first covenant' (Heb. 9:15; cf. 5:5–10)'.

3. *Prophet*. With the people in and out of exile, the anticipation of this humble servant creates a tension: Israel awaits the promised One, but God is silent. After hundreds of years pass, one last prophet arrives on the scene and his mission is to announce that the silence is over: the age of the Messiah is now at hand. In accordance with Isaiah, John the Baptist proclaims repentance in the wilderness, baptizing the people of Israel, all so that they are ready to meet the King and enter his kingdom (John 1:19–34; see chapters 3 and 4). The time when God spoke to and through his prophets is over: he now speaks to his people through his Son, Christ Jesus. Hebrews may capture the bridge from the prophets to the Messiah best when the author begins his book, writing, 'Long ago, at many times and in many ways, God spoke to our fathers by the prophets, but in these last days he has spoken to us by his Son' (1:1–2).

But did Jesus himself read history with such a wide-angle lens, one that narrows with his own coming? Do we have reason to believe Jesus read the canon with such a conceptual unity and Christological *telos* in mind?

The answer is yes. Since the next two chapters will focus on Matthew and John, briefly consider Luke's presentation of Christ and his use of the prophets at the beginning and end of his Gospel. First, on the heels of his baptism and temptation, Jesus begins his ministry by entering the synagogue in Nazareth. The 'scroll of the prophet Isaiah was given to him' (Luke 4:17). Unrolling the scroll, Jesus 'found the place where it was written' in the prophet Isaiah (61:1–2):

---

[114] For other aspects of this redemptive, messianic work, see Wellum 2016: 141.

The Spirit of the Lord is upon me,
  because he has anointed me
  to proclaim good news to the poor.
He has sent me to proclaim liberty to the captives
  and recovering of sight to the blind,
  to set at liberty those who are oppressed,
to proclaim the year of the Lord's favour.
(Luke 4:18–19)

The speaker in Isaiah 61 is none other than the messianic servant. Verses 1 and following describe his ministry. As the Lord's anointed one, he is the one on whom the Spirit of the Lord will dwell. What is his mission? It is that of a prophet, one who proclaims the word of the Lord. That word is good news, liberty to captives, the arrival of the Lord's favour, and justice and comfort for those who mourn. The messianic servant, then, is the Spirit-anointed prophet whose word brings good news of covenant blessing.

Having been baptized with the Father's vocalized approval and the Spirit's descending presence, how does Jesus interpret Isaiah 61? After rolling up the scroll, and with the eyes of all on him, Jesus says, 'Today this Scripture has been fulfilled in your hearing' (Luke 4:21). Jesus believes he is none other than Isaiah's Spirit-anointed servant. But notice, his messianic identity is inseparable from his prophetic responsibility, just as Isaiah 61:1–2 describes. When his listeners reject his claims, Jesus makes his prophetic identity clear: 'Truly, I say to you, no *prophet* is acceptable in his home town' (4:24; emphasis added). This pericope at the start of Luke's Gospel sets the trajectory for all that follows. Jesus starts his ministry announcing that he is the Spirit-anointed prophetic servant Isaiah wrote about, and now, in his person and work, the Scriptures – this Scripture in particular – will be fulfilled. The inscripturated word will be fulfilled in him who is the Word.

Second, consider the end of Jesus' ministry, Luke 24 to be exact. This passage alone records the resurrected Christ on the road to Emmaus. A distance of 7 miles (11 km) from Jerusalem Jesus appears to two men, whose 'eyes were kept from recognizing him' (24:16). As Jesus enquires as to their conversation, Cleopas explains how this 'Jesus of Nazareth, a man who was a prophet mighty in deed and word before God and all the people' was delivered up by the chief priests and rulers 'to be condemned to death, and crucified' (24:20). Cleopas is full of disappointment because he 'had hoped that he [Jesus] was the one to redeem Israel' (24:21). Evidently, Cleopas believes the Scriptures of Israel warrant his messianic hope that the redeemer promised to Israel has come in Jesus. Yet Cleopas finds himself perplexed that Israel's anointed One has been crucified and all the more disturbed at the report that Jesus' tomb is found empty.

While Cleopas fails to see how Jesus' apparent defeat by death on a cross could be the mission of the true Messiah who effects the redemption of Israel, Jesus opens their eyes to the wide-angle lens and one that has himself as its *telos*:

> 'O foolish ones, and slow of heart to believe all that the prophets have spoken! Was it not *necessary* that the Christ should suffer these things and enter into his glory?' *And beginning with Moses and all the Prophets, he interpreted to them in all the Scriptures the things concerning himself.*
> (Luke 24:25–27; emphases added)

Later, Jesus appears to a larger gathering of his disciples, showing them his hands and feet, and Luke records a similar response from Jesus:

> Then he said to them, 'These are my words that I spoke to you while I was still with you, that everything written about me in the Law of Moses and the Prophets and the Psalms must be fulfilled.' Then he opened their minds to understand *the Scriptures*, and said to them, '*Thus it is written*, that the Christ should suffer and on the third day rise from the dead, and that repentance and forgiveness of sins should be proclaimed in his name to all nations, beginning from Jerusalem. You are witnesses of these things.'
> (Luke 24:44–48)

In this resurrection narrative Jesus not only assumes the Old Testament is characterized by a canon consciousness, but teaches his disciples that the entire canon was conscious of him. In that sense, *Jesus is the canon*, for all the Scriptures typologically point forward to him.[115]

---

[115] To see this close identification between Jesus and the canon developed in more depth, see Gaffin 1988: 165–183.

Scholars have often wondered how this can be and where in the Old Testament Jesus took his disciples to demonstrate such a radical claim. Yet Luke gives the reader a taste in his sequel, the book of Acts. Acts unveils one of the greatest mysteries of the canon: the prophetic, eschatological promise of the new covenant centres around a *person*, namely the Messiah of Israel. It is this anointed one that Israel is told to anticipate. He is the one who brings eschatological hope to Israel in their state of exile; he will be the one to deliver his people; he will be the definitive word from God; and his arrival will mean the fulfilment of the covenant promises made not only to David and Moses but to one as far back as father Abraham. His arrival will usher in the last days so that God's covenant blessings may not only be manifested among his people Israel but be taken to the nations.

While a variety of cases in the book of Acts serve this point, consider as an example Acts 3 and its use of Deuteronomy 18. For the prophets, the Messiah to come is one who is a prophet himself, bringing the final word of redemption from God to his people. As God promises through Moses in Deuteronomy 18, he will 'raise up' for Israel a prophet like Moses (18:18): 'I will raise up for them a prophet like you from among their brothers. And I will put my words in his mouth, and he shall speak to them all that I command him' (18:18).

In one sense, Deuteronomy 18:17–18 has in mind the immediate prophet(s) who followed Moses, starting with Joshua; the entire prophetic office may be in view.[116] Yet these prophets could not compare to Moses.[117] Granted, they mediated Yahweh's word but never like Moses, who encountered God face to face, and with whom God spoke like a friend. Deuteronomy concludes with the death of Moses and this striking contrast between Moses and the prophetic line that was to follow him: 'And there has not arisen a prophet since in Israel like Moses, whom the LORD knew face to face' (Deut. 34:10).

Deuteronomy 18:17–18 has a greater vision in view, one that looks to a *prophet* who will be greater than Moses and mediate God's word in the

---

[116] Young (1985: 29–31) argues that the singular 'prophet' does not preclude many succeeding prophets to be in view, and by consequence the prophetic office as an entire institution. Young believes Deut. 18:19 is in view in Luke 11:50–51, when Jesus refers to the 'blood of all the prophets', from Abel to Zachariah. A 'prophetic line' is assumed.

[117] Is Moses himself aware of this? Yes, says Sailhamer: Moses' 'brief comments at the close of the book tell us in no uncertain terms that the prophet that Moses spoke of in Deuteronomy 18 was not any of the later prophets of Israel. There was still a prophet yet to come. In other words, the author who gave us the "final" ending of the Pentateuch understands the words of Moses in Deuteronomy 18 exactly as they were understood by the NT authors. That "prophet like Moses" was the expected Messiah and he had not yet come.' Sailhamer 2001: 18.

most direct manner yet to be seen. Any immediate prophet that was raised up after Moses was but a type and shadow of the Prophet who would come not only with the word of Yahweh but as Yahweh himself to dwell and tabernacle with his covenant people (cf. Matt. 1:23).

It is on the basis of texts like Deuteronomy 18 that Jesus can say to his accusers, 'For if you believed Moses, you would believe me; for he wrote of me' (John 5:46). Peter followed suit in the book of Acts.[118] Addressing the Jews in Solomon's Portico, Peter not only turns attention to the prophets as those who 'foretold' that this Jesus, the Christ, would suffer – a prophetic word that was 'thus fulfilled' when Christ died on the cross (3:17–18) – but Peter even quotes Deuteronomy 18:15, 18 and 19 to say that the prophet the prophetic office foreshadowed has come in Jesus:

> Repent therefore . . . that he may send the Christ appointed for you, Jesus, whom heaven must receive until the time for restoring all the things about which God spoke by the mouth of his holy prophets long ago. Moses said, 'The Lord God will raise up for you a prophet like me from your brothers. You shall listen to him in whatever he tells you. And it shall be that every soul who does not listen to that prophet shall be destroyed from the people.' And all the prophets who have spoken, from Samuel and those who came after him, also proclaimed these days.
> (Acts 3:19–24; cf. Deut. 18:19–24)[119]

The use of Deuteronomy 18 in Acts 3 to demonstrate the prophetic role of Christ is but the tip of the Christological iceberg in Luke 24 (cf. Acts 2:14–41; 10:43; 13:13–41; Rom. 15:4; 1 Cor. 10:6; 2 Cor. 1:20; 3:14–16;

---

[118] Deut. 18 is also quoted by Stephen in Acts 7:37. For similar appeals either to Moses or the Prophets, see Matt. 11:13; Acts 28:23; Gal. 3:6–8; Heb. 1:1; 3:1–6; 2 Peter 1:20–21.

[119] Did Moses grasp the full depth of his Spirit-inspired words in Deut. 18? Maybe not, or at least not exhaustively. We are not told regardless. Young believes Moses at least knew that 'God would raise up a body of prophets which was to find its supreme expression in one great prophet, who would stand in peculiar relationship to himself.' Young 1985: 32–33. Yet, as mentioned already, Moses speaks not merely according to his own mind but is carried along by the Spirit as he writes. 'Hence, no mere finite creature, not even Moses, could ever completely fathom their profundity.' Ibid. 33. Young's statement creeps towards *sensus plenior*, and it is not unjustified since the divine intention for Deut. 18 to foreshadow Christ is confirmed by Christ and his apostles. In the end, the NT proves to be the God-inspired interpretation of the OT, and Jesus' prophetic role is but one example of such a principle at work. 'When finally Christ appeared upon earth, the promise was fulfilled in its highest and fullest sense. It is, therefore, a Messianic promise.' Ibid. 35.

Col. 1:16; Heb. 11:13–16).[120] Christ is not only the great *prophet* who mediates the word of the Lord, but is a *priest* who intercedes for Israel's sins by means of his own sacrifice (Isa. 53; Zech. 3:1–5; Mal. 4:2), and ushers in God's kingdom rule and reign as Israel's Davidic *king* (Zech. 3:6–10).

Conclusion

With the voice of Jesus in Luke 24 echoing in the background, the chapters that follow will dwell on the Gospels to see how Jesus and the Evangelists turn to the Old Testament to craft a mosaic of Christological prefigurement. In doing so, it will become clear that Jesus sees himself as the rightful heir to Israel's Scripture, the continuation of Israel's story, and the long-anticipated fulfilment of Israel's covenant treatise. Yet by listening to Jesus explain how he brings the Scriptures to fulfilment, we will also perceive his own attitude towards the Scriptures as the inspired word of God. And who better to listen to than to him who is the Word, revelation embodied in the flesh?

---

[120] For an extensive presentation of the prophetic office as typological of Christ, see Goppelt 1982: 61–82.

3

The Scripture must be fulfilled: the Matthean witness (case study 1)

Contrary to the conclusions of modern critical scholarship, there is an intrinsic continuity between the Gospels and the Scriptures of Israel. That continuity is the agenda of the Gospel writers: their aim is to demonstrate that Jesus is the fulfilment of the Law and the Prophets. For the Evangelists, the story of Israel has reached a tipping point in the coming of Israel's Messiah. As H. von Campenhausen explains, Christ 'stands at the convergence point of the entire preceding salvation history, which he brings to its goal'.[1] If von Campenhausen is right, then the Gospels are pivotal as revelatory witnesses. If everything in the life of Christ, from his teaching to his works, 'constituted the continuation and climax of the ancient biblical story', then the Scriptures of Israel, explains Hays, are the *generative milieu* for the gospels, the original environment in which the first Christian traditions were conceived, formed and nurtured'.[2]

This generative milieu affects the way the Evangelists tell the story of Jesus; they do so in a way that typologically corresponds to persons, events and institutions in Israel. They require their readers to read intertextually, with the story of Israel in one hand and their Gospel narratives in the other in order to see how Jesus brings the Scriptures of Israel to fulfilment. While fulfilment can refer to the completion of direct prediction, it more often than not refers to the way 'Jesus deepens, explains, fills out, and reveals the true intent' of the Scripture, explains Pennington. It may be implicit at times but 'the evangelists tell the stories of Jesus in ways that mimetically correspond to events in Israel's history. The tools and habits of reading intertextually help us unearth these riches.'[3]

---

[1] Campenhausen 1970: 110.
[2] Hays 2006: 53. Emphasis original.
[3] Pennington 2012: 250.

Such intertextuality also means the Evangelists have a certain *attitude* towards the Old Testament. Their Gospels do not seek to displace the Old Testament but show its true fulfilment in Jesus the Christ. 'They assume', says Stuhlmacher, 'that the Christ event is an event of messianic fulfillment and that, as such, it can only be properly understood with reference to and with the help of the Holy Scriptures.'[4] This attitude not only defines the Evangelists, but Jesus himself. To be more accurate, the Evangelists' attitude to the Scriptures, and their figural reading of the Old Testament, stems from Jesus himself. As seen in Luke 24, the disciples struggle to see Christ in the Old Testament, but once Jesus opens their eyes, they see his sufferings and resurrection prefigured throughout its covenantal corpus, transforming their view of the canon and eschatology (see conclusion of chapter 4).

Approach to fulfilment

Presupposed in the Gospel accounts is the belief that only one who has inspired the writers of the Old Testament can claim to bring what the Old Testament authors prophesied and prefigured to fulfilment. The unity of history and the continuity of the canon from Adam to Christ entirely depend on a divine author who has not only breathed out the Scriptures of Israel but is bringing them to fulfilment through Jesus, who is the definitive revelation from God. To see this presupposition in full colour, the theme of 'fulfilment' will occupy the attention of this chapter.

Before a study of specific texts begins, it is necessary to clarify at the start that 'fulfilment' in the Gospels is not uniform in its delivery. It is not as if, for example, every fulfilment motif occurs in the form of direct prophecy. Rather, there are diverse forms of fulfilment. Here we have in mind not the use of the Old Testament as a medium of expression, the application of its moral principles or the representation of its diverse points of view.[5] There is something, indeed a mosaic of options, that sits between direct prophecy on the one end of the spectrum and mere applications on the other end. Fulfilment in the Gospels often occurs through *intertextual echoes* and *typological correspondence*, both of which will be the focus moving forward.

---

[4] 'Because they saw the Christ event as the high point and goal of the revelation of the one God, the references of the early Christians to the Scriptures were tradition-historically and theologically foundational from the very beginning.' Stuhlmacher 2018: 750.

[5] On each of these and for examples of each, see Moo and Naselli 2016: 707–710.

Additionally, not all Evangelists bring out these echoes and types in the same manner. At times the Evangelists will quote from the Old Testament or announce that something Jesus said or did was in fulfilment of the prophets. At other times they will allude to fulfilment in a way their Jewish readers will naturally identify (but contemporary readers unfamiliar with the Jewish world may struggle to follow).[6] 'The New Testament's reference to the Old Testament is not exhausted therefore by scriptural quotations and allusions,' Stuhlmacher explains, 'but extends to the very foundations of the language of faith and leaves its mark on the entire testimony about Christ.'[7]

With that diversity in mind, Matthew and John will be the focus, serving as two case studies out of the four Gospels.[8] That is not because fulfilment is not present in Mark and Luke – indeed, fulfilment pervades their accounts. Rather, it is because what Mark and Luke so often assume Matthew makes explicit.[9] While Mark, for example, insinuates an Old Testament echo, Matthew quotes the Old Testament passage in view and at times even provides an explanatory comment. Not only does Matthew quote the Old Testament at length but he tells his reader that something has happened to fulfil the prophets (e.g. cf. Mark 11:1–10 with Matt. 21:1–9 and its quotation of Zech. 9:9). Matthew follows Mark's narrative but chooses to expand on it with overt appeals to the Old Testament to make it plain to the reader that everything happening, down to the smallest detail, is in fulfilment of the Scriptures.[10] Hays also observes that Matthew's prediction and fulfilment approach has an 'apologetic thrust'. This 'rhetorical tactic seeks to validate his [Matthew's] affirmations about the identity of Jesus by grounding them in Israel's authoritative texts, presumably in opposition to other interpreters who would see Matthew's Christological claims as incongruous with Israel's Scripture'.[11] As will be seen, from start to finish, Matthew exhibits continuity between the

---

[6] Given this subtlety, typically present in Mark and not so present in Matthew, Hays is right to call such instances allusive echoes. Here is Hays's definition: 'When a literary echo links the text in which it occurs to an earlier text, the figurative effect of the echo can lie in the unstated or suppressed (transumed) points of resonance between the two texts.' Hays 1989: 20.

[7] Stuhlmacher 2018: 751.

[8] It is not the purpose of this study to defend the legitimacy of engaging the Gospels; nevertheless, as to their inspiration, historicity and accuracy, see Hill 2010.

[9] I have also chosen to confine this chapter to Matthew because space is limited. Other studies seek to exhaust the Gospels' use of the OT, but this study looks merely to test cases to make a larger point about the Scriptures of Israel.

[10] Hays 2016: 106.

[11] Ibid. 107.

Scriptures and the identity of Jesus, which speaks volumes about what Matthew believes the Scriptures to be in the first place.

That continuity and correlation is relevant for this study because it validates the high view of Scripture Jesus and the Evangelists presuppose in their apologetic, Christological accounts.

Introducing the 'fulfilment' theme

Matthew is well known for his 'fulfilment' theme: it is prevalent throughout his Gospel and colours his presentation of Jesus. Ten passages use a form of the verb *plēroō* and in many of these texts a specific Old Testament passage is in view.[12]

1. The birth of Jesus:

All this took place *to fulfil what the Lord had spoken by the prophet*:

> 'Behold, the virgin shall conceive and bear a son,
>   and they shall call his name Immanuel'

(which means, God with us).
(1:22–23; cf. and Isa. 7:14)

2. Mary and Joseph flee Herod into Egypt:

This was *to fulfil what the Lord had spoken by the prophet*, 'Out of Egypt I called my son.'
(2:15; cf. Hos. 11:1)

3. Herod kills all male children:

Then *was fulfilled* what was spoken by the prophet Jeremiah:

> A voice was heard in Ramah,
>   weeping and loud lamentation,
> Rachel weeping for her children;
>   she refused to be comforted,
> because they are no more.

(2:17–18; cf. Jer. 31:15)

---

12 Emphasis added to each passage that follows.

4. Joseph flees from Archelaus into Nazareth:

And he [Joseph] went and lived in a city called Nazareth, *so that what was spoken by the prophets might be fulfilled*, that he would be called a Nazarene.
(2:23; cf. Judg. 13:5, 7 and Isa. 11:1)

5. Jesus starts his ministry in Capernaum:

Now when he heard that John had been arrested, he withdrew into Galilee. And leaving Nazareth he went and lived in Capernaum by the sea, in the territory of Zebulun and Naphtali, *so that what was spoken by the prophet Isaiah might be fulfilled*:

> The land of Zebulun and the land of Naphtali,
>   the way of the sea, beyond the Jordan,
> Galilee of the Gentiles –
> the people dwelling in darkness
>   have seen a great light,
> and for those dwelling in the region and shadow of death,
>   on them a light has dawned.

From that time Jesus began to preach, saying, 'Repent, for the kingdom of heaven is at hand.'
(4:12–17; cf. 4:15–16 and Isa. 9:1–2)

6. Jesus casts out demons and heals the sick:

This was *to fulfil what was spoken by the prophet Isaiah*: 'He took our illnesses and bore our diseases.'
(8:17; cf. Isa. 53:4)

7. Many come to Jesus and he heals them all:

This was *to fulfil what was spoken by the prophet Isaiah*:

> 'Behold, my servant whom I have chosen,
>   my beloved with whom my soul is well pleased.

I will put my Spirit upon him,
> and he will proclaim justice to the Gentiles.
He will not quarrel or cry aloud,
> nor will anyone hear his voice in the streets;
a bruised reed he will not break,
> and a smouldering wick he will not quench,
until he brings justice to victory;
> and in his name the Gentiles will hope.'

(12:17–21; cf. Isa. 42:1–4)

8. Jesus speaks in parables only:

This was *to fulfil what was spoken by the prophet*:

> 'I will open my mouth in parables;
>> I will utter what has been hidden since the foundation
>>> of the world.'

(13:35; cf. Ps. 78:2)

9. Jesus rides into Jerusalem on a donkey:

This took place *to fulfil what was spoken by the prophet*, saying,

> 'Say to the daughter of Zion,
> "Behold, your king is coming to you,
>> humble, and mounted on a donkey,
>> and on a colt, the foal of a beast of burden."'

(21:4–5; cf. Isa. 62:11 and Zech. 9:9)

10. Judas hangs himself:

Then was *fulfilled what had been spoken by the prophet Jeremiah*, saying, 'And they took the thirty pieces of silver, the price of him on whom a price had been set by some of the sons of Israel, and they gave them for the potter's field, as the Lord directed me.'
(27:9–10; cf. Jer. 32:6–9 and Zech. 11:12–13)

In other instances, slightly different 'fulfilment' vocabulary captures the same fulfilment theme.

1. Jesus is baptized by John:

But Jesus answered him, 'Let it be so now, for thus it is fitting for us *to fulfil all righteousness.'*
(3:15)

2. The Sermon on the Mount:

Do not think that I have come to abolish the Law or the Prophets; I have not come to abolish them but *to fulfil them.*
(5:17)

3. Jesus speaks in parables:

This is why I speak to them in parables, because seeing they do not see, and hearing they do not hear, nor do they understand. Indeed, in their case *the prophecy of Isaiah is fulfilled that says*:

'You will indeed hear but never understand,
    and you will indeed see but never perceive.'
For this people's heart has grown dull,
    and with their ears they can barely hear,
    and their eyes they have closed,
lest they should see with their eyes
    and hear with their ears
and understand with their heart
    and turn, and I would heal them.'
(13:13–15; cf. Isa. 6:9–10)[13]

4. Jesus goes to the cross willingly:

Then Jesus said to him, 'Put your sword back into its place. For all who take the sword will perish by the sword. Do you think that I cannot appeal to my Father, and he will at once send me more than twelve legions of angels? But how then should *the Scriptures be fulfilled, that it must be so?'*
(26:52–54)[14]

---

[13] Also see Mark 4:10–13.
[14] No OT text is quoted here by Matthew.

5. Jesus arrested as if a criminal:

At that hour Jesus said to the crowds, 'Have you come out as against a robber, with swords and clubs to capture me? Day after day I sat in the temple teaching, and you did not seize me. But all this has taken place that *the Scriptures of the prophets might be fulfilled.*' Then all the disciples left him and fled.
(26:55–56)[15]

At other times, Jesus uses phrases like 'have you never read' to convey fulfilment.
1. Children in the temple cry Hosanna:

And the blind and the lame came to him in the temple, and he healed them. But when the chief priests and the scribes saw the wonderful things that he did, and the children crying out in the temple, 'Hosanna to the Son of David!' they were indignant, and they said to him, 'Do you hear what these are saying?' And Jesus said to them, 'Yes; *have you never read,*

'"Out of the mouth of infants and nursing babies
    you have prepared praise"'?
(Matt. 21:14–16; cf. Ps. 8:2)

2. The Son is rejected (parable of the tenants):

Jesus said to them, '*Have you never read in the Scriptures:*

'"The stone that the builders rejected
    has become the cornerstone;
this was the Lord's doing,
    and it is marvellous in our eyes"'?
(Matt. 21:42; cf. Ps. 118:22–23)

Although less common in Matthew's Gospel, sometimes Jesus directly identifies a 'prophecy'.

---

[15] No OT text is quoted here by Matthew.

1. Jesus rebukes the Pharisees and scribes for elevating their traditions above the word of God:

You hypocrites! Well did Isaiah prophesy of you, when he said:

> ' "This people honours me with their lips,
> but their heart is far from me;
> in vain do they worship me,
> teaching as doctrines the commandments of men." '
> (Matt. 15:7–9; cf. Isa. 29:13)

Out of ten uses of the verb *plēroō* in the first list, Matthew 1:22 and 2:15 are the only two where Matthew says something has occurred 'to fulfil what the Lord had spoken by the prophet'. The other texts say only 'what was said by the prophet'. Assumed is Matthew's belief that the oral and written witness of the prophets is one of dual authorship. As Garland explains, these formulas point

> to a dual-authorship view of Scripture where the human prophet is the channel through which the divine agency speaks (cf. Matt. 15:4, 7; 22:43; Acts 1:16; 4:25; 28:25; Rom. 1:2; 2 Tim. 3:16; 2 Peter 1:19–21). Passages such as these are foundational for evangelical views of biblical inspiration and authority.[16]

Yet what does 'fulfilment' mean for Matthew?

While there are cases where direct prophetic prediction is in view, many occurrences are indirect, as seen with typological fulfilment.[17] Fulfilment in Matthew, says Garland, 'has as much to do with historical patterns as with prophetic predictions'.

> Prophetic prediction contains the prophet's revelational foresight of a future event (cf. 2:4–6), but Matthew's fulfillment quotations more often contain Christian hindsight in which a historical event from the Hebrew Bible serves as a pattern for a NT event that it

---

[16] Garland 2008: 21.

[17] It would be a mistake to assume that prophecy and prediction are synonymous. While the former includes the latter, the latter does not exhaust the former. Prophecy is a much broader category.

anticipated. Historical events, whether past, present, or future, are viewed as the providential outworking of God's plan. Also, biblical prophecy is primarily not prediction but covenantal admonition, which utilizes the rehearsal of past events as well as the prediction of future events to motivate present covenant loyalty. Fulfillment in Matthew includes ethical and historical matters as well as predictive prophecy.[18]

Garland categorizes Matthew's fulfilment motif into (1) ethical, (2) historical and (3) prophetic.[19] At various points in Matthew's Gospel, one may become primary (e.g. ethical in Matt. 3:15; 5:17; 'biblical prediction' in 4:14; 8:17; 12:17; 21:4; 26:54, 56). Nevertheless, 'the most prevalent aspect of fulfillment in Matthew concerns historical patterns (1:22; 2:15, 17, 23; 13:14, 35; 23:32; 27:9)'. In other words, events 'in biblical history anticipate events in Jesus's ministry in that Jesus fills them with new significance'. This involves the patristic concept of recapitulation. 'By recapitulating these biblical events, Jesus demonstrates the providence of God in fulfilling his promises to Israel.'[20]

In most instances 'fulfilled' does not occur on the lips of Jesus (though note Matt. 3:15; 5:17; 26:54), but it is a mistake to think Jesus is unaware of such a theme or that he does not see himself as the fulfiller. The fulfilment theme surfaces so often in Matthew's Gospel that Jesus not only believes his teaching, but his works bring to completion and fill up what his Father foreshadowed through Israel's fathers (hence Matt. 5:17–18). More often than not, it is a particular healing that is said to 'fulfil what was spoken' (Matt. 8:17; Isa. 53:4; Matt. 12:17–21; Isa. 42:1–3), and it is such healings that are tied to the gospel Jesus is proclaiming (Matt. 9:25; 10:7; 12:28).

The pervasiveness of the fulfilment theme and its reflective nature, what some have called *Reflexionszitate* (reflection citations), reveals one of Matthew's main intentions in writing his Gospel, namely that 'the gospel of the kingdom', as Hagner calls it, is 'the fulfillment of the OT expectation'.[21] Matthew's quotations of the Old Testament, then, are deeply

---

[18] Garland 2008: 23.
[19] He qualifies, 'These categories are not discrete but overlapping; individual fulfillments may contain elements of all three aspects.' Ibid. 25.
[20] Ibid.
[21] Hagner 1993: liv.

theological in nature.[22] Through them Matthew demonstrates that the covenant promises of the Old Testament reach their fulfilment in the gospel of Jesus Christ. Indeed, Matthew's entire account is written for this purpose. Not only his quotations of the Old Testament but entire events in the life and ministry of Jesus demonstrate that the gospel of the kingdom is at hand in the person and work of Christ.

Several of these 'fulfilment' passages deserve consideration. Yet rather than limiting what follows to explicit fulfilment language or quotations from the Old Testament, other subtle (but sometimes just as overt) indicators will be considered, many of which draw on intertextual and typological correspondence between Jesus and an Old Testament person, event or institution. My purpose is not to exhaust them all (some count over sixty quotations of the Old Testament in Matthew alone, and that does not include allusions). Rather, I will touch on the broad contours for the purpose of understanding the attitude Jesus and the Evangelists have to the scriptural witness.[23]

New genesis, new king: son of Abraham, son of David (Matt. 1:1–17)

Chapter 5 will engage Matthew's genealogy and temptation narrative at length. Nevertheless, it should at least be acknowledged here that Matthew begins his Gospel by connecting Jesus' coming to the Old Testament heritage. This much is plain in Matthew's choice to begin with a genealogy that traces Jesus' lineage back not only to David but to Abraham. By doing so, Matthew's story is immediately connected to the story of Israel. The connection to David and Abraham indicates that this Jesus is the one who will fulfil the covenant promises Yahweh made to Abraham (Gen. 15) and will do so as the much-anticipated Davidic king who establishes David's eternal kingdom and dynasty (2 Sam. 7).

Scholars like Hays and Crowe have pointed out, as well, that even Matthew's opening words echo Genesis 1: 'the book of the genesis of Jesus

---

[22] Ibid. lv. Poythress (2016: 236–237) prefers 'promise' over 'prediction', if he is to choose the vocabulary we use, because today there are too many misconceptions of what prediction entails (e.g. merely human guessing, mere foresight [not power], mere foretelling). For the OT authors, 'prophesying' is far more than direct prediction but includes indirect prediction of all kinds.

[23] What follows will be a brief treatment of select passages. For a much fuller treatment of each passage, see Carson 1984: 3–602; Blomberg 1992: 1–110; Hagner 1993; 1995; Osborne 2010; France 2007; Turner 2008; Morris 1992. Also patristics: Hilary 2012; Augustine 2012a; Jerome 2008.

Christ'.[24] Although it is Luke in his genealogy who explicitly connects Jesus to Adam (Luke 3:38), Matthew's choice of vocabulary may assume the same correspondence, a subtle indication that Jesus is not only the son of David and the son of Abraham, but the son of Adam; that is, the last Adam. If so, then Matthew ties Jesus' entrance to a 'new Genesis', the 'story of an eschatological redemption that begins the world anew'.[25] When further tied to Israel's patriarch and most seminal king, the 'identification links the new creation inextricably to the past of Israel, as signified by references to Abraham, the patriarchal *Urvater* of the nation, and David, its great iconic royal figure'.[26]

Again, in chapter 5 we will return to this passage to see how it further communicates Jesus' Adamic obedience as God's faithful son, much in contrast to Israel's unfaithfulness as a son who has breached the covenant. For now, it is sufficient to recognize how Israel would have read this genealogy: as a tale of his own tragic history, and yet at the same time, through Matthew's eyes, as a sign of hope that Abraham's son and David's greater king has arrived to bring Israel out of exile with a new genesis. Both Abraham and David, then, are but types; Jesus is the antitype who ushers in the covenant blessing and kingdom rule these fathers could only anticipate in faith. As Matthew will quickly reveal, the son of Abraham and David will accomplish this mission by *saving* God's people from their sins (Matt. 1:21), a theme to which we now turn.

The virgin shall conceive and bear a son (Matt. 1:22–23)

Retelling the birth of Christ, Matthew highlights the supernatural nature of this birth (Mary 'was found to be with child from the Holy Spirit'; 1:18) but also chooses to focus on the angel's appearance to Joseph, who is the 'son of David' (1:20), again reiterating the preceding genealogy. Joseph is told that the son Mary gives birth to is to be named 'Jesus, for he will save his people from their sins' (1:21). The restoration, renewal and redemption of Israel the prophets promised is finally at hand. Jesus will be the one to bring to fulfilment God's saving promises from Adam to Abraham, from Moses to David.

---

[24] Hays 2016: 110. This is Hays's translation.
[25] Ibid.
[26] Ibid.

To headline such a fulfilment, Matthew takes the reader back to Isaiah:

All this took place to fulfil what the Lord had spoken by the prophet:

> 'Behold, the virgin shall conceive and bear a son,
>   And they shall call his name Immanuel'

(which means, God with us).
(1:22–23; cf. Isa. 7:14; 8:8, 10)

'Immanuel' solidifies the meaning behind Jesus' name. God's presence is a saving presence, the angel announces to Joseph. Yet most surprising of all is the way the Lord descends to make himself present. No longer will his presence come down in a cloud or pillar of fire, no longer will it be mediated through the mercy seat in the tabernacle or temple, but now the Son of God himself will descend to be with his people. His incarnate presence is the greatest proof that his saving purpose, which the prophets foretold, has been inaugurated. As Mary will later sing:

> He has helped his servant Israel,
>   in remembrance of his mercy,
> as he spoke to our fathers,
>   to Abraham and to his offspring for ever.
> (Luke 1:54–55)

New exodus (Matt. 2)

In Matthew's second chapter he will move beyond Jesus' genealogical ties to Abraham and David to identify Jesus now with Israel, God's covenant people and firstborn son. Jesus is, in other words, not only the greater son of David but the true Israel, and, since Israel is considered everywhere in the Old Testament to be God's son, Jesus is God's true Son.

Right away, Matthew 2 begins with the wise men telling Herod that the prophet Micah (5:2) foretold that Bethlehem would give birth to this great 'ruler who will shepherd my people Israel' (Matt. 2:6). The wise men are guided to Jesus by the star and when they leave, the angel of the Lord informs Joseph that Herod is on the hunt; Joseph is to take Jesus and Mary by night and depart for Egypt. In Egypt they are to remain until Herod is no more. But Matthew adds, 'This was to fulfil what the Lord had spoken by the prophet, "Out of Egypt I called my son"' (Matt. 2:15). Again, chapter 5 will explore this narrative in fuller depth. For now, suffice it to say that Matthew is quoting Hosea 11:1, a passage in which 'son' refers to Israel and his pending exodus from exile, in order to identify Jesus as the one who inaugurates a *new exodus*. Matthew's figurative reading is a type of 'fulfilment' and one that is Christologically oriented for the sake of recapitulating Israel's exodus story in the redemptive mission of the true Israel, Jesus Christ.[27]

Matthew's use of Hosea assumes the validity of *sensus plenior* (see chapter 2). The divine authorial intent in Hosea 11:1 goes beyond what Hosea understood at the time: a fuller meaning is present, though Hosea is unaware of it. It is doubtful Hosea had the Messiah in view, but it is certain the divine author did, as Hosea spoke of God's 'son'.[28] Yet, as mentioned before, this is not an appeal to some mystical, secret knowledge, nor does *sensus plenior* mean later writers interpret earlier texts in a roughshod, proof-text manner. As was argued in chapter 1, *sensus plenior* is not to be divorced from the progressive nature of revelation and history. The category of firstborn son, a label Yahweh gives to express his covenantal love for his people, was not foreign to Hosea. As Carson says:

> building on existing revelation, [Hosea] grasped the messianic nuances of the 'son' language already applied to Israel and David's promised heir in previous revelation so that had he been able to see Matthew's use of 11:1, he would not have disapproved, even if messianic nuances were not in his mind when he wrote that verse.[29]

Carson concludes that Hosea 'provided one small part of the revelation unfolded during salvation history; but that part he himself understood to be a pictorial representative of divine, redeeming love'.[30] In this sense, fulfilment occurs when out of Egypt God calls his son, Jesus the Christ, the true Israel.

That connection between Jesus and Israel is further explicated when Matthew records Herod's reaction. Discovering the wise men manoeuvred

---

27 Hence Hays (ibid. 113) calls this 'figural correspondence' a 'Christological fulfillment'.
28 Carson 1984: 92; LaSor 1978a: 49–60.
29 Carson 1984: 92.
30 Ibid.

around his deceitful strategy, Herod turns aggressive, killing all male children two years and under (2:16). Yet Matthew says this all happened in fulfilment of Jeremiah 31:15 ('A voice was heard in Ramah, / weeping and loud lamentation'; 2:18). Israel, knowing their history, would have resonated deeply with 'Rachel is weeping for her children' (Jer. 31:15). Now Rachel weeps once more as rulers on earth seek to destroy God's Son, Israel's true heir. As will be seen in chapter 5, sonship is a key theme in the Gospels, and here the sonship of Israel is alluded to in the sonship of Jesus. As God's son, Israel is taken into exile for his covenant unfaithfulness, which results in cries of great suffering, but now God's Son is called out of exile for the purpose of leading a new exodus, one in which his covenant obedience will result in Israel's redemption. Matthew's choice to quote both Hosea 11:1 and Jeremiah 31:15 is not arbitrary, but intentionally brings to the surface the typological continuity between Israel and Jesus. '*By evoking these two prophetic passages in the infancy narrative, Matthew connects both the history and the future destiny of Israel to the figure of Jesus, and he hints that in Jesus the restoration of Israel is at hand.*'[31]

The figural fulfilment and Israel-sonship typology continues in Matthew 3 and 4. As will be seen in chapter 5, Jesus, like Israel, must go through the waters of baptism before entering the wilderness. John the Baptist will go into the wilderness first, however, to prepare the way, preaching a message of repentance and administering baptism because the 'kingdom of heaven is at hand' (Matt. 3:2). It is now at hand because David's son has come to inaugurate his kingdom reign (Matt. 1:1). John is the one Isaiah spoke of, says Matthew, the voice in the wilderness who makes straight the path of the Messiah (note the quotation of Isa. 40:3 in Matt. 3:3).

To John's surprise, however, Jesus must start his ministry with baptism not because Jesus himself needs forgiveness for his sins but because he is Israel's representative, identifying with God's chosen son and that son's covenant unfaithfulness. His baptism is vicarious for he will obey, where Israel (and Adam) failed, and be washed for Israel's sake. His baptism is to 'fulfil all righteousness' (Matt. 3:15). Chapter 5 will explore the last Adam and true Israel imagery in this baptism account but notice here that such a baptism visibly identifies Israel with Jesus.

The typological correspondence continues when Jesus is then led by the Spirit from the waters of the Jordan into the wilderness, where he, like Israel

---

[31] Hays 2016: 116. Emphasis original.

(and Adam) is tempted to determine whether he, unlike Israel (and Adam), will be God's *obedient* Son. As chapter 5 will show at length, his covenant obedience is driven by his adherence to the Torah, as Jesus' repeated quotations from Deuteronomy demonstrate. Whereas Israel grumbled for food in the wilderness, the food of God's obedient Son, the true Israel, is the word of God (Matt. 3:4; cf. Deut. 8:3). By depending on the word of the covenant, Israel's mediator and representative fulfils the stipulations of the covenant, procuring salvation for the covenant people of God.

At this point it is worth observing that not only Israel but Moses is a type whose presence is felt in Matthew's temptation narrative. Jesus fasts forty days and nights, which could represent Israel's forty years of wandering, but may also represent the forty days and nights Moses fasted on Mount Sinai. Deuteronomy 9:25–26 says Moses interceded for Israel due to the iniquity Israel committed. Having just been vicariously baptized for Israel's sin, the subtle tie between Deuteronomy 9 and Matthew 4 may be in Matthew's purview. Could Jesus, like Moses, be interceding with his Father on behalf of the sins of Israel, the people Jesus has come to save?[32] If so, then Jesus has not only represented Israel typologically in his baptism, passing through the waters as Israel did when God called his son out of Egypt through the Red Sea, but now, before he experiences temptations like Israel did in the wilderness, he must first enter the presence of God as Moses did at Sinai to intercede on behalf of the people's idolatry.

New Moses, greater Moses: not an iota will pass from the Law (Matt. 5:17–18 [Luke 16:17])

As the new Moses who leads Israel's new exodus, it is fitting for Jesus, like Moses in Deuteronomy, to lay before the people the way to righteousness. As Moses ascended the mountain, so too Jesus 'went up on the mountain' (Matt. 5:1) to deliver his sermon. While the intricacies of the sermon, and the many discussions over how to interpret it, need not detain us here, most agree that the sermon sets before the Israelites what covenant life in the Messiah's kingdom is to be like. Jesus' sermon will provide the

---

[32] To see an affirmative answer to this question worked out in detail, consult Hays (ibid. 116–118).

authoritative interpretation of the Torah and accentuate that obedience to the law Christ articulates in Matthew 5 must come *from the heart* (e.g. 5:21–30).

Again, much could be explored: this sermon addresses the standard of righteousness, the nature of true covenant love, the priority of mercy in the Beatitudes, the posture of prayer, the eschatological orientation of one's treasure, the necessity of regular trust in the Father, and much more. For our purposes, however, it is the start of the sermon that is relevant due to what Jesus says about the Torah and its fulfilment.

If there is a *propositio* to the Sermon on the Mount, 5:17–20 is a strong contestant.[33] These verses not only tell Jesus' listeners what he thought of the Old Testament Scriptures and their fulfilment, but who Jesus believes himself to be and how such Scriptures find their culmination in his new covenant ministry. On a larger scale, these verses also identify the relationship between Israel and Christianity, the old covenant and the new covenant, Moses and Jesus.

The Law and the Prophets

First, what does Jesus mean by the 'Law' and 'the Prophets'? In contemporary idiom, 'Prophets' is a narrow designation, referring to minor and major prophets. However, in Jesus' day 'Prophets' is far more encompassing. If the Law is the Pentateuch, then the Prophets are everything thereafter. 'Prophets' is not so much a reference to major or minor prophets but to any and all writings by prophets. For example, 'Prophets' not only include someone like Samuel during the reign of Saul but David, a title Peter is not hesitant to attribute to the king after God's own heart (Acts 2:30). To be clear, then, by the 'Law' and 'the Prophets' Jesus means all the Hebrew Scriptures, and with them the entire storyline from Adam to Moses to Israel's exile.

Furthermore, the 'Law and the Prophets' is not only a reference to the entire canon of the Hebrew Scriptures as well as the storyline within that canon, but also refers to the Law *as interpreted* by the Prophets. As Dumbrell says, Jesus refers to the Law 'not only as it was given in its essence but as it was prophetically interpreted'.[34] Or as Pennington clarifies, 'It is Torah understood within the context of the whole canon,

---

[33] Pennington 2017: 170.
[34] Dumbrell 1981: 17.

with the prophets as interpreters of the Law, calling people back to wholehearted and eschatologically oriented faithfulness to the covenant.'[35] The phrase, then, not only assumes the *analogia scriptura*, but insinuates a progressive nature to revelation through redemption. As God further manifests himself through his redemptive acts, so too does he further reveal himself through prophets, prophets who interpret and apply the Law to their own day as well as foretell a day to come when all that the Law spoke of will come to its culmination in the long-awaited Messiah and Davidic king.

Jesus' use of the phrase 'the Law or the Prophets' has special, covenantal connotations. He is not only saying that the Prophets of old interpreted the Law and pointed forward to a day when the Law will reach its fulfilment, but it is his claim that such a day has arrived. As the one who inaugurates the kingdom, ushers in the new age, cuts the new covenant, he will now specify how this Law is fulfilled and what it means for citizens of his new covenant community.[36] Matthew 5:17–20, in other words, is eschatologically driven: what previously was a future reality promised and anticipated is now a present reality in the advent of the Messiah. The new covenant age Jeremiah (31:31–34), Ezekiel (36:22–38) and Isaiah (40 – 66) could only imagine has now been ushered into the present as Jesus addresses Israel with a new kind of authority ('But I say to you').[37]

With such an eschatological emphasis in mind, it makes sense then that Jesus' address, or Moses-like sermon, is concerned with what life in this new covenant era is to look like. The ethics of the sermon do not merely parallel the ethics of the Law, nor do they merely re-establish the original or true intention of the Law, but they articulate how that Law has reached its culmination in the person of Christ. At issue is not only how Jesus interprets the Law but how that Law is to be perceived with the arrival of its true heir, not to mention the kingdom and (new) covenant he inaugurates. While commandments and ethics are in view – both in the Law and in Jesus' Sermon – they are always issued within the framework of the divine covenant.[38]

---

[35] Pennington 2017: 172.

[36] The use of 'covenant' is intentional, for the first-century Jew would understand 'Law' in the light of the history of God's covenant with Israel. See ibid. 173. Also cf. Hilary 2012: 66.

[37] As Mark (1:27) records, 'And they were all amazed, so that they questioned among themselves, saying, "What is this? A new teaching with authority! He commands even the unclean spirits, and they obey him."'

[38] Pennington 2017: 173.

Not abolish but fulfil: Jesus as eschatological goal

If there is a covenantal, eschatological context that is organic to the Sermon itself, as seen in Jesus' use of 'Law or the Prophets', then the reader is better equipped to interpret Jesus' opening statement: 'Do not think that I have come to abolish the Law or the Prophets; I have not come to abolish them but to fulfil them' (5:17). Announcing the arrival of the kingdom of heaven (Matt. 3:7; etc.) and establishing the ethics of the new covenant community are *not* attempts to set aside the Law or the Prophets as irrelevant. Nor are these ways of dismissing the Law given to Moses as that which is misguided. Jesus has not come to abolish the Law as if he were a first-century antinomian. Moving forward in Matthew's Gospel, as well as Mark and Luke's, Jesus will exhibit his fidelity to the Mosaic Law in a way that surpasses the scribes and Pharisees.

The issue, rather, is one of *fulfilment*. How will the Law operate now that the Christ has come and with him a new era in the history of redemption? And has the Law's purpose now reached a point of intended culmination with the arrival of the kingdom of heaven?

Countless commentators have debated the meaning of fulfilment. Leon Morris outlines three interpretations, while recognizing that there is truth to each:

1　It may mean that he would do the things laid down in Scripture.
2　It may mean that he would bring out the full meaning of Scripture.
3　It may mean that in his life and teaching he would bring Scripture to its completion.[39]

Davies and Allison enlist nine, though they are persuaded mostly by interpretations 5 and 9:

1　The Greek could [be translated to mean] . . . 'I did not come to destroy the law of Moses nor did I come to add to the law of Moses.'
2　[Jesus means] . . . 'establish', 'make valid', 'bring into effect'.
3　[Jesus means] . . . 'to do', 'to execute'.
4　Jesus 'fulfils' the law by observing it perfectly and completely in his own person and ministry.

---

[39] Morris 1992: 108.

5 Jesus 'fulfils' or 'completes' the law by bringing a new law which transcends the old.

6 The Torah is 'fulfilled' when Jesus, explaining God's intention, brings out its perfect or inner meaning or expands and extends its demands.

7 Jesus 'fulfils' the law because, through his coming, he enables others to meet the Torah's demands.

8 When Jesus 'fulfils' the law or the prophets, he does it by bringing the new righteousness, which is the new spirit of love: love is the fulfilling of the law.

9 The 'fulfilment' is eschatological: the *telos* which the Torah anticipated, namely, the Messiah has come and revealed the law's definitive meaning.[40]

Interpretations 5 and 9 certainly are core aspects, but Davies and Allison have neglected 4: 'Jesus "fulfils" the law by observing it perfectly and completely in his own person and ministry.' The eschatological factor (number 9) makes little sense if the Messiah is only another prophet, revealing the 'law's definitive meaning'. He must also be a priestly mediator, a theme the Gospels accentuate, one who fulfils the Law 'by observing it perfectly and completely in his own person and ministry'. As mentioned already, the Sermon's eschatological gravitas is seen in both; or perhaps we should say the Messiah comes to reveal the Law's *telos*, revealing its definitive meaning, but that *telos* and *definitive meaning* are encapsulated in his own person and work. Only on that basis is Jesus able to claim authority as one who '"fulfils" or "completes" the law by bringing a new law which transcends the old' (number 5 above).

Davies and Allison are on target in their conclusion 'So when Jesus declares, "I came ... to fulfil", he means that his new teaching brings to realization that which the Torah anticipated or prophesied: its "fulfiller" has come.[41] Such Christocentrism in Matthew's Gospel reorients how the Law and the Prophets are perceived in a radical way. Christ may not dissolve or abolish the Law or the Prophets but fulfilling them does reposition where the centre is to be located in the new covenant that he establishes:

---

40 Davies and Allison 1988: 486.
41 Ibid. 487. Also see Blomberg 1992: 104.

He who fulfils the law and prophets displaces them in so far as he must become the centre of attention: the thing signified (Jesus) is naturally more important than the sign (the law and the prophets) pointing to it. This is why Matthew's book is firstly about Jesus, not about the law and the prophets.[42]

So, when Jesus says he has come to fulfil the Law and the Prophets he cannot merely have in mind his obedience to the Law (as true as that is; see chapter 5), nor merely that he will reveal its true intent (which no doubt had been obscured by the oral traditions of some scribes and Pharisees). He must mean something more fundamental. The Law and Prophets pointed forward to his day, his teaching and his redemptive work. The eschaton has been ushered into the present, so that everything anticipated has now reached its *telos* in the Messiah. 'Jesus presents himself as the eschatological goal of the OT,' says Carson, 'and thereby its sole authoritative interpreter, the one through whom alone the OT finds its valid continuity and significance.'[43] Hence there is strong continuity with all that came before. Jesus not only means there is *prediction* and *completion*, but *prefiguration* and *consummation*, prefiguration involving the much larger concept of typology.[44]

At the same time, such continuity is not without discontinuity. The Messiah comes not merely to reveal the Law's *telos* but to go beyond and transcend it for the sake of establishing a new code or constitution for a covenant that surpasses the old.[45] It is 'significant that, after declaring he has not come to abolish Torah, Christ does not state that he has come to preserve it unchanged'.[46] In part, that explains why Jesus' Sermon does not merely focus on the external, but, as Jeremiah and Ezekiel anticipated, moves within, addressing the heart. It is not enough to avoid murder: one

---

[42] Davies and Allison 1988: 487.

[43] Carson 1984: 144.

[44] Pennington 2017: 175. Beale's definition of typology fits well with Matthew: 'Typology therefore indicates fulfillment of the indirect prophetic adumbration of events, people and institutions from the Old Testament in Christ who now is the final, climactic expression of all God ideally intended through these things in the Old Testament (e.g. the law, the temple cultus, the commissions of prophets, judges, priests, and kings). Everything which these things lacked by way of imperfections was prophetically "filled up" by Christ, so that even what was imperfect in the Old Testament pointed beyond itself to Jesus.' Beale 1994: 396.

[45] It would take us too far off track to engage with the question of whether the Law is to be obeyed in the new covenant in the light of v. 17, but see Schreiner 1993; Thielman 1994; Meyer 2009.

[46] Blomberg 2016: 683.

must not even become angry. It is insufficient to refuse adultery: one must not lust within. And so on.

> What Jesus requires of his followers surpasses what has traditionally been regarded (by the scribes and Pharisees) as the requirement of the Torah. So although there is continuity with the past, the Messiah also brings something new, and it does not surprise when 5.21–48 goes beyond the letter of the law to demand even more.[47]

Jesus is, then, the Law's 'sovereign interpreter'.[48]

Not an iota

If Jesus fulfils the Law, is Jesus' own view of the Law revealed in the process? That is a most pertinent question for the present study, and verses 18–19 hand the reader an answer in the affirmative.

Yet one need not even arrive at verse 18 to see this affirmation already present in verse 17. To say, as Jesus does, that he has not come to abolish but fulfil the Law and the Prophets, is not only to say much about the continuity and discontinuity between the old and the new but is to recognize the original and abiding authority the Law and Prophets carry. 'If the law is fulfilled, it cannot on that account be set aside,' explain Davies and Allison.

> Fulfilment can only confirm the Torah's truth, not cast doubt upon it. And while Jesus' new demands may surpass the demands of the OT, the two are not contradictory . . . Rather do the words of the Torah remain the words of God (cf. 15.4), their imperatival force undiminished (cf. 5.18; 23.23).[49]

The 'imperative force' that remains 'undiminished' is a force that originates in the divine author himself. Jesus and the Jews consider the Torah, as well as the writings of the Prophets, so forceful in authority because they believe that behind a Moses or David is Yahweh, the divine voice speaking

---

[47] Davies and Allison 1988: 482.
[48] Blomberg (2016: 683), reflecting on Matt. 5:33–42, where Jesus forbids vows that the Torah commands, says, 'It is better, therefore, to recognize Jesus' role with Scripture as being its sovereign interpreter, rather than making sweeping generalizations about *either* changing the Law *or* his leaving it unchanged. Each category or topic will have to be examined on a case-by-case basis.' Emphases original.
[49] Davies and Allison 1988: 487.

concurrently, confluently and concursively with and through the human author. For Jesus to abolish or disregard what the Law and Prophets say is to disregard what Yahweh himself says through them. Jesus would be dismissing the one from whom the Law and Prophets originate.

That such abiding authority stems from Yahweh himself is discernible in verse 18. Yet here Jesus not only identifies the divine source but the extensiveness and efficacy of his word. It may be tempting to say that the completion and consummation the Law prefigured is to be seen in the larger narrative. The small matters of the Law are less relevant, so the argument goes. Jesus, however, has little patience for such a view because it (1) misunderstands and insults the extensiveness of the Law's authority and truthfulness, and (2) belittles the significance of his own Christological fulfilment mentioned in verse 17.

For Jesus, his fulfilment of the Law means the fulfilment of the Law not only in whole but in every part, no matter how small or insignificant the details may be. 'For truly, I say to you, until heaven and earth pass away, not an iota, not a dot, will pass from the Law until all is accomplished' (Matt. 5:18; cf. Luke 16:17). Here Jesus issues one of the strongest, if not the strongest, affirmations of the Torah's authority in all of Christian Scripture. The iota refers to the letter in the Greek alphabet that is the smallest. The equivalent in Hebrew would be the yodh.

Some have estimated that 66,420 yodhs exist in the Hebrew Scriptures.[50] It may seem that the loss of one yodh is meaningless, even insignificant. But Jesus says just the opposite: not one will pass until all find their fulfilment. Without qualification, Jesus asserts both the plenary nature of Scripture's inspiration, reliability and authority, as well as its perpetual efficacy. Behind these Scriptures not only stands a divine author but a divine author whose purpose has been inscripturated down to the smallest letter, a purpose that will be fulfilled only when every iota and yodh is accomplished in his Son. As Leon Morris says, verse 18 'forms a very emphatic assertion of the permanent validity of Scripture. None of it will pass away, Jesus says, until *all has taken place*. The divine purpose in Scripture will be fully worked out.'[51] The emphatic assertion is equally accented in Luke's account: 'But it is easier for heaven and earth to pass away than for one dot of the Law to become void' (16:17).

---

[50] Morris 1992: 109, n. 67.
[51] Ibid. 110. Emphasis original. Also see Augustine 2012a: 1.8 (p. 10).

One can see, then, why Jesus warns anyone who dares to relax even the least of God's commandments (Matt. 5:19). If every iota or yodh of the Law is God given, trustworthy and awaiting its accomplishment, then one would have to defy God himself to change his Law or teach others to 'do the same'. The consequence is serious: he 'will be called least in the kingdom of heaven'. Yet those who do them will be named greatest.[52]

'Relaxes' could be translated 'loosens', for Jesus is warning anyone who considers even the smallest part of the Scriptures to be void, nullified or lacking purpose from the divine author.[53] Such a warning applies to those, like the Pharisees, who are negligent, which explains Jesus' righteous indignation in Matthew 23:23: 'Woe to you, scribes and Pharisees, hypocrites! For you tithe mint and dill and cumin, and have *neglected* the weightier matters of the law: justice and mercy and faithfulness. These you ought to have done, *without neglecting the others*' (emphasis added). While Jesus may acknowledge a distinction – that is, 'weightier matters of the law' – he does so without compromising the rest of the law (i.e. 'without neglecting the others'), which only demonstrates his point in Matthew 5:19.[54]

While verse 20 begins to move the listener into the ethics of covenant life in Jesus' kingdom (i.e. 'unless your righteousness exceeds that of the scribes'), one should not miss how verses 17–18 preclude any assumption that Jesus considered any part of the Scriptures exempt from the divine author's hand. The responsibility of Jesus' ministry entails that every iota or yodh will be accomplished, and that accomplishment begins with Jesus and the kingdom he inaugurates.[55]

Miracles and exorcisms: the fulfilment of Isaiah (Matt. 8 and 12)

Matthew's fulfilment theme not only colours the beginning and end of Jesus' ministry but everything in between. Consider the two major facets of Jesus' ministry: his miracles and teaching (usually in parables).

It would be a gross misunderstanding to assume that Jesus' many miracles are random occurrences merely meant to exhibit his power. Like everything

---

[52] The seriousness of Jesus' warning is not foreign to the Torah. Consider Deut. 18:20: 'But the prophet who presumes to speak a word in my name that I have not commanded him to speak, or who speaks in the name of other gods, that same prophet shall die.'

[53] Morris 1992: 111.

[54] Hays 2016: 121.

[55] There are differences of opinion as to *when* all is accomplished; see Pennington 2017: 176–177.

else in Matthew's Gospel, the miracles of Jesus are rooted in the Hebrew prophetic heritage, performed *in fulfilment* of God's promises through the prophets. The miracles of Jesus also validate his messianic and divine identity, verifying that God's promise to establish his kingdom and covenant is being fulfilled. In short, Jesus' signs and wonders, his power over the demonic realm, all convey to the people of Israel that their king has come and with him God's kingdom. The inauguration of the kingdom is at hand.

For instance, in Matthew 8 Jesus heals a leper (8:1–4), the servant of a centurion (8:5–13), as well as two demon-possessed men (8:28–34). In between the servant of the centurion and the demon-possessed men, Matthew includes the healing of Peter's mother-in-law, who has a severe fever that leaves her the minute Jesus touches her hand (8:14–15). Matthew then adds a comment that could have occupied several more chapters if described in detail:

> That evening they brought to him many who were oppressed by demons, and he cast out the spirits with a word and healed all who were sick. *This was to fulfil what was spoken by the prophet Isaiah*: 'He took our illnesses and bore our diseases.'
> (8:16–17; emphasis added)[56]

Matthew is quoting Isaiah 53:4, in which Isaiah describes the suffering servant – or *'ebed yahweh*, 'Servant of Yahweh' – in substitutionary categories. In its entirety verse 4 reads:

> Surely he has borne our griefs
>   and carried our sorrows;
> yet we esteemed him stricken,
>   smitten by God, and afflicted.

Isaiah goes on to say that 'he was pierced for our transgressions; / he was crushed for our iniquities' (53:5), a passage on the mind of the Gospel writers, and Jesus, as the cross approaches. Yet Matthew believes the whole ministry of Jesus fits within the context of Isaiah 53. The substitutionary nature of his sufferings is not restricted to the cross but is present

---

[56] Many commentators believe Matthew has provided his own translation to reflect the meaning he believes is present in Isaiah. Likewise, with Matt. 12:18–21.

throughout the ministry of Christ, defining his constant absorption of pain and sickness in those he heals. In the mind of Matthew Jesus is the one ultimately prefigured in Isaiah's words, describing one who would carry man's griefs, sorrows, illnesses and diseases.

Yet Matthew is not importing an interpretation Jesus would have disagreed with. As will be seen, Jesus himself will respond to John the Baptist's enquiry by telling him to look at the way he (Jesus) has healed the sick (Matt. 11:5–6). Such healings serve as an announcement: 'the Messiah is here and the kingdom of heaven is now at hand!' Or with God's promises through the prophets in mind: 'Look at the way Jesus is healing the sick; the one prophets like Isaiah spoke about has finally arrived!' For Matthew and Jesus, God promised the Messiah would take away his people's diseases; what Yahweh promised through the prophets must be true because Yahweh has come through on his word in the healing power of his Davidic king and royal son.

Matthew makes a similar statement in 12:18–21. Again, the pattern is similar. Matthew records a specific miracle, in this case the healing of a man with a withered hand, and then gives a summary statement: 'And many followed him, and he healed them all and ordered them not to make him known' (12:15–16). Matthew then instructs the reader as to the meaning of Jesus' perpetual healing ministry:

This was to fulfil what was spoken by the prophet Isaiah:

> 'Behold, my servant whom I have chosen,
>> my beloved with whom my soul is well pleased.
> I will put my Spirit upon him,
>> and he will proclaim justice to the Gentiles.
> He will not quarrel or cry aloud,
>> nor will anyone hear his voice in the streets;
> a bruised reed he will not break,
>> and a smouldering wick he will not quench,
> until he brings justice to victory;
>> and in his name the Gentiles will hope.'
>
> (12:17–21)

While Matthew 8:16–17 quoted Isaiah 53:4, now Matthew quotes Isaiah 42:1–4. Here the messianic role is expanded so that Matthew not only says

Jesus, in the heritage of Isaiah, bore their illnesses but this Jesus is the *Spirit-anointed* servant, chosen by Yahweh to preach and restore justice but by means of his meekness and peace-bearing spirit.

In Matthew 12:14 the reader is told that the Pharisees conspired to destroy Jesus after healing the man with the withered hand. Aware, Jesus retreats, and yet all those sick seeking to be healed still find him (12:16). The picture is upside down: while the Pharisees expect a Messiah whose authority will be forcefully paraded (much like their own), Jesus' authority, reflecting Isaiah 42, is manifested and acknowledged by the way he stoops down in humility to care for the helpless, ushering in a peace that is but a taste of the eternal peace he offers to all who will have him.[57] His is an authority exercised through servanthood, lowliness and meekness, just as God told their fathers through his prophet Isaiah.

The Prophets and the Law prophesied until John (Matt. 11)

When John the Baptist sends messengers to Jesus to ask whether he is the one who is to come – a question that itself reveals the type of canonical unity presupposed among those Jews mindfully awaiting the advent of the Messiah – Jesus responds by pointing to the miracles he has performed:

> Go and tell John what you hear and see: the blind receive their sight and the lame walk, lepers are cleansed and the deaf hear, and the dead are raised up, and the poor have good news preached to them. (Matt. 11:4–5)

Blomberg and Kvalbein find support in the DSS for the Jewish belief that Isaiah 35:5–6 was messianic in orientation.[58] If true, then Jesus is recruiting the language of Isaiah 35 to communicate that these signs and wonders serve to announce him as the Messiah Isaiah had in view. Is Jesus the 'one who is to come', asks John? The answer is undoubtedly 'yes' if John remembers Isaiah. The works of Jesus are all the proof John needs.

---

[57] 'In popular expectation messiahs exercised their authority by crushing opposition, but Jesus showed his authority in his concern for the helpless and downtrodden.' Morris 1992: 309; cf. Hagner 1993: 339; Turner 2008: 316–317.

[58] 4Q521 is in view. See Blomberg 2016: 678; Kvalbein 1998: 87–110.

Jesus then turns attention to John as one who is a 'prophet' foretold by the prophets. Quoting from Malachi 3:1, Jesus says:

This is he of whom it is written,

> 'Behold, I send my messenger before your face,
>   who will prepare your way before you.'
> (Matt. 11:10)

Jesus clarifies further, saying, 'For all the Prophets and the Law prophesied until John, and if you are willing to accept it, he is Elijah who is to come' (11:13–14).

Yet Jesus does not leave himself out of this fulfilment:

> For John came neither eating nor drinking, and they say, 'He has a demon.' The Son of Man came eating and drinking, and they say, 'Look at him! A glutton and a drunkard, a friend of tax collectors and sinners!'
> (11:18–19)

John is but the messenger; Jesus is the Son of Man himself, the one whom all the prophets pointed forward to with eager anticipation. But to the surprise of many, his mission does not concern the righteous but the unrighteous and the ungodly, the lost sheep of Israel (Matt. 10:6), not those who are well but those who are sick and in need of a doctor (Matt. 9:12).

Something greater than the temple is here: the new David is lord of the Sabbath (Matt. 12:1–8; 12:41–46)

In Matthew 12 Jesus again faces conflict with the Pharisees, this time over the Sabbath since Jesus' disciples pluck heads of grain to eat. Accused of breaking the day of rest, Jesus asks, with 1 Samuel 21:1–5 in mind:

> Have you not read what David did when he was hungry, and those who were with him: how he entered the house of God and ate the bread of the Presence, which it was not lawful for him to eat nor for

those who were with him, but only for the priests? Or have you not
read in the Law how on the Sabbath the priests in the temple profane
the Sabbath and are guiltless?
(12:3–5)

The Pharisees are so focused on the letter of the law that they have misunderstood the spirit of the law. As Jesus says in verse 7, 'And if you had
known what this means, "I desire mercy, and not sacrifice", you would not
have condemned the guiltless.' The Pharisees, observes Hays, 'are at fault
because they demand punctilious observance of the law at the expense of
basic human need, represented by the disciples' hunger'.[59] Already they
have forgotten Jesus' Sermon on the Mount, that those who are blessed are
those who are merciful (5:7).

It is fitting that Jesus quotes Hosea 6:6.[60] In the context of Hosea the
prophet is delivering a word of judgment due to Israel's unfaithfulness as
Yahweh's bride. Yet within that oracle of condemnation comes a word of
hope. Should his bride repent and turn back, the Lord will bring restoration.
But Israel and Judah alike must understand what God truly desires; if his
bride is truly repentant then she will not merely perform the required
rituals but demonstrate the same steadfast love that characterizes Yahweh.
Applied to Jesus and the Pharisees, Hosea 6:6 is a striking indictment
against the religious leaders: they have missed the heart of God. Sacrifices
and burnt offerings do not matter if God's mercy is vacated from the law.
'Thus, Jesus himself is asserting, as Lord of the sabbath, his right to declare
the priority of merciful action over other construals of the sabbath that
focus chiefly on the prohibition of work.'[61]

Assumed in Jesus' reply is a typological correspondence with David, a
prophetiae ratio as Hilary of Poitiers calls it.[62] Like David, Jesus too has
authority as David's kingly son, the Messiah of Israel, to supersede the
written prescriptions of the law to fulfil its true intent (i.e. human flourishing).
'The analogical argument suggests that Jesus is, like David, the Lord's
anointed one whose mission and authority can override ordinary legal

---

[59] Hays 2016: 126.
[60] Back in Matt. 9:9–13 Jesus also quoted Hosea when the Pharisees baulked at him for eating
with tax collectors and sinners: 'Those who are well have no need of a physician, but those who
are sick. Go and learn what this means: "I desire mercy, and not sacrifice." For I came not to
call the righteous, but sinners' (9:12–13).
[61] Hays 2016: 126.
[62] Hilary 2012: 139.

restraints.'[63] The new David transcends the law because he is its culmination and, as we will see, its original author. Jesus' authority also goes beyond that of David. 'I tell you, something greater than the temple is here . . . For the Son of Man is lord of the Sabbath' (12:6, 8). The Pharisees are so focused on external conformity that they fail to see that the one the Law and the temple foreshadowed has arrived. (Their fixation with the type leads them to over-look the reality of the antitype.) In Jesus, therefore, is an authority to determine what the law means and how it should be applied because he is its divine author and its intended fulfilment. With him God's kingdom has been inaugurated and the messianic age has dawned. The Lord himself has come.

That Jesus transcends the law and the temple is further evidenced in Matthew 22:41–46, when Jesus poses to the Pharisees a messianic question: 'What do you think about the Christ? Whose son is he?' (22:42). When they answer that he is the son of David, Jesus throws a textual riddle at them that exposes their Christological deficiency. Quoting Psalm 110:1, Jesus asks:

> How is it then that David, in the Spirit, calls him Lord, saying,
>
> > 'The Lord said to my Lord,
> > Sit at my right hand,
> > > until I put your enemies under your feet'?
>
> If then David calls him Lord, how is he his son?
> (22:43–45)

The Pharisees are right that the Christ is the son of David, but they fail to see that he is also far more. He is not only David's son but David's Lord! The 'function of the narrative', comments Hays, 'is to emphasize yet again that Jesus both fulfills and transcends the expectation of the messianic Son of David'.[64]

Parables and the prophecy of Isaiah (Matt. 13:14–15)

It was said that the fulfilment pattern is present in Jesus' works (miracles) and words (parables). If Matthew 12:18–21 exhibits the former, Matthew

---

[63] Hays 2016: 150.
[64] Ibid. 151.

13:14–15 demonstrates the latter; both are two of the ten fulfilment passages in Matthew.

Matthew 13 opens with the parable of the sower. Yet Jesus leaves the parable uninterpreted for his listeners, not an uncommon move for the rabbi. Seemingly frustrated, the disciples ask Jesus afterward, 'Why do you speak to them in parables?' (13:10). The question appears to be asking, 'Why do you not tell them plainly?' In response Jesus reminds his disciples that a divine purpose is at work. As mysterious as it may appear, not everyone has been given the 'secrets' of the kingdom. 'To you it has been given to know the secrets of the kingdom of heaven, but to them it has not been given' (13:11). Or in Mark's account, 'To you has been given the secret of the kingdom of God, but for those outside everything is in parables, so that "they may indeed see but not perceive . . ."' (Mark 4:11–12).

Whose eyes are opened is left to the sovereign prerogative of his Father. Revelation is given but it is God given; therefore, his Father will decide to whom it is given and with whom it will be effective. Not all eyes have been opened to the identity of Jesus as have the eyes of the disciples. Hence Jesus uses the word *mystēria* from *mystērion*; the presence of the divine passives ('has been given' and 'has not been given') conveys that God alone reveals such a 'secret' when and to whom he wills. 'Only when he does so does the truth become available,' France states.[65] 'The doctrine of election lies behind these words,' says Morris.

> It is not a merit in the disciples that they understand where others do not; their comprehension is due to the fact that God has chosen them and given them the gift of understanding. They have received a gift that outsiders have not received (*to you* is emphatic), and the perfect tense signifies that the gift remains with them.[66]

This is not the first time Matthew has emphasized the sovereignty of God in revelation. As Jesus prays to his Father, having just pronounced judgment on those listeners who do not believe (Matt. 11:20–24):

> I thank you, Father, Lord of heaven and earth, that you have hidden these things from the wise and understanding and revealed them to

---

[65] France believes these divine passives and the 'whole tenor of the passage' is in the vein of Dan. 2. See France 2007: 511.

[66] Morris 1992: 339 (cf. 341). Similarly, see Turner 2008: 340. But contra Hagner 1993: 373.

little children; yes, Father, for such was your gracious will. All things have been handed over to me by my Father, and no one knows the Son except the Father, and no one knows the Father except the Son and anyone to whom the Son chooses to reveal him. (11:25–27)[67]

It should be concluded, then, that revelation, being so tied to the sovereign decision of God, is a gracious gift and one that originates from God himself. No doubt this is exactly how Jesus perceives not only the Scriptures but his own revelation and teaching from the Father. Revelation could not be more closely connected to the being of God, who is its source.

While much of Jesus' teaching ministry is meant to reveal, here Jesus says his teaching ministry is designed to conceal. The means by which such a concealing occurs is through the literary medium of parables. As Jesus says, 'This is why I speak to them in parables, because seeing they do not see, and hearing they do not hear, nor do they understand' (13:13). Again, the sovereign choice of God is assumed in the medium; in a sense, the message is the medium. He speaks to them in parables because they do not see and so that they will not see but will remain in their blind state. 'Matthew, no less than Mark and Luke,' says France, 'has the secrets given to some and not to others in v. 11, and his v. 12 has compounded the inequality.'[68]

At the same time, if 13:11 stresses divine sovereignty and the gratuity of election with regard to the disciples, 13:14 also emphasizes human responsibility in the disbelief of the crowds and religious leaders. As Jesus says in 13:12, 'For to the one who has, more will be given, and he will have an abundance, but from the one who has not, even what he has will be taken away.' Here the maxim of medieval interpreters like Augustine and Anselm is relevant for hermeneutics: 'I believe in order to understand.' Yet for those who do not believe, they will not understand. Morris adds:

It was precisely because they had accepted the revelation that Jesus was the Messiah who would bring in the kingdom that the disciples

---

[67] Apparently, Matthew does not believe the sovereign choice of God in divine revelation eliminates the responsibility of the hearer, for Jesus says next, 'Come to me, all who labour and are heavy laden, and I will give you rest' (11:28). To explore this further, see Turner 2008: 340.

[68] France 2007: 513. France does not believe that changes as one moves to Mark and Luke. 'The basic theme of "to some and not to others" remains.' Ibid. 515.

were able to understand and respond to the teaching in the parables. And it was because people like the Pharisees had not accepted it that they did not understand.[69]

The medium of parables only ensures that the unbelieving remain unregenerate; the continuing use of parables, even though the listeners clearly do not understand, is a divine decision, even a Christological one. Yet, at the same time, 13:11–12 places ultimate responsibility with the unbeliever himself. The refusal to believe leaves the doubter culpable.

Whereas it is typically Matthew who interrupts the narrative to explain that an Old Testament passage is being fulfilled, this time it is Jesus himself:

Indeed, in their case *the prophecy of Isaiah is fulfilled that says*:

'You will indeed hear but never understand,
    and you will indeed see but never perceive.
For this people's heart has grown dull,
    and with their ears they can barely hear,
    and their eyes they have closed,
lest they should see with their eyes
    and hear with their ears
and understand with their heart
and turn, and I would heal them.
(13:14–15; cf. Mark 4:12; Luke 8:10; emphasis added)[70]

Citing Isaiah 6:9–10 is an indictment most severe. In context Isaiah is called to take God's message to a people who will not listen but reject it. To be more precise still, it is the message God puts in Isaiah's mouth that brings about Israel's resistance and rebellion against Yahweh. By way of analogy and further culmination, the Jews of Jesus' day bring such hard-heartedness to its climax. The irony is that Jesus' listeners hear him but do not understand the significance of what he says or its true meaning. His listeners see him, but they remain blind to the person and message right in front of them. Like Israel of old, they have hearts that are spiritually lifeless and unreceptive. For that reason, they will not receive the healing the

---

[69] Morris 1992: 340.
[70] Also see Matt. 13:35 and Ps. 78:2. And see Mark 4:10–13.

Messiah brings. Similar to other fulfilment passages in Matthew, says Osborne, this passage is 'typological and says the situation behind Isa 6 is being reenacted in the current generation. The hardness of the nation in Isaiah's day is "fulfilled" or "comes to completion" in the hardness of the people in Jesus' day.'[71]

To further the irony, it is the people of Jesus' day who bring Isaiah's words to fulfilment. Isaiah's judgment against those with a dull heart, deaf ears and blind eyes is a 'prophecy', says Jesus, that has been fulfilled by those who reject him and his message. In what appears to be the lengthiest passage quoted from the Old Testament, Jesus himself demonstrates that his ministry – and even the consequences it has for how his listeners react to it – is the typological fulfilment of the divine purpose as revealed in the prophetic writings. Jesus not only believes God spoke through prophets like Isaiah but that such 'prophecy', as Jesus calls it, is active, the divine plan revealed in the Scriptures being worked out in the very words and works of Jesus. To make such a connection, says Hagner, Jesus must assume inspiration. 'The typological correspondence, wherein the former situation [Israel in Isaiah's day] foreshadows the latter, is seen to be divinely intended and rests upon the divine inspiration of the Scriptures.'[72] Jesus' eschatology, therefore, is entirely contingent upon his belief in divine inspiration; the fulfilment of God's words in Isaiah's words has arrived in Jesus, the messianic prophet who ushers in the last days.[73]

The conclusion Jesus draws is oriented to the prophets as well: 'For truly, I say to you, many prophets and righteous people longed to see what you see, and did not see it, and to hear what you hear, and did not hear it' (13:17). Isaiah was restricted to his time and day, but how he longed to see the very things God had spoken through him. What the prophets would have given to hear Jesus explain the Torah and then, by his very deeds, bring it to fruition.[74] 'Jesus is saying that his mission in the world is the culmination of the purpose of God made clear in prophecies from of old.'[75] In John's account Isaiah himself is said to have known, even seen, the glory of Christ (John 12:41). To be sure, the disciples sit in a privileged position, though they do not always realize it.

---

[71] Osborne 2010: 511.
[72] Hagner 1993: 374.
[73] See ibid. 374.
[74] Osborne 2010: 512.
[75] Morris 1992: 344.

The sign of Jonah (Matt. 16)

Jesus utilizes a similar tactic in other conflicts with the religious leaders. Previously the theme of 'fulfilment' manifests itself in the miracles of Jesus. In Matthew 16 (cf. Luke 11:29–32) the Pharisees and Sadducees question such a fulfilment by insisting Jesus perform yet another miracle at their demand. Testing him, they require Jesus to give them 'a sign from heaven' (16:1). Jesus exposes the tragic irony in such a demand, for these men can read the weather forecast ahead of time by looking at the colour of the sky, yet cannot 'interpret the signs of the times' (16:3; cf. Luke 12:54–56). Will they be given a sign? Yes and no. 'An evil and adulterous generation seeks for a sign, but no sign will be given to it except the sign of Jonah' (16:4).

Even when Jesus refuses to accommodate those with evil, unbelieving intent, he is displaying fulfilment. At other points in Jesus' ministry Jonah is said to prefigure Jesus' death and resurrection (Matt. 12:40). Here, however, the 'sign of Jonah' brings to remembrance how a wicked nation repented at the message of judgment; yet the people of Jesus' day will not repent even though one greater than Jonah is present. The sign they receive carries judgment alone. Jesus has appealed not only to a historical moment but to a prophet, and in doing so embodies not only the salvation of Israel but their judgment for refusing to repent. Whether it is his miracles or his refusal to perform miracles, Jesus is clear that what was typologically foreshadowed (as with Jonah) is now at hand, resulting for some in eternal life and for others in eternal judgment. Whether it is his miracles or his teaching, Jesus' mission presupposes a continuity with the story of Israel that Jesus, Israel's Saviour and Judge, is bringing to its culmination.

Moses, Elijah and the transfiguration of Jesus (Matt. 17:1–13)

That continuity with the Scriptures and the story of Israel shines at its brightest in the transfiguration of Christ in Matthew 17. Technically the language of 'fulfilment' is not used, but it proves unnecessary in view of the two men who appear by Jesus' side during the revelation of his divine glory.

The transfiguration, unlike so many other miracles and exorcisms, is a private affair, one that only Peter, James and John witness (17:1). Also, certain Matthean themes mentioned earlier show themselves once again.

For example, Jesus leads his inner circle of three 'up a high mountain' like a new Moses or new Elijah (17:1; cf. Exod. 19 and 24; 1 Kgs 19).[76] Except, when they arrive it becomes clear that he is someone far greater than Moses and Elijah, for his ordinary human appearance is eclipsed by his divine, pre-incarnate and future glory: 'And he was transfigured before them, and his face shone like the sun, and his clothes became white as light' (17:2).

On the one hand, this narrative harkens back to Moses descending Sinai with a face that glowed and had to be veiled (Exod. 34:29–30). On the other hand, the glow of Jesus' face is no mere recapitulation. Rather than a mere reflection of divine glory, Jesus undergoes a transfiguration revealing divine glory itself. 'The verb *metamorphoō* ("transfigure," "transform," "change in form")', says Carson, 'suggests a change of inmost nature that may be outwardly visible', as it is in Matthew 17:1-13 and Exodus 34:29 'or quite invisible (Rom 12:2; 2 Cor 3:18).'[77]

For what purpose does this transfiguration occur? *Revelation.* Jesus intends to reveal who he is and what he will do so that the faith of his disciples will be solidified. 'That Jesus was transfigured "before them" implies that it was largely for their sakes: whatever confirmation the experience may have given Jesus, for the disciples it was revelatory.' Revelation of what, exactly? 'As they would come to realize, they were being privileged to glimpse something of his [Jesus'] preincarnate glory (John 1:14; 17:5; Phil 2:6–7) and anticipate his coming exaltation (2 Peter 1:16–18; Rev 1:16).'[78]

The revelation of his pre-incarnate glory and coming exaltation is timely. Six days earlier Jesus told his disciples that he was going to Jerusalem to die (16:21). The disciples, as exemplified in Peter's rebuke (16:22), struggled to see how this could be if Jesus is, as Peter confessed, none other than the Christ (16:16). Yet if they had ears to hear, they would have noticed that Jesus not only predicted his sufferings but his resurrection on the third day (16:21). Witnessing his transfiguration not only manifests the humility of the Son – the Son who enjoys the glory of divinity with the Father will lower himself to suffer death! – but also confirms the resurrection glory on the other side of the cross. 'Therefore they had reason to hope that they would

---

[76] Carson (1984: 384) also believes Matthew is giving a literary clue to Moses' and Elijah's journeys up a mountain.

[77] Ibid. 385.

[78] Ibid.

yet see the Son of Man coming in his kingdom (16:28).'[79] Transfigured before their eyes, the disciples have every reason to believe that this is the Christ, the anointed One whom the Law and the Prophets promised and prefigured.

That confirmation is further corroborated when two Old Testament representatives join Jesus. Shocked by the sheer radiance of his divine glory, the disciples see two others appear next to Jesus, Moses and Elijah, both of whom talk with Jesus (17:3). Why Moses and Elijah? There may be many reasons but three stand out.

1. Moses and Elijah represent the Law and the Prophets, which Jesus has said, at the start of Matthew's Gospel, he has come to fulfil (5:17). Furthermore, both men had, what Carson calls, 'eschatological roles': 'Moses was the model for the eschatological Prophet (Deut 18:18) and Elijah for the forerunner (Mal 4:5–6; Matt 3:1–3; 11:7–10; 17:9–13).'[80] So not only do they represent the entire Old Testament, from the Law to the Prophets, but their prophetic functions were eschatologically geared, pointing forward to the coming of a greater Prophet.

2. It follows as well, then, that both men serve as types of Christ in the Old Testament, which is supported only by this transfigured encounter. This can be seen in countless ways, but given the transfigured glory of Jesus in Matthew 17 it is anything but accidental that Moses and Elijah witnessed the divine glory, veiled as it might have been (Exod. 31:18; 1 Kgs 19:1–18). Their presence at Jesus' transfiguration communicates that the glory of God himself, namely God's beloved Son, has been enfleshed, but now for but a moment that glory is unveiled for the disciples' benefit. The divine glory is Jesus himself; his transfiguration says that much, for he 'radiates the glory of Deity'.[81]

3. In their prophetic, eschatological and typological representation, Moses and Elijah also serve as identity markers of God's covenant with his people and the covenant's redemptive–historical progression and fulfilment. Moses represents the covenant ratified at Sinai, while Elijah represents the covenant renewed.[82] Their presence next to Jesus insinuates that the covenant promises of God have not failed but are about to reach their fulfilment in his death and resurrection, a point Jesus himself will make at his last Passover meal with his disciples.

---

[79] Ibid.
[80] Ibid. Also see Hilary 2012: 186.
[81] Carson 1984: 385.
[82] Ibid.

Witnessing Jesus, Moses and Elijah converse, the disciples then see a 'bright cloud' overshadow these three, and with it a voice from the cloud speaks (17:5). In the Old Testament, the book of Exodus in particular, the glory of Yahweh appeared to Israel in the wilderness by means of a cloud; its overshadowing presence indicated to Israel that Yahweh himself had descended and was present. Here, in Matthew 17, the cloud reappears but this time Yahweh speaks from the cloud concerning his only begotten Son and Messiah, the one he has sent: 'This is my beloved Son, with whom I am well pleased; listen to him' (17:5). This is not the first time this language – 'my beloved Son' – is heard. Similar, if not identical language is used at Jesus' baptism (Matt. 3:17). But with Jesus' prediction of his suffering just prior to the transfiguration, it seems the 'beloved Son' language repeated in Matthew 17:5 only heightens the reality of Psalm 2:7 and Isaiah 42:1: Jesus is the Davidic king but his exaltation to that throne will be as a servant who suffers.[83]

In that light, typology has now met its antitype. As Carson says, Matthew 17:5 goes beyond Matthew 3:17 to elevate Jesus 'above Moses and Elijah'.[84] Israel was to listen to Moses, her prophet, but now Moses' antitype has arrived, and Yahweh instructs the disciples to 'listen to him' (John 17:5). One far greater than Moses is now present; the prophetic office has met its eschatological point of fulfilment. Previously, God spoke through his prophetic mediator Moses, but now God has sent his beloved Son to speak to his people, and he speaks with unequivocal authority.[85]

Your king is coming (Matt. 21)

Fulfilment in Matthew begins to peak as Jesus enters Jerusalem and prepares for suffering. In Matthew 21 Jesus stops on the Mount of Olives, telling two of his disciples to enter the nearby village where they will find a donkey and her colt. If asked why they are taking them, the disciples are to respond, 'The Lord needs them' (21:3). Matthew then comments:

---

[83] Ibid. 386.

[84] Ibid.

[85] 'The additional words "Listen to him" – an allusion to Deuteronomy 18:15 – confirm Jesus is the Prophet like Moses (Deut. 18:15–18; cf. Acts 3:22–23; 7:37). This does not mean Jesus is another prophet of Moses' stature but the eschatological Prophet patterned on Moses as a type . . . Moses' primary role here is typological, whereas Elijah's, not explained till vv. 9–13, is eschatological.' Ibid.

This took place to fulfil what was spoken by the prophet, saying,

> Say to the daughter of Zion,
> 'Behold, your king is coming to you,
>   humble, and mounted on a donkey,
>   and on a colt, the foal of a beast of burden.'
> (21:4–5)

Matthew is quoting from Isaiah 62:11 and Zechariah 9:9, the latter prophet being a favourite of Matthew's Gospel. In the passion narrative Matthew will cite from Zechariah six more times (see Matt. 21:12–13 and Zech. 14:21; Matt. 26:15–16 and Zech. 11:12; Matt. 26:26–29 and Zech. 911; Matt. 26:30–35 and Zech. 13:7; Matt. 27:3–10 and Zech. 11:12–13; Matt. 27:51–53 and Zech. 14:4–5). Jews in Jesus' day understood Zechariah 9:9 in messianic-Davidic categories.[86] Yet notice, Matthew leaves out the phrase in Zechariah 9:9 that this humble king on a donkey is 'righteous and having salvation'. Hays does not believe this omission is a metalepsis, but instead a 'deliberate editing-out of a phrase' since king Jesus is about to undergo crucifixion. His moment of triumph awaits the empty tomb; for now, his victory will be masked as he goes to the cross. He is 'not a conquering military hero', as perhaps many Jews expected the new son of David to be, but instead a 'lowly, gentle figure who is reshaping Israel's messianic hope in a way that could hardly have been anticipated – a way, indeed, that will lead to the cross'.[87]

John makes the connection to Zechariah and Isaiah as well but introduces these Old Testament passages with 'just as it is written'. However, John then explains how the disciples later come to see this fulfilment for what it is: 'His disciples did not understand these things at first, but when Jesus was glorified, then they remembered that these things had been written about him and had been done to him' (John 12:16).

Whereas John begins with shouts of 'Hosanna', Matthew concludes with those shouts. As Jesus rides on the donkey and the colt, the crowd spreads branches on the road, shouting, 'Hosanna to the Son of David! Blessed is he who comes in the name of the Lord! Hosanna in the highest!' (Matt. 21:9).[88] Echoed in 21:9 is Psalm 118:25–26. Situated within the Hallel

---

[86] Ibid. 437.

[87] Hays 2016: 153.

[88] Compare to Mark 11:9–11, who does not use 'Son of David' but instead 'the coming kingdom of our father David'.

psalms, 118:25–26 is a psalm that not only resounds with praise but anticipation and hope that the Lord will act as Israel's deliverer. 'Save us, we pray, O LORD!' (118:25). They cry out, longing for one 'who comes in the name of the LORD!' (118:26). In Matthew 21 Israel's Davidic king comes in the name of the Lord, for he is the one who will 'save' the people of his kingdom.

However, in this fulfilment passage Matthew intends to convey not only that Jesus is the Messiah, the Son of David, but that he is a king entering Zion *with humility*. Zechariah pictures the Lord as a King who brings justice to his people as well as peace. Here, however, Matthew focuses on the latter.[89] Rather than Jesus entering Jerusalem on a war horse leading an army after conquering his enemies, the messianic king rides a beast of burden, a lowly donkey symbolizing peace.[90]

Was Jesus himself aware of such symbolism and fulfilment? It would seem so. Morris asserts:

> The mention of the prophecy that was fulfilled right at the beginning of this incident (and not after Matthew has related what happened), may be meant to indicate that Jesus consciously fulfilled the words of the prophet. This does not mean the disciples understood ... But Jesus knew what he was about, and his action proclaimed boldly to all who had eyes to see that Jesus was indeed the Messiah, but a Messiah of a very different stamp from any that the deliriously happy crowds had imagined.[91]

His choice of this humble beast is a deliberate enactment of prophetic fulfilment.[92]

We should also observe how this fulfilment passage at the start of the passion narrative emphasizes divine control. From Jesus' knowing just where his disciples should retrieve the donkey to the quotation from Zechariah indicating that all this took place to fulfil what the prophet said, Yahweh's sovereignty is seen in the way he brings what he previously said through the prophets to fulfilment. 'This is the ninth of ten such passages,' says Osborne:

---

[89] In his quotation of Zech. 9:9 notice his omission of 'just and saving is he', which Hagner takes as intentional 'to focus on the humility of Jesus'. Hagner 1995: 594.
[90] Ibid.; Morris 1992: 521; Carson 1984: 437.
[91] Morris 1992: 521.
[92] Blomberg 2016: 678; Keener 2009: 259–260; Tan 1997: 138–143.

all of which stress Jesus as the one prophesied in OT expectation, the one who reenacts the life of Israel. God's sovereign control (note the divine passive, which means, 'that God might fulfill') denotes that Jesus is the centerpoint of history, bringing to completion God's plan of salvation and OT hope.[93]

God's sovereign control is but another subtle indication not only that the Scriptures of Israel are imbued with his divine intention throughout, but he has brought those same Scriptures to their fulfilment in the life and mission of Jesus.

Have you never read? (Matt. 21:12–17)

Having received a king's welcome, David's greater son returned to his temple but only to find it was not ready for his arrival.[94] What was meant to be a place of worship, sacrifice and devotion, the very place in which the presence of the Holy One would descend to dwell with his people, has been turned into a market. Infuriated, Jesus drove out the money-changers and overturned their tables. With a righteous indignation, and an eschatological authority, Jesus appealed to Isaiah 56:7 and Jeremiah 7:11: 'It is written, "My house shall be called a house of prayer", but you make it a den of robbers' (Matt. 21:13).[95]

This incident has been titled a 'cleansing' for good reason. The temple's external, ritual defilement reflected the people's internal, spiritual corruption. The anointed one has returned to his Father's house but not to find the people praying for his coming, nor being a light to the nations. 'The temple was meant to be a house of prayer, but they made it "a nationalist stronghold"', writes Carson.[96]

The temple was not fulfilling its God-ordained role as a witness to the nations but had become, like the first temple, the premier symbol of a superstitious belief that God would protect and rally his people irrespective of their conformity to his will.[97]

---

[93] Osborne 2010: 754.

[94] Matthew chooses to place the temple cleansing after Jesus' entry into Jerusalem (cf. Matt. 21:13–16; Luke 19:45–48).

[95] Cf. Carson 1984: 442.

[96] 'Den of robbers' is translated by Carson as 'nationalist rebel' (cf. Matt. 27:16). Ibid.

[97] Ibid.

Such a judgment is seen in Mark's Gospel when he chooses to mention the *nations*: 'Is it not written, "My house shall be called a house of prayer for all the nations"? But you have made it a den of robbers' (11:17). Quoting Isaiah 56:7 with the 'Court of the Gentiles' in plain sight must have been especially damning to those receiving Jesus' rebuke. Yet it also reveals Jesus to be the Messiah Isaiah promised would bring salvation *to the nations*, fulfilling God's covenant promise to Abraham that through him all the nations would be blessed (Gen. 15:18). The coming of God's Messiah meant the nations 'would stream to Jerusalem in unprecedented numbers to worship her God'.[98]

With the cleansing initiated, the blind and lame can now come into the temple to receive healing from the king of Israel, the Son of David (Matt. 21:14). For one greater than the temple is now present with God's people (Matt. 12:6). Failing to understand how such healings signify that the last days have arrived, that the kingdom has come and that David's greater son has returned to restore the presence of Yahweh, the chief priests and scribes grow indignant when they hear children crying out, 'Hosanna to the Son of David!' (Matt. 21:15). 'Do you hear what these are saying?', they protest to Jesus (21:16).

Notice, it is the title 'Son of David' that these leaders cannot stand to hear attributed to Jesus. This is ironic: the chief priests and scribes, who study the Scriptures of Israel day and night, cannot recognize David's greater son and king when he arrives, but the blind, the lame and the children can. This is not the first time this has happened: in Matthew 9:27 two blind men cry out, 'Have mercy on us, Son of David,' and are healed by Jesus. Yet this time even the children sing, 'Hosanna to the Son of David!' Jesus responds to the unbelief of the chief priests and scribes by quoting Psalm 8:2:

Yes; have you never read,

> 'Out of the mouth of infants and nursing babies
> you have prepared praise'?
(Matt. 21:16)

Psalm 8:2 reads in its entirety:

---

98 Blomberg 2016: 679.

Out of the mouth of babies and infants,
you have established strength because of your foes,
to still the enemy and the avenger.

Psalm 8 is a hymn of praise, one in which David exalts the Lord for his work in creation. The glory of the Lord in creation also manifests his strength over his enemies. That strength and glory reaches its culmination when the Davidic king, David's greater son, enters his temple to hear infants praising him. As in Psalm 8, so too in Matthew 21, those who are weak and helpless – babes and infants – shut up the mouths of Jesus' enemies because on their lips are shouts of praise to their Creator and Davidic saviour.

Jesus relies on the typology of the psalm to justify his actions, defend the God-ordained intention behind the temple and even bring to further fruition his Father's plan not merely for the temple itself but on a wider scale for Israel as a covenant people. The latter point assumes not only that there is a unity to the Scriptures but that this unity is due to Yahweh himself being the author and orchestrator of Israel's story and covenant canon.

From stone to cornerstone: Mark 12 and Matthew 21:33–46

By this point the tension between Jesus and the religious leaders is reaching a breaking point. In Mark 11:27–33, for example, the chief priests, scribes and elders challenge the authority of Jesus, questioning who gave him authority to do the works he is doing (11:28). Mark follows this encounter with the parable of the tenants (12:1–12; cf. Matt. 21:33–46), a parable that not only echoes the vineyard language of Isaiah (1:8; 5:1–7; 27:2; cf. Ezek. 19:10) but is designed to declare the Father's judgment against the Sanhedrin.

The owner of a vineyard leases his winepress to tenants as he leaves the country. When the seasons change, he sends servants to collect the 'fruit of the vineyard', only for the tenants to beat the first two servants and kill the third. This pattern continues for some time until the owner decides to send his own 'beloved son' (12:6; cf. Mark 1:11; 9:7); surely they will show respect for his own heir, especially since he carries a legal authority, representing his father. The absurdity of the owner sending his own son is meant to display how outrageous and radical the Father's benevolence and grace are towards his wayward covenant people.[99]

Given the history of Israel, the tenants, as one might expect, are once again vicious, this time murdering the owner's beloved son and heir so that they instead will receive the inheritance.[100] Jesus asks, 'What will the owner of the vineyard do?', and answers, 'He will come and destroy the tenants and give the vineyard to others' (12:9).[101] Jesus is drawing a parallel to describe what has taken place and will take place. Yahweh sent his servants the prophets, from the 'blood of righteous Abel to the blood of Zechariah the son of Barachiah', as Jesus will later say (Matt. 23:35), to call Israel back to repentance and covenant renewal. Yet they did not listen but instead killed the prophets (cf. Acts 7:52). Now he has sent the heir, his own 'beloved son', but Jesus they will kill as well. One might say the situation is worse than the parable; at least in the parable the tenants recognized it was the owner's son. In Jesus' case, as Mark 11:28 demonstrates, the religious leaders do not even recognize Jesus to be the *Son of the Father* but question his authority and heavenly origin.

Nevertheless, the owner of the vineyard is not without vindication. He will 'come and destroy' these wicked tenants, giving his vineyard to another (12:9). By application, judgment is coming and through judgment Yahweh will bestow salvation on others. Here Jesus transitions from the parable to his present ministry, and does so by switching metaphors and quoting Psalm 118:22–23:

> The stone that the builders rejected
>> has become the cornerstone;
> this was the Lord's doing,
>> and it is marvellous in our eyes.

---

[99] Stein 2008: 531–540; Strauss 2014: 516; Edwards 2002: 537–558. These commentators and others note how such a theme is prevalent throughout the OT (Ps. 86:5; Isa. 53; 54:5; 62:5; Jer. 3:12–14; 4:1; Hos. 2:19; Mal. 2:11) and NT (John 3:16; Rom. 2:4; 5:6–8; Phil. 2:1–11; Titus 3:4–5).

[100] 'The religious leaders are acting just like the tenants, viewing the nation of Israel as *theirs* rather than God's. They foolishly refuse to submit to Jesus, God's Son, or to respond to his proclamation of the kingdom of God.' Strauss 2014: 516. Emphasis original.

[101] 'Others' includes Gentiles, especially since the context includes the temple scene, where Jesus quotes Isa. 56:7's saying regarding his father's house being a house of prayer for all nations. Edwards 2002: 360. However, it is not limited to Gentiles, but also refers to the new covenant people and church Jesus establishes by his blood. See Strauss 2014: 520.

140

In context, the psalmist could be referring to a stone cast aside as insignificant and irrelevant in the building of the temple, yet one that, to everyone's surprise, becomes central, even the head stone.[102] Jesus is this stone, the cornerstone of a new temple, as not only Mark intends to convey but many other New Testament authors, demonstrating how central this imagery was to the early church (Luke 20:17; Acts 4:11; Rom. 9:33; 10:11; 1 Cor. 3:11; Eph. 2:20–22; 1 Peter 2:6–8).

What Mark describes in brief, expecting his readers to understand, Matthew elaborates and makes explicit. In Matthew 21 Jesus provides the interpretation of the parable:

> Therefore I tell you, the kingdom of God will be taken away from you and given to a people producing its fruits. And the one who falls on this stone will be broken to pieces; and when it falls on anyone, it will crush him.
>
> (21:43–44)

Although they will put the Son to death, he will be vindicated, a sovereign plan the Father has every intention of accomplishing. Those who crush the Son will then be crushed by the cornerstone.

What is relevant for the purposes of this study is the way Jesus chooses to make such a point: 'Have you not read this Scripture . . . ?', Jesus asks (12:10). Or in Matthew's Gospel: 'Have you never read in the Scriptures . . . ?' (21:42). As we have seen, Jesus' parable resembles the vineyard imagery of Isaiah (1:8; 5:1–7; 27:2), but his specific quotation is from Psalm 118:22–23. Some think Psalm 118 positions David as the type – after all, David is overlooked by his own people and belittled by his enemies but is chosen to be Yahweh's cornerstone/capstone and to reign as his royal mediator over God's covenant people. But there is also good reason to believe the psalm refers to Israel as a type.[103] Israel is a people the nations discount and ridicule, yet Israel is Yahweh's firstborn son, chosen to receive the patriarchs, the covenants, the law and the Messiah himself. Against all appearances, Israel is made the cornerstone/capstone, a type of the true Israel yet to come who will re-enact Israel's history for the purpose of

---

[102] Edwards 2002: 360. There is diverse opinion as to whether Jesus has in mind a cornerstone, capstone, keystone, etc. Regardless, the point is that the stone is foundational to the rest of the building. See Strauss 2014: 517; Gray 2008: 76.
[103] Carson 1984: 453.

redemption (see chapter 5). Like David and Israel, Jesus will be opposed, ridiculed and persecuted, yet in his demise Yahweh will raise him up as the true cornerstone/capstone.[104]

Not only is there an expectation that Jesus' listeners (and especially his religious opponents) should know what the Old Testament says and how its typology will come to maturity in Christ, but Jesus assumes that the Old Testament witness, in its specifics and as a whole bears the divine author's stamp. This divine author is now accomplishing his plan of redemption through his Son, the cornerstone.

The Son of Man goes as it is written of him: the blood of the covenant (Matt. 26:17–29)

As the hour of death approaches, Jesus prepares for the Passover. The typology thickens: Jesus is to be laid on the altar as a sacrifice for the sins of the people; he *is* the Passover meal (Exod. 12:1–28). Hence the symbolism instilled in his words 'Take, eat; this is my body' (26:26). The sacrificial language of Passover is explicit when he introduces the cup as well: 'Drink of it, all of you, for this is my blood of the covenant, which is poured out for many for the forgiveness of sins' (26:28).

By pouring out his blood, Jesus secures the salvific promises and blessings of the covenant, first of which is forgiveness. Jesus does so as the antitype of Passover, the meal that inaugurated Israel's exodus and entry into the covenant at Sinai. However, Luke's Gospel specifies that the covenant Jesus cuts is the 'new covenant in my blood' (Luke 22:20). This is the new covenant Yahweh promised through Jeremiah the prophet: 'Behold, the days are coming, declares the LORD, when I will make a new covenant with the house of Israel and the house of Judah' (31:31). The Passover meal, therefore, was but a type of the final sacrifice yet to come, a sacrifice to end all sacrifices. Passover's covenantal context pointed forward to a new covenant. It is the new covenant 'in my blood' because unlike the blood of the lamb at Passover, the blood of this Lamb will definitively take away sins.[105] As the sacrifice to end all sacrifices, he is the final Passover lamb.

---

[104] Ibid.
[105] On this point, the book of Hebrews capitalizes. What is but a short reference in Matthew and Luke becomes Hebrews' Christology.

This sacrificial imagery not only takes the reader back to Exodus 12, to Passover itself, but to Exodus 24 where the covenant is confirmed (see chapter 2). When Moses 'wrote down all the words of the LORD', he 'rose early in the morning and built an altar at the foot of the mountain' and his young men 'offered burnt offerings and sacrificed peace offerings of oxen to the LORD' (24:4–5). Taking the blood in his hands, Moses put half the blood in basins and the other half he 'threw against the altar', for there the presence of God descended among a sinful people (24:6). With the 'Book of the Covenant' in hand, Moses read it so that all Israel could hear it and swear to uphold it (24:7). Then 'Moses took the blood and threw it on the people and said, "Behold the blood of the covenant that the LORD has made with you in accordance with all these words"' (24:8). But in Matthew 26, the blood and the Mediator are one: as the new Moses, Jesus spills his own blood for the forgiveness of the people. His blood covers them so that their guilt is taken away and their sins are no more; through his sacrifice the people have peace with God.[106] The end note of Jeremiah's new covenant promise is ratified: 'For I will forgive their iniquity, and I will remember their sin no more' (31:34). Is this not what the angel promised at the start of Matthew's Gospel: 'you shall call his name Jesus, for he will save his people from their sins' (Matt. 1:21).[107]

Additionally, it is no small matter that Jesus is characterized by a self-consciousness in this whole affair. He understands that his body and blood will bring the Scriptures and all their typological symbolism to their culmination. As he reclines with his disciples, he announces that one of his disciples will betray him (Matt. 26:21). It will be the one who dips his hand in the dish with Jesus (26:23). Yet even his betrayal is no accident: it too is to fulfil the Scriptures. Jesus says, 'The Son of Man goes as it is written of him, but woe to that man by whom the Son of Man is betrayed!' (26:24).

---

[106] Could Exod. 24 be alluded to when Peter says 'for obedience to Jesus Christ and *for sprinkling with his blood*' (1 Peter 1:2; emphasis added)?

[107] Hays 2016: 136. Hays also claims Zech. 9:11 could be in view: 'As for you also, because of the blood of my covenant with you, / I will set your prisoners free from the waterless pit.' Since Matthew already quoted Zech. 9:9 in Matt. 21:5, Hays believes 9:11 must be in view in this later narrative. 'Matthew's last supper scene creates a complex overlay of intertextual echoes, recalling both the blood-spattered covenantal banquet of Exodus 24 and the blood-secured messianic promise of deliverance found in Zechariah 9.' Ibid. With those two texts in mind, Hays says the people's cry – 'his blood be upon us' – means more than the people know. I find Hays's intertextuality fascinating, but also somewhat difficult to demonstrate with certainty. He may be right, however, since Matthew's Gospel is loaded with intertextual connections. At the same time, Matthew tends to be explicit and direct when he makes an intertextual connection, which is not the case with Zech. 9:11.

His death may be the result of betrayal, but Jesus is clear that such betrayal is itself in accordance with the Scriptures.[108] He must lay down his life as the Scriptures of Israel confirm.

How then should the Scriptures be fulfilled? (Matt. 26:47–56)

As Jesus draws near to the hour of his execution, he is betrayed by Judas and arrested by the chief priests and the elders. They approach Jesus with clubs and swords, as if they are arresting a violent criminal. In the moment of his arrest, Peter seizes his sword and cuts off the ear of the high priest (Matt. 26:51). Jesus rebukes Peter, reminding him that Jesus is in sovereign control; if he so desires, he can call on his Father who will send twelve legions of angels to his defence (26:53). 'But how then should the Scriptures be fulfilled, that it must be so?' (26:54).

The fulfilment theme is repeated when Jesus then asks the crowd at large:

> Have you come out as against a robber, with swords and clubs to capture me? Day after day I sat in the temple teaching, and you did not seize me. But all this has taken place that the Scriptures of the prophets might be fulfilled.
> (26:55–56)

No specific passage is cited by Jesus: he may have in mind the whole scope of Scripture or simply all those Old Testament texts that either directly or typologically point forward to this hour (e.g. Pss 22; 69; Isa. 52:12 – 53:12; Zech. 13:7).[109]

Jesus underlines the predetermined nature of his death, but it should also be emphasized that such an ordained, predestined fate is not merely a voluntary covenant or pact between Jesus and his Father; it is one that has been charted by the prophets in the Scriptures, as Jesus himself says. More precisely still, the mission of redemption agreed upon in eternity between the Father and the Son (see chapter 4) was revealed progressively in the

---

[108] 'No OT quotation explains "as it is written of him"; but one may think of OT passages such as Isaiah 53:7–9; Daniel 9:26, or else suppose that an entire prophetic typology (see on 2:15; 5:17–20) is in view, such as the Passover lamb, or some combination of the two.' Carson 1984: 534.

[109] Osborne 2010: 986.

prophetic writings and now must happen just as described in the Scriptures of Israel. If not, not only is it the case that the 'Scriptures are not fulfilled, the faithfulness of God could be called into question'.[110] Hence, throughout Matthew's Gospel, as well as Mark, Luke and John, there is a divine-scriptural necessity to Jesus' sufferings, so that he can repeatedly emphasize that the Son of Man must suffer if the Scriptures and the covenant promises of God are to be fulfilled.

Conclusion: Matthean fulfilment and the Scriptures

The fulfilment motif reveals a foundational commitment of Matthew's Jesus: in the Scriptures of Israel God has spoken through the Law and the Prophets to prefigure his Davidic king. Those Scriptures are fulfilled in Jesus, the Christ, the Son of God. The Scriptures, therefore, are God given and God breathed, according to Matthew's Jesus, and on this basis, they are loaded with Christological intent in the promise–fulfilment pattern they present. With astuteness, Hagner explains:

> Together, Jews and Christians shared such convictions as the sovereignty of God, the inspiration of the Scriptures, and the unity of God's saving purpose resulting in the interconnectedness of his redemptive acts. To these the Christians added the one supreme conviction that Jesus was the *telos*, the goal, of what the OT had promised.[111]

Hagner draws the appropriate conclusion:

> With these presuppositions, Christians like Matthew saw correspondences between events of the past and the time of Jesus not as coincidental, as we moderns might, but as divinely intended, with the earlier foreshadowing the latter, much in the sense of prophecy and fulfilment.[112]

---

[110] Hagner 1995: 790; cf. Morris 1992: 676.
[111] Hagner 1995: lvi.
[112] Ibid.

4

The ultimate fulfilment and self-disclosure of God – the Word made flesh: the Johannine witness (case study 2)

Each Gospel author has a specific angle and theological agenda, which has led many biblical scholars to distinguish the Gospel of John from the Synoptics, as if the former is less interested in the promise–fulfilment motif. However, the Synoptics have no monopoly on the fulfilment theme. John too paints the life of Christ with such a motif, even if it is less conspicuous than it is in Matthew, for example. John's unique use of the fulfilment motif adds another colour to the mosaic seen so far.

On the one hand, John touches on some of the same accounts where the fulfilment theme is manifested. On the other hand, he also incorporates the fulfilment theme in places left unexplored by the Synoptics, adding insight to Jesus' own reception and interpretation of the Scriptures and their origin. However, there are notable differences between John's approach and that of the Synoptics. While Matthew tends to telegraph when, where and why an Old Testament text is being quoted, John paints word pictures (e.g. Jesus is the Word, the lamb of God, living water, the bread of life, the good shepherd, the vine, etc.), using metaphors and allusions to show how the types in the Old Testament are fulfilled in Christ, the antitype.[1] John may not directly quote the Old Testament as much as

---

[1] This chapter will focus more on outright metaphors than allusions. Nevertheless, Köstenberger (2007: 419–420) observes how John's Gospel is full of OT allusions: 1:1 (Gen. 1:1); 1:14 (Exod. 34:6); 1:17 (Exod. 34:6); 1:18 (Exod. 33:20); 1:21 (Deut. 18:15, 18); 1:23 (Isa. 40:3); 1:29, 36 (Isa. 53:6–7); 1:45 (Deut. 18:15, 18); 1:49 (Ps. 2:7; 2 Sam. 7:14; Zeph. 3:15); 1:51 (Gen. 28:12); 2:5 (Gen. 41:55); 2:17 (Ps. 69:9a); 3:5 (Ezek. 36:25–27); 3:8 (Eccl. 11:5); 3:13 (Prov. 30:4); 3:14 (Num. 21:9; Isa. 52:13); 3:16 (Gen. 22:2, 12, 16); 3:28 (Mal. 3:1); 4:5

Matthew – John's explicit allusions to the Old Testament number around 27, while Matthew's total 124. Yet John is just as adamant to situate Jesus within the story of Israel but does so through a cornucopia of types rather than always promise–fulfilment vocabulary. Hays says it this way: *'If Luke is the master of the deft, fleeting allusion, John is the master of the carefully framed, luminous image that shines brilliantly against a dark canvas and lingers in the imagination.'*[2] There is a larger reason for this: 'For John, the story of Israel has no independent significance; it finds a place in John's narrative as the symbolic matrix for his portrayal of Jesus.' Rather than an explicit promise–fulfilment approach (like in Matthew's Gospel), John *'summons the reader to recognize the way in which Israel's Scripture has always been mysteriously suffused with the presence of Jesus*, the figure who steps clearly into the light in the Gospel narrative'.[3]

In this chapter, John's approach will be explored but for the purpose of understanding further how such a fulfilment motif sheds light on Jesus and the Evangelists' understanding of the Scriptures. The choice of passages adumbrated will be selective for two reasons: I do not want to trespass into chapter 5 where we will explore the covenant obedience of Christ in John, nor chapter 6 where the divine identity of Christ in John is elaborated at length. Nevertheless, once the fulfilment motif is established, we will conclude this chapter by asking and answering an eschatological question: did Jesus and the church adopt the canon or did the canon give birth to Jesus and his church?

(note 1 *cont.*) (Gen. 33:19; 48:22; Exod. 13:19; Josh. 24:32); 4:10 (Num. 20:8–11; cf. 21:16–18); 4:14 (Isa. 12:3; Jer. 2:13); 4:20 (Deut. 11:29; 12:5–14; 27:12; Josh. 8:33; Ps. 122:1–5); 4:22 (Isa. 2:3); 4:36 (Amos 9:13); 4:37 (Mic. 6:15); 5:27 (Dan. 7:13); 5:29 (Dan. 12:2); 5:45 (Deut. 31:26–27); 5:46 (Deut. 18:15, 18); 6:14 (Deut. 18:15, 18); 6:29 (Mal. 3:1); 6:31 (Ps. 78:24b); 6:45 (Isa. 54:13a); 7:22 (Gen. 17:10–13; Lev. 12:3); 7:24 (Lev. 19:15); 7:40 (Deut. 18:15, 18); 7:42 (2 Sam. 7:12; Ps. 89:3–4; Mic. 5:2); 7:51 (Deut. 1:16–17; 17:4; 19:18); 7:58 (Neh. 9:15, 19–20; cf. Num. 20:11; etc.; Ps. 77:16, 20 LXX; Isa. 58:11; Zech. 14:8); 8:12 (Isa. 9:1–2; cf. 49:6); 8:15 (1 Sam. 16:7); 8:17 (Deut. 17:6; 19:15); 8:28 (Isa. 52:13); 8:35 (Gen. 21:1–21); 8:44 (Gen. 3:4; cf. 2:17; Isa. 14:12); 9:2 (Exod. 20:5; Ezek. 18:20); 9:5 [= 8:12] (Isa. 9:1–2; cf. 49:6); 9:24 (Josh. 7:19); 9:34 (Ps. 51:5); 10:3–4 (Num. 27:15–18); 10:8 (Jer. 23:1–2; Ezek. 34:2–3);10:16 (Isa. 56:8; Ezek. 34:23; 37:24); 10:33 (Lev. 24:16); 10:34 (Ps. 82:6a); 12:8 (Deut. 15:11); 12:13 (Ps. 118:26a); 12:15 (Zech. 9:9); 12:27 (Pss 6:3; 42:5, 11); 12:32 (Isa. 52:13); 12:34 (Ps. 89:4, 36–37); 12:38 (Isa. 53:1); 12:40 (Isa. 6:10); 12:41 (Isa. 6:1); 13:18 (Ps. 41:9b); 15:1 (Isa. 5:1–7; cf. Jer. 2:21); 15:25 (Pss 35:19; 69:4); 16:22 (Isa. 66:14); 16:32 (Zech. 13:7); 17:12 (Ps. 41:9); 19:7 (Lev. 24:16); 19:18 (Isa. 22:16; cf. 52:13); 19:24 (Ps. 22:18); 19:28–29 (Ps. 69:21; cf. 22:15); 19:31 (Deut. 21:22–23); 19:36 (Exod. 12:46; Num. 9:12; Ps. 34:20); 19:37 (Zech. 12:10); 19:38 (Isa. 53:9); 20:22 (Gen. 2:7); 20:23 (Isa. 22:22).

[2] Hays 2016: 284. Emphasis original. Luke totals 109 OT references; Mark, 70. Hays's point is not an absolute. As we will see at the end of this chapter, John does use 'fulfilment' language in John 19 to quote the psalms directly.

[3] Ibid. 289. Emphasis original.

The supreme self-disclosure of God: the Word became flesh (John 1:1–34)

John's Gospel does not begin with a human genealogy, as does Matthew's (i.e. Abrahamic), but with a divine genealogy. Jesus is the Word who not only was *with* God in the beginning but *was* God (John 1:1). John's strong attestation to the divinity of this Word will be explored further in chapter 6. Here we need instead to draw attention to the way this Word relates to the revelation of God.

'Word' is chosen by John because it captures Jesus as *revelation personified*. In other words, as the Word, Jesus is the 'ultimate self-disclosure' of God.[4] '*Logos*', says Geerhardus Vos, 'means both reason and word, owing to the fine Hellenic perception, that the two processes of thinking and speaking are intimately related, thinking being a sort of inward speech, speaking a sort of outward thought.' What does this entail when applied to Jesus? 'The *Logos* is, therefore, the outward Revealer of the inward mind of God.'[5]

Jesus himself makes this claim throughout John's Gospel, but Jesus does not mean, nor does John, that he is but one more in a long line of prophets who speak the word of God to the people of God. Jesus certainly is a prophet, as well as a priest and king, but is unlike the prophets that preceded him. In his case, God does not use a human intercessory agent: the Son of God himself became flesh. The one who 'was with God' and 'was God' has spoken *as a man*. Divinity itself has tabernacled with God's people to speak to them *directly*. Revelation himself has become incarnate: the Word has descended to men but as a man himself. Since Jesus is the Word who not only was 'with God' but who 'was God', Jesus

> disclosed God through what He was; His nature, His character were God-revealing; ultimately this involves and postulates His being divine in His nature, His being God. On the other hand Jesus also revealed God through the speech He brought from God, through the words He spoke.[6]

---

[4] Carson 1991: 114.
[5] Vos 1948: 345.
[6] Ibid. 346.

Labelling Jesus the Word assumes continuity with the Old Testament – he is, after all, the climactic speech of God in a long history of God's speech to Israel; he is the definitive Word that proves God's covenant word is true. In the Old Testament it is God's word that creates, reveals and redeems.[7] 'God's "Word" in the Old Testament', says Carson, 'is his powerful self-expression in creation, revelation and salvation, and the personification of that "Word" makes it suitable for John to apply it as a title to God's ultimate self-disclosure, the person of his own Son.'[8] As seen in chapter 2, divine revelation brings redemption and redemption only furthers divine revelation. What is so remarkable about Jesus' being the Word is not only that he is the *personal* agent of *creation* – 'All things were made through him, and without him was not any thing made that was made' (John 1:3) – but God's *revelation* and *redemption* are embodied in this one person, this God-man. 'In him was life, and the life was the light of men' (John 1:4). As will be seen as we progress through John's Gospel, the words of this Word are redemptive in nature, offering life to all who will hear them. That is because this Word is himself the redemption of Israel. His words not only offer life, but as the Word he is life.

However, labelling Jesus the Word also insinuates discontinuity, setting Jesus apart from how 'word' is used in the Old Testament. 'Both psalmists and prophets portray God's word in close-to-personified terms (Ps. 33:6; 107:20; 147:15, 18; Isa. 55:10–11),' says Köstenberger, 'but only John claims that this word has appeared in space-time history as an actual person, Jesus Christ (1:14, 17).'[9] John does depict, however, the efficacy of the Word in the Old Testament in him who is the Word. Just as the word is sent out by God not to return void (Isa. 55:11), so is the Word, the Son, sent by the Father to a world in need of saving.[10] His mission will be effective.

Unprecedented as well is the medium through which this sending will occur, namely human 'flesh', to use John's vocabulary. Although this Word was with God and was God, this 'Word became flesh and dwelt among us' (1:14). Here is the miracle of the incarnation. John's use of *eskēnōsen* – 'dwelt' (ESV, NASB) or 'dwelling' (NIV) – has been understood by some as

---

[7] For a helpful summary of the word's activity in creation, revelation and redemption, see Carson 1991: 115.

[8] Ibid. 116.

[9] Köstenberger 2007: 421.

[10] Ibid.

pitching a tent. John means to picture the tabernacle and temple, where God's holy presence descended to dwell with his covenant people: 'And let them make me a sanctuary, that I may dwell in their midst' (Exod. 25:8).[11] Nevertheless, in the Old Testament the inner sanctuary of God's dwelling place could be entered only by the priest, and even then under strict instructions, lest God's transcendent holiness be polluted by human hands. How shocking, then, that John can say the 'Word was made flesh and dwelt among us.' God now tabernacles among his people *as one of his people*. The Glory of Israel, which no man can see and stay alive, has now been seen in the form of a man (John 1:14).[12] Never has the revelation of God been so personal and so direct.

The purpose of this incarnate mission is to dispense grace (the 'Word' is said to be 'full of grace and truth'; 1:14). 'For the law was given through Moses; grace and truth came through Jesus Christ' (1:17). John's opening may seem radically different from those in the Synoptics, but John quickly transitions to the history of Israel that defines the Christ of the Synoptics. Already John is approaching the fulfilment theme in 1:14 and 17, but does so in a unique way, namely through the history of redemption. John will present Jesus as greater than Abraham (8:53), Jacob (4:12) and Moses (5:46–47; 9:28), but at the start of his Gospel John positions Jesus as the culmination of these types. He is the revelation to fulfil all prior revelations. Instead of Paul's law–grace contrast, John's point is to announce Jesus as the 'climactic eschatological revelation of God's covenant love and faithfulness'.[13] Calling the Word 'grace and truth' is John's way of saying 'that this covenant faithfulness found ultimate expression in the sending of God's one-of-a-kind Son (1:14, 18)', his only begotten Son.[14] John is setting Jesus up as the new Moses, enacting a new prophetic era in which the grace Moses longed for is now distributed to all God's people (Num. 11:29).

When John the baptizer enters John's stage and is asked by the Jerusalem priests and Levites who he is, the response given indicates that the fulfilment of the Scriptures (Scriptures these religious leaders know so well) is now at hand. 'I am not the Christ,' says John; nor is he Elijah or the Prophet (1:20–21). 'I am the voice of one crying out in the wilderness,

---

[11] On the development of this language across the OT, see Exod. 33:9; 40:34–35; 2 Sam. 7:6; Pss 15:1; 26:8; 27:4–6; 43:3; 74:7; 84:1; Ezek. 37:27–28; Köstenberger 2007: 421.

[12] Chapter 6 will address the latter half of v. 14, which speaks of the Son's being from the Father.

[13] Köstenberger 2007: 423.

[14] Ibid. 422. I believe 'begotten' is more faithful to the context. See Irons (2017): 98–116.

"Make straight the way of the Lord", as the prophet Isaiah said' (1:23). John is quoting Isaiah 40:3, clarifying that he is not the promised Messiah or the Lord, but is the one who clears the path for the Christ that the prophets promised would bring salvation and redemption to Israel.

As seen already, Isaiah is a favourite among the synoptic authors, and they turn to him repeatedly to explicate the fulfilment the Christ brings to Israel and her Scriptures. John is no exception. When Isaiah 40:3 is read in context, one can see why this passage in particular is appropriate. The same voice that cries out to prepare the way of the Lord says that the

> glory of the LORD shall be revealed,
>   and all flesh shall see it together,
>   for the mouth of the LORD has spoken.
> (Isa. 40:5)

The revealed glory this voice in the wilderness references is not unfamiliar to John, who writes, 'And the Word was made flesh, and dwelt among us, (and *we beheld his glory*, the glory as of the only begotten of the Father,) full of grace and truth' (1:14, KJV; emphasis added). When Jesus performs his first miracle in Galilee, turning water to wine, John says Jesus 'manifested his glory' and 'his disciples believed' (John 2:11). As he approaches the cross, Jesus himself will refer to this revealed glory as well (e.g. 11:40; 12:41–43; 17:5, 22, 24). Jesus will not only refer to the glory he had with the Father before the world existed (17:5), but to the glory he received from the Father, which he has also given to his disciples (17:22). His desire is Godward in the greatest sense of the word: 'Father, I desire that they also, whom you have given me, may be with me where I am, to see my glory that you have given me because you loved me before the foundation of the world' (17:24).

Yet one must not forget that in John's Gospel the glory of the Christ is the glory of *the Word*. This Word imagery also fits within the context of Isaiah 40. For not only does this wilderness voice cry out that the 'glory of the LORD shall be revealed' (40:5) but this voice also says that the word of God is established for all eternity.

> The grass withers, the flower fades,
>   but the word of our God will stand for ever.
> (40:8)

While Isaiah is not using 'word' here as John does, giving 'word' personal attributes and identity, nevertheless the escalation is detectable. The voice in the wilderness prepares the way for the Lord, that his glory may be revealed, and does so on the basis that the word of God will stand for ever. John opens his Gospel by declaring that this glory has been revealed by the Word's becoming flesh (1:14), which is unprecedented since this Word has an eternal identity not only with God but as God (John 1:1).

Yet again, John transitions with ease between the metaphysics of Christology and the mission of this Word in the history of Israel. John the baptizer sees himself bringing to fulfilment the role Isaiah typologically assigned to him, making straight the way of the Lord (1:23), which is explicit the moment Jesus approaches John for baptism. Told by God that this is the Christ (1:31), John identifies Jesus as the 'Lamb of God, who takes away the sin of the world!' (1:30). For both John the Evangelist and John the Baptist, the arrival of Jesus is the inauguration of salvation for the nations, just as God first promised to Abraham.

'Lamb' imagery is deeply embedded in Israel's heritage. If John the Baptist was aware of Isaiah 40:3 as he circumscribed his own identity, he was aware of Isaiah 53:7 in his attestation to Jesus' identity:

> He was oppressed, and he was afflicted,
>   yet he opened not his mouth;
> like a lamb that is led to the slaughter,
>   and like a sheep that before its shearers is silent,
>   so he opened not his mouth.

Isaiah 53:7 is the text being read by the Ethiopian eunuch when Philip arrives and identifies Christ as the one Isaiah has in view (Acts 8:30–35). Isaiah's lamb, John's readers will soon discover, will go to the cross but will not protest: he will be slaughtered in silence.

Yet John may also have in mind Exodus 12, where the imagery of the Passover Lamb fits John's own portrait of Jesus:

> Tell the congregation of Israel that on the tenth day of this month every man shall take a lamb according to their fathers' houses, a lamb for a household . . . Your lamb shall be without blemish, a male a year old. You may take it from the sheep or from the goats, and you shall keep it until the fourteenth day of this month, when the

whole assembly of the congregation of Israel shall kill their lambs at twilight.
(Exod. 12:3, 5–6)

That John the Evangelist chooses to mention this exclamation concerning the 'lamb of God' with Exodus 12 in mind is not a stretch since he will conclude his Gospel by highlighting the fact that none of Jesus' bones were broken, just like the Passover lamb (John 19:33). Quoting Exodus 12:46, he comments, 'For these things took place that the Scripture might be fulfilled: "Not one of his bones will be broken"' (19:36).

In sum, the antitype foreshadowed by the type has come, and though this lamb has yet to be slaughtered, already John announces salvation to Israel and the world by means of this lamb's blood. He is the sacrificial, substitutionary, Passover lamb, whose death will secure the forgiveness of sins.[15] But as we will find out later, John will return to this 'lamb' language to say Jesus is also the shepherd who lays down his life for the sheep (John 10:15). Lamb or shepherd, the point is that the Old Testament typology of the substitutionary sacrifice is a song that crescendos the closer the reader approaches the cross.

It is within this Johannine introduction that Jesus begins his ministry and does so as one who fully believes the Scriptures are being fulfilled in his own ministry.

We have found him: Son of God, Son of Man (John 1:43–51)

The fulfilment theme introduced so far continues when Jesus calls his first disciples. Philip runs to find Nathanael because he is convinced this Jesus is the one the Scriptures said would come to redeem Israel: 'We have found him of whom *Moses in the Law and also the prophets wrote*, Jesus of Nazareth, the son of Joseph' (1:45; emphasis added). Philip's excitement reveals the anticipation so many Jews in his day felt as they read the Scriptures. What sets Philip apart is his conviction that the Messiah, whom the Law of Moses and the Prophets – a larger category broad enough to include both former and latter prophets, whether they be Samuel or David – prophesied about, had arrived in Jesus of Nazareth. While

---

[15] On the substitutionary nature of this lamb's sacrifice, see Morris 1995: 130.

Philip does not identify specific passages, his reference to the Law of Moses could very well have in mind a passage like Deuteronomy 18, where Yahweh promises that he will raise up a prophet like Moses: one in whom Yahweh has implanted his words (18:15, 18). If so, Philip's hope will be confirmed when Jesus says Moses 'wrote of me' (5:46).

Philip's reference to the prophets could include an array of prophetic passages. Carson and Köstenberger, for example, wonder whether the prophet Isaiah could be in view (Isa. 9:1–7; 11:1–5, 10–12; 52:13 – 53:12).[16] They may be right; after all, in Acts 8:32–35 Philip clarifies for the Ethiopian that the passage he is reading, Isaiah 53:7–8, has been fulfilled in Jesus.

Philip assumes that these prophecies awaiting fulfilment are not dead artefacts of a superstitious age dependent on a written testimony that is mythological, due to the primitive perspectives of their ancestors. Rather, Philip is looking for their fulfilment and with anticipation because he believes God himself spoke through the Law and the Prophets. Their words and writings are *living* in the sense that what God declared through them will be brought to fulfilment at the divinely appointed time. 'That is the stance', says Carson,

> of the entire Gospel: Jesus fulfils the Old Testament Scriptures (*cf.* 5:39). The earliest disciples could not have identified Jesus as the promised Coming One, the Messiah, without believing that the Scriptures pointed to him, for that was part of the common stock of Jewish messianic hope.[17]

Furthermore, the Scriptures Philip relies on for his messianic hope reflect the God who has authored them, so much so that Philip can make what must have been the most radical statement a Jew in Israel could ever make: 'The Messiah the Scriptures promised is right here!' Such a claim would have been dismissed as originating from someone who had lost his mind; even if paid attention to by the religious leaders, such a claim would have invited scorn due to its deeply theological, even political, motive.

In contrast to Philip, however, Nathanael doubts. Yet when he meets Jesus and Jesus tells him that he saw him under the fig tree even before Philip called him (an impossible feat for someone who is not Israel's

---

16 Carson 1991: 159; Köstenberger 2007: 429.
17 Carson 1991: 159.

Messiah), Nathanael becomes just as much, if not more, radical with his words than Philip: 'Rabbi, you are the Son of God! You are the King of Israel!' (1:49). Nathanael's exclamation is the first of many others in John's Gospel. For example, Martha will confess, 'Yes, Lord; I believe that you are the Christ, the Son of God, who is coming into the world' (John 11:27).[18] The title Son of God serves as bookends to John's Gospel as a whole: while Nathanael begins John's Gospel with this title, John will conclude his Gospel with it when he outlines the purpose for which he wrote:

> Now Jesus did many other signs in the presence of the disciples, which are not written in this book; but these are written so that you may believe that Jesus is the Christ, the Son of God, and that believing you may have life in his name.
> (20:30–31)[19]

Son of God

The title 'Son of God' is prolific across the Old and New Testament.[20] It is used in the Old Testament to refer to a variety of human beings, but for our purposes its use of the Davidic king matters most. As seen in chapter 2, in 2 Samuel 7 God promises that David's son will be God's son; through him he will establish a for-ever kingdom and cut an everlasting covenant (7:14). Or consider Psalm 2, the installation of the Davidic king. Here the Davidic king is anointed and crowned by God, who chooses to portray this event in sonship language:

> As for me, I have set my King
>   on Zion, my holy hill.
> I will tell of the decree:
> The LORD said to me, 'You are my Son;
>   today I have begotten you.'
> (Ps. 2:6–7)

---

[18] Also, John the Baptist will exclaim after baptizing Jesus, 'I have seen and have borne witness that this is the Son of God' (John 1:34).

[19] In Matthew's Gospel the same confession appears, but from Peter: 'You are the Christ, the Son of the living God' (Matt. 16:16). Also note Satan's temptation of Jesus in Matt. 4:3: 'If you are the Son of God, command these stones to become loaves of bread.'

[20] Matt. 14:33; 17:5; Mark 9:7; Luke 1:35; 9:35; John 3:36; 5:23; 14:13; Acts 9:20; Rom. 5:10; 8:29; 1 Cor. 1:9; Gal. 4:4–6; Col. 1:13–14; 1 Thess. 1:10; Heb. 1:2; 4:14; 7:28; 1 John 1:3; 1:7; 5:11; Rev. 2:18; etc.

Both 2 Samuel 7 and Psalm 2 situate sonship in royal categories: the Davidic king may be David's son, but he is also God's son, representing God's rule to his people and the nations, as seen in Psalm 2:8–12, when God gives the nations to his kingly son as his heritage. 2 Samuel 7 ensures that this heritage will be one of peace, with God's kingly son sitting on the throne, reigning over an everlasting kingdom in covenant concord:

> When a Davidide assumes the throne, he does so under God's kingship. The reign of the Davidic king is meant to reflect God's reign, including his passion for justice, his commitment to the covenant, his hatred of idolatry, and his concern for the oppressed.[21]

Therefore, says Carson,

> the peacemaker may be called the son of God because he enters into the identity of the supreme Peacemaker, God himself. Similarly, the Davidic monarch is called the son of God because he enters into the identity of the supreme Monarch, God himself.[22]

In that light, when the title is applied to Jesus, it takes on these royal, sonship connotations and more. This is the case in John 1:49 when Nathanael couples 'Son of God' with 'King of Israel' as if the two are synonymous. By using these titles Nathanael confesses Jesus to be Israel's Christ, but as Christ he is God's royal Son.[23] In their immediate context, 2 Samuel 7 has Solomon in view and although Psalm 2 does not list an author, Acts 4:25 says David is its speaker. Nevertheless, both 2 Samuel 7 and Psalm 2 escalate in their typological fulfilment, which is why the New Testament will reference or allude to both as if they speak of Christ himself (for 2 Sam. 7, see Luke 1:32–33, 69–70; Acts 4:30–31; for Ps. 2, see Matt. 3:17; 17:5; Acts 4:25–27; 13:33; Rom. 1:4; Heb. 1:5; 5:5).

Promised and foreshadowed through the typology of David's kingship was the hope of a superior Davidic king, David's greater son; indeed, God's Son, who will establish the eternal covenant God made with David (2 Sam. 7:14).

---

[21] Carson 2012: 32.
[22] Ibid.
[23] Köstenberger 2007: 429; Barrett 1978: 186; Ridderbos 1997: 91.

He is the Lord's 'Anointed' (Ps. 2:2), the 'King' Yahweh has set in Zion (Ps. 2:6). This is why Mary is told by the angel that the child conceived in her womb

> will be great and will be called the Son of the Most High. And the Lord God will give to him the throne of his father David, and he will reign over the house of Jacob for ever, and of his kingdom there will be no end.
> (Luke 1:32–33)

It is also why Zechariah is characterized by a similar response to that of Nathanael – but one that echoes 2 Samuel 7, Psalm 2 and the prophets – when the old man's mouth is opened by the Lord:

> Blessed be the Lord God of Israel,
>   for he has visited and redeemed his people
> and has raised up a horn of salvation for us
>   in the house of his servant David,
> as he spoke by the mouth of his holy prophets from of old,
> that we should be saved from our enemies
>   and from the hand of all who hate us.
> (Luke 1:68–71)[24]

What prophets could Zechariah have in mind? What prophets reiterate that David's greater son will for ever establish God's covenant and kingdom and reign as God's begotten son? We need not revisit chapter 2 here, but it should be recalled that Isaiah, Ezekiel and Jeremiah all speak of this greater Davidic king as God's son, either by direct prophecy or, more often than not, by typology.

Isaiah 9, for example, refers to a child who will be born:

> Of the increase of his government and of peace
>   there will be no end,
> on the throne of David and over his kingdom,
>   to establish it and to uphold it

---

24 One should also notice how Zechariah goes on in v. 72 to say the salvation that comes through David's house is in fulfilment of the covenant promises God made with Abraham.

with justice and with righteousness
    from this time forth and for evermore.
(9:7)

Luke 2:1 will refer to Jesus as this child who sits on David's throne. Later Isaiah promises 'There shall come forth a shoot from the stump of Jesse, / and a branch from his roots shall bear fruit' (11:1), one on whom the Spirit rests (cf. Isa. 61:1–2 and Luke 4:18–19), one who judges with righteousness (11:2–5). Through him God's 'everlasting covenant' and 'steadfast, sure love for David' is exhibited (Isa. 55:3–4; cf. 54:10; Ps. 18:50).

Jeremiah too will refer to a 'righteous Branch' whom God will 'raise up for David', one who will 'reign as king and deal wisely, and shall execute justice and righteousness in the land' (Jer. 23:5). His name will be 'The LORD is our righteousness' (23:6; cf. 33:14–18), a shepherd, like David, who leads God's sheep in the way of the covenant (23:1–4). Ezekiel will speak of a Davidic shepherd in that same vein. God will summon his sheep from the nations and have them lie down in peace under 'one shepherd, my servant David' (34:23).[25]

The list of prophets could continue, but the point is, whether it be Nathanael or Zechariah, to be the 'Son of God' is to be David's greater son, the Messiah who comes to his people announcing his kingdom is at hand.

However, in John's Gospel Son of God not only identifies Jesus as Israel's Messiah and Davidic king, but also goes beyond the history of Israel into eternity. In other words, John uses the title to convey that this messianic king is also the eternal Son from the Father. As will be seen in chapter 6 with passages like John 5, this king is also 'my Son' who is 'begotten' so that the nations will bow in homage (Ps. 2:7, 12). As will be argued there, it is his eternal sonship that grounds his messianic, kingly mission. Such is the diversity of Son of God language.

In John 1:49 it seems Nathanael uses the title primarily to convey Jesus' messianic, Davidic kingship; nevertheless, it is possible John intends the title to start transcending mere kingship since Nathanael's praise is in response to the miraculous omniscience of Jesus. This will be a pattern in John's Gospel, as seen in John 4 when Jesus, never having met her before, reveals his knowledge of the Samaritan woman's private life. Her response will be similar to Philip's and Nathanael's.

---

[25] For a more extensive exploration of these connections, see Carson 2012: 36–38.

Jacob's ladder (Gen. 28)

Now that Nathanael believes, Jesus returns to the 'glory' he has come to reveal:

> 'Because I said to you, "I saw you under the fig tree", do you believe? You will see greater things than these.' And he said to him, 'Truly, truly, I say to you, you will see heaven opened, and the angels of God ascending and descending on the Son of Man.'
> (John 1:50–51)

Jesus takes the reader back to Jacob, who is later given the name Israel, and to his dream (vision) in particular, where a ladder from the heavens reaches the earth as angels ascend and descend on Jacob-Israel (Gen. 28:12). These angels were a sign to Jacob that Yahweh would carry on his covenant promises to Abraham through Jacob.[26] Now, however, angels ascend and descend on Jesus, the Son of Man, Abraham's (and Israel's) true Son and final heir.[27] 'What the disciples are promised, then, is heaven-sent confirmation that the one they have acknowledged as the Messiah has been appointed by God.'[28] As the Son of Man, Jesus is the new Israel, the true Israel, the one through whom Yahweh has made himself known. 'Jesus is', says Klink, 'Heaven open.' 'What is unique about Jesus is not only his sonship or that he is God or intimate with the Father, but also that he provides for some to "see" God,' a point Jesus explicitly makes in John 14:9. The way to the Father and to heaven is through Jesus, the Word from God and the Word who is God. 'Jacob saw a vision; the disciples saw the Word-become-flesh.'[29] What Jacob could see only dimly in that which was typologically pictured, the disciples now see with crystal clarity. Who Jesus is and what he has come to accomplish was foreshadowed in Israel's Scripture (hence John's reference to the Law of Moses and the Prophets) but now has been revealed in the one who is revelation itself, the Word who has descended from heaven to earth to bring God's covenant promises to Abraham to fulfilment.

If one finishes Genesis 28, one will also discover that when Jacob wakes up he is so overflowing with excitement over this confirmation of God's covenant blessing and presence that he says, 'Surely the LORD is in this place,

---

[26] Köstenberger (2007: 429) calls this Yahweh's 'reaffirmation'.

[27] Köstenberger (ibid.) argues that the proper translation should be 'on him'. On the meaning of the title 'Son of Man', see Carson 1991: 164–165.

[28] Carson 1991: 163–164.

[29] Klink and Lockett 2016: 154.

and I did not know it . . . How awesome is this place! This is none other than the house of God, and this is the gate of heaven' (28:16–17). He names the place Bethel the next morning (28:19), which means 'house of God'. When the angels ascend and descend on Jesus, he is the new Jacob, the new Israel, and the *new Bethel*, the very location of God's presence, and the fullest manifestation of God's revelation.[30] As will soon be seen, this is news the Samaritan woman will receive unexpectedly when she attempts to set Jesus over against 'our father Jacob' (4:12). While she clings to Jacob's well for water, Jesus will announce that one greater than Jacob stands in front of her, one who gives living water (4:13). The revelation Jacob receives is but a small picture of the revelation Israel receives in him whom John calls the Word.

Son of Man

Last, the promise Jesus makes to Nathanael that he will see 'greater things than these' (1:50) is not unrelated to Jesus' self-designation as the 'Son of Man' (John 1:51). Son of Man is a title that takes John's readers back to Daniel 7:13–14, where 'one like a son of man' is featured and prophesied about:

I saw in the night visions,

> and behold, with the clouds of heaven
>> there came one like a son of man,
> and he came to the Ancient of Days
>> and was presented before him.
> And to him was given dominion
>> and glory and a kingdom,
> that all the peoples, nations, and languages
>> should serve him;
> his dominion is an everlasting dominion,
>> which shall not pass away,
> and his kingdom one
>> that shall not be destroyed.

(Dan. 7:13–14)

---

[30] 'Correspondingly, Jesus' message to Nathanael and the other disciples is that he himself will be the place of much greater divine revelation than that given at previous occasions (cf. Heb. 1:1–3).' Köstenberger 2007: 430, who builds on the works of Carson 1991: 163–164; Witherington 1995: 72; Burge 2000: 79; Borchert 1996: 149; Schnackenburg 1990: 1.320; Ridderbos 1997: 93–94.

With overtones of Daniel 7, this title 'Son of Man' is used in John and the Synoptics, and sometimes in ways that build on John 1:50–51. For example, in Matthew 26:63 the high priest puts Jesus on trial and demands to know if he is 'the Christ, the Son of God', to which Jesus responds, 'You have said so. But I tell you, from now on you will see the *Son of Man* seated at the right hand of Power and coming on the clouds of heaven' (26:64; emphasis added). In the vein of Daniel 7 Jesus pictures the Son of Man as an eschatological, heavenly figure, one who will descend from the heavens with the authority of God himself. Jesus' statement is so offensive because he applies Son of Man to himself, insinuating that he is the one who will descend from the 'right hand of Power' to judge the living and the dead, and to establish God's for-ever dynasty of peace.

However, that end-time reality has already been ushered into the present. Jesus shows himself to be the Son of Man from heaven by casting out demons, exhibiting his victory over the evil powers and by performing a multitude of signs and wonders (e.g. Matt. 4:24). But in John's Gospel, this Son of Man will finally bring the glory of heaven to earth when he is lifted up on the cross.[31] 'No one has ascended into heaven except he who descended from heaven, the Son of Man. And as Moses lifted up the serpent in the wilderness, so must the Son of Man be lifted up' (John 3:13–14). As much as the Son of Man's eschatological work is not yet, it is already inaugurated in Jesus' miracles and crucifixion and will be confirmed once for all in his victorious resurrection and ascension to his heavenly throne, where he will reign as the one who has defeated death and established the 'everlasting dominion' of God's kingdom (Dan. 7:14). As will soon be seen, John uses Daniel's 'Son of Man' title (Dan. 7:13) and the ascending-descending imagery (John 3:13) to push the title beyond Daniel: as the Son of Man who descends from heaven, Jesus is the revelation of God incarnate. He is, in other words, the Revealer come down from heaven, the Word made flesh (John 1:14) who reveals 'heavenly things' (John 3:12).[32]

There is, then, a certain elasticity to the title: it was 'sufficiently malleable to allow Jesus to define its content in Christological terms'.[33] John 1:50–51

---

[31] Köstenberger 2007: 430.

[32] Hays (2016: 333) qualifies, with John 1:51 in mind, that 'the Son of Man is not himself the figure who moves between the two realms; rather, the angels are the heavenly messengers, while Jesus is the intermediary figure who makes the connection possible'. True enough, as long as we recognize that the only way Jesus can be this intermediary (and stationary) figure is *if he has first descended from heaven*.

[33] Köstenberger 2007: 430.

is the first use of the title, and sets the rest of John's narrative within the context of typological fulfilment.

The serpent in the wilderness: John 3

That Jesus is who Nathanael thinks he is will be confirmed for John's readers in John 3 when a 'man of the Pharisees' and a 'ruler of the Jews' named Nicodemus approaches Jesus. Nicodemus saw the signs and wonders and confesses that Jesus must be a 'teacher come from God' (3:2). Nevertheless, he comes to Jesus at night, likely because he fears the judgment of his fellow Pharisees.

In response to Nicodemus's recognition that Jesus could not do such signs 'unless God is with him' (3:2), Jesus turns to the metaphor of birth to convey to Nicodemus that one must be 'born again' to enter the kingdom of God (3:3). Nicodemus takes Jesus literally, 'How can a man be born when he is old? Can he enter a second time into his mother's womb and be born?' (3:4), failing to perceive that Jesus is using birth to picture a spiritual reality. The response Jesus gives communicates to Nicodemus that the birth Jesus has in mind is not one of human origin but one from the Spirit:

> Truly, truly, I say to you, unless one is born of water and the Spirit, he cannot enter the kingdom of God. That which is born of the flesh is flesh, and that which is born of the Spirit is spirit.
> (3:5–6)

Jesus' reference to water and Spirit may allude to the prophet Ezekiel, where Yahweh promises a new covenant in which all God's covenant people will be washed within and indwelt by the Spirit. Water pictures the cleansing, renewing and regenerating work of the Spirit in this new covenant age:

> I will sprinkle clean water on you, and you shall be clean from all your uncleannesses, and from all your idols I will cleanse you. And I will give you a new heart, and a new spirit I will put within you. And I will remove the heart of stone from your flesh and give you a heart of flesh. And I will put my Spirit within you, and cause you to walk in my statutes and be careful to obey my rules.
> (Ezek. 36:25–27)

Nicodemus is to understand Ezekiel's new covenant promise as now being fulfilled in Jesus, who comes baptizing with the Holy Spirit (John 1:33). The nature of the regeneration or new birth described by Jesus (e.g. John 3:8) has been thoroughly explored elsewhere and need not detain our attention here.[34] What is striking, however, is the conversation that follows when Nicodemus remains ignorant, 'How can these things be?' (3:9), even after Jesus has explained this new birth from the Spirit.

Jesus' response to Nicodemus's ignorance and perplexity is a rebuke: 'Are you the teacher of Israel and yet you do not understand these things?' (3:10). Nicodemus was a 'ruler of the Jews' and should have known what Jesus was saying, precisely because such a teaching was not new but rooted in the Scriptures of Israel. Nicodemus's lack of understanding of 'earthly things' (like the new birth, which is basic to entering God's kingdom) will keep him from moving up to 'heavenly things' (3:12); that is, deeper realities of the kingdom.[35]

Jesus knows of such 'heavenly things' because he is the one who is from heaven. He is the Word from heaven who *reveals* heavenly things.[36] As the one who has come down from his heavenly home, his authority is unmatched. 'No one has ascended into heaven except he who descended from heaven, the Son of Man' (3:13). Whereas previously Jesus was described as 'Son of God' (1:34), now Jesus uses 'Son of Man' to describe his heavenly identity. Like John 1:51, Jacob's ladder (Gen. 28) and Daniel's son of man vision (Dan. 7) may be echoed in 3:13; however, this time it is not angels who descend and ascend on the Son of Man but Jesus himself is said to ascend and descend from heaven. The reason why Jesus, the Son of Man, has descended from heaven is conveyed typologically: 'And as Moses lifted up the serpent in the wilderness, so must the Son of Man be lifted up [*hypsōthēnai*], that whoever believes in him may have eternal life' (3:14–15). The Son of Man has descended from the heavenlies to ascend to the cross before he finally ascends back into heaven, all for the purpose of securing salvation and granting eternal life to all who believe (cf. 3:36).

For John, this mission concerning eternal life is connected to Jesus' identity as the Word (of truth: John 1:14; 3:33). As John the Baptist says later on, Jesus the Christ 'comes from above' (3:31) to bear witness to 'what he has seen and heard' (3:32), a statement that echoes what Jesus said in

---

[34] For an extended treatment of this passage and the nature of regeneration, see Barrett 2013.
[35] Carson 1991: 199.
[36] Note a similar point from John the Baptist in John 3:31–32.

3:12–13. He who believes in Jesus' testimony 'sets his seal to this, that God is true' (3:33). 'For he whom God has sent utters the words of God, for he gives the Spirit without measure' (3:34; cf. Isa. 11:2; 42:1; 61:1). Therefore, belief in the Son means eternal life, while rejection of Jesus' true testimony as the Word results in death and wrath (3:36).

For the present purposes, 3:14 has particular relevance, for there Jesus ties his future suffering ('lifted up') to the snake in the desert, a type loaded with Christological import. The reference, Numbers 21:9, is infamous. When Israel left Mount Hor and travelled by way of the Red Sea, the people 'became impatient on the way' and 'spoke against God and against Moses', saying, 'Why have you brought us up out of Egypt to die in the wilderness? For there is no food and no water, and we loathe this worthless food' (21:4–5). Here is a shocking complaint to make against the God who not only delivered this people from endless years of slavery in Egypt but provided (apparently 'worthless') food to a people who would otherwise starve, guaranteeing that better food awaited them ('milk and honey'; Exod. 3:17) in the land he promised to their father Abraham.

While Israel is shaking her fist in the air at Yahweh, 'the LORD sent fiery serpents among the people, and they bit the people, so that many people of Israel died' (21:6). Confessing their lack of humility ('We have sinned, for we have spoken against the LORD and against you'; 21:7), the people beg Moses to pray to the Lord to do away with these lethal snakes. Merciful and gracious, the Lord does so but only through a mediating symbol that is an image of the curse itself. 'Make a fiery serpent', the Lord says to Moses, 'and set it on a pole, and everyone who is bitten, when he sees it, shall live' (21:8). All those who have faith and look to the bronze serpent are healed and live.

Jesus' use of the snake imagery in Numbers 21 is labelled by Carson as 'theological adaptation of the literal ("to lift up") and the figurative ("to enhance") meanings of the verb'.[37] Theological adaptation and figurative meanings move the reader beyond mere parallels, as if Jesus were only providing his listeners with an illustration. Jesus is doing far more, indicating that the physical life restored to Israel by means of a mediator was but a small taste of the forgiveness and eternal life Jesus brings when he is 'lifted up' for transgressors. Such humiliation and suffering on the cross (i.e. 'lifted up') will be the means of Jesus' exaltation whereby he

---

[37] Carson 1991: 201.

will once again enjoy the glory he had with his Father before his incarnate state.

There is, then, a double entendre at play. Jesus will be lifted up on a cross and put to death, yet it is by means of his crucifixion that the Son of Man is also lifted up, that is, exalted and glorified, as will be further explained in John 17:1–4. By fulfilling the mission of his Father, succeeding in his humble covenant obedience (see chapter 5), Jesus glorifies his Father and his Father glorifies his Son. In the end, Jesus' death will result in a resurrection and ascension by which he is lifted up into glory to enjoy the trinitarian fellowship he had with his Father in eternity (cf. John 17:5, 24).[38]

It should be concluded, then, that the atonement itself is a type of exaltation, one that leads to the Son's exaltation from the grave. For this reason, it is likely John has Isaiah in mind, who pictures the Servant's procuring atonement for sin by means of his suffering, yet in doing so is exalted as well:

> Behold, my servant shall act wisely;
>> he shall be high and lifted up,
>> and shall be exalted.
> (52:13)

Verse 14, then, begins Isaiah's lengthy discourse on this Servant's brutal suffering for the sake of Israel's transgressions. John will pick up on Isaiah's paradoxical emphasis: the Servant who suffers death is the same Servant who is exalted; through his sufferings he achieves his exaltation.

It is not surprising John might have Numbers 21 and Isaiah 52:13 in mind, since he will allude to both again in John 12 as Jesus' focus on his coming sufferings becomes acute. There Jesus cries out in distress, 'Now is my soul troubled. And what shall I say? "Father, save me from this hour"? But for this purpose I have come to this hour. Father, glorify your name' (12:27–28). At that moment, a voice from heaven is heard, confirming that the Father has not only heard his Son but has glorified and will glorify his name (12:28). Jesus then announces that his hour has come: 'Now is the

---

[38] There is even a sense in which the Son accrues glory by fulfilling his mission. In John, 'Jesus' death is not a moment of ignominy and shame, but rather a glorious event that not only brings glory to God, Jesus' sender (12:28; 17:1, 4), and accrues glory to the Son owing to his obedience to the Father's will (12:23; 17:1), but also becomes the way by which Jesus returns to the glory that he had with the Father before the world began (17:5; cf. 17:24; see also 13:1; 16:28).' Köstenberger 2007: 436–437. On this point, also see Hays 2016: 334.

judgment of this world; now will the ruler of this world be cast out. And I, *when I am lifted up from the earth*, will draw all people to myself' (12:31–32; emphasis added). John then explains why Jesus said this: 'He said this to show by what kind of death he was going to die' (12:33). Like John 3:15, though not as elaborate, Jesus uses the imagery of Numbers 21:8 to convey how he will be lifted up on the cross as the necessary means by which sinners will be drawn to his Father. Spiritual healing and life will come only by looking up to him who is lifted up for the sins of the people. Isaiah knew this, for, as Jesus explains in John 12:41, Isaiah 'saw his glory and spoke of him' (cf. Isa. 6:1).

> It would appear that John has performed an astonishing intertextual fusion of Daniel 7:13–14, Numbers 21, and Isaiah 52:13 . . . the theological result of this fusion is explosive: it generates an interpretation of Jesus' death on a cross as the triumphant exaltation of the Son of Man.[39]

Living water from the Christ: John 4, the new Bethel and the new Israel

Jesus' encounter with the woman of Samaria at Jacob's well may be one of the most scandalous in the Gospel accounts. Jesus, a Jew, is not only stopping in Samaria (Sychar) but conversing with a Samaritan woman. The intense, sometimes ferocious, ethnic and religious animosity between Jews and Samaritans in the first century is no secret. Associating oneself could have been interpreted as ethnic or religious apostasy, or at least defilement. The woman herself recognizes this much when she questions how Jesus, a Jew, could even think to ask her, 'a woman of Samaria' for a drink (4:9). Similarly, John adds his commentary: 'For Jews have no dealings with Samaritans' (4:9). No Jew would have dared to speak to this woman, nor even approach her, as Jesus does, asking for a drink. There were many reasons for this, some religious (the place of proper worship) and others ethnic (associating with a Samaritan could result in ritual pollution).

For Jesus, however, who he is and what he has to offer supersedes any longstanding ethnic or religious barrier. 'If you knew the gift of God, and who it is that is saying to you, "Give me a drink", you would have asked

---

[39] Hays 2016: 335.

him, and he would have given you living water' (4:10). The promise of 'living water' has a rich heritage up to this point. Water equalled life in Israel's wilderness travels. At critical points in their pilgrimage, God provided water to keep his people alive in a dry wilderness (e.g. Num. 20:8–11; 21:16–18). It became, naturally, a fitting symbol for spiritual life and salvation, a symbol of eschatological hope that Israel, despite her sin and waywardness, would still drink the waters of salvation (Isa. 12:3; 49:10; 44:3; Zech. 14:8; Ezek. 47:9), and from none other than Yahweh himself, who is described as the spring of living water (Jer. 2:13).[40]

With that background in view, Jesus uses water to convey the salvation he offers. As was seen in John 3 with Nicodemus, Jesus describes the new birth in terms of water to convey the washing, cleansing power of the Spirit, echoing Ezekiel 36:25–27. Here, in John 4, he returns to the symbolism water carries since it is Jacob's well where Jesus encounters this Samaritan woman. The living water Jesus offers to this woman is not merely for physical refreshment but eternal salvation. The living water or salvation the prophets said Israel would drink in the eschaton has now gushed into the present. Yahweh, in Isaiah's day, summoned all those thirsty to come and drink of the waters he gives, waters that will pour life into the soul (Isa. 55:1–3), but Jesus announces to this woman that living water is now available in himself.[41] Forgiveness and eternal life are promised to all those who drink of him.

Both Carson and Köstenberger wonder whether this Samaritan woman 'appreciated such allusions to the Prophets, although John's Jewish readers would have done so'.[42] Remember, the Samaritans restricted their canon to the Pentateuch, which put them at odds with Jesus, who often referred to the Law *and the Prophets*. Nevertheless, even if restricted to the Pentateuch, the symbolism would have resonated, for 'even in the Samaritans' own liturgy it is said regarding the Taheb (the Samaritan equivalent to the Messiah) that "water shall flow from his buckets" (cf. Num. 24:7; see Bruce 1983: 105)'.[43]

Nonetheless, like Nicodemus, this woman can only interpret Jesus' words through the corporeal world in which she lives ('Sir, you have nothing to draw water with, and the well is deep'; 4:11). Nevertheless, 'living

---

[40] Köstenberger 2007: 438.
[41] Ibid. 438–439.
[42] Ibid. 439; cf. Carson 1991: 220.
[43] Köstenberger 2007: 438; cf. Bruce 1983: 105.

water' has her curious for obvious reasons and she seems at least to perceive something spiritual or miraculous is being referenced instead, as seen in her question 'Are you greater than our father Jacob?' (4:12). This woman is scrutinizing Jesus against the greatest father in her own heritage. After all, the two of them are at Jacob's well (John 4:6), which sat in the 'field that Jacob had given to his son Joseph' (4:5; cf. Gen. 33:18–19; 48:1–22; Josh. 24:32).

Jesus will answer this question of identity, though not yet. First, he pushes on the metaphor once more to stress the difference between what he gives and what this world gives:

> Everyone who drinks of this water will be thirsty again, but whoever drinks of the water that I will give him will never be thirsty again. The water that I will give him will become in him a spring of water welling up to eternal life.
> (4:13–14)

As water was a familiar metaphor to Ezekiel's readers, so Jesus appeals to such imagery to convey the type of life he gives to those spiritually thirsty.

Previously, Jesus introduced eternal life as the reason why he was sent by the Father (John 3:16). Jesus continues that line of thought but now uses water, which every creature needs to live, to convey that same message. Unlike the water this woman draws from the well, water that quenches thirst for a short time only, the water (life) Jesus gives is eternal (3:14). Later in John's narrative, Jesus will return to this imagery but extend his offer to the public. At the Feast of Booths, Jesus stands up and, quoting the prophet Ezekiel, cries out, 'If anyone thirsts, let him come to me and drink. Whoever believes in me, as the Scripture has said, "Out of his heart will flow rivers of living water"' (John 7:37–38; cf. Ezek. 47:1).[44]

The question that lingers for this woman, as it did for Nicodemus, is whether she can see her own need for this water of eternal life. By exposing the sinfulness of her marital life, Jesus makes her need for this water apparent. Furthermore, by revealing the array of husbands she has had, knowledge no stranger from a land foreign to Samaria could have known, Jesus also manifests his messianic identity.

---

[44] Notice too that John adds his commentary that Jesus was referring to the Spirit (7:39), which, building on Ezekiel, serves only to confirm the correspondence and synonymity between water and Spirit in John 3.

Realizing he is some kind of prophet, she defaults to a heated religious dispute between Samaritans and Jews, identifying the mountain on which the well sits as the place of her forefathers, the only appropriate place of worship. 'Our fathers worshipped on this mountain, but you say that in Jerusalem is the place where people ought to worship' (4:20). Behind this well stands Mount Gerizim. In Deuteronomy 11 God promises covenant blessings to Israel should they obey the Lord (11:26–28). One such blessing is entering into the land of promise. When the people of Israel enter the land, they are to 'set the blessing on Mount Gerizim' (11:29). On Mount Ebal, however, Israel is to set 'the curse on Mount Ebal'. In John 4 not only is Mount Gerizim hovering over Jacob's well but Mount Ebal is not far off either. In Deuteronomy 27 Moses again mentions this mountain when he tells Israel they are to write the law on stones as soon as they enter the land God is giving them (27:2–3). These stones are to be used in the construction of an altar to the Lord on Mount Ebal (27:5), and when the people see this altar they will see 'all the words of this law very plainly' (27:8). Here we are reminded of chapter 2 once again, and the inseparable identity between the covenant and God's word.

Davies refers to these mountains as a 'holy geography'; that reverence is seen when this woman, like her fellow Samaritans, argues that worship is to occur on 'this mountain' as opposed to Jerusalem.[45] Her statement could not be more inflammatory in view of recent history. In 128 BC, about a century and a half before Jesus met this Samaritan, the Jews destroyed the temple the Samaritans built on Mount Gerizim (400 BC).[46] Jerusalem, not Gerizim, was where the temple of God was to be located and where proper worship was to take place, said the Jews.

Jesus is not afraid to correct this woman where she has erred: 'You worship what you do not know; we worship what we know, for salvation is from the Jews' (4:22). In other words, the Jews are Yahweh's chosen people, to whom he has revealed his law and sent his prophets, and therefore it is through them that God's salvation (for the world) will be manifested. 'The idea', says Carson,

is that, just as the Jews stand within the stream of God's saving revelation, so also can it be said that they are the vehicle of that

---

45 Davies 1994: 298–302; cf. Köstenberger 2007: 438.
46 Köstenberger 2007: 488.

revelation, the historical matrix out of which that revelation emerges. 'In Judah God is known; his name is great in Israel' (Ps. 76:1).[47]

At the same time, Jesus moves her beyond her immediate surroundings to once again see her situation – and that of the world – through an eschatological lens. 'Woman, believe me, the hour is coming when neither on this mountain nor in Jerusalem will you worship the Father' (4:21). And again:

> But the hour is coming, and is now here, when the true worshippers will worship the Father in spirit and truth, for the Father is seeking such people to worship him. God is spirit, and those who worship him must worship in spirit and truth.
> (4:23–24)

Hays captures the shift: 'John's theology of the incarnate Word will insist that Jesus himself is now the locus of God's presence in the world, the site of true worship and revelation.'[48] This much was evident back in John 2 ('Destroy this temple, and in three days I will raise it up'; 2:19). In other words, Jesus is the *new temple*: the presence of God has descended and now walks among men.

Therefore, salvation may be from the Jews but salvation originates from God himself, who is a spiritual being. Beyond the barriers of geographical location, Jesus opens this woman's eyes to the type of worship 'their fathers' longed for and could only anticipate, namely one where the worshipper is drawn to the Father in 'spirit and truth'. Jesus' message is this: true worship depends on what lies within – whether one is spiritually devoted to Yahweh. Since Yahweh is spirit, unlike the material idols of the nations, his first concern is not geographical location but spiritual devotion.

Already the woman acknowledges Jesus to be a prophet. Given Jesus' emphasis on the future and the worship that awaits God's people, the woman's mind is oriented towards messianic categories. Jesus has detailed the type of worship that will come, but she now identifies who it is that will

---

[47] Carson 1991: 225. Also see Hays 2016: 296. Köstenberger (2007: 439) quotes Carson with approval but also clarifies what Jesus does not mean: 'Jesus' response . . . does not imply the salvation of all Jews, nor is its primary point of reference that the coming Messiah (or Taheb) will be Jewish.'
[48] Hays 2016: 296.

usher in this new era of true worship. 'I know that Messiah is coming (he who is called Christ). When he comes, he will tell us all things' (4:26). Seemingly attempting to get around Jesus' direct eschatological statements, this woman appeals to the highest office: the Messiah himself. He will clarify any confusion over these matters, present or future.

What she does not expect is what she hears next: 'I who speak to you am he' (4:26). At those words, all ethnic and religious barriers disappear as she runs to tell her fellow Samaritans about Jesus: 'Come, see a man who told me all that I ever did. Can this be the Christ?' (4:29). When they return, many Samaritans believe (4:39).

Here is one of the most lucid self-attestations by Jesus in all the Gospels. He is none other than the Christ, the Messiah. On that basis, he has eternal life to give. The fulfilment of the Old Testament covenant promises are at hand because the one the Law and the Prophets foreshadowed has arrived and offers salvation to all those who will drink his water.

Bread from heaven: John 6 and the new Moses

John and Jesus' use of imagery to convey Jesus' identity only continues in John 6. If Jesus bore witness to his messianic identity in Samaria and Jerusalem, then it is on the other side of the Sea of Galilee, by the Sea of Tiberias, that he recapitulates the history of Israel to demonstrate that just as he offers water of eternal life so now does he offer bread of life. Indeed, he *is* the bread of life. Although John has hinted at it already in the signs and wonders Jesus performs, John 6 will lay the exodus typology on thick, as Jesus is cast as Israel's *new Moses*, bringing Deuteronomy 18 to its culmination.[49]

Like Moses, in John 6 Jesus ascends the mountain as the crowds await his return (6:2). With the Passover at hand (6:4), Exodus 11 – 16 is in the background as Jesus then feeds the five thousand with but five barley loaves and two fish (6:5–14).[50] Left over are twelve baskets full, which may represent the twelve tribes of Israel now being renewed by the new Moses,

---

[49] Köstenberger (2007: 437) points out that the 'entire Johannine Farewell Discourse (chaps. 13–17)' is 'patterned after Moses' final words to the Israelites in the book of Deuteronomy'.

[50] Some commentators believe the reference to five loaves and two fish is meant to echo 2 Kgs 4:42–44, where Elisha uses loaves and grain to feed one hundred men. See Ridderbos 1997: 211–212; Barrett 1978: 275; Köstenberger 2007: 444.

who feeds them through his twelve disciples, who themselves picture Israel's new covenant community.[51]

Already, at this point in the narrative, typology is present. This feeding is rich in symbolism as Jesus, the new Moses, feeds the people of God with a sign that corresponds to Yahweh's miraculous provision in the wilderness. As will be seen, just as Israel grumbled, so too will the Jews of Jesus' day respond with unbelief and complaint. There is, as one expects with types, escalation; as will now be seen, the manna Yahweh rained down from heaven filled their stomachs but now the manna from heaven is God's own Son. Yet, like their fathers in the wilderness, they will reject this gracious gift. Both in the feeding and in the response, there is positive and negative typological fulfilment.[52]

Filling their stomachs on this miracle, the people are astonished: 'This is indeed the Prophet who is to come into the world!' (6:14). The Prophet they refer to is the one mentioned in Deuteronomy 18:15–22, a new prophet like Moses (a new Moses), who has the words of Yahweh in his mouth (18:18). Their enthusiasm cannot be curbed, for Jesus perceives they are about to 'come and take him by force to make him king', which motivates him to withdraw, for his time is not yet at hand (6:15).

In between this miraculous feeding and Jesus' confession that he is the bread of life, John situates a more personal encounter with Jesus that only his disciples experience, yet one that leaves them just as astonished as the crowds who want to crown Jesus king. The evening after the feeding of the five thousand, Jesus' disciples sail across the sea to Capernaum. When darkness descends, the waters surge with the wind behind them. Seemingly out of nowhere Jesus appears, walking towards them on the water. Although John's account is brief (Jesus says, 'It is I; do not be afraid'; 6:20), Matthew's narrative adds further insight. For not only does Peter attempt to walk to Jesus only for Jesus to save him from drowning, but Matthew concludes with a response by the disciples most consistent with John's own Christology: 'And when they got into the boat, the wind ceased. And those in the boat worshipped him, saying, "Truly you are the Son of God"' (Matt. 14:32–33).

Carson and Köstenberger believe there are a variety of possible Old Testament allusions present, including Jesus' 'It is I' (John 6:20) echoing

---

[51] See Carson 1991: 271; Köstenberger 2007: 444.
[52] On the presence of typology and escalation here, see Köstenberger 2007: 447.

the divine name 'I AM' (Exod. 3:14) and 'do not be afraid' being a constant Old Testament refrain (Gen. 26:24; Deut. 1:21, 29; 20:1, 3; Josh. 1:9). They point to the Psalms as well, for Psalm 77:16, 19 describes the Lord as the one whose 'way was through the sea', and Psalm 107:29 says the Lord 'made the storm be still, / and the waves of the sea were hushed' (cf. 107:30).[53] These and others may be alluded to as Jesus walks on the sea as the Lord who created and continues to reign over the created order. He multiplied bread; now the sea bows at his command (see Ps. 77:16).

The next day, John reports, the crowds travel to Capernaum to seek Jesus once more, but this time are met by Jesus who exposes their true motive: 'you are seeking me, not because you saw signs, but because you ate your fill of the loaves' (6:26). Similar to his approach to Nicodemus and the Samaritan woman, Jesus moves from the physical to the spiritual by means of metaphor, this time using the bread the crowds just ate. Issuing a warning that sounds similar to Isaiah 55:1–3, Jesus says, 'Do not labour for the food that perishes, but for the food that endures to eternal life, which the Son of Man will give to you' (6:27). Still, Jesus does so within the context of his relation to his Father: 'For on him', that is, Jesus, the 'Son of Man', 'God the Father has set his seal' (6:27).

The response Jesus requires is no different from that addressed in John 5: belief in the one whom the Father has sent, or, in the words of John 6, the one on whom the Father has set his seal. When the crowds ask how they can do the 'works of God', Jesus responds, 'This is the work of God, that you believe in him whom he has sent' (6:29). They pretend to be concerned with 'doing the works of God' but Jesus admonishes them simply to believe he is the Messiah their Scriptures prefigured.[54]

However, trust in Jesus as the Messiah and the Son the Father has sent is not within their hearts, for they demand a sign first. To add insult to injury, they appeal to their 'fathers', who 'ate the manna in the wilderness', quoting Nehemiah 9:15, saying, 'He gave them bread from heaven to eat' (6:31; cf. Num. 11:7–9; Ps. 78:24). The demand for a sign cannot be more ironic: in John 6:14 Jesus fed over five thousand with five loaves and two fish. The demand for a further sign may seem right in their eyes; after all,

---

[53] Carson 1991: 276; Köstenberger 2007: 444.

[54] On this contrast between 'doing' and 'believing', see Köstenberger 2007: 445: 'Jesus' answer is nothing less than stunning: God's requirement is summed up as believing in "the one he has sent" (the language may reflect Mal. 3:1) – that is, the Messiah. This contrasts with the people's apparent confidence that they are able to meet the demands of God.' Cf. Carson 1991: 285; Morris 1995: 319; Barrett 1978: 287.

if Jesus is the one Deuteronomy 18 promised, then what is another sign?[55] But that logic only reveals their unbelief: no matter how many signs Jesus performs they will not believe. For they are not born again.

At their demand for another sign, Jesus responds:

> Truly, truly, I say to you, it was not Moses who gave you the bread from heaven, but my Father gives you the true bread from heaven. For the bread of God is he who comes down from heaven and gives life to the world.
> (6:32–33)

In their appeal to the Old Testament, they have overlooked who gave them bread from heaven; Moses was but the mediator, God the true provider. This oversight is significant because if they understand that it is the Father who provided this bread in the wilderness, then they may believe in his Son, the true bread from heaven. He is bread because, unlike the manna in the wilderness, Jesus gives life, and this life is not just for the Jews but for the nations, bringing to fulfilment God's covenant promises to Abraham.

Notice, as well, that Jesus uses the present instead of the past tense when he says, 'my Father *gives* you the true bread from heaven'. Jesus intends his listeners to move from the past to the present because the bread in the wilderness is the type and he its antitype. The bread, in other words, prefigures the true, living bread, Jesus Christ. The tense change, says Hays, indicates a 'paradigm shift': 'the manna story is not just about a past event in salvation history; rather, it points forward *figurally* to a different kind of bread altogether'.[56] Hays adds that this prefigurement is also supported by a substantive reading of ὁ *katabainōn ek tou ouranou* in 6:33:

> *ho gar artos tou theou estin ho katabainōn ek tou ouranou kai zōēn didous tō kosmō.*

> For the bread of God is he who comes down from heaven and gives life to the world.

---

[55] Carson (1991: 285) and Köstenberger (2007: 445) spell out this logic well, depending on the research of Beasley-Murray 1999: 91; Barrett 1978: 288; Brown 1966; 1970: 265; Moloney 1998: 212.

[56] Hays 2016: 322. Emphasis original.

If an attributive is in view, 6:33 would read, 'the bread of God is *that which* comes down from heaven'. But a substantive reading is far more in line with the typological point Jesus is making: 'the bread of God is *the One who* comes down from heaven'.[57]

When the Jews ask for this bread that comes from heaven, a response that shows their ignorance of the typology at play (much like the Samaritan woman and the 'living water' Jesus offers), Jesus responds by pointing to himself as the true antitype. 'I am the bread of life; whoever comes to me shall not hunger, and whoever believes in me shall never thirst' (6:35). The bread from heaven their fathers received was a sign of God's gracious provision, but it was a bread that did not last. Jesus, building on the metaphor, is a bread that grants life, life that will not end. To eat this bread is never to hunger again; this is why he was sent by his Father in the first place. 'For this is the will of my Father, that everyone who looks on the Son and believes in him should have eternal life, and I will raise him up on the last day' (6:40). And again:

> I am the bread of life. Your fathers ate the manna in the wilderness, and they died. This is the bread that comes down from heaven, so that one may eat of it and not die. I am the *living bread* that came down from heaven. If anyone eats of this bread, he will live for ever. And the bread that I will give for the life of the world is my flesh.
> (6:48–51; emphasis added)

Notice, the salvation and life Jesus offers, in the context of John 6, is spurned. The Jews reject Jesus as the bread of life and grumble in unbelief as did their fathers (6:41). Nevertheless, Jesus knows those who are his; those who do not believe do not come to Jesus because the Father has not drawn them, says Jesus (6:44). Yet there are many who hear and do believe (and many who have yet to hear but will believe); they are drawn by the Father. Despite the unbelief of some, Jesus can claim Isaiah 54:13 is being fulfilled: 'It is written in the Prophets, "And they will all be taught by God"' (John 6:45). As was seen in chapter 2, in Isaiah 54 and 55 Yahweh declares that he will be a faithful husband to Israel despite her unfaithfulness (54:5–6). Due to his 'steadfast love' and 'compassion', says Yahweh, 'my covenant of peace

---

[57] Ibid. Emphasis original.

shall not be removed' (54:10). The promise is bold: 'All your children shall be taught by the LORD' (Isa. 54:13). Using imagery that will not be foreign to John's readers, Isaiah then presents Yahweh's invitation:

> Come, everyone who thirsts,
> come to the waters.
> (Isa. 55:1; cf. John 4:10–15; 7:37–38).

The unbelief of these Jews demonstrates that they are not truly 'children' 'taught by the LORD'. Nevertheless, the fulfilment of Isaiah 54:13 is at hand because the Father is drawing a people to Jesus and all those whom he draws are 'taught by God'; in other words, they are true disciples, not grumbling but receiving the bread from heaven, he who is eternal life (John 6:50–51). 'Great shall be the peace' of these 'children' (Isa. 54:13) because they are recipients of the 'everlasting covenant' of peace (Isa. 55:3) procured by the Servant who offers his own flesh as the bread that gives life to the world (Isa. 6:51).[58]

Much like Nicodemus and the Samaritan woman, John 6:52 presents the Jews as sceptical of Jesus because they cannot think beyond the corporeal and thus miss the spiritual significance of the metaphor itself (e.g. 'How can this man give us his flesh to eat?'). Just as Jesus promised 'living water', now he promises 'living bread'. But the Jews need not look for something outside Jesus: he is the water that quenches thirst and the bread that satisfies the hungry. He not only offers life; he *is* life. Eternal life cannot be separated from who he is:

> Truly, truly, I say to you, unless you eat the flesh of the Son of Man and drink his blood, you have no life in you. Whoever feeds on my flesh and drinks my blood has eternal life, and I will raise him up on the last day.
> (6:53–54)

Jesus continues, 'For my flesh is true food, and my blood is true drink. Whoever feeds on my flesh and drinks my blood abides in me, and I in him' (6:56).

---

[58] My mention of Isa. 54 – 55 is brief, but see an extended treatment in Köstenberger 2007: 448–451.

Earlier in the dialogue, the Jews could not grasp how Jesus could say this given his apparently ordinary origins. 'Is this not Jesus, the son of Joseph, whose father and mother we know? How does he now say, "I have come down from heaven"?' (6:42). Given their unbelief, the crowd questions the relation between who Jesus is and what he claims to offer, asking on what basis he can claim such a prerogative. But Jesus refuses to operate by such a misconception on their part. What he offers (eternal life) cannot be separated from who he is (the Son sent from the Father). Again, Jesus will return to trinitarian vocabulary to justify his claim: 'As the living Father sent me, and I live because of the Father, so whoever feeds on me, he also will live because of me' (6:57; cf. 7:28–29). The life he has from the Father grounds the life he gives to those who trust in him. As one sent from the Father, Jesus is bread in a way that far surpasses the bread of their fathers. 'This is the bread that came down from heaven, not like the bread the fathers ate and died. Whoever feeds on this bread will live for ever' (6:58).

The response of the Jews throughout this narrative is full of typological flavour. John 6:41 says 'the Jews grumbled' just like their fathers (6:41). Jesus noticed that many of his own disciples 'were grumbling' as well (6:61). For they struggled with Jesus' teaching, turning away to follow him no longer (6:66). What they need is the same thing Nicodemus needs: the Spirit. Only the Spirit can cause them to be born again so that they see Jesus for who he is. They need, in other words, spiritual eyesight. 'It is the Spirit who gives life; the flesh is no help at all' (John 6:63). How does the Spirit give life? Through Jesus' words. The very 'words' he has spoken to them 'are spirit and life' (6:63), says Jesus. The revelation of his identity and the salvation he brings are conveyed through the words he speaks; therefore these are words of life, words through which the Spirit brings about spiritual rebirth. Just as God efficaciously spoke life into existence, so he speaks spiritual life into the darkness of the human soul and through those words of life the Spirit creates a new creature in Christ.[59]

Despite the unbelief of so many, Peter does not fail to see at least the essence of what Jesus has said and how it relates to who Jesus is and where he has come from. 'Lord, to whom shall we go? You have the words of eternal life, and we have believed, and have come to know, that you are the Holy One of God' (6:68–69). Although Peter will later show signs that he

---

[59] On the nature of regeneration by the Spirit through the word, see Barrett 2013.

does not entirely understand the type of mission Christ has come to accomplish, nevertheless here he expresses the type of belief that can come only from the Father (i.e. 'no one can come to me unless it is granted him by the Father'; 6:65; cf. 6:44). Peter's is the type of belief that has as its object none other than the 'Holy One of God', the Son sent from the Father.

Such an identity is heavenly, to be sure, but it is one the Father revealed through the Prophets; hence the Jews should have known who Jesus is by the Scriptures they adhered to so faithfully. 'It is written in the Prophets,' Jesus says quoting Isaiah 54:13, '"And they will all be taught by God." Everyone who has heard and learned from the Father comes to me – not that anyone has seen the Father except he who is from God; he has seen the Father' (6:45–46). There is no doubt in Jesus' mind that he alone has seen the Father and has been sent by the Father to grant eternal life to all those his Father gives him (6:65). And given what we learned in chapter 2, it is fitting that he decides to make that point by appealing to the Scriptures of Israel, which typologically speak of his identity.

Israel's good shepherd: John 9 and 10

It is palpable by now that John's account is a Gospel filled with Christological metaphors, metaphors that build on the typology of Old Testament Israel. As seen already, Jesus is living water and living bread from heaven.[60] In John 10 the figure of speech changes to the good shepherd. John is strategic, positioning this metaphor on the heels of the enormous opposition Jesus receives for healing a man born blind (John 9). It is strategic because John has already broached the metaphor of light, introducing back in John 1:9 and 8:12 Jesus as the 'true light' of the world. Now he who is the light of the world (9:5) opens the eyes of a blind man, while those who claim to be enlightened are spiritually blind, walking in darkness (John 9).[61]

Questioned by the Pharisees, the blind man is astonished that the Pharisees can be so clueless as to where this healer comes from:

---

[60] He is also the light of the world (John 8:12), but we will explore this metaphor in chapter 6.

[61] Since my purpose is to arrive at John 10, I will not rehearse the details of John 9, but it should be noted that the narrative is filled with OT allusions: e.g. Jesus tells the blind man to wash the mud from his eyes in the Pool of Siloam (John 9:7), which alludes to the command Elijah gave to Naaman with regard to the Jordan (2 Kgs 5:10–13); 'Siloam' or 'Shiloah' in Hebrew means 'Sent' (John 9:7, 11); and Gen. 49:10 promises the 'scepter will not depart from Judah until Shiloh comes'. See Köstenberger 2007: 460, building on Carson 1991: 364–365, who also notes how Isa. 8:6 records the Jews' rejection of Shiloah, and here, in John 9, the Jews reject the one sent by the Father.

Why, this is an amazing thing! You do not know where he comes
from, and yet he opened my eyes . . . Never since the world began has
it been heard that anyone opened the eyes of a man born blind. If this
man were not from God, he could do nothing.
(9:30, 32–33)

The story is dripping with irony: the one born blind has spiritual sight,
understanding that Jesus must be God sent to heal him. Yet the Pharisees –
who witness this man's recovered vision are spiritually blind, and should
have remembered prophets like Isaiah who speak of the Messiah as a healer
of the blind (Isa. 29:18; 35:6; 42:7; 61:1–2) – are unable and unwilling to
accept Jesus as one who has come from the Father.[62] When confronted
with the blind man's simple yet profound observation 'If this man were not
from God, he could do nothing,' the Pharisees become defensive: 'You were
born in utter sin, and would you teach us?' (9:34).

When Jesus appears once more to the man born blind, asking him
if he believes in the 'Son of Man' (9:35), Jesus is forthright in saying that
he is this Son of Man ('it is he who is speaking to you'; 9:37). Hearing
this, the man exclaims, '"Lord, I believe", and he worshipped him' (9:38).
Jesus receives this man's worship; he does not correct him as if he were
committing blasphemy. The Synoptic Gospels attest to the same (Matt.
2:11; 14:33; 28:17–18), which leads John McIntyre to conclude that we
should 'not be satisfied with any christological analysis which eliminates
from its conception of who he [Jesus Christ] is all valid basis for an
attitude of worship to him'. Such an approach has its own agenda and
differs from the Christology of John (and the Synoptics) for this fundamental reason:

It is on this very score that humanistic interpretations of the person
of Jesus Christ fail, that they present to us someone who cannot
sustain human *worship*; admiration, perhaps, even a sense of wonder
at the courage he had in the face of danger and death, but never
worship. That is given only to God.[63]

---

[62] On the OT expectation that the Messiah would open blind eyes, see Carson 1991: 375;
Morris 1995: 422; Köstenberger 2007: 459.

[63] McIntyre 1966: 45. Emphasis original. Hays (2016: 175; emphasis original) draws a similar
conclusion but with regard to Matthew's Gospel: '*Matthew highlights the worship of Jesus for
one reason: he believes and proclaims that Jesus is the embodied presence of God and that to*

With the Pharisees in view, Jesus indicates in John 9 that his ministry is one that saves as well as condemns. 'For judgment I came into this world, that those who do not see may see, and those who see may become blind' (9:39). When the Pharisees ask if they are blind, Jesus does not correct them but only confirms their blindness, a blindness, he says, that perpetuates and sustains their guilt before his Father (9:41). Again, the irony is blatant: the blind man's guilt is removed when he sees Jesus for who he truly is, the Son of Man (John 9:35–39); but the Pharisees' guilt remains because, though they see, they remain blind to his Christological identity (9:41). This is a reminder that the light of the world not only opens spiritually blind eyes but blinds those who are in spiritual darkness; the light both distributes grace and executes judgment (9:39; cf. John 1:9–10).

Such an encounter is the context, in John's Gospel, for Jesus' claim to be the good shepherd, a shepherd whose mission looks different from those who are but thieves and robbers, an accusation directed against the religious elite. The religious leaders are those who walk in darkness due to their spiritual blindness (9:39–41). To change imagery, they are false shepherds, leading the people astray (the blind leading the blind). Jesus, by contrast, is the true and good shepherd (10:14), who leads the sheep to drink from streams of living water.

Yet before Jesus describes himself as the good shepherd, he first describes himself as the *door*:

> I am the door. If anyone enters by me, he will be saved and will go in and out and find pasture. The thief comes only to steal and kill and destroy. I came that they may have life and have it abundantly. (10:9–10)

---

worship Jesus is to worship YHWH – not merely an agent or a facsimile or an intermediary.' Hays says elsewhere, 'In the midst of Matthew's artful weaving of correspondences, however, he always reminds us that Jesus is more than a successor to Moses, more than a new Joshua, far more than a prophet like Moses who continues Moses' ministry in some derivative fashion. Jesus is, in a way that Moses never was, "Emmanuel," God with us. That is why Jesus can declare that he has come not merely to remind people of the law and the prophets but to fulfill them. That is why he can cite Moses and then add, "but I say to you," asserting his own authority as definitive source and interpreter of Torah. And that is why he can promise to be present to his followers to the end of the age, in a way that never could have been claimed for Moses. Moses, then, is a *foreshadowing* of Jesus, a forerunner who prefigures some facets of the identity of Jesus. Jesus takes up into his own story line all that Moses signified for Israel, while also surpassing his precursor.' Ibid. 145. Emphasis original. We will explore Jesus' divinity further in chapter 6.

The image of a door comes close to capturing what Jesus will later communicate in John 14:6: 'I am the way, and the truth, and the life. No one comes to the Father except through me.' While those who came before Jesus were 'thieves and robbers' (10:8), Jesus has come not to take but to give. What he gives is truth and life. Yet *the way* to such life is through him alone. He is the door one must enter through to receive this life.

In John 10:11 Jesus adjusts his figure of speech from a door to a shepherd who cares for the sheep, one who even lays down his life for the sheep. Unlike the hired hand who runs at the first sight of danger, abandoning the sheep and leaving them for the wolves (10:12–13), the good shepherd stays to care for and protect his own. In the context of the Son's mission from the Father, there is a soteriological commitment the Son will not renege on. Those sheep given to him by the Father have been entrusted to his care; as their shepherd, he will even give himself up to secure their salvation: 'I am the good shepherd. I know my own and my own know me, just as the Father knows me and I know the Father; and I lay down my life for the sheep' (10:14–15). In doing so, the Son receives the benevolence only his Father can give. 'For this reason the Father loves me, because I lay down my life that I may take it up again' (10:17). Such is the charge Jesus has received from his Father (10:18). It is a mission Jesus takes on voluntarily and with full control ('I lay it down of my own accord'); it is a mission that reflects the authority Jesus possesses as well ('I have authority to lay it down, and I have authority to take it up again'; 10:18).

Like John's previous metaphors, this one too is rich in Old Testament allusions.

1. *By claiming to be the good shepherd, Jesus identifies himself with Yahweh, who is throughout the Old Testament referred to as the shepherd of Israel, his flock* (Gen. 48:15; 49:24; Pss 28:9; 74:1; 77:20; 78:52; 79:13; 80:1; 95:7; 100:3; Isa. 40:11; Jer. 31:9; Ezek. 34:11–31).[64] In Psalm 23, for example, David calls the Lord his shepherd, the one who makes him 'lie down in green pastures' and 'leads' him 'beside still waters' (23:2). This shepherd 'restores my soul' (23:3). David took comfort in the staff of his shepherd (23:4); so too does Jesus promise to protect his sheep from those who are thieves and wolves, even if he must lay down his own life for their sake (John 10:10, 12–15). Like David's shepherd, Jesus brings life and

---

64 For more on these OT allusions, see Köstenberger 2007: 462.

restoration to the lost sheep of Israel (John 10:10; cf. Matt. 10:6; 15:24), the type of restoration life the prophets anticipated (see chapter 2).

2. *By claiming to be the good shepherd, Jesus typologically identifies himself as the eschatological shepherd Moses hoped for and anticipated.* Many commentators believe John 10:3–4 has Numbers 27:15–18 in view.[65] In Numbers 27 Moses' time leading the people is at an end and Joshua will take his place. The Lord tells Moses to go up the mountain of Abarim to see the land of promise, the land Israel will enter with Joshua (27:12). 'When you have seen it, you also shall be gathered to your people' (27:13). Moses replies:

> Let the LORD, the God of the spirits of all flesh, appoint a man over the congregation who shall go out before them and come in before them, who shall lead them out and bring them in, that the congregation of the LORD may *not be as a sheep that have no shepherd.*
> (27:16–17; emphasis added)

Joshua is then appointed as Israel's new leader and shepherd (27:18), but, taking Jesus into account, this passage escalates in meaning. Matthew, for instance, says of Jesus, 'When he saw the crowds, he had compassion for them, because they were harassed and helpless, like sheep without a shepherd' (9:36). John capitalizes on this shepherd allusion all the more by devoting a lengthy section of his Gospel to Jesus as the good shepherd who cares for his sheep and knows them as his own (e.g. 10:13–14).

3. *By claiming to be the good shepherd, Jesus sets himself apart from the hired hand, the thief and the wolf, and distinguishes himself as Israel's true messianic leader, Davidic shepherd-king and covenant mediator.* Israel had many shepherds who led them, as sheep, astray. Ezekiel even prophesied against these 'shepherds of Israel' (Ezek. 34:2), as did prophets like Zechariah (11:4–17):

> Thus says the Lord GOD: Ah, shepherds of Israel who have been feeding yourselves! Should not the shepherds feed the sheep? . . . The weak you have not strengthened, the sick you have not healed, the injured you have not bound up, the strayed you have not brought back, the lost you have not sought.
> (Ezek. 34:2, 4)

---

[65] E.g. Carson 1991: 383; Barrett 1978: 369; Köstenberger 2007: 462.

As a result, the sheep 'were scattered, because there was no shepherd, and they became food for all the wild beasts' (34:5). Yahweh takes this personally: 'My sheep were scattered; they wandered over all the mountains and on every high hill. My sheep were scattered over all the face of the earth, with none to search or seek for them' (34:6).[66]

Yahweh will not leave his sheep as prey for wild beasts, but will take a stand against these shepherds and hold them accountable (Ezek. 34:7–9); he will then 'rescue' his sheep (34:10). The Lord himself will become their shepherd, in order to 'seek them out' (34:11). 'As a shepherd seeks out his flock when he is among his sheep that have been scattered, so will I seek out my sheep, and I will rescue them from all places where they have been scattered' (34:12). Once he finds his lost sheep, he will 'gather them from the countries' and he will 'feed them' (34:13–14). 'I myself will be the shepherd of my sheep, and I myself will make them lie down, declares the Lord GOD' (34:15).

Yet Yahweh also promises that he will raise up a new shepherd, one like the iconic shepherd-king, David. 'And I will set up over them one shepherd, my servant David, and he shall feed them: he shall feed them and be their shepherd' (Ezek. 34:23). With this Davidic, shepherd-king in place, Yahweh promises to make 'a covenant of peace and banish wild beasts from the land' (34:25; cf. Isa. 54:10; 55:3).

Likewise, Yahweh says through the prophet Jeremiah that he will destroy those shepherds who scattered his sheep (Jer. 23:1), and 'gather the remnant of my flock' and 'set shepherds over them' (Jer. 23:3–4). But in the end, Yahweh will 'raise up for David a righteous Branch, and he shall reign as king and deal wisely, and shall execute justice and righteousness in the land' (Jer. 23:5). From David, who was a shepherd turned king, will rise up a righteous king who will shepherd Israel with compassion and bring their enemies to justice.

The prophets, therefore, long for the day of the Messiah, the new Davidic king, because he will prove to be a good shepherd. Like King David, this messianic shepherd will care for and protect the sheep from intruders and posers; his rod and staff will not only gather the lost sheep of Israel to be fed but bring down judgment on their predators to ensure they enjoy the peace of the covenant. In the words of Micah, Yahweh promised to assemble his people 'like sheep in a fold, like a flock in its pasture' (2:12), as their 'king passes on before them, / the LORD at their head' (2:13).

---

[66] Other prophets make similar pronouncements; e.g. Zech. 11:4–17.

In John 10 Jesus goes to great lengths to describe himself as the good shepherd, the archetype shepherd-king who brings to fulfilment the hopes of Israel as voiced by the prophets. 'The "good shepherd" is not simply a consoler who promises to care for the souls of those who believe . . . Rather, Jesus is staking symbolic claim to be the new David, the restorer and ruler of Israel.'[67] But like previous metaphorical allusions, typological fulfilments and predictive prophecies, John 10 demonstrates Jesus' belief in the Scriptures of Israel; these originated from the mouth of his Father and what his Father spoke concerning the Christ in the Law and the Prophets Jesus is now bringing to fulfilment.

Isaiah saw the glory of Christ: John 12

Despite Jesus' teaching from John 2 – 11, the crowds still entertain doubt concerning his origin and identity. The typology present in Numbers 21 (John 3:14) is not on the forefront of their minds when they question Jesus, saying, 'We have heard from the Law that the Christ remains for ever. How can you say that the Son of Man must be lifted up? Who is this Son of Man?' (12:34). Apparently, these sceptics did not resonate with Philip's reaction when he discovered Jesus and said, 'We have found him of whom *Moses in the Law* and also the prophets wrote, Jesus of Nazareth, the son of Joseph' (1:45; emphasis added). The crowd fails to see where in the Law a suffering Messiah is found. Yet Jesus is adamant that he is bringing the Law to fulfilment, and is about to be lifted up in accordance with Moses and the Law.

In the end, Jesus traces the crowd's lack of perception to their spiritual condition and blindness. Jesus is the light, but his listeners remain in darkness, despite his instruction not to let the darkness overtake them (12:35–36). Notwithstanding his many miraculous signs, they remain in unbelief (12:37). Yet, says John, such unbelief, such spiritual blindness, was preordained and orchestrated by God:

they still did not believe in him, so that the word spoken by the prophet Isaiah might be fulfilled:

'Lord, who has believed what he heard from us,
    And to whom has the arm of the Lord been revealed?'

---

[67] Hays 2016: 319.

Therefore they could not believe. For again Isaiah said,

> 'He has blinded their eyes
>   And hardened their heart,
> lest they see with their eyes,
>   and understand with their heart, and turn,
>   and I would heal them.'

Isaiah said these things because he saw his glory and spoke of him. (John 12:37–41; cf. Isa. 53:1; 6:10)

As seen in Matthew's account (ch. 3), so too in John's account a salient feature of the text is the way John utilizes a theology of divine sovereignty in what appears to be Jesus' defeat. Certainly, Yahweh is judging Israel for their hardness of heart, but John's quotations from Isaiah demonstrate that Yahweh is much more than a judge reacting to the sinfulness of his people: he is the one who has predestined and preordained such unbelief in the first place, only to send Isaiah to preach a message that will harden Israel in their unbelief.[68] 'God *is* the cause of the unbelieving response to Jesus, not merely the judge of it,' asserts Klink.[69] The emphasis on God's sovereignty does not remove man's responsibility nor does it annul his culpability. Nevertheless, this text makes God the primary cause of the people's blindness and hardness of heart, as perceivable in John's use of the active voice in verse 40 ('He has blinded their eyes / and hardened their heart, / lest they see').[70]

The connection between 6:64–65 (you 'do not believe . . . This is why I told you that no one can come to me unless it is granted him by the Father') and 12:40 ('He has blinded their eyes / and hardened their heart . . .') should not be lost on the reader either. 'Not only has God not "drawn" these people or "given them faith",' says Michaels, 'but he has "blinded their eyes and hardened their hearts" to make sure they would *not* repent and be healed!'[71] Carson says something similar: 'God commands Isaiah to undertake this ministry in the full knowledge that the results will be

---

[68] Here is not the place to unpack a doctrine of predestination. However, see Barrett (2017: 107–109), where I address how God can reprobate while not committing evil himself.

[69] Klink and Lockett 2016: 560. Emphasis original.

[70] Ridderbos 1997: 444.

[71] Michaels 2010: 710. Emphasis original.

negative; indeed, such preaching to these people *evokes* a negative response, is in some sense the *cause* of the negative response.'[72] If God is the cause, then what might this mean for the way John appeals to Isaiah? 'In that sense God himself, through the prophet, hardens the heart of people – a point later recognized by the prophet when he begs the Almighty to display himself in more merciful ways (Is. 63:15–19).'[73]

Divine sovereignty is not irrelevant to the theme of this present project, because in John's mind such predetermination on God's part to guarantee such blindness is exactly what ensures that the Scriptures are true and brought to fulfilment as God intended. In other words, with the fulfilment of God's salvific plan comes the fulfilment of his spoken and written word. To be more precise, God's salvific plan is accomplished *through* his revelatory, inscripturated speech, and his revelatory, inscripturated speech brings about his salvific plan. Revelation and redemption are inseparable for John. Sometimes his revelation redeems, but at other times God has purposed it to condemn. The latter is the case here, and the surrounding context demonstrates that in blinding the eyes of the Jews God will usher in the Gentiles (cf. the Greeks who approach Jesus in John 12:20–26 in the context of 12:32: 'And I, when I am lifted up . . . will draw all people to myself'). So even in the act of blinding Israel's eyes, God has opened the eyes of the nations to see his Son for who he is; redemption, counter-intuitive as it seems, comes through judgment. When the revelation of God's Son is hidden from some, it is revealed to others that they might have life in his name.

Like the synoptic authors, John is strategic in the way he turns to the prophet Isaiah to communicate that the rejection Jesus is experiencing – a rejection that will soon lead to being 'lifted up' in death – is predetermined and foreshadowed in the unbelief of Israel during the days of Isaiah. 'The Evangelist intends not merely to refer to the similarity between unbelief in Isaiah's day and in Jesus' day,' clarifies Ridderbos, 'but rather places this unbelief in the light of God's continuing dealings with his backsliding people in the whole history of revelation.'[74] Such is the purpose of John's intertextual hermeneutic.

John's first quotation is from Isaiah 53:1, recapitulating the astonishment of Isaiah at the unbelief of God's people. Just as Isaiah's gospel was rejected, so will Jesus' gospel be repudiated. The second quotation is from Isaiah

---

[72] Carson 1991: 448. Emphases original.
[73] Ibid.
[74] Ridderbos 1997: 444.

6:10, a passage alluded to and quoted often by the New Testament authors (e.g. Matt. 13:13–15; Mark 4:12; Luke 8:10; Acts 28:26–27; Rom. 11:18). Matthew appeals to Isaiah 6:10 as a fulfilment text that explains why Jesus taught in parables (Matt. 13:14–15). John, however, quotes this text to explain the people's reaction in unbelief to Jesus' miracles and his assertion that the Messiah must be lifted up. John, like Matthew, uses the language of 'fulfilment' ('fulfilled' in 12:38) because he too believes that what Jesus is doing and teaching is analogous to Isaiah, prophetically foreshadowed in what Isaiah portrayed. They could not believe because God had blinded their eyes (12:39), which is another way of saying, since it is God himself who is behind Isaiah's prophecy, that they could not believe because Isaiah's prophecy was to be fulfilled (12:38). Put simply, Jesus' listeners could not believe (12:39) because 'Isaiah had prophesied in Scripture that they would not (vv. 38–41)'.[75]

John's interpretation of Isaiah's statement is found in 12:41, but it may not be instinctual to modern interpretative methods: 'Isaiah said these things because he saw his glory and spoke of him.' What does John mean that Isaiah saw the glory of Christ? It is shocking statements like these that incriminate Jesus with the religious leaders (e.g. Jesus says in 8:56–59 Abraham 'saw' Jesus' day). In Isaiah's vision Isaiah is standing before the Lord as his glory fills the temple. Yahweh is the one in view, it would seem. But John reads with a trinitarian lens, as demonstrated at the start of his Gospel by his unequivocal assertion that the Word, the Son, existed with God. Pre-existence is not foreign to John, nor is he quiet concerning its implications for Jesus' identity.

Furthermore, the glory Isaiah refers to is not absent from John's Gospel; except John applies this divine glory to the Son, Jesus the Christ. Jesus too is high and lifted up (Isa. 6:1) but in John's narrative the elevation of this glory will be seen at the cross, though that type of glory is anticipated by Isaiah as well.[76] Yahweh's statement through Isaiah 'Behold, my servant shall act wisely; / he shall be high and lifted up, / and shall be exalted' (52:13) is followed by 'He was despised and rejected by men' (53:3), which is a contextual fit for John's narrative. 'From the Gospel writer's perspective, the "glory" of the Lord (Isa 6:1, 3) and the "glory" of his servant (Isa 52:13) seem to have merged into one.'[77]

---

[75] Michaels 2010: 707.
[76] Ibid. 711.
[77] Ibid.

Commentators debate, nevertheless, whether Isaiah actually sees the glory of the pre-incarnate Son or whether Isaiah sees divine glory, glory that is appropriated by all three members of the Godhead but is applied to the Son specifically in the context of John's narrative. Ridderbos provides a mediating position:

> The Evangelist does not mean that Isaiah already foresaw Jesus' (later) glory, but that the glory of God as the prophet foresaw it in his vision was no other than that which the Son of God had with the Father before the world was and that was to be manifested before the eyes of all in the incarnation of the Word (17:4; 1:14, 18).[78]

Ridderbos's interpretation is at least consistent with the pervasive emphasis of John and Jesus concerning the latter's glory with the Father in eternity.[79] Carson believes there is, therefore, a 'Christian reasoning' at play:

> if the Son, the Word, was with God in the beginning, and was God, and if he was God's agent of creation, and the perfect revelation of God to humankind, then it stands to reason that in those Old Testament passages where God is said to reveal himself rather spectacularly to someone, it must have been through the agency of his Son, his Word, however imperfectly the point was spelled out at the time.[80]

That glory is characteristic in John who begins his Gospel claiming Jesus is the agent of creation (John 1:2).

Klink adds that there is an intertextual parallel between Jesus' day and Isaiah's day both in the blindness God causes and the message proclaimed:

> The narrator has just made an intra-Scriptural connection not merely between the Father and the Son but also between the responses of the

---

[78] 'For that reason ("because") the prophetic judgment of hardening on account of the unbelief of the people was fully applicable to the rejection of Jesus by Israel, and even came to fulfillment therein.' Ridderbos 1997: 445.

[79] John's testimony that Isaiah saw the glory of Christ in his vision is not a Johannine anomaly: previously Jesus claimed that Abraham saw the day of Jesus and was glad (John 8:56). Jesus' divine identity and existence do not begin in Nazareth: as Jesus says, 'before Abraham was, I am' (8:58).

[80] Carson 1991: 450.

people in Isaiah's day and Jesus' day . . . God 'blinded' and 'hardened' (John 12:40) even though it was not fully manifested until Jesus revealed it, just as we can say that Isaiah saw Jesus even though it was not fully manifested in Isaiah.[81]

Klink presumes, 'Isaiah and Jesus proclaim the same message of God, now made known as the gospel of Jesus Christ, the one who finally and more fully reveals it (1:18).'[82]

To conclude, John 12 establishes that behind the prophets is a divine author and one who speaks through his prophets with the full intention of his words giving birth to prophetic fulfilment in the words and works of his Son. John 12 is extraordinary because this principle is demonstrated by John's unpredictable statement that when Isaiah saw the glory of the Lord, it was the glory of Jesus he saw; therefore when he spoke he spoke of him. Not only, then, does the prophet speak the words of God but the prophet is said to have seen and spoken about the Christ whom the vision and prophecy prefigured.

The Scripture will be fulfilled: John 13 and 17[83]

If the language of fulfilment is apparent at the beginning of John's passion narrative in John 12, that pattern only intensifies as the narrative progresses, pervading the events of Jesus' suffering the closer he approaches that epochal event of being lifted up.

In John 13:18 Jesus reveals that one will betray him; it is one who has not been 'chosen' (13:18). As surprising as such a betrayal may seem, Jesus believes it is as determined as God's election of Jesus' other disciples:

> I am not speaking of all of you; I know whom I have chosen. But the Scripture will be fulfilled, 'He who ate my bread has lifted his heel

---

[81] Klink and Lockett 2016: 559.

[82] Ibid. 561.

[83] For the sake of space, I am bypassing John 15. But like the metaphors seen so far (water, bread, etc.), 'vine' and 'branches' are ones grounded in the Scriptures of Israel. Notice too how John 15 ends with the Jews hating Jesus so that the 'word that is written in their Law' is 'fulfilled' (15:25). John then quotes Pss 35:19 and 69:5. We will turn to John's quotations of the psalms in John 19.

against me.' I am telling you this now, before it takes place, that when
it does take place you may believe that I am he.
(13:18–19)

Jesus does not conceal his confidence. Just as he knows whom his Father
has chosen, so does he know not only who will betray him but how such a
betrayal will fulfil God's preordained plan as vocalized in the Scriptures.
Jesus is quoting David in Psalm 41:9, who says:

Even my close friend in whom I trusted,
   who ate my bread, has lifted his heel against me.

Jesus uses David's betrayal to describe his own, but is not merely observing
the similarity of his own betrayal to that of David's betrayal. Jesus believes
that what David wrote in the Scripture is now being fulfilled; there is, then,
some form of typological correspondence and fulfilment.

In his high-priestly prayer (John 17) Jesus will make the same
interpretative manoeuvre when he tells the Father that he has been faithful
to accomplish the mission given to him, a mission set out in the Scriptures:
'While I was with them, I kept them in your name, which you have given
me. I have guarded them, and not one of them has been lost except the son
of destruction, *that the Scripture might be fulfilled*' (17:12; emphasis added).
Jesus is not directly quoting in full any Scripture, so it would seem, but his
statement may once again be a reference to Psalm 41:9.

In John 13 and 17 the reader can sense the heavy emphasis Jesus places
not only on his Father's plan and sovereign will, but on the way that plan
and will were articulated through the scriptural authors, whether via
direct prophecy or, more often than not, through typological correspondence. It does not seem that strict prediction is present in Psalm 41:9
but rather, based on Jesus' use of the text, a type that escalates. David is
a type of Christ, so much so that his words can be adopted by Christ,
applied to his own betrayal and interpreted as a 'fulfilment' of the betrayal
David himself experienced. The analogical is prophetically loaded for
John.

One could object, however, that Psalm 41:9 cannot be typological of
Christ nor is Christ justified in saying this Scripture is 'fulfilled' since other
parts of this psalm admit wrongdoing. For example, in verse 4 David pleads
for grace because he has disobeyed God:

As for me, I said, 'O LORD, be gracious to me;
  heal me, for I have sinned against you!'

Such logic, however, fails to recognize that a text can be messianic in its prophetic nature or typological in the way it prefigures the archetype to come without being so in all its minute comprehensibility.

What factors, then, must be present for a portion of a text, in this case a psalm, to be *typologically messianic*? Carson identifies two. 'First, because of 2 Samuel 7:12–16, Psalm 2 and other passages, David himself became a "type", a model of "great David's greater Son", the promised Messiah.' Carson qualifies that such Davidic typology 'did not mean that *everything* that happened to David had to find its echo in Jesus'.[84] Nevertheless, it

> meant that many of the broad themes of his life were understood that way – especially where language was so hyperbolic when applied to David alone that many readers of the Scriptures, Jews and Christians alike, were driven to seeing in such texts an anticipation, an adumbration, of the coming King.[85]

Anticipation, adumbration – these are present in Psalm 41:9 as seen in the way Jesus not only quotes and alludes to such a text in John 13:18–19 and 17:12 but sees himself as the greater son of David, the one who brings to culmination the eternal kingdom God promised to David by means of a covenant (2 Sam. 7:12–16).

Carson also elaborates on this first feature with yet a second one:

> Second, amongst the great themes of David's life that are repeatedly picked up in the New Testament are those that focus on his suffering, weakness, betrayal by friends, discouragement (*e.g.* the use of Ps. 22 in the passion narratives). Great David suffered; his greatness did not exempt him from pain and tears.[86]

Hence, when Christ suffers betrayal, naturally he personifies David's suffering in betrayal though in far greater measure and with far more

---

[84] Carson 1991: 470. Emphasis original.
[85] Ibid.
[86] Ibid.

historical significance as the Davidic king God promised would come to establish his kingdom for ever.

> Christians who came to see that the greatest display of the glory of the incarnate Word lay in the suffering and death so despised by the blind world, could not help but emphasize the similar strand in David's life, and see in it part of the mosaic that established a Davidic 'typology'.[87]

This typological pattern that accompanies scriptural fulfilment not only reveals Jesus' belief that the Scriptures originate from a divine author but that through them the divine author is bringing to culmination the plan of redemption revealed through the Law and the Prophets. This much is plain not only in extended quotations from prophets like Isaiah, but in subtle, pithy statements Jesus makes in John, such as 'But the Scripture will be fulfilled' (13:18) and 'that the Scripture might be fulfilled' (17:12). That concise vocabulary continues throughout the passion narrative of John's Gospel when Jesus is delivered over for crucifixion, to which we now turn.

John's use of the Davidic psalms in the crucifixion of the King of the Jews: John 19

Throughout John's passion narrative, the reader is told that the smallest, seemingly most insignificant, details happen 'to fulfil the Scriptures'. Some of these details lead John even to quote from specific scriptural passages that he believes are being intentionally, if not typologically, fulfilled by Jesus. Consider the following three instances.[88]

1. Casting lots for Jesus' tunic in fulfilment of Psalm 22:18:

> When the soldiers had crucified Jesus, they took his garments and divided them into four parts, one part for each soldier; also his tunic. But the tunic was seamless, woven in one piece from top to bottom, so they said to one another, 'Let us not tear it, but cast lots for it to see whose it shall be.' This was *to fulfil the Scripture* which says,

---

[87] Ibid.
[88] Emphases added.

'They divided my garments among them,
and for my clothing they cast lots.'
(John 19:23–24)

2. Jesus, to fulfil Psalm 69:21, says he thirsts:

After this, Jesus, knowing that all was now finished, said (*to fulfil the Scripture*), 'I thirst.' A jar full of sour wine stood there, so they put a sponge full of the sour wine on a hyssop branch and held it to his mouth. When Jesus had received the sour wine, he said, 'It is finished', and he bowed his head and gave up his spirit.
(John 19:28–30)

3. Pierced but bones not broken in fulfilment of Exodus 12:46; Numbers 9:12; Psalm 34:20; Zechariah 12:10:

But when they came to Jesus and saw that he was already dead, they did not break his legs. But one of the soldiers pierced his side with a spear, and at once there came out blood and water. He who saw it has borne witness – his testimony is true, and he knows that he is telling the truth – that you also may believe. *For these things took place that the Scripture might be fulfilled:* 'Not one of his bones will be broken.' And again another Scripture says, 'They will look on him whom they have pierced.'
(John 19:33–37)

What at first glance appear to the modern interpreter as random proof texts turn out to be strategic citations to complete John's typological canvas. Read within John's wider context, these Psalms citations communicate that this crucified Jesus is the *Davidic king and Messiah*.

As was seen in our look at John 1:49, Nathanael's eyes are opened to the messianic identity of Jesus, and Nathanael responds by calling Jesus the Son of God and King of Israel, two titles used synonymously, with strong overtones of Psalm 2:7 and 2 Samuel 7:12–14 in the background.[89] This royal motif does not stop here, however, but continues in John 6:15. Seeing Jesus take a small lunch and feed over five thousand, the crowd

---

[89] In chapter 6 we will see that Nathanael's confession has implications for Jesus' deity as well.

attempts to take him by force 'to make him king'. Jesus escapes because it is not yet time for such a public affirmation; that time arrives in John 12:15 when this 'king' enters Jerusalem with shouts of 'Hosanna!'. John concludes that Jesus rode into Jerusalem 'just as it is written' in Zechariah 9:9:

> Fear not, daughter of Zion;
> behold, *your king* is coming,
>   sitting on a donkey's colt!
> (Emphasis added)

On that account Pilate will ask Jesus at his trial whether he is the 'King of the Jews' (John 18:33). Jesus responds by correcting misconceptions: 'My kingdom is not of this world' (18:36). To which Pilate asks, 'So you are a king?' (18:37). Although it is unlikely that Pilate understands the type of king Jesus is and the type of kingdom he inaugurates, Jesus gives an affirmative answer: 'You say that I am a king. For this purpose I was born and for this purpose I have come into the world – to bear witness to the truth' (18:37). Nevertheless, the crowd detests this self-proclaimed king. They shout, 'Crucify him!', but Pilate asks, perhaps intending to insult the Jews, why he should crucify 'your King?' (19:15). The chief priests resent Pilate's rhetorical question: 'We have no king but Caesar' (19:15).

With this royal motif in view, John intentionally paints the crucifixion account in Davidic colours. Israel has rejected Jesus as their king: his crucifixion, they believe, is proof that he is no king of theirs. God promised a king on David's throne whose reign would be for ever. However, they have forgotten Jesus' earlier prediction, namely that he would be exalted by being lifted up (John 3:14; 8:28; 12:32).[90] This king ascends to his royal throne by descending to the grave: his crucifixion is his exaltation. For that reason, John incorporates a splintering of 'fulfilment' passages from the psalms of David. John is intent to demonstrate that it is through his death that Jesus typologically fulfils his office as the new Davidic king.

For example, consider just one of the three references above: John 19:23–24 (fulfilling Psalm 22:18). It is David who expresses his anguish in Psalm 22, crying out to God, asking God where he is in Jesus' moment of

---

[90] That is why they protest, 'We have heard from the Law that the Christ remains for ever. How can you say that the Son of Man must be lifted up? Who is this Son of Man?' (John 12:34).

despair and why God remains silent as the enemies mock Jesus (22:1–8). David is specific about his suffering, which is not only spiritual but physical (Ps. 22:14–15). So near to death is David that he says he can count his bones as his enemies gloat over him (22:17). So sure are they that David is defeated by death that they divide his garments among them, and cast lots for his clothing (Ps. 22:18).

As the new and greater David, Jesus undergoes such sufferings but on a cosmic scale. Typologically represented, what David experienced escalates in the agony of Christ on the cross, as seen not only in John but in the Synoptics (Matt. 27:35–43; Mark 15:34). Those who put him to death gloat over him as they divide his garments. Nevertheless, John says they do not tear his garments but cast lots to see who will get them, perhaps unintentionally signifying the unity of Christ's kingdom even in his moment of death.

Daley-Denton and Köstenberger wonder if there is an allusion here to 1 Samuel 15:27–28, where God tears the kingdom from Saul, an act symbolically portrayed when Saul clings to Samuel's robe only to tear it, and again symbolized when David tears Saul's robe at Engedi (1 Sam. 24). By contrast, Jesus' robe remains unified, symbolizing the indivisibility of his kingdom even in his moment of death. If so, God's covenant promise to set on David's throne an eternal king who establishes an eternal kingdom is brought to the pinnacle of its fulfilment (2 Sam. 7:13).[91] But whether 1 Samuel 24 itself is alluded to or not, John's use of Psalm 22 positions Jesus as the Davidic king who fulfils and escalates the suffering David experienced. In this sense, David's suffering prefigured Christ's suffering. 'There is', says Hays, 'an implicit suggestion here that Jesus paradoxically fulfils the role of Davidic kingship precisely through his conformity to the extreme suffering portrayed in these Davidic lament psalms.'[92]

As to the big picture of this current study, such fulfilment manifests not only John's belief in the inspiration of these Scriptures but in their persistent canonical trustworthiness. Given how small these details appear to be in the narrative (casting lots for a tunic rather than tearing it, asking for a drink, piercing Jesus' side but not breaking his legs, etc.), it is hard to see how John and Jesus could have believed in anything but the verbal and plenary nature of the Scripture's inspiration and inerrancy. Blomberg is on the mark:

---

[91] They also propose 1 Kgs 11:29–31, where Ahijah's torn robe pictures the separation of the kingdom of Solomon. Daley-Denton 2004: 133; Köstenberger 2007: 501.

[92] Hays 2016: 326.

What we do *not* see in Christ's teachings based on the Scriptures of his people is anything that would point to a canon within a canon – viewing only certain parts of the Bible as authoritative . . . We find nothing to suggest that Jesus distinguished between following the Bible on matters of faith and practice, or of doctrine and ethics, while allowing for mistakes in details of history that we can ignore.[93]

Apart from such attributes of Scripture, it is doubtful John or Jesus would have so readily believed and taught others that such Scriptures were being fulfilled in the very midst of their listeners and observers.

The relationship between Israel's Scriptures and this 'new movement': from eschatology to Christology

With an in-depth (though selective) look at Matthew and John's Gospels now complete, are there wider conclusions to be reached concerning the Scriptures that Jesus' disciples and their associates would write once Jesus ascended into the heavens? Consider but a few.

If the Old Testament Scriptures find their *telos* in Jesus Christ, and if he is their fulfilment, then an important implication follows for the church of the first century. It is this: *the Old Testament Scriptures are not adopted by Jesus and the church (that is the approach of most sects and cults), but the Old Testament Scriptures give birth to Jesus himself and are the genesis of his church.* As mentioned earlier, for Luther they are the swaddling clothes in which Christ is born.[94]

---

[93] Blomberg 2016: 698. Emphasis original.
[94] Luther 1960: 236. Stuhlmacher (2018: 6; emphasis original) captures a similar point from the perspective of the NT's background: 'Jesus and the apostles were born Jews. They read Israel's Bible as the word of God, which remained equally valid for them. They gave the Christian churches that sprang up after Easter a stake in this Bible, and they referred to it as the (Holy) Scripture(s), even as the Jews did. This expression is characteristic. The Scriptures are *God's holy word for all of early Christianity* . . . They read this Bible as the Spirit-inspired living word of the one God who created the world, chose Israel to be his own people, and sent the promised Messiah and Savior of the world in the person of Jesus of Nazareth. Individual New Testament books admittedly use the Scriptures of the Old Testament eclectically or with varying degrees of intensity. But their common appeal to these Scriptures cannot be denied: it was and is fundamental to Christian faith.'

It is beyond the scope of this study to move into dogmatic discussions of canon and tradition.[95] However, the last two chapters demand that the above point be clarified and stressed. This same point has been elaborated by Robert Jenson, who contests the popular idea that the church 'somehow "took over" or "accepted" old Israel's Scripture'.[96]

The neo-Protestant theology of the nineteenth and twentieth centuries, that spoke so much about 'history,' often used its invocation of history to relativize the authority of the Old Testament. That the gospel identifies itself as the culmination and content of the Old Testament's story can be made to mean that the Old Testament now serves to provide historical background for the gospel. On this construal, we do not need the Old Testament to understand the New, but it is only in the New that we find the message itself.[97]

This conception makes the Scriptures of Israel irrelevant to Christ and the New Testament. Theology is divorced from history whenever the Old Testament becomes mere historical background, adopted by the church merely for the purpose of providing a context for that which is really important, the gospel of the New Testament.[98] Yet such a view has everything backwards. 'On the contrary,' Jenson exclaims, '*Israel's Scripture accepted – or did not accept – the church.*'[99]

---

[95] See Barrett 2016: 332–371.

[96] Jenson 2010: 20.

[97] Ibid. 23. Dempster demonstrates how this approach leads to specific canonical conclusions: 'The standard historical explanation for canon is that at best it is simply a product of the believing community, a fortuitous result of historical circumstances, or at worst a product of political power, the result of the victors in internecine theological struggles. Thus the documents have no inherent transcendent value as such but for various reasons were considered important, and the community or communities gave them a "divine" stamp of approval. External forces operating within the communities produced the canon. This is for the most part the "master narrative" within the academic community. Canon is simply a "human repertoire": documents *considered* sacred and special became canon. Viewed from a distinctly immanent frame, the chief mark of canon is its enumerative nature: it is simply a special list. Thus there is no distinct ontology of canon. Frequently the points are made that canon does not signify *a collection of authoritative documents* but *an authoritative collection of documents*, and that it is wrong to confuse the two. An external process of canonization made a collection of authoritative documents into an authoritative collection through a series of decisions by councils and groups.' Dempster 2016: 135. Emphases original; cf. Webster 2003: 95–126.

[98] Krentz (1975: 16) calls this the 'process of objectification'. Also see Bartholomew (2015: 211), who blames Semler in particular and the history of religions school of thought, as well as de Wette, who learned from Kant, that the 'contingent truths of history cannot be revelatory', which resulted in a full-on assault on the OT (214).

[99] Jenson 2010: 20. Emphasis added.

The logical order Jenson describes may seem trivial but the integrity of the Old Testament witness and the organic unity (and progression) of the entire canon in the person and work of Christ depend on such an order.

> The church initially could not ask and still should not ask: 'Why should/did we adopt Israel's Scripture?' 'What do we need it for?' The Law, the Prophets, and the Writings were Scripture for those who first believed the resurrection, and in that role they were antecedent to and indeed independent of this new conviction.[100]

Jenson proposes that our mindset must be totally reoriented if we are to understand not only the first-century Christian but the unity of the canon from Old to New Testament. 'The real question was and is this: *"Can Israel's Scripture accept this proclamation of Jesus' resurrection and this new movement within Israel?" "Why does Israel's Scripture need Jesus and his disciples?"*'[101] Christopher R. Seitz has made a similar observation:

> In the early church the problem was not how to square faith with an Old Testament regarded as outmoded but the reverse. How, in the light of Scripture regarded as authoritative and a privileged witness to God and His truth, could it be said that Jesus was in accordance and was one with the Father who sent him?[102]

Was this not the nucleus of the conflict between Jesus and the religious leaders? They all presupposed the Old Testament Scriptures originated from God, yet disagreed on their messianic fulfilment in Christ; in other words, *the difference was one of eschatology, not canon.* Nevertheless, because the religious leaders of Jesus' day rejected him as the one the Old Testament prefigured, many Jews did not, indeed would not, become *Christ*-ians. Therefore, although the disagreement between the religious leaders and Jesus was one of eschatology, it did have significant canonical consequences, chief being the Jewish rejection not only of Christ but of his apostles and their writings. 'Thus a view of the canon as a whole basically originates in the Christ event itself.'[103] As De Lubac says, 'Jesus Christ

---

[100] Ibid.
[101] Ibid. Emphasis added.
[102] Seitz 2001: 65.
[103] Bartholomew 2015: 54. Also see Gaffin 1988: 165–183; Rad 1979: 19.

effects the unity of Scripture because he is its end and its fullness. Everything in Scripture is related to him. And he is its unique Object. We could even say that he is the totality of its exegesis.'[104]

That said, Jenson is right to target the resurrection, for the empty tomb is but the beginning of a movement that claimed the Old Testament witness not merely as a text to complement its own message (that methodology would align more with Gnostic groups). Rather, those who belonged to 'the Way' (Acts 9:2) saw themselves as the true heirs of the Old Testament, true Jews, true sons of Abraham, even if they were ethnically Gentiles (Gal. 3:7). Why? The tomb was found empty; the Scriptures were fulfilled.

After the destruction of the temple, observes Jenson, the rabbis asked these types of questions when confronted with the claims of the gospel by first-century Christians: 'Can Israel's Scripture accept this proclamation of Jesus' resurrection and this new movement within Israel?' and 'Why does Israel's Scripture need Jesus and his disciples'? But their answer was negative:

> the Torah does not support this message, and the last thing that yet again distressed and dispersed Israel needs is this new sect, which does not uniformly keep the law and may even be heretical with respect to the singleness of God.[105]

The great divide between Jews who rejected Jesus and Jews who followed him comes down to this: the former did not believe Jesus was the fulfilment of the Scriptures of Israel, but the latter did and based everything on that foundational belief. While there might have been many qualities that distinguished first-century Christian Jews from non-Christian Jews, *the core issue was the gospel itself.* The divide was theological: it was *Christological* through and through.

And the divide was tense, as not only the crucifixion of Jesus demonstrated but also the martyrdoms of his disciples, because these Christ-followers were claiming the same Scriptures every Jew adhered to for religious belief and practice. The difference was that the church followed the hermeneutic of Christ by rereading the Old Testament only to discover that Jesus was typologically prefigured and prophesied about just about

---

[104] De Lubac 2000: 105.
[105] Jenson 2010: 20.

everywhere. It was not a matter of reading Jesus *back into* the Old Testament: the Old Testament itself was the seed that blossomed into its own fulfilment with the coming of the messianic king.

Yet what was the proof of such a scriptural–Christological presupposition? The Jewish religious leaders believed they had proved otherwise by crucifying this supposed 'King of the Jews': Christology was buried with Christ in the tomb. That confidence was shattered three days later when this King rose victorious over his enemies. The resurrection, in other words, was the announcement to Jerusalem, Judea, Samaria and the ends of the earth that the Scriptures of Israel did in fact speak of Christ as the Messiah. That is a claim Jesus made in his own lifetime, but it is one powerfully demonstrated when he appeared to hundreds of eye-witnesses before ascending to the right hand of his Father. Jesus'

> preaching and actions manifestly claimed that he and his community were uniquely and exactly what Israel according to its Scripture needed; and when he was executed on account of this claim, the God of Israel confirmed it by raising him up.[106]

Therefore, as Christ's disciples spread this good news, it was only good news because that which was promised in Israel's Scriptures had come true in Christ. For 'a hundred years or more it was always the new gospel that was justified by Israel's Scripture, never the other way around'.[107]

---

[106] Ibid.
[107] Ibid. Here Jenson is in debt to Von Campenhausen. Also see Gaffin 2008: 61–81; Sailhamer 2001: 15.

5

Living by every word from the mouth of God: what Christ's covenant obedience to the Scriptures says about the Scriptures

In chapter 2 I argued that the interpreter's hermeneutical approach to Jesus and the Scriptures needs to be reoriented and reconfigured so that Jesus' understanding of Scripture's ontology is not forced through a Pauline grid (as if Jesus must always address the nature of Scripture *directly*). Instead, Jesus' understanding of Scripture is perceived far more *indirectly*, via the promise–fulfilment pattern intrinsic to the Old Testament and the typological tapestry that escalates across the canon only to blossom in the Gospels. Chapters 3 and 4 examined the plethora of ways Jesus and the Gospel writers claim the Scriptures to be fulfilled. By focusing on typology, for example, it became clear that Jesus and the Gospel writers presuppose not only inspiration, but divine authorial intent and canonical unity. They see themselves, as did the first-century church, as the rightful heirs to the Old Testament and believe they continue its story as Yahweh intended from the beginning.

Now it remains to be seen how Jesus fulfils the redemptive promises and types of the Old Testament, how the covenant word of Yahweh reaches its fulfilment in the one who inaugurates the new covenant, namely Christ Jesus. In what follows it will be concluded that Jesus does so, in part, by his *life of obedience*, an obedience meant to secure righteousness and eternal life for all those who trust in him.[1] To see this, we will turn to the way the

---

[1] I say 'in part' because we should not forget the passive obedience of Christ; i.e. Christ's suffering by which he pays the penalty of our transgressions. See e.g. chapter 4.

Gospels describe Jesus as the last Adam, the true Israel, the son of Abraham and David, and Son of God, to see that Jesus is the obedient, Adamic Son, fulfilling the stipulations of God's covenant word to win back God's covenant people.

For our purposes, this redemptive obedience, which is a Christological and soteriology reality (what theologians have labelled the 'active obedience' of Christ), has major implications for understanding Jesus' view of the Scriptures. *In the Gospels Jesus is on a mission as the incarnate and Adamic Son to fulfil all righteousness and attain redemption for God's covenant people, but that mission is only successful if he is obedient to the Scriptures. It is by means of his trust in the Scriptures and his obedience to them that Jesus secures a perfect record of obedience that is then reckoned to those who trust in him. Therefore, some of Jesus' most direct affirmations of Scripture's inspiration and authority are not manifested in pithy sayings extracted from the context of his incarnation but instilled within the redemptive mission he came to accomplish as our covenant Mediator and federal head. In other words, the very mission of the Son reveals the ontology of the Scriptures according to the Son.*[2]

If right, then the claim at the start of this project – that Jesus and the Gospels' hermeneutic needs reorientation – is substantiated. Instead of looking for a direct reflection on Scripture, as one can with Paul or Peter, one looks most fundamentally to the mission of the Son – indeed, the gospel itself – to discover Jesus' scriptural presuppositions. As mentioned at the start, one need not pedal through the Gospels looking for an uncharacteristic statement about Scripture's ontology. Rather, one need but look to the *mission* of the Son to discover the *attitude* of the Son towards the Scriptures of Israel.

In what follows, the focus will be restricted to the Synoptic accounts. That is not because the present theme is absent from John; indeed, John has an important place for the Son's obedience to the Scriptures. However,

---

[2] I have worded this paragraph carefully for a reason: when I associate obedience with sonship here and going forward, I am referring to the economy of salvation. In other words, I have in mind the *incarnational, covenantal* and *Adamic* obedience of Christ as a *servant*, not an eternal obedience or subordination of the eternal Son to the Father's authority within the immanent Trinity. I reject the latter, which is the view of EFS (Evangelical Functional Subordination). EFS is a social trinitarianism that cannot be supported by Scripture or the creeds, substituting a modern definition of person and roles (in its case hierarchy) for biblical, classical categories (eternal relations of origin). EFS compromises the Son's equality. To see my critique of EFS, consult my forthcoming book, *Simply Trinity*. Also see the critiques of Giles 2012; Sanders and Swain 2017; Bird and Harrower 2019.

John chooses to zero in on the Son's fulfilment of his Father's mission ('For I have come down from heaven, not to do my own will but the will of him who sent me'; 6:38) and does not focus, as much as the Synoptics do at least, on the obedience of Jesus *to the Scriptures* in particular, though John no doubt would have agreed with this synoptic emphasis. That said, Matthew, Luke and Mark will be at the centre of this chapter, while John – and his focus on the filial identity of the Son – will occupy chapter 6.

Matthew

Covenant obedience and Adamic sonship

In chapter 2 it was concluded that Adam acts within the framework of a covenant (i.e. covenant of creation/works). Created by God and made in God's very image, Adam is a son, and one God designs to live in covenant relationship with him. This covenant relationship, like all covenants, has certain stipulations; for example, Adam can eat from every tree, but is not to eat from the tree of the knowledge of good and evil. This command or word from God put Adam to the test. Would he listen to the word of God or to the word of the serpent?

The reader of the whole canon also knows, as Paul reveals (Rom. 5:12–21), that Adam is not an isolated actor in this drama near the beginning of creation. He acts not just for himself but for all humanity. He is, in other words, humankind's first and most important father. In that moment of testing Adam represents his progeny. Given the covenantal nature of the relationship in the garden, it is appropriate to say that Adam is federal head to all those born in his wake. His covenant unfaithfulness results in the downfall not only of himself but all to come. His guilt, his corruption, will now be that of all humanity.

The disaster and curse Adam's disobedience creates results in a humanity desperate for a new, second and last Adam, one who acts just as vicariously as Adam did but this time to obey the word of God and remain faithful to the covenant on behalf of the ungodly. As Calvin comments:

> Accordingly, our Lord came in order to take Adam's place in obeying the Father, to present our flesh as the price of satisfaction to God's

righteous judgment, and, in the same flesh, to pay the penalty that we had deserved.[3]

In that sense, all of history can be summarized by two Adams: a first Adam, whose covenant representation resulted in the condemnation of humanity, and a second or last Adam, whose covenant representation results in the justification of the ungodly. Eternal life hangs in the balance of Adam's choice: if he obeys, he will for ever enjoy a Sabbath rest, eating indefinitely from the tree of life. His disobedience to the word of God, however, necessitates a second Adam who can win back the life Adam and his fallen race forfeited. In the last Adam paradise lost is paradise regained.[4]

The Genesis account is not lost on the Old Testament authors. They too will retell the history of Israel through an Edenic and Adamic lens. Scholars from G. K. Beale and Brandon Crowe to N. T. Wright, despite certain differences, have all recognized the many ways creation imagery is utilized by Old and New Testament authors alike.[5] This much is seen, for example, in the continual command to be fruitful and multiply (Gen. 9:1, 7; 35:11–12) or the way the land of promise is painted in new creation vocabulary (Lev. 26:6–12; Jer. 3:16; 23:3; Ezek. 36:11).[6] What is more, Adam's sin as Israel's first father becomes the ultimate reference point for sin's inception and covenant transgression (Josh. 7:21; 1 Chr. 1:1; Job 31:33; Isa. 43:27; Hos. 6:7).

Crowe, building on the work of Vos and Beale, claims that this theme of covenant obedience is naturally tied to *Adamic sonship*. Crowe only confirms what has been asserted so far when he writes, 'As the one who stands at the head of original humanity in Scripture, Adam was created to be God's son who would be faithful to God's (covenantal) commands.' Yet notice the way Crowe ties faithfulness and sonship together:

When Adam failed as the protological vice-regent, he acted contrary to his status as righteous son of God who was created in the glorious image of God. Sonship in Scripture is consistently paired with

---

[3] Calvin 1960: 2.12.3; cf. 4.16.18.

[4] This reading of Genesis has been articulated by a plethora of Reformed commentaries and NT scholars. See the bibliography for examples. Also see chapter 2.

[5] Beale 2011: 46–54; 2004: 81–121; Wright 1992: 21–26. To see a fuller case for Edenic and Adamic language throughout the texts mentioned, consult Crowe 2017: 57–63. It should be qualified, however, that Wright does not go so far as to affirm the covenant of creation in the way I have above. Nevertheless, he sees creation language throughout the OT.

[6] Crowe 2017: 57–58.

obedience, and it is highly significant that the requisite relationship between sonship and obedience is properly traced scripturally back to Adam.[7]

The proof that covenant obedience and Adamic sonship are interrelated in Scripture is demonstrated in the transition from Genesis to Exodus, from Adam to Israel. In Adam's heritage Israel too is God's son.[8] And like Adam, as well as all the little 'Adams' that followed (Noah, Abraham, Isaac, Jacob, Joseph), Israel lives and breathes covenantal air. Brought to the foot of Sinai, Israel is corporately inducted into the covenant and, as seen in chapter 2, the book of the covenant becomes the constitution of Israel's covenant, their daily bread (Deut. 8:3). Yet unlike some ANE treaties, the *pactum* Israel enters into with Yahweh could not be more personal.[9] Even before Israel is liberated and reaches Sinai, the nation is called by God to be his firstborn son. Moses, Israel's big brother, is to tell Pharaoh, 'Thus says the LORD, Israel is my firstborn son, and I say to you, "Let my son go that he may serve me." If you refuse to let him go, behold, I will kill your firstborn son' (Exod. 4:22–23). So filial is Israel's relationship to Yahweh, his father, that when Pharaoh's heart proves to be hard and stubborn, God does just that: he takes the life of Pharaoh's firstborn, and that death sentence is so personal that Pharaoh finally releases his grip on Yahweh's firstborn. Pharaoh's son is taken to preserve God's son.

The language of 'firstborn son' is not merely for Pharaoh's benefit but continues as a theme across the Old Testament. For example, when Israel is on the edge of entering the land of promise, he cowers in fear at the sight of the nations. He has forgotten that he is the privileged, chosen son of God. So the Lord corrects his son, reminding Israel how he has acted as his father:

> The LORD your God who goes before you will himself fight for you, just as he did for you in Egypt before your eyes, and in the wilderness, where you have seen how the LORD your *God carried you, as a man carries his son.*
> (Deut. 1:30–31; emphasis added)

---

[7] Ibid. 61.

[8] That is not to say the parallel between Adam and Israel is exact. On differences, see ibid. 65–67.

[9] See my engagement with Kline in chapter 2 on ANE treaties and covenants.

In Deuteronomy 8, a passage we will return to, the Lord again reminds Israel that he has led him through the wilderness. Like Adam in the garden, Yahweh tested his son for forty years 'that he might humble you' and 'know what was in your heart' (Deut. 8:2). Yahweh let his son go hungry so that he learned to trust in his father for manna from heaven and discover that 'man does not live by bread alone, but man lives by every word that comes from the mouth of the LORD' (8:3).

Nevertheless, Israel's grumbling and distrust of his father's covenant word made discipline necessary. Yet Yahweh disciplined as a father would his son: 'Know then in your heart that, as a man disciplines his son, the LORD your God disciplines you' (8:5). As a son is to listen to the word of his father, so too Israel is to 'keep the commandments of the LORD your God by walking in his ways and by fearing him' (8:6). The irony of Israel's story is that they keep wandering after the gods of foreign nations, nations that have no special filial privileges from Yahweh. Yet Israel alone is God's chosen son, God's called-out nation. He has no need to long for what the nations have: Israel is God's firstborn. Hence all the unique identity markers: from his clothing to his haircut (e.g. Deut. 14:1) Israel is meant to stand out because he alone is God's firstborn, 'a people holy to the LORD your God', a people the 'LORD has chosen' to be his 'treasured possession, out of all the peoples who are on the face of the earth' (Deut. 14:2).

For that reason, Moses can respond to the foolishness of Israel and sing:

> Is not he your father, who created you,
> > who made you and established you?
> Remember the days of old;
> > consider the years of many generations;
> ask your father, and he will show you . . .
> (32:6–7)

Yet Israel rebelled against his father, who 'found him in a desert land, and . . . cared for him' as the 'apple of his eye' (32:10).

> You were unmindful of the Rock that bore you,
> > and you forgot the God who gave you birth.
> (32:18)

Israel grew into a 'perverse generation, / children in whom is no faithfulness' (32:20). The Lord sent disaster on his son, the plague and the sword (32:23–25). Nevertheless, Yahweh promises to avenge the 'blood of his children', and repay his son's adversaries; in the end, he will cleanse the land for his people (32:43). That cleansing is not just retributive, punishing Israel's enemies, but is meant to wash the sons of Israel as well so that they and their land will experience peace and covenant renewal.

The covenant structure of Deuteronomy oscillates around this father–son dynamic, a dynamic that hinges in large part on the son's covenant obedience to his father, much like Adam's filial (dis)obedience to his Father-Creator, and the creation covenant he graciously set in place. When Israel disobeys his Father's word, failing to uphold the covenant obligations, the curses threatened by the covenant treaty are unleashed. Yet when Israel is faithful to the covenant obligations, living in communion with his father, the blessings of the covenant treaty are lavished on Israel. In this filial covenant, holiness cannot be neglected, for Israel is to reflect the holiness of his father. In other words, '*because* the sons of Israel are sons of the Lord their God, *therefore* they must be holy'. Yet such filial obedience is to be heartfelt, internally driven and moved by love itself as both the Prophets (Jer. 31:31–34; Ezek. 36:22–38) and Jesus (Matt. 5) specify. As Deuteronomy 7 and 11 demonstrate, 'Love is tantamount to obedience in the context of the covenant . . . and this love is to characterize the devotion and fealty of Israel as son to its divine father.'[10]

As will be seen in my discussion of the temptations of Jesus (Matt. 4), no one exhibits this filial, covenantal and obedient love like the incarnate, Adamic, and messianic Son, Jesus Christ. He is the last Adam, the true Israel, the Son who never fails to obey and from the heart. He does so not for himself but for others, for, like Adam, he is tested according to a new covenant, but unlike Adam and Israel he succeeds. His federal representation procures the salvation of all those found in the second Adam; his obedience results in the inauguration of a new covenant, one in which all God's people know the Lord.

Lest one think this obedience of the last Adam is an invention of Paul, consider the Gospel accounts in brief.[11]

---

[10] Crowe 2017: 62.

[11] Crowe believes an 'Adam Christology' pervades the Gospels, meaning that 'Christ is a *representative* figure'. Should we understand Christ as the new Adam who represents us, who is our covenant mediator, then we will also understand how this Christ relates to Israel.

'Out of Egypt I called my son' (Matt. 1 – 2)

As seen in chapter 3, Matthew may be the most explicit of the Evangelists with his Old Testament references, ensuring his reader understands how Jesus brings to fulfilment promises and types foreshadowed in the Old Testament.

Right away Matthew situates Jesus within the lineage of David and Abraham (1:1). The stress on David continues when the angel of the Lord addresses Joseph as 'son of David' (1:20). Having announced that Mary will give birth to a son conceived in her by the Holy Spirit, Matthew comments that all 'this took place to fulfil what the Lord had spoken by the prophet' Isaiah (1:22; see Isa. 7:14; 8:8, 10). The son Mary gives birth to is to be called Immanuel because he is 'God with us' (Matt. 1:23). He is not merely another son of David but is David's greater son who is the Lord himself (Ps. 110:1). The Lord has not merely sent another prophet to his people: the Lord himself has come to his people to dwell with them. 'Hosea 11:1–11 thus resonates richly with the Matthean Emmanuel theme: the God who called his Son out of Egypt is the same God who is present *in their midst*.'[12] In other words, God's presence has been embodied in his own Son. As will be seen in chapter 6, this explains why worship of Jesus is such a prevalent theme throughout Matthew's Gospel.[13]

That this is God's own Son becomes plain when Mary and Joseph flee with Jesus due to the rising threat of Herod. Worried at the news of a new king, one whose name is written in the books of the prophets (see Matt. 2:6 and Mic. 5:2), specifying even the town of this king's birth, Herod becomes the persecutor of Immanuel. Warned by the angel of the Lord, Joseph is told to flee to Egypt until further instruction. Matthew sees just how thick the typology has become and observes that all this occurred 'to fulfil what the Lord had spoken by the prophet' Hosea: 'Out of Egypt I called my son' (Matt. 2:15; Hos. 11:1).

It is worth noting that Hosea 11:1 reads in full:

> *When Israel was a child, I loved him,*
> and out of Egypt I called my son.

(note 11 *cont.*) With both Adam and Israel, 'Christ is portrayed in covenantal terms: as the last Adam, Christ is the covenantal (or *federal*) head of his people, the mediator of the new covenant.' Ibid. 16. Emphases original.

[12] Hays 2016: 166. Emphasis original.

[13] E.g. Matt. 2:2, 11; 8:2; 9:18; 14:32–33; 15:25; 20:20; 28:9, 17.

Here is a father–son relationship that is bound in love. Yahweh loves his son, Israel, the 'apple of his eye' (Deut. 32:10). Yet born to Mary and Joseph is a son who is the true Israel, the one on whom all the promises of the prophets find their hope and culmination. He is the Son on whom the Father's love rests.[14]

The correspondence between these two sons in Matthew 2 is anything but accidental: Israel was oppressed by Pharaoh in Egypt until Yahweh called his son out of Egypt. Now the new exodus has arrived. Herod may be the new pharaoh, forcing God's Son into hiding, but out of Egypt Yahweh calls his son yet again. Yet Jesus is not only the antitype to Israel but to Moses as well. For the same son who is called out of Egypt to be a new Israel is also a new Moses, one who ushers in a new exodus for the people of God. Jesus' ministry is still to come but already the exodus he inaugurates is at hand as he lies in his mother's arms.

Baptism to fulfil all righteousness: Matthew 3:13–17 (Mark 1:9–11; Luke 3:21–22; John 1:29–34)

Matthew does not wait until Jesus is in the full swing of his ministry but conveys at its inception that Jesus is the obedient, incarnate Son from the Father. Matthew 3 begins with the prophet John the Baptist and his preaching of repentance ('Repent, for the kingdom of heaven is at hand'; 3:2). John is the one 'who was spoken of by the prophet Isaiah':

The voice of one crying in the wilderness:
'Prepare the way of the Lord;
   make his paths straight.'
(3:3; cf. Isa. 40:3)

According to Isaiah (and Matthew), John is not the Messiah but the one who clears the way. John himself understands this to be the case, for he clarifies his identity and role when he says, 'I baptize you with water for repentance, but he who is coming after me is mightier than I, whose sandals I am not worthy to carry. He will baptize you with the Holy Spirit and fire' (Matt. 3:11). John's baptism is but the opening act; the baptism that the Lord himself performs, the baptism with the Spirit, will

---

[14] On fatherly love being the central motif here, see Carson 1984: 92.

be received only when the one John proclaims, the Christ, comes to his people, Israel. John's message and baptism will, at the proper time, be surpassed by him who is 'the Lord'.

What John does not expect, however, is that 'the Lord', the one who baptizes with the Holy Spirit, will himself be baptized by John. Matthew says John tried to prohibit Jesus from entering into the waters: 'John would have prevented him, saying, "I need to be baptized by you, and do you come to me?"' (Matt. 3:14). John's humility, which is just as explicit in Mark's account (see 1:7), is appropriate given the identity of the one who baptizes with the Spirit. However, what John does not yet realize is that Jesus must be baptized by John if Jesus is to identify with Israel and represent Yahweh's people in his obedient life. Jesus responds to John's resistance, 'Let it be so now, for thus it is fitting for us *to fulfil all righteousness*' (Matt. 3:15; emphasis added).

There is a substitutionary, vicarious aspect to Jesus' being submerged under the waters of the Jordan. John's Gospel is direct in this regard: when John the Baptist sees Jesus, he utilizes the imagery of the Passover, and perhaps the sacrificial system of the Old Testament as a whole, when he declares, 'Behold, the lamb of God, who takes away the sin of the world!' (1:29; cf. Exod. 12:5; Lev. 16; Isa. 53:6–7). Matthew does not say so in that many words, but expects his readers to see the vicarious element in the way he presents the baptism account, and especially in Jesus' claim ('to fulfil all righteousness'), which John chooses to omit. Jesus is being baptized on behalf of the people of Israel, and for the forgiveness of their sins. He is the one who is without sin, but since he comes as the covenant representative, he must be baptized for the sake of his people's transgressions. 'Jesus' identification with the people in their baptism', explains Vos, 'had the proximate end of securing for them vicariously what the sacrament aimed at, the forgiveness of sins.'[15]

Yet not only is forgiveness in view but the fulfilling of righteousness as well. The fulfilment of righteousness is in accord with Yahweh's promise in Jeremiah that the righteous Branch of David will be called 'The LORD is our righteousness' (Jer. 23:6). Jesus comes, therefore, on behalf of the people and for the people. 'By participating in John's baptism', says Crowe, 'Jesus identifies with God's people as their representative, which is part of the logic for why his obedience can be counted vicariously.'[16]

---

[15] Vos 1996: 320.
[16] Crowe 2017: 68.

That Jesus fulfils all righteousness as the obedient, incarnate Son is confirmed when he rises from the waters:

> And when Jesus was baptized, immediately he went up from the water, and behold, the heavens were opened to him, and he saw the Spirit of God descending like a dove and coming to rest on him; and behold, a voice from heaven said, 'This is my beloved Son, with whom I am well pleased.'
> (Matt. 3:16–17; cf. Mark 1:9–13; Luke 3:21–22; John 1:29–34)

The trinitarian nature of this narrative is arresting. The Son is baptized, the Father voices his approval and the Spirit rests on the Son. The Father not only identifies his Son but expresses his pleasure with him. The Son is loved by the Father and the Son's incarnational, covenantal obedience to fulfil the mission of his Father only honours the Father all the more.

In this event, the reader sees both Messiah and sonship kiss, so that when the Father delights in his incarnate Son it is also a delight in his Messiah, who stands in Israel's stead. Chapter 3 looked at instances where 'Son of God' is a title that features Jesus as the messianic, Davidic king, and chapter 6 will look at examples (e.g. John 5) where sonship language features Jesus as the eternal Son of the Father. But here we meet one of those unique points in Matthew's Gospel where it appears both are being featured or at least presupposed. The first half of Matthew 3:17 ('This is my beloved Son') echoes Psalm 2 where the Lord's 'anointed' one, the Davidic king, is said to be God's Son ('You are my Son; / today I have begotten you'; 2:7), and the second half of 3:17 ('with whom I am well pleased') echoes Isaiah 42:13 – 53:12.[17] Yet because it is the Father speaking, this can be none other than the eternal Son come down from heaven as God incarnate.

Crowe captures this duality in all its richness:

> The contours of Jesus' sonship are multifaceted, at once communicating Jesus' ontological-filial relationship to his Father, announcing Jesus' messiahship (Pss. 2:7; 89:27; 2 Sam. 7:14), evoking corporate Israel (Exod. 4:22–23), and recalling Adam's royal-filial sonship.

---

17 Ibid. 39.

Crowe concludes:

> As messianic Son, Jesus represents Israel, and sonship is also the
> primary rubric by which the Gospel writers communicate Jesus'
> obedience. One can therefore concur with Ulrich Luz ... 'The Son
> of God is the just man who is fully and representatively obedient to
> God's will.'[18]

The richness of this imagery (i.e. messianic sonship) is only furthered by
echoes of Isaiah 42, where the Lord voices his delight in his chosen servant
by placing his Spirit upon him:

> Behold my servant, whom I uphold,
>   my chosen, in whom my soul delights;
> I have put my Spirit upon him;
>   he will bring forth justice to the nations.
> (Isa. 42:1)

While Matthew will not explicitly quote Isaiah 42 until chapter 12
(cf. 12:18–21), the language and imagery of Isaiah pervade the baptism
narrative. While Israel is God's chosen servant, Isaiah 42 is taken by
Matthew to speak ultimately of a servant who does what Israel did not do,
namely obey the covenant treaty. To take Israel's place, and figuratively step
into Israel's place in this baptism event requires the mentality of a servant,
and one who will, as the Gospel narratives advance, suffer for the people
to secure their redemption and bring justice to the nations. Matthew 3 is
but the beginning of many other instances in which the messianic Son will
be referred to as the obedient suffering servant (Luke 9:51 and Isa. 50:7;
Luke 23:47; Acts 3:14; 7:52; 22:14 and Isa. 53:11).[19]

At this point, one should notice two relevant features. (1) Although
neither Jesus nor the Gospel writers explicitly quote the Old Testament,
echoes of the Old Testament are present. It is hard to imagine Jesus being
unaware of these Isaianic echoes until he rises out of the waters and the
Spirit descends on him and he hears his Father's approval. (2) Jesus has not

---

[18] Ibid. 70–71.
[19] The point has been made, so I will not explore these instances, but see ibid. 71–72. Crowe
also makes the observation that while Luke 23:47 refers to Jesus as righteous, Matt. 27:54 and
Mark 15:39 refer to Jesus as Son of God. 'This also corroborates the view that sonship and
servanthood are complementary concepts, both of which underscore the representative
obedience of Jesus.' Ibid. 72.

yet quoted the Scriptures (though he will shortly) but already it is clear that he sees himself as the messianic, obedient, servant Son whom the Scriptures anticipated.[20] That self-consciousness is essential because we will now see that the *means* by which Jesus is to fulfil all righteousness is his continuing trust and dependence *on the Scriptures* as nothing less than the word his Father has breathed out by the same Spirit who descended on him.

Living by every word from the mouth of God: Matthew 4:1–11 (cf. Mark 1:12–13; Luke 4:1–13)

Having been baptized by John in the Jordan to 'fulfil all righteousness' (Matt. 3:15), the same 'Spirit of God' that descended 'like a dove' on Jesus then sent him into the wilderness (4:1). In Matthew 4 (cf. Luke 4:1–16) the obedient messianic Son is tempted by Satan; yet, as we will see, God's Son undergoes such a temptation as the last Adam and the true Israel. Jesus is recapitulating Israel's history as both the son of Adam (Gen. 3:15) and the Son of God (since Israel was God's son). Except, rather than breaking the covenant by transgressing the book of the covenant, Jesus will be an obedient son, reversing Adam's curse and Israel's damnation.

This much is plain when Jesus chooses to quote Deuteronomy, which is, to reiterate chapter 2, the book of the covenant. Through Moses Israel is instructed according to the words or commandments of God so that Israel will, as God's son, enter the land God promised to his father Abraham (Deut. 6:1–3). In Deuteronomy 6:5 Israel is given the greatest of commands: 'You shall love the LORD your God with all your heart and with all your soul and with all your might.' Yahweh says 'these words' are to penetrate within, so that they are 'on your heart' (Deut. 6:6). They are always to be present: the Israelite family is to talk of them when they sit down in their house, walk along the way, and lie down to sleep (Deut. 6:7). If not, Israel will forget them, and by forgetting them will forget the Lord (6:12). Israel is to fear the Lord and serve him only (6:13), rather than pant after other gods from the surrounding nations (6:14). Furthermore, Israel is not to put the Lord to the test by flirting with idolatry (6:16). Instead, they are to 'diligently keep the commandments of the LORD your God, and his testimonies and his statutes, which he has commanded you' (6:17), doing that which is 'right and good in the sight of the LORD' (6:18).

---

[20] For more on Jesus' self-consciousness, see Vos 1953.

If they are obedient, Yahweh will bless Israel in the land (6:18–19; 8:1). In Deuteronomy 8 Israel is told to remember the forty years spent in the wilderness; as God's covenant son, Israel was humbled by God, who tested his son to know what resided in their heart (8:2). Yahweh

> humbled you and let you hunger and fed you with manna, which you did not know . . . that he might make you know that man does not live by bread alone, but man lives by every word that comes from the mouth of the LORD.
> (8:3)

Yahweh warns that Israel dare not 'forget' who Yahweh is and what he has done; hence the importance of his spoken and inscripturated word. It is this covenantal word that is Israel's safeguard against all temptation in the land of promise. Israel was to cling to the book of the covenant for covenant life.

In similar fashion, before Jesus can enter his ministry he must be tempted and tested as God's Son. Notice the correspondence: Israel passed through the waters of the Red Sea and entered the wilderness for a time of testing. Likewise, Jesus passed through the waters of John's baptism to be led into the wilderness for testing as God's Son.[21] Yet also notice the difference: Israel passed through the waters of the Red Sea unharmed, only to fall into idolatry and walk away from the Book of the Covenant the people were given at Sinai. Jesus, however, is a new Moses, representing a new covenant people, and his temptations will not have the same result. Jesus has risen out of the waters of baptism, yet his baptism is 'to fulfil all righteousness'.

In all three Synoptics it is the wilderness that is the stage for this cosmic battle between Jesus and the serpent. The wilderness is not without symbolism, as hinted at by Mark when he says Jesus was 'with the wild animals' (Mark 1:13).[22] In other words, Jesus is reliving Israel's testing in the wilderness.[23] If Israel was God's covenant son, then it is little surprise why Matthew opens his Gospel citing Hosea 11:1 in reference to Christ:

---

[21] For more on this parallel, see Crowe 2017: 76; Hays 2016: 117–119.

[22] There is further symbolism when Matthew mentions forty days of fasting, representational of Israel's forty years (although Hays [2016: 117] believes the forty days and nights could refer to the forty days and nights Moses was on Mount Sinai fasting [Exod. 34:28; Deut. 9:9]). 'Like Israel, Jesus is tempted by hunger. And like Israel, Jesus is tempted to idolatry.' Davies and Allison 1988: 352.

[23] On the nature of this recapitulation, see Garland 2001: 39–40.

'Out of Egypt I called my son' (2:15). Israel's history is being recapitulated by Jesus, but this time with an entirely different outcome. His success will mark him as the true Israel, the Son of God who listens to and obeys the word of the covenant.[24]

The 'tempter', approaching the fasting Jesus, turns to the Scriptures. Augustine argued that sin is always parasitic, preying on that which is good.[25] If we take Augustine's insight further, we might add that evil, and the deception that temptation brings, thrives on the truth, but only the truth in part. That is the case in the wilderness temptations: as the devil appeals to the Scriptures, he does so to manipulate Jesus into breaking another part of the Scriptures. What Jesus demonstrates throughout these temptations, however, is that Satan hides the *analogia scriptura*, failing to interpret one passage of Scripture in the light of another, neglecting to allow Scripture to interpret Scripture. In short, the reason these appeals to the Scriptures have little effect is because Jesus exposes Satan's neglect of Scripture's inherent, comprehensive unity. To set one Scripture over against another is not only hermeneutically problematic, but Satan's way of excusing covenant unfaithfulness.

Such an erroneous hermeneutic is at work in each temptation.[26] In the first Matthean temptation the devil says, 'If you are the Son of God, command these stones to become loaves of bread' (4:3). The tempter has taken one scriptural truth (Jesus is the Son of God) and used it to excuse Jesus from fasting, which is a physical demonstration of trust in his Father's provision. He has the divine right and power to fill his hunger immediately, Satan reasons. The temptation is to act like Adam in the garden and eat from the forbidden tree, feasting upon its prohibited fruit.[27] The temptation is to act like Israel in the wilderness, who did not trust in the word of God, and its covenant promises, but grumbled against the Lord because he grew hungry and thirsty (Exod. 16; Num. 11).[28] Similarly, the 'devil's aim is to break Jesus' perfect trust in his Father's good care (cf. 6:24–34) and thereby alter the course of salvation-history'.[29]

---

[24] Morris 1992: 71–72.

[25] Augustine 2005: 11.

[26] I am following Matthew's account. Luke's account, by comparison, reverses the second and third temptations. See Luke 4:1–13.

[27] To see this parallel teased out more, see Crowe (2017: 77), who believes the temptations of Jesus have more typological references to Adam than to Israel.

[28] Davies and Allison 1988: 362.

[29] Ibid.

Furthermore, Satan knows exactly where to attack: he tempts Jesus to turn stones into bread since he is the 'Son of God'. As mentioned, this title is used in Matthew 3:17 when the Father expresses his pleasure over his Son's baptism to fulfil all righteousness. 'Son of God' in that passage captures not only Jesus' filial identity as the eternal Son of the Father but his messianic identity as the Davidic king. Jesus, the Son of God, is baptized on behalf of Israel, God's firstborn son. Now Jesus, the Son of God, is tempted on behalf of Israel, God's firstborn son. To throw this title at Jesus is an alluring temptation because it appeals to Jesus' prerogatives as the eternal Son and the greater son of David.

Jesus may be tempted as the Son of God, the one his Father loves and as Israel's King and Messiah, but Jesus remains determined not only to represent Israel in his baptism but now to represent Israel in his temptation. Jesus will respond as every Israelite should respond: by depending on the word of God. 'Satan tempts Jesus as the Son of God, the King of Israel, but Jesus defends himself as should any Israelite, as should Israel as a whole, without actually using the word "son" in this way.'[30] Jesus knows that the Scriptures, in this case Deuteronomy 8:3, not only support his identity but his mission of obedience:

But he answered, 'It is written,

> "man shall not live by bread alone,
>> but by every word that comes from the mouth of God."'
(4:4)

Satan has tried to persuade Jesus to use his power for self-gratification; after all, he is the Son of God and does he not have the right to gratify his hunger? Yet Jesus demonstrates that his mission is not to be a magician: he has come to serve others by his miracles, which are themselves a sign that the kingdom has come (e.g. Matt. 14:15–21; 15:32–38; cf. 8:1–17; 8:28–34; 9:1–8, 18–34; etc.).[31] To perform such a miracle would display a distrust in his Father's word, which is his food. While there are times when performing a miracle serves to fulfil his mission (e.g. feeding of the five thousand; Matt. 14:13–21), at other times a miracle would forfeit Jesus' mission; this is one

---

30 Carson 2012: 40.
31 Morris 1992: 70–73.

of those times. Jesus recapitulates Israel's experience but, unlike Israel, Jesus is a son who keeps 'the commandments of the LORD your God by walking in his ways and by fearing him' (Deut. 8:6).

Next:

> the devil took him to the holy city and set him on the pinnacle of the temple and said to him, 'If you are the Son of God, throw yourself down, for it is written,
>
> > '"He will command his angels concerning you,"
>
> and
>
> > '"On their hands they will bear you up,
> >   lest you strike your foot against a stone."'
> (4:5–6)

Satan is perceptive: if Jesus is going to rely on his Father, as in the last temptation, then Satan will take advantage of such dependence. The tempter is quoting from Psalm 91:11–12, providing textual justification, it would seem, for Jesus to throw himself into the hands of his Father's angels. Such a feat would also demonstrate Jesus' own power as the Son of God.

Yet Jesus sees through the way Satan has twisted Scripture to give the appearance that Jesus will be acting in obedience to God.[32] Like before, Jesus turns to Scripture, this time Deuteronomy 6:16, saying, 'Again it is written, "You shall not put the Lord your God to the test"' (4:7). Satan uses Scripture in a fallacious manner, for Jesus' throwing himself down would not be dependence on his Father but putting his Father to the test. Putting God to the test was an egregious habit Israel committed in the wilderness (e.g. Exod. 17:2–7), but not one Jesus will commit in his wilderness temptation. Israel demanded God perform a miracle at Massah, testing him by saying, 'Is the LORD among us or not?' (Exod. 17:7), but Jesus will not make the demand Satan wishes.[33] Once again, Jesus will not demand anything from his Father but humble himself to fulfil the mission he has received from his Father. A time will come when Jesus will lay down his life, but this

---

[32] Davies and Allison 1988: 366.
[33] Morris 1992: 76.

is not that time. 'Any peril he must face – and he will face the cross – and any miracle he is to do – and he will do plenty – must arise solely from obedient service to God's purpose.'[34]

Before Jesus encounters the final temptation, it should also be observed just how ironic it is that Satan has chosen to quote Psalm 91:11–12 but not verse 13, which says 'the serpent you will trample underfoot'. By resisting Satan's temptation, Jesus is effectively bringing to fulfilment Genesis 3:15 as the offspring of the woman who crushes the head of the serpent.[35] 'Jesus's refusal to follow Satan's advice during the wilderness temptations', observes Beale, 'was the beginning victory over Satan professed in [Ps. 91].'[36] With Beale's insight in mind, Crowe is justified to identify in Christ the marriage of an Adam–Israel recapitulation. 'Thus, in light of the Old Testament context, Matthew's second temptation, and Luke's third, bespeak a fusing of Son of God and Adam imagery to communicate an Adam Christology of obedience.'[37]

From the 'holy city' the tempter takes Jesus to the top of a mountain to view 'all the kingdoms of the world and their glory' (4:8). Rather than quoting Scripture, the tempter, whom John calls the 'ruler of this world' (John 12:31; 14:30; 16:11), appeals to his own authority and power: 'All these I will give you, if you will fall down and worship me' (4:9). Here is a shortcut to glory and victory, to lordship and dominion, one by which Jesus can accomplish the same ends if only he will make one concession. Jesus can have all that the Father has promised him, and he can have it right now, without the long road of suffering. He simply must give his allegiance to Satan, and then the empire will be his. But Satan is tempting the same Jesus who will say in Matthew 16:26, 'For what will it profit a man if he gains the whole world and forfeits his soul?' Jesus returns to Scripture once more, quoting Deuteronomy 6:13:

Be gone, Satan! For it is written,

> 'You shall worship the Lord your God
>   and him only shall you serve.'
> (4:10)

---

34 Davies and Allison 1988: 367.
35 Crowe 2017: 77.
36 Beale 2011: 420.
37 Crowe 2017: 77.

Jesus need not look to Satan for lordship: once he defeats Satan at the cross he will rise victorious, declaring from a mountain top, 'All authority in heaven and on earth has been given to me' (Matt. 28:18).[38]

Several conclusions deserve to be highlighted at the end of this temptation narrative. To begin with, in the first temptation it is noticeable not only that Jesus quotes Scripture as that which 'is written', but when he quotes Deuteronomy 8:3 he dispels Satan's manoeuvre by his reliance on the totality of Scripture's authority and sufficiency. Jesus is depending on 'every word that comes from the mouth of God'. The plenary nature of Scripture is not to be overlooked. Jesus did not think some parts of Scripture were from God but not others: all of it is food man is to live by. '*Every word* is comprehensive,' says Morris.

> Jesus is not suggesting that parts of Scripture may safely be neglected, but affirming that it is profitable in its entirety. The reason is apparent in the words *that go out through God's mouth*. Jesus views God as the author of Scripture, and because of this it must be heeded carefully.[39]

Not only does Jesus believe *all* Scripture is authoritative and to be adhered to but he traces the Scriptures back to their source as the ultimate explanation as to why they are authoritative. That source is none other than the 'mouth of God'. As much as critics of biblical authority have sought to disconnect its origins from its divine author, Jesus draws the connection as tightly as one can. One need not rest an entire theory of inspiration on this observation, but one should also not underplay the import of Jesus' assumption for a theory of inspiration. For him, the Old Testament in its entirety was authoritative because it originated in its entirety from God's own mouth and finger. The God-breathed nature of the Scriptures is not a Pauline invention, but is affirmed by Jesus himself and originates as early as Deuteronomy 8:3. On the basis of Scripture's divine origin Jesus resists the tempter and instead relies on the food his Father feeds him, and that food is synonymous with the Scriptures.

---

[38] Donaldson (1985: 92) summarizes the three temptations: 'Jesus was called to live out in his own experience the Sonship that was to have characterized Israel – a relationship with God which invites dependence on him for provision of needs, trust in his presence without the need for demonstration, and acceptance of sovereignty only on his terms.'

[39] Morris 1992: 74. Emphases original.

Last, the trust in the Scriptures that Jesus exemplifies is the very means to his covenant obedience as the last Adam, true Israel and faithful Son of God. In other words, it is through Jesus' vicarious covenant obedience to the word of his Father that we see his unflinching, unreserved reliance on his Father's word. The reason Jesus not only surpasses but overcomes Adam and Israel's disobedience is because he, the new covenant head, trusts in the covenant word of his Father.[40]

One could continue on in Matthew to see this sonship theme through to the end of his Gospel, but the texts inspected are sufficient to make the point.[41] It remains to be seen whether the other Gospels appeal to these last Adam, true Israel and sonship themes and whether these themes reveal the identity of the Scriptures.

Luke

Much like Matthew and John, Luke has much to say concerning the mission of Christ and how that mission is accomplished through Jesus' dependence on the Scriptures. However, Luke adds yet another dimension, by tracing Jesus' lineage all the way back to Adam.

Jesus as last Adam in Luke's genealogy: Luke 3:38

Luke begins with a genealogy, but unlike Matthew's genealogy that starts with Abraham, Luke's begins with Adam, whom Luke calls the 'son of God' (3:38). Tracing Jesus all the way back to Adam is an intentional identification on Luke's part, one that marks Jesus as the new and last Adam at the start of his ministry. Doing so communicates to the reader not only who Jesus is but what he has come to accomplish.

To begin with such typology leads the reader to enter Luke's Gospel by first considering the ways Christ is like and unlike Adam. Like Adam, Christ has come to represent God's covenant people; and like Adam, Christ will be put to the test (Luke 4:1–15) to see if he will remain obedient to the covenant. Yet unlike Adam, Christ will obey where Adam disobeyed, so that by his obedience to the word of God the people of God are redeemed

---

[40] Crowe (2017: 79) makes the point that Jesus not only surpasses but overcomes.

[41] Another title that is connected to Christ as the last Adam is 'Son of Man'. To see how this title reveals the Son of Man's redemptive mission, consult Crowe (ibid. 37–53).

from Adam's curse. As the last Adam, Jesus reveals himself to be the true son of God Adam never was.[42]

Garden temptation recapitulated: Luke 4:1–13

Like his genealogy, Luke's temptation narrative also features Christ as the last Adam. Luke's emphasis on the Adam–Christ correspondence is seen in the way he transitions: after featuring Adam, the son of God (3:38), in the genealogy of Jesus, Luke 4 then recapitulates the testing of Adam in the temptations of Jesus (4:1–13). Since they were explored in Matthew's Gospel, those temptations need not be repeated here; the point is that Luke's transition from genealogy to temptation is meant to position Christ at the start of Luke's Gospel as the new and last Adam who will, by his obedience to the word of God, usher in the new creation. With God as his Father, Christ is the son of God who recapitulates Adam's trial but with success. His identity, as seen in Matthew and John, is both filial and Adamic.[43]

However, there is a sense in which every temptation and spiritual battle Jesus faces from Luke 4 onwards reveals him to be Adam's antitype (e.g. Luke 11:14–23; 13:15–16; 22:53).[44] Yet his testing as the last Adam is most intense as he enters his own passion. In Luke 22:39–46, for example, the reader wonders whether Jesus will be obedient to the end as this Son of God

---

[42] Does Luke's direct lineage back to Adam mean that Matthew, who does not mention Adam, has no place for Christ as the last Adam? Not necessarily. It is true, Matthew traces Jesus specifically back to David and ultimately to Abraham, and does so to introduce Christ not only as the righteous branch of David (2 Sam. 7:14; Pss 89; 132) foretold by the prophets (Isa. 11; Jer. 23; 33:15–16), but as the one who fulfils the covenant promises God made to Abraham (Gen. 12:1–3; 15). Nevertheless, Matthew may give other indications of an Adamic heritage. E.g. the 'book of the genealogy' in Matt. 1:1 is similar to the genealogy that traces Adam to Noah: 'This is the book of the generations of Adam' (Gen. 5:1; cf. 2:1). 'What Luke communicates by the phrase "son of Adam, son of God" (Luke 3:38)', asserts Crowe, 'Matthew communicates by means of verbal parallels to Genesis 5:1, along with new-creational imagery. This includes the role of the Holy Spirit in the conception of Jesus (Matt. 1:18, 20) and at his baptism (Matt. 3:16; cf. Gen. 1:2), echoes to Genesis elsewhere in Matthew, and Matthew's explicit "new creation" language (e.g. *palingenesia* [Matt. 19:28]).' Ibid. 35. Additionally, like Adam, Jesus is a covenant representative who is to undergo a covenant obedience, as his ties back to David and Abraham presume. Crowe lists three more reasons: 'First, Jesus's promise in Matthew to provide rest from heavy labors (Matt. 11:28–30) provides an answer to the curse of Adam's toil (Gen. 3:16–19) . . . Second, Jesus on several occasions appeals to God's original created order . . . Third, and more briefly, Jesus's miracles recall the original creative power of God.' Ibid. 36–37.

[43] Ibid. 29; Beale 2011: 418.

[44] Crowe 2017: 32.

prays to his Father and asks to remove the cup (of suffering) from him (22:42). Even his disciples are told to pray lest they fall into temptation, and at the most critical hour (22:41). But again, unlike the first Adam, the second Adam does not give way to temptation: 'Nevertheless, not my will, but yours, be done', he prays to his Father (22:42). And just like his wilderness temptations, Jesus' obedience to the will of his Father is rewarded with an angel from heaven who strengthens Jesus (22:43). This time, however, his suffering is far from over; in fact, it has only begun (see 22:44).

Paradise reopened: Luke 23:43

The pinnacle consequence of the Son's filial, Adamic faithfulness to his Father's covenant word is the crucifixion and its echoes of Eden at every turn. With two criminals crucified next to Jesus, one criminal mocks Jesus while the other begs him to remember him when Jesus enters his kingdom (23:42). Jesus responds, 'Truly, I say to you, today you will be with me in paradise' (23:43). In the dark shadow of Calvary it would seem Eden has been eclipsed. Not so. The Son of God may be defeated in his body, but not in his loyalty to the mission of his Father.

Therefore, he dies only to rise; paradise is recovered and those in Christ will experience its true blessing because the second Adam has conquered sin once and for all. 'Whereas Adam was exiled from paradise because of his sin, Jesus as the obedient, last Adam has the authority to reopen paradise for those who believe – even the brigand on the cross next to him.'[45]

Mark

It is clear by now that Matthew and Luke see Jesus' filial, Adamic obedience to the word of God – that is, both the Scriptures of Israel and the intra-trinitarian word between the Father and the incarnate Son – as key to the redemptive mission of Jesus. Whether he accomplishes salvation and secures a new covenant by his blood depends on his faithfulness to the covenant word of his Father.

---

[45] Ibid. Are there other parallels from Adam to Christ in Luke's Gospel? Possibly. E.g. Crowe (ibid. 32–33), building on Evans and Sanders (1994: 39–40), believes it is the Holy Spirit who is the breath of God that brings Adam to life in Gen. 2:7, and this same Spirit is the one who comes upon Jesus at his birth (Luke 1:35), and remains on him throughout his ministry, empowering him to obey his Father and fulfil the mission of redemption (Luke 4:1–13).

Yet it should not be forgotten that Matthew and Luke build on the foundation Mark has laid, though with their own theological agendas. It is no surprise, then, to discover that such a theme is not foreign to Mark; some might even say it originates in Mark. Regardless, Mark's presentation of the obedient life of Christ is far subtler and is characterized by shades that may or may not also be present in Matthew and Luke, at least not in the same way.

While many variations of this theme in Mark could be explored, we will limit ourselves to four: (1) Mark's last Adam imagery in his brief temptation narrative (Mark 1:13); (2) Mark's repeated notation of Jesus' passion predictions encapsulated by servant and ransom language in Mark 10:45; (3) Mark's extended narration of Jesus' conflict with the Pharisees over their traditions (Mark 7:1–23);[46] and (4) Mark's description of Jesus' adherence to the Scriptures throughout Jesus' miracles.

With the wild animals: Mark's last Adam (Mark 1:13)

At the start of Mark's Gospel, the reader is presented with the temptation of Jesus in the wilderness; yet, unlike parallel Gospels (Matthew and Luke), Mark's account is brief: but two verses long. Mark's language is distinctive in many ways. After being baptized by John, Mark says the 'Spirit immediately drove him [Jesus] out into the wilderness' (1:12). Added to this brief account is Mark's unique comment 'And he was with the wild animals, and the angels were ministering to him' (1:13).

What is one to make of this wilderness language? Though out of vogue to say so, Mark may be opening his Gospel and, in very Marklike fashion, insinuating that this Jesus is a new Adam. There are elements of continuity. For example, both Adams are driven into the *wilderness*; Adam is driven out of Eden and Jesus is driven out of the Jordan. The major difference – and this is what makes Jesus the antitype – is that Adam's wilderness exile is due to his sin while Jesus' exile is due to his Adamic obedience, as marked by the presence of the Holy Spirit. Additionally, Mark's choice to mention wild animals is supportive. Like Adam, Jesus dwells with animals, but does so peacefully, which is an indication that he is recovering the dominion Adam lost. The new creation the prophets foretold (e.g. Isa. 43:20; 65:22)

---

[46] For Matthew's account, see Matt. 15:1–20. I have chosen to focus on Mark's because it is more expansive due to its inclusion of Exod. 20:12 and 21:17. In this sense it is original.

has been inaugurated in the second Adam, who has turned the wilderness into an Edenic temple-kingdom once more.[47]

Crowe summarizes this reading of Mark well:

> whereas Adam failed the temptation in the *garden* and was cast out, Jesus is led by the Spirit into the *wilderness* – a setting redolent of both the place of Israel's testing and the desolation resulting from the fall – where Jesus does not succumb to the temptation of Satan. And in both cases – in Adam's expulsion from the garden, and Jesus' being thrust into the wilderness – the strong term *ekballō* is employed.[48]

Building on an observation by Richard Bauckham, Crowe acknowledges that this interpretation was the consensus at one time but is no longer so.[49] A comparison to Elijah (1 Kgs 19:4–8) is more common today. Nevertheless, Crowe does not think Elijah typology must be precluded to see also an Adamic Christology present in Mark 1 (or the rest of Mark for that matter).[50]

G. K. Beale has devoted the most space to arguing for an Adam–Christ correspondence in the Gospels, Mark included.[51] For Beale, the Jesus Mark presents is one who embodies the true image of God and returns humanity to the end-time blessings first promised to Adam had he obeyed. Jesus is the

> complete and perfect reflection of God's image, the absolutely righteous last Adam who obtained the eschatological blessings and glory. Thus, not only did Jesus recapitulate what Adam did, 'but also he went beyond that in his faithfulness and obedience to succeed in the task at which Adam had failed.'[52]

Having addressed Mark's pictorial, zoological allusion to Jesus as the last Adam, and therefore Israel's representative in his covenant obedience,

---

[47] Crowe 2017: 26; cf. Beale 2011: 418–420.
[48] Crowe 2017: 24. Emphases original.
[49] Ibid.; cf. Bauckham 1994: 7.
[50] Crowe is pushing back against someone like Stein (2008: 65), who argues that Adam–Christ typology is absent not only from Mark 1 but from the rest of his Gospel as well.
[51] Beale 2011: 357–468.
[52] Crowe 2017: 28; quoting Beale 2011: 386.

Mark's narrative moves from Edenic imagery to more conspicuous declarations from Jesus himself.

The Son of Man goes as it is written of him: surrender to the cross as adherence to the Scriptures

Each Gospel, in some form, displays the self-awareness of Jesus concerning his coming passion. In each Gospel Jesus shows his full control over his forthcoming death by predicting its arrival and necessity.

In Mark one encounters repeated occurrences of such predictions. In Mark 8 Jesus begins to teach his disciples that the 'Son of Man must suffer many things and be rejected by the elders and the chief priests and the scribes and be killed, and after three days rise again' (8:31–32; cf. Matt. 16:21–28; Luke 9:22–27). It is this prediction that causes Peter infamously to 'rebuke' Jesus. Having just confessed Jesus to be none other than the Christ (8:29), Peter now corrects this Christ. Jesus must be mistaken: How could the anointed one suffer and die? Peter's rebuke receives a rebuke of its own from Jesus: 'Get behind me, Satan! For you are not setting your mind on the things of God, but on the things of man' (8:33). Jesus then proceeds to spell out the cost of discipleship. To follow the soon-to-be crucified Jesus, his disciples must also pick up their cross (8:34). If not, they are not true followers, nor do they understand the mission and message of Christ to a world in need of salvation.

In Mark 9 another passion prediction falls off the lips of Jesus. Mark tells the reader that as Jesus and his disciples passed through Galilee, Jesus

> did not want anyone to know, for he was teaching his disciples, saying to them, 'The Son of Man is going to be delivered into the hands of men, and they will kill him. And when he is killed, after three days he will rise.'
> (9:30–31; cf. Matt. 17:22–23; Luke 9:43–45)

However, Jesus' disciples are just as clueless as Peter was in Mark 8. They 'did not understand the saying, and were afraid to ask him' (9:32).

Yet a third time, in Mark 10, Jesus predicts his fate. This time they travelled up to Jerusalem. They 'were amazed', Mark says, 'and those who followed were afraid' (10:32). Taking his disciples aside, Jesus reminds them yet again of the doom that is ahead of him:

> See, we are going up to Jerusalem, and the Son of Man will be
> delivered over to the chief priests and the scribes, and they will
> condemn him to death and deliver him over to the Gentiles. And
> they will mock him and spit on him, and flog him and kill him. And
> after three days he will rise.
> (10:33–34; cf. Matt. 20:17–19; Luke 18:31–33)

If one presses on to the rest of Mark 10, one will also discover that
Jesus reveals the ultimate reason why he has come and why this hard,
fatal road to the cross is necessary. The context of Mark 10:35–45
concerns the request from James and John, the sons of Zebedee, to
sit at the right and left hand of Jesus in glory (10:37). Jesus questions
whether they know what they ask because the road to glory must first
enter through the gates of death: 'Are you able to drink the cup that I
drink, or to be baptized with the baptism with which I am baptized?'
(10:38).

When Jesus assures James and John that they will drink his cup and be
baptized with his baptism, he nevertheless corrects their presumption that
they could occupy his right and left hand in glory, which ignites the fury
of the other ten disciples towards these sons of Zebedee (10:39–41). Calling
all his disciples to him, Jesus deconstructs their assumption as to what it
means to enter glory. The path to glory is humility, not self-acclamation.
They are not to be like the rulers of the Gentiles, who 'lord it over them',
but instead must take on the mindset of a servant: 'whoever would be great
among you must be your servant, and whoever would be first among you
must be slave of all' (10:43).

Could the lowliness of a servant even define the mission of the Son of
Man? Indeed: 'For even the Son of Man came not to be served but to serve,
and to give his life as a ransom for many' (10:45).[53] While scholars have
been reticent to see the atonement motif in Mark, verse 45 demonstrates
its presence.[54] Here Jesus moves beyond a mere factual prediction of his
death to the essence of its purpose. This is why he has come, to ransom
sinners by giving his own life over. Such selflessness requires that he not
safeguard his royal rights but become as lowly as a servant. To give his life
over to death for the sake of ransoming God's people means the Son of Man

---

[53] By comparison, Luke's Jesus says, 'For the Son of Man came to seek and to save the lost'
(19:10).
[54] See Bolt 2016.

must humble himself, fulfilling the mission he has come to accomplish in the most sacrificial way possible.

Mark 10:45, in the context of the preceding three passion predictions, is pivotal for our purposes because it not only acknowledges Jesus' obedience to the point of death on a cross but provides insight into his mindset or attitude as the obedient Son, the last Adam. It was seen in Matthew and John that Jesus takes on a mission granted to him by the Father and foretold by the Scriptures of old, yet Mark reveals the same. For Jesus says at his betrayal, 'For the Son of Man *goes as it is written of him* . . .' (14:21; emphasis added). Jesus consciously subjects himself to death in order to bring the Scriptures to fulfilment. Put otherwise, *by surrendering himself to the cross, Jesus is adhering to the Scriptures of Israel.*

It is this mission that will bring the Scriptures to fulfilment, but it is a mission that requires absolute humility.[55] Echoing throughout Jesus' statement is the verbiage of Isaiah. In Isaiah 53 Yahweh speaks of a suffering servant, one who 'was despised and rejected by men, / a man of sorrows and acquainted with grief' (53:3). Through his grief God's people are ransomed. For this servant is one who 'was pierced for our transgressions' and 'crushed for our iniquities; / upon him was the chastisement that brought us peace' (53:5). That servant is like a humble lamb who willingly goes to the slaughter, silent before its shearers, refusing to open his mouth (53:7). The death of the lamb, however, is the redemption of God's people. His 'soul makes an offering for guilt' (53:10).

Echoing Isaiah, Mark explicates the type of humility and obedience that characterize Jesus.[56] Mark is not as explicit as Matthew, who directly acknowledges Jesus' faithfulness to his Father's covenant word. Yet Mark need not always mention the Scriptures of Israel: he expects his readers to read between the lines and hear Isaiah when he paints Jesus as a servant who gives up his life as a ransom. What is faint in Mark becomes vocalized in the end. As Jesus eats the Passover meal with his disciples, he says to them, holding up the wine, 'This is my blood of the covenant, which is poured out for many' (14:24). Jesus believed he was establishing the new covenant God had promised through the prophets (see chapter 2), and he was doing so by means of a sacrificial obedience, the giving of his life for the salvation of God's people.

---

[55] Such Christological humility may not be stated outright in the Gospels, but its presence is so important that the NT writers consider it a defining feature of the church. See e.g. Phil. 2:1–11.

[56] Luke does too: 'But I am among you as the one who serves' (22:27).

Recovering the authority and intent of the law: Mark 7:1–13

If, as argued to this point, the *mission of Jesus to ransom a people involves a life of servant-minded obedience to the word of God and the Scriptures of Israel*, then one would expect Mark to pinpoint, at a strategic point in his narrative, Jesus' unqualified loyalty to that word over against his opponents. That strategic moment arrives in Mark 7, sandwiched as it is within Jesus' healing miracles, and preceding Jesus' bold exposure of the Pharisees' 'leaven' (8:14–21).

In Mark 7 the reader is told that the Pharisees are drawn to Jesus, although their interest precludes a faith seeking understanding. Joined by scribes from Jerusalem, these Pharisees become irritated and offended, even outraged, that Jesus' disciples are eating without previously washing their hands.[57] For the Pharisees, eating with unwashed hands means eating with 'defiled' hands (7:2). In an editorial comment that conveys his readership also consists of Gentiles, Mark clarifies that

(For the Pharisees and all the Jews do not eat unless they wash their hands properly, holding to the tradition of the elders, and when they come from the market-place, they do not eat unless they wash. And there are many other traditions that they observe, such as the washing of cups and pots and copper vessels and dining couches.) (Mark 7:3–4)[58]

It is doubtful that these Jews are merely concerned with responsible hygiene. In the context of Jewish religious custom, such a practice has far more to do with ceremonial cleansing and ritual consecration.

What becomes plain in Jesus' reaction is that such a custom did not originate in its present form from within the law, but instead was the product of later attempts to fence the law and preserve the distinction between Jew and Gentile. 'Rituals concerning cleanness and uncleanness reflect rabbinic developments more than actual Torah prescriptions.'[59] As James Edwards

---

[57] France (2002: 280) thinks Jerusalem is meant to indicate these religious leaders have come to 'investigate and/or to dispute with Jesus'. Stein (2008: 338) is less certain.

[58] Vv. 3–4 are not the only clue Mark's reader's may be primarily Gentiles; see vv. 14, 18 and 19.

[59] Edwards 2002: 205.

observes, Exodus 30:19–21 and 40:12–13, 30–32, as well as Leviticus 22:1–6, required washing to enter the tabernacle, and Leviticus 15:11 made washing a necessary consequence of contact with physical discharge. France also notices that ritual purity was mandatory for priests prior to offering a sacrifice (Exod. 30:18–21; 40:30–32).[60] Strauss goes further, believing the Pharisees and scribes not only had such texts in mind but applied them universally since 'all God's people were meant to be holy', although this might not have been their motivation when Jesus' disciples were confronted.[61]

Regardless, what is clear is that the reaction to Jesus' disciples goes beyond these Old Testament texts, assuming adherence to an oral law beyond the Torah but one equally binding.[62] There are various speculations as to how this extra-scriptural oral law developed. 'As Judaism's encounter with Gentile culture increased in the postexilic period,' says Edwards, 'the question of ritual cleanliness took on new significance as a way of maintaining Jewish purity over against Gentile culture.'[63]

The phrase 'new significance' is fitting, for the tension between Jesus and the Jews in Mark 7 is one that pivots on the additional prescription established, one that goes beyond the law as law. That point we will return to, but here it is sufficient to note that the stigma of unwashed hands was one of defilement, where the unwashed failed to observe a rule established by the Jews to ensure religious, social and cultural segregation and consecration. 'This practice was seen as an important expression of faithfulness to being Jewish in a context where Hellenistic practices risked overwhelming Jewish distinctiveness.'[64] Unwashed hands meant defilement and defilement meant one's distinct status – and perhaps, by association, the *community's* distinct status – had been surrendered, even compromised.[65]

All that becomes vocalized once the scribes and Pharisees join company for the purpose of confronting Jesus as to why his disciples do 'not walk

---

[60] France 2002: 280.

[61] Strauss 2014: 298.

[62] France (2002: 280) says, 'The extension of this principle to the eating of ordinary food, and to Jewish people other than priests, was a matter of scribal development.' Yet France doubts ritual washing of hands was the norm by Jesus' day, though it was expected by the group Jesus encountered.

[63] Edwards 2002: 205. Edwards lists the Qumran community (see the DSS) as an example but acknowledges that the Pharisees were just as strict. Also see Bock 2015: 222.

[64] Bock 2015: 220–221.

[65] While our focus has an eye for the way the law itself comes into this debate, Mark is likely utilizing this confrontation to demonstrate the cessation of the law as well, including additions to the law with regard to food, for Gentile believers. In Christ Gentiles are no longer bound to a law fulfilled by the object of their faith. See Strauss 2014: 298; Edwards 2002: 204.

according to the tradition of the elders, but eat with defiled hands?' (7:5). Verse 5 confirms Mark's editorial comments, namely that the scribes and Pharisees assume the authority of an oral tradition grounded in rabbinic Judaism (and as Mark makes clear, it is a tradition not merely concerned with one law, like the washing of hands, but with many, including the washing of utensils).

Violating the 'tradition of the elders' was no small infraction either. We learn from Josephus that it is this tradition that distinguished the Pharisees. While the Torah was the sufficient authority for the Sadducees, and a written authority at that, the Pharisees saw their oral traditions just as binding. Such traditions were not instantaneously handed down, however, but continued to change and accumulate with time. With the establishment of the Old Testament canon, these oral traditions became far more solidified, as one can tell by the strong reaction to Jesus' disciples by the scribes and Pharisees.[66] Various commentators have recognized how the rabbis believed Moses descended Sinai with not one but two laws. The Mishnah

> was believed to preserve an unbroken chain of authorized tradition extending from Moses to the 'Great Synagogue' of Jesus' day (*m. Avot* 1:1–13). The Mishnah called the oral interpretation 'a fence around the Torah' (*m. Avot* 3:14) – 'fence' being understood as preservation of the integrity of the written law by elaborating every conceivable implication of it.[67]

If the Torah is the view of the forest – giving to Israel the general principles by which to live, such as prohibitions against worshipping anyone but Yahweh – then the Mishnah is the view on the ground, among the trees, giving Israel the specifics, even making pronouncements where the Torah is silent. These two laws, Torah and Mishnah, it was argued, go together, the oral law, the Mishnah, designed to assist Israel with adherence to the written law, the Torah acting as a fence around the latter.

However, this two-source theory also led to a reformulation of the Torah's perspicuity. The Mishnah was necessary precisely because the

---

[66] Edwards 2002: 208. See Josephus, *Ant.* 13.297.

[67] Edwards 2002: 208; cf. Bock 2015: 221. Stein (2008: 339) adds that the traditions were 'supposedly given orally by God to Moses on Mount Sinai (*m. 'Abot* 1.1ff.; Josephus, *Ant.* 13.10.6 §297), that were codified into the Mishnah (ca. AD 200), which along with its Aramaic commentary, the Gemara, make up the Jerusalem Talmud (ca. AD 400) and the larger Babylonian Talmud (ca. AD 500)'.

Torah was not always clear, and certainly did not articulate the exact application of its instruction for all matters of holy living:

> The Torah alone, according to advocates of the oral tradition, was believed to be too ambiguous to establish and govern the Jewish community. The oral tradition as preserved in the Mishnah, on the other hand, prescribed in infinite detail how the intent of the Torah ought to be fulfilled in actual circumstances.[68]

That which is not entirely clear cannot be entirely sufficient either. Therefore, the oral tradition took on a life (and authority) of its own.

True, the original intention of the Mishnah was commendable, although the rabbinical belief that its origins stemmed directly from Sinai cannot be substantiated from the book of Exodus. A fence serves a good purpose, guarding the purity and original design of the object within its borders. However, as Jesus' comments reveal, that intention had been taken to an extreme and in some cases lost altogether. If the oral tradition 'in theory' was 'intended to express the intent of the law', unfortunately 'in practice' this oral tradition 'tended to shift the center of gravity from the intent of the Torah to an increasing array of peripheral matters that either obscured or perverted that intent'.[69]

Despite their noble adherence to the 'tradition of the elders', Jesus considered these traditions (1) extra-scriptural in origin, rooted in a man-made oral heritage, not a written, God-inspired one as with the Torah, and (2) so misguided in their application that they served to challenge that which alone is from God, namely the Torah. Both show themselves in Mark 7:6–13.

Jesus' response to the question (really, more of an objection) posed by the scribes and Pharisees begins with sarcasm: 'Well did Isaiah prophesy of you hypocrites . . .' Jesus then quotes Isaiah 29:13 to ascribe such hypocrisy to the Pharisees and scribes:

> This people honours me with their lips,
>> but their heart is far from me;
> in vain do they worship me,
>> teaching as doctrines the commandments of men.[70]

---

[68] Edwards 2002: 208.

[69] Ibid.

[70] Jesus appears to be utilizing only part of v. 13, which reads, 'Because this people draw near with their mouth and honour me with their lips, while their hearts are far from me, and

Jesus then adds his own condemnation: 'You leave the commandment of God and hold to the tradition of men' (Mark 7:8). Jesus may have a specific commandment in view, but more likely has in mind the general tendency of the scribes and Pharisees to nullify God's commands in the Scriptures by means of their own traditions.[71]

There are a variety of reasons why Jesus issues this condemnation. First, as seen already, the confrontation between the scribes and Pharisees and Jesus centres on the assumption – and for Jesus it is a dangerous, erroneous assumption – that this oral tradition, for all its good intent, is equal in authority to the Torah itself.[72] For Jesus, one originates from man; the other, from God. Nonetheless, this first issue is more or less assumed in the condemnation itself, though it becomes explicit in verses 8 and 9.

Second, and perhaps more to the point, adhering to 'the tradition of men' over against the 'commandment of God' (the contrast is evident when Jesus says, 'You *leave* the commandment of God and *hold* to the tradition of men'; 7:8; emphasis added) reveals a type of hypocrisy Jesus finds repulsive. The nature of the hypocrisy itself will surface in Mark 7:10–13 and 14–23. As 7:14–23 reveals, the scribes and Pharisees are judgmental towards those who do not follow their traditions *externally* (e.g. washing hands), while *internally* the spiritual condition of their heart is anything but Godward. Such is the very essence of hypocrisy, namely an outward appearance that does not match an inward condition of the soul, all the while claiming to possess the latter.

As Jesus says elsewhere:

Woe to you, scribes and Pharisees, hypocrites! For you are like whitewashed tombs, which outwardly appear beautiful, but within are full of dead people's bones and all uncleanness. So you also outwardly appear righteous to others, but within you are full of hypocrisy and lawlessness. (Matt. 23:27–28)

In Mark 7 the scribes and Pharisees may look uber-religious, going beyond the Torah even to wash their hands, but inwardly their spiritual condition

---

(note 70 *cont.*) their fear of me is a commandment taught by men . . .' His quotation can be traced back to the LXX. France (2002: 284) looks at the LXX and concludes that 'those condemned are seen as teaching, not merely following, human commands'.

[71] Stein 2008: 342.

[72] 'By Jesus' day, adherence to the unwritten oral tradition was as important for the Pharisees as was adherence to the Torah itself.' Edwards 2002: 208.

fails to reflect such an external cleansing, as their opposition to Jesus and his message evidences.

However, the type of hypocrisy Jesus identifies in his opponents is not one merely of *spiritual discontinuity* (between the heart and outward appearance) but one of *theological incongruity*. What makes this hypocrisy so outrageous is that these scribes and Pharisees, as if they are following the commandments of God, claim to pass judgment on Jesus' disciples in the name of God. Jesus exposes the incongruity repeatedly. The ending of the Isaiah quotation underscores that the reason their worship is in vain is because they teach 'as doctrines the commandments of men' (Mark 7:7; Isa. 29:13). Twice Jesus emphasizes the problem when he follows the Isaiah quotation with

> You leave the commandment of God and hold to the tradition of men.
> (7:8)

> You have a fine way of rejecting the commandment of God in order
> to establish your tradition!
> (7:9)

The fundamental issue, in other words, is not merely adding to the Torah that which is not Torah but rejecting the Torah by means of human, contrived doctrines, laws that are *at odds with* the true intention of the Torah itself. The assumption on Jesus' part is that human traditions, interpretations and doctrines have replaced that which is from God himself. Such a replacement has undermined that which is divinely given and authoritative *because such traditions are antithetical to the God-intended* meaning of the Torah. The issue is not whether the scribes and Pharisees are zealous enough; indifference is not the problem, at least not primarily. Rather, the issue is that in their zeal they have opposed the law of God, and for this reason Jesus labels them 'hypocrites'.

That such hypocrisy is grounded in opposition is seen in the Greek itself. For instance, Edwards does not prefer the NIV translation of verse 9 because it does not bring out the full force of the verbs. 'The Pharisees do not simply "set aside" God's commandments, that is, favor something in their place; they "reject" (Gk. *Athetein*) them by making a conscious choice *against* them.' For example, the

> NIV says that the Pharisees do this in order 'to observe your own
> commandments.' If the Gk. *stēsēte* is the proper reading in v. 9, then

it is more definite and stronger: the Pharisees do this to erect (*stēsēte*) or cause something to stand in the place of the Torah.[73]

And since the verbs in verses 8–9 are in the present tense, observes Edwards, such an opposition is considered to be continuing. Jesus has in mind not merely a manufactured heritage or system that these scribes and Pharisees have imbibed, but one incongruous with the law of God and one they are determined to follow. 'The oral tradition is thus exposed and censured as a willful substitution of human contrivance for the word and will of God.'[74]

Jesus does not leave his accusation in the abstract but enlists a specific example to prove his point in verse 9. In Mark 7:10–13 Jesus exposes the way the religious leaders justify breaking a commandment of God by the supposedly honorable appeal to 'Corban'. The fifth commandment says people are to honour their father and mother (Exod. 20:12; cf. Deut. 5:16). According to Moses, dishonouring one's parents is punishable by death (Exod. 21:17; cf. Lev. 20:9). Seemingly, there is no way around this commandment or its penalty. Nevertheless, the religious leaders found a way.

Although it is obligatory to care for one's mother and father, should one claim 'Corban' then the commandment is no longer in effect. Corban is a transliteration of the Hebrew and Aramaic. In passages like Leviticus 2:1–14 Corban refers to a vow or an offering made.[75] Mark says that to call something Corban is to say it is 'given to God'. As it came to be used in the oral Jewish tradition, Corban was a way of devoting to God an object that would then be off limits to others. To devote something to God was to set it apart from usual or ordinary use by others. However, there is a way to use Corban to one's own advantage. By claiming something is Corban, one keeps it for oneself and precludes others from having it. Motivation is everything, determining whether an appeal to Corban is God-honouring or self-centred.

Corban relates to one's parents because one could say, for example, that his property or funds were Corban, thereby restricting them to himself rather than having to make them available to his parents as needed. The rabbis were clever enough to anticipate such a problem, which is why it became a matter of debate, some arguing that such an oath should be

---

[73] Edwards 2002: 209–210. Emphases original.
[74] Ibid. 210.
[75] Strauss 2014: 302.

broken or rescinded in order to preserve a commandment, while others denying such an exception.[76] It appears that Jesus' opponents did not allow for the breaking of Corban, which only served to deepen their hypocrisy, for not only were they aware of the oath taker's corrupt motives but indirectly supported those motives by guarding their oath from annulment.

By doing so, as Jesus exclaims, the religious leaders nullified the commandment of God (!) in their attempt to avoid nullification of their human tradition. Worse still, they were keeping, even prohibiting, others from obeying a clear commandment of God to preserve that which was not from God but the creation of men.[77] Furthermore, in their legalism they cultivated the opposite intention of the law; while the fifth commandment is meant to serve, honour and care for one's parents, this use of Corban harms one's parents, and probably at their most vulnerable point in life.

For these reasons, Jesus is outraged. By permitting the oath taker not 'to do anything for his father or mother', you are 'making void the word of God by your tradition that you have handed down' (Mark 7:12–13). Yet this is just one way God's word is subverted by oral human traditions. For Jesus concludes, 'And many such things you do' (7:13). There is no end to this erroneous theology and hypocrisy. Jesus, in Mark 7:14–23, then proceeds to expose such hypocrisy by returning once more to the real issue in God's sight, which is not outward religiosity but inward conformity; that is, a conformity that stems from the heart.

To summarize, not only have these religious leaders elevated a human law, one of man's traditions, to the level of the commandments of God, but have elevated the one at the expense and perversion of the other.

High view of Scripture

Jesus' immediate point concerns the hypocrisy of the religious leaders, yet when he exposes such hypocrisy he also makes lucid the nature of the Scriptures in comparison with the nature of their oral traditions.[78] The religious leaders certainly had a high view of Scripture – as initial attempts to fence the Torah demonstrate – believing the Scriptures to be God given,

---

[76] Strauss (ibid.), who sites *m. Ned.* 8.1 – 9.1, where 'the Mishnah favors release of the vow for the sake of the parents'. Also see France (2002: 286–287), who points to the example of a son and his father in *m. Ned.* 5.6, and Stein (2008: 342), who turns to Josephus (*Ant.* 4.4.4 §§72–73; *Ag. Ap.* 1.22 §167).

[77] Stein 2008: 342–343.

[78] There is another factor: Jesus' own authority in interpreting and bringing to fulfilment the true intent of the law. On this point, see Strauss 2014: 307; Edwards 2002: 214.

not merely products of Moses but the word of Yahweh himself. Nevertheless, over time such fencing had evolved into a mindset that elevated oral tradition to the level of Scripture, and consequently skewed the intentions of the covenant. Jesus will tolerate such an epistemology as much as he will tolerate the hypocrisy within their hearts. Although the narrative is driven by the confrontation of hypocrisy, such a confrontation is established on the foundational premise that they have left 'the commandment of God and hold to the tradition of men' (7:8). Three times Jesus accentuates such a conflict between man's and God's words (7:8–9, 13).

It must be concluded, therefore, that in the mind of Jesus he not only considered the Scriptures to have originated from God, but upon such a belief Jesus could then argue that the Scriptures, unlike the traditions of the elders, are inherently a different type of document. Jesus did not merely believe the Scriptures to be greater in authority, but to be altogether of a different type of authority. The oral traditions were man-made; the Scriptures were God made. For that reason, when Jesus rebukes the religious leaders for elevating their oral traditions, his rebuke carries force because such an elevation is the perversion of that which is no mere human command but the very command of God. As seen in chapter 2, to violate or undermine such commands is to transgress the covenant itself, for the Scriptures of Israel are the constitution of the covenant.

That rebuke assumes, naturally, that the written Scriptures *are* by nature of their origin the very commandments of God, commandments Jesus is intent on obeying and bringing to fulfilment. In Mark 7:10–13 it is one command (the fifth commandment) in view, but as verse 13 reveals, this is but one example of the many ways these leaders undermine the nature and authority of the Scriptures as a whole. Whether it is washing with unclean hands (7:1–6) or appealing to Corban (7:10–13), Jesus assumes in his reply that the written Scriptures originate from Yahweh and as such are the words of Yahweh *in toto*. They possess, then, the type of authority that has no equal; to break them is to rebel against Yahweh himself. They are, after all, the 'commandment *of God*' (7:8–9; emphasis added), the very 'word *of God*' (7:13; emphasis added).[79]

---

[79] France (2002: 288; emphasis original) denies that 'word of God' in v. 13 refers to the Scriptures, but instead argues that it refers more broadly to the 'Christian message and its proclamation' as seen in Luke–Acts. He then draws the conclusion 'Here, therefore, it is unlikely that the scribes' fault is to be understood specifically as contravening *Scripture*, but rather as undermining a specific divine pronouncement (the fifth commandment) in favour of their own human tradition.' France is mistaken for a variety of reasons: (1) There is no need

To conclude, Jesus has a high view of Scripture, and it serves the practical purpose of distinguishing between his message and that of his opponents, between his covenant obedience and their covenant unfaithfulness. There is no contest between the two since Jesus not only interprets the Scriptures for what they intrinsically are (the 'word of God'; 7:13) but submits himself to them as the one whose own words are not only found to be in conformity with their divine author but to originate from the divine author himself.

Christ's obedience to the Law

It has been demonstrated so far that Jesus' adherence to Scripture as that which is God inspired and authoritative is essential to fulfilling his redemptive mission from the Father as the last Adam. Furthermore, his determination to purchase our salvation by his covenant obedience brings him into heated conflict with the religious leaders. Their obedience to the Scriptures, it turns out, is fraudulent since they have elevated their traditions to justify their hypocrisy. Jesus' adherence to scriptural authority, on the other hand, reveals him to be, once more, the true Israel, the Son who is faithful to the book of the covenant.

In this last section, Jesus not only shows his understanding of Scripture by his obedience to the Scriptures but by the way he corrects,

---

to choose between the Scriptures and the 'Christian message and its proclamation' in a text like Mark 7. Jesus did not intend these two to be set over against one another. While we may distinguish them, the one includes the other and cannot be severed from the other. (2) To contravene a commandment (like the fifth) is to contravene Scripture. A first-century Jew would not have so strongly differentiated between the two, especially since the commandments were given to Moses and inscripturated. Where do the commandments of God come from if not from the Scriptures, and specifically the Torah? Jesus seems to assume this much in vv. 8 and 9, so why would the same assumption not be in view in v. 13. (3) When Jesus says the religious leaders are 'making void the word of God' (v. 13), he is doing so in the immediate context of the fifth commandment. Why would Jesus say that they 'leave the commandment of God' (v. 8) and are 'rejecting the commandment of God' (v. 9), and then give a specific example from the fifth commandment (vv. 10–12), but then conclude in v. 13 that they are not breaking the Scriptures specifically but only the broader message of Christ? (4) The entire context of Mark 7 has to do with whether or not Jesus' disciples are following the oral traditions of the scribes and Pharisees. Yet those oral traditions are supposed to be based on that which they fence, namely the Scriptures. This is why the rebuke of Jesus is so shocking to them: they think they are following the Scriptures. Hence the narrative can conclude by comparing their word, which is from man, to the Scriptures, which are words from God. (5) Yes, France is right, 'word of God' does not often refer specifically to the Scriptures throughout the NT. However, this must be taken on a case-by-case basis because various authors use the phrase for various reasons and in various ways. We need not read Mark's use as if it must conform to Luke's, as France assumes. In sum, while Jesus may not be directly referring to *all* the OT Scriptures in v.13, nevertheless it is a step too far to say he is not referring to the Scriptures at all, for the context concerns the commandments of God, which originate from the Torah, and at times even specific commandments (like the fifth).

rebukes and instructs others *according to the Scriptures*, and the Law in particular.

Adherence to what Moses commanded

At the start of Mark's Gospel, Jesus encounters a leper who implores him to make him clean. Jesus pities the leprous man and at his command the man's leprosy disappears. Yet, rather than just send the man away, Jesus instructs him to follow the instructions of the Law prescribed in Leviticus 14:2–32: 'See that you say nothing to anyone, but go, show yourself to the priest and offer for your cleansing what Moses commanded, for a proof to them' (Mark 1:44; cf. Luke 17:14).

Commentators debate whether Jesus intends to convey the necessity of obedience to the law or whether he is merely assisting the leper with the initial and official process of returning to society. It is unclear, however, why these two are mutually exclusive; in fact, the latter appears to be included in the former in the context of Leviticus. Adherence to the law also brings restitution into the society of Israel. Regardless of this quibble, there is a broader point presupposed by the text: Jesus' insistence that this leper follows through on the priestly process stems from his conviction that the law carries the authority of its divine architect and therefore should instruct covenant life for Israel.[80]

Similarly, consider Mark 10, where Jesus is tested by the Pharisees, yet this time about whether it is lawful to divorce one's wife (10:1; cf. Matt. 19:3–6). Jesus responds by turning to the authority of Moses: 'What did Moses command you?' (10:3), he asks. The Pharisees find security in the fact that Moses 'allowed a man to write a certificate of divorce' (10:4; cf. Deut. 24:1–4), but Jesus corrects them, explaining that such a certificate was due to their 'hardness of heart' (10:5). Jesus then goes beyond Moses to the God-intended design behind marriage at the start:

> But from the beginning of creation, 'God made them male and female.' 'Therefore a man shall leave his father and mother and hold fast to his wife, and the two shall become one flesh.' So they are no longer two but one flesh. What therefore God has joined together let not man separate. (10:6–9; cf. Gen. 1:27; 5:2)

---

[80] Blomberg (2016: 685) believes there is a Christological emphasis, so that Jesus does not merely teach obedience to the law but implies his own superiority to the law as the Christ: Jesus does not need the priestly process to make this man whole again.

Jesus moves beyond the immediate context of Moses' certificate, a context grounded in the depravity of the human heart, to the beginning of creation, for it is there that one finds the true intention of marriage and the law. In doing so, it is transparent that Jesus not only reveals the true intention of the Law, but the Law itself stems from Genesis, where the marriage institution God established with Adam and Eve can be found. Jesus not only exhibits a right interpretation of Deuteronomy 24:1–4 but displays the intertextual intention of Deuteronomy 24 by grounding it in revelation up to that point, in this case Genesis 2:1 and 5:2.

Assumed in such an exegetical move is the authorship and authority of Yahweh. The only reason Jesus can make such an intertextual manoeuvre is because even his opponents assume that the Lord who gave his law to Moses intended that law to be interpreted in full view of God's prior revelation in Genesis, in this case, his revelation at creation concerning the institution of marriage. In short, Jesus holds the trump card, for unless the Pharisees can demonstrate that their interpretation of Deuteronomy 24 is grounded in the divine author's intention in Genesis, they are without a rejoinder.

Also, in Mark 10 is Jesus' encounter with the rich young man, who asks Jesus, 'Good Teacher, what must I do to inherit eternal life?' (10:17; cf. Matt. 19:18; Luke 18:18–30). Jesus responds:

> Why do you call me good? No one is good except God alone. You know the commandments: 'Do not murder, Do not commit adultery, Do not steal, Do not bear false witness, Do not defraud, Honour your father and mother.'
> (10:18–19)

Jesus considers these commands in Exodus 20:12–16 and Deuteronomy 5:16–20 binding covenant precepts God gave to Moses and Moses gave to the people. What God spoke to Moses was inscripturated, canonically binding, and authoritative not only in Moses' day but in Jesus' own day. Jesus' Jewish audience would have assumed the same.

Jesus is aware, however, that this rich young man knows these commands (see 10:19) and the response given is expected: 'Teacher, all these I have kept from my youth' (10:20). What Jesus says next catches the young man off guard: 'You lack one thing: go, sell all that you have and give to the poor, and you will have treasure in heaven; and come, follow me' (10:21). The man walks away 'disheartened' and 'sorrowful' because 'he had great possessions' (10:22) and apparently was unwilling to follow Jesus at such a cost.

Again, Jesus' attitude towards the Scriptures, in this case the Law specifically, is apparent. To Jesus these are living commandments with continuing, binding, covenantal authority in his own day because they are not merely from Moses but from Yahweh, their covenant Maker himself. The rich young man assumes this as well, for his original question is Godward in orientation: 'what must I do to inherit eternal life?' (10:17). Furthermore, the true test is not how many commandments this young man has kept (though that is certainly a factor) but whether he understands what is required of God's covenant members, namely wholehearted obedience and devotion at any cost. While the young man is focused on whether he has broken any laws, Jesus reveals that this affluent youth has not kept the one thing that matters most regardless of what law is in focus: wholehearted, unconditioned devotion to God. The young man's heart is elsewhere in the end. The tragic ending of this encounter not only speaks with clarity to the type of disciple Jesus is after, but also exemplifies the way the law was intended to be interpreted and applied, as well as the type of authority it had, or at least was supposed to have, in the covenant life of corporate Israel.

Have you not read? Mark 12:18–27

Mark 12:18–27 is somewhat of a unique pericope in Mark's Gospel because it represents an extended dialogue between Jesus and the Sadducees, as opposed to the Pharisees.

The Sadducees test Jesus as to who will possess a woman in the afterlife if she has multiple, successive husbands in the present life. Mark tips off the reader that the Sadducees are setting a rhetorical trap for Jesus since they do not believe in the resurrection in the first place. Jesus knows that and his response reveals a deeper problem:

> Jesus said to them, 'Is this not the reason you are wrong, because you know neither the Scriptures nor the power of God? For when they rise from the dead, they neither marry nor are given in marriage, but are like angels in heaven. And as for the dead being raised, have you not read in the book of Moses, in the passage about the bush, how God spoke to him, saying, "I am the God of Abraham, and the God

of Isaac, and the God of Jacob"? He is not God of the dead, but of the
living. You are quite wrong.'
(12:24–27)

Like Mark 12:10, but with greater public visibility, Jesus rebukes his
opponents for not knowing what they should know from the Old Testament.
Jesus quotes from Exodus 3:6 to argue that there is a resurrection because
the God behind the Scriptures, the same God who covenanted with
Abraham, Isaac and Jacob, is a *living* God. Jesus interprets Yahweh's self-
identification at the burning bush as a witness that he is the living God,
and if he lives so will his people, lest his covenant promises fail.

Furthermore, not only is he the God of the living as opposed to the dead,
but the resurrection state is not what the Sadducees assume it to be. The
saints will not be occupied with marriage but will be more like 'angels in
heaven'. Not only have the Sadducees failed to recognize the power of the
God behind the resurrection but have misunderstood the purpose of
the resurrection state altogether, and all because they do not know the
Scriptures as they should.

Notice as well that the Old Testament is once again referred to as 'the
Scriptures', but this time more explicitly associated with the divine author.
Jesus does not merely rebuke the Sadducees for not knowing the Scriptures
but for not knowing the *God-intended meaning* in those Scriptures. Hence
Jesus not only references 'the Scriptures' but the 'power of God', a phrase that
he then uses to highlight a basic metaphysical tenet of first-century Judaism:
the God of Abraham, Isaac and Jacob is the God of the living. Jesus dismantles
their theological misconception by appealing to the Scriptures to reveal the
doctrine of God therein; doing so robs the Sadducees' argument of any
hermeneutical force. In the end, Jesus' argument about the afterlife and its
ethics rests on a theological presupposition that Jesus brings to the surface:
the author behind these authoritative Scriptures and the one they portray is
Yahweh; he is the God of the living and the living had better pay attention to
his living word, the Scriptures of Israel.[81] Jesus, by contrast, is their model
for what faithful, covenant obedience to these Scriptures looks like.

---

[81] In the passages examined, the dialogue between Jesus and the religious leaders over the
Scriptures is almost always negative. However, Mark 12:28–34 is a rare exception. There Jesus
encounters a scribe who asks Jesus to identify the most important commandment, to
which Jesus responds by quoting Deut. 6:4–5 and Lev. 19:18 (cf. Matt. 22:34–40). The scribe
praises Jesus' response and Jesus concludes that this scribe is not far from the kingdom (12:34).
The outcome is positive in large part because Jesus and the scribe agree as to the true nucleus

In the Holy Spirit: Mark 12:37–40

In the final text to consider, Jesus goes on the offensive rather than being put on the defensive, as is usually the case. In Mark 11:27 – 12:24 Jesus is questioned and tested by the religious leaders, but in Mark 12:25–40 Jesus tests his opponents. In an account recorded by all three Synoptics (Matt. 22:41–46; Mark 12:35–37; Luke 20:41–44), Jesus is teaching in the temple when he asks the question 'How can the scribes say that the Christ is the son of David?' Jesus then quotes from Psalm 110:1:

> 'The Lord said to my Lord,
> Sit at my right hand,
>> until I put your enemies under your feet.'

Jesus follows up his quotation of Psalm 110:1 by observing how 'David himself calls him Lord', only to ask, 'So how is he his son?' (Mark 12:37). The riddle is perplexing for the Jews: How is it that the Christ is both the son of David and the Lord of David? How can he be inferior to David (as a son) yet superior to David (as his Lord)?

Jesus' exegetical question demonstrates that his Jewish opponents have a much lower view of the Messiah than they should have. They do understand that the Messiah is to be the 'son of David' (2 Sam. 7:11–16; Isa. 11:1; 9:2–7; Jer. 23:5–6; 30:9; 33:15–16; Ezek. 34:23–24; 37:24–28; Hos. 3:5; Zech. 3:8; 6:12); nevertheless, he is not merely another David or greater David. They fail to see that Jesus' identity does not begin with David but precedes David as the one who is the Son of God himself, a title pervasive in Mark's narrative (1:1, 11; 3:11; 5:7; 9:7; 12:6; 14:61). Perhaps this is why Matthew's version records Jesus also asking, 'Whose son is he?' (22:42).

> Jesus is indeed the Son of David, the messianic King from David's line who will fulfil the promises of the Hebrew Scriptures (cf. Isa. 11:1–9). But he is much more than the Son of David: he is the Son of God and Lord of all.[82]

(note 81 *cont.*) of the law: 'to love him with all the heart and with all the understanding and with all the strength, and to love one's neighbour as oneself, is much more than all whole burnt offerings and sacrifices' (12:33). Somehow this scribe escaped the elevation of man's traditions over the Scriptures, as well as the hypocrisy of many religious leaders who paraded external conformity without internal conviction.

[82] Strauss 2014: 552; cf. Morris 1992: 377; Stein 2008: 569.

What is salient, yet without direct attention, is the way Jesus introduces Psalm 110:1: 'David himself, in the Holy Spirit, declared . . .' (Mark 12:36). Or in Matthew's account: 'How is it then that David, in the Spirit, calls him Lord, saying . . .' (22:43). As discovered in Matthew 5:18–19, the concept of concursus is not foreign to Jesus, and here again it is ingrained in his quotation of the Old Testament. That David is considered a prophet is conspicuous in the book of Acts (2:29–30). Yet the book of Acts also follows Jesus' lead by saying David, as a prophet, spoke by the Holy Spirit (Acts 1:16; 4:25). At other times, the correlation between prophet and Spirit is so close that the two voices are considered one and the same. 'The NT authors', concludes Strauss, 'viewed the Holy Spirit's guidance in the production of Scripture as so intimate that OT quotes in the NT are sometimes introduced with phrases like, "The Holy Spirit spoke . . ." (Acts 28:25; cf. Heb. 3:7; 10:15).'[83]

Jesus' language for the Old Testament authors becomes increasingly theological when we consider how he not only refers to the Old Testament witness as the 'Scriptures' and introduces Psalm 110 with 'It is written' but also subordinates human authorship to the third person of the Godhead and his divine rhetoric. To say, as Jesus does, that David spoke 'in the Spirit' is not merely to recognize that the prophet David was influenced by the Spirit but that the Spirit's words became David's words. Jesus need not tell the reader *how* that concursus occurs; the fact that it does occur and that the Spirit has power over David is enough to rest assured that the inspiration that results is *verbal* in nature (notice how Jesus rests his identity on the minute differentiation of lordship vocabulary).

Contrary to those who assume such a synonymity between the human and the divine author was an invention of early Christianity, we see here that there are textual reasons to conclude that such a belief does not originate from the apostles but stems from Jesus himself. Paul (2 Tim. 3:16) and Peter (2 Peter 1:21) believed that what the prophets said God said, having been carried along by the Spirit, yet the Spirit's role is presupposed in Mark 12:36 and Matthew 22:43 as well.[84] As Jesus articulates, in veiled form, his Christological identity, his pre-understanding concerning scriptural identity also reveals itself.

In sum, Jesus assumes a congruous correlation between the human and divine author. As a prophet, David not only speaks for God and on behalf

---

[83] Strauss 2014: 550.
[84] Luke is the only one of the three who does not mention the Holy Spirit.

of God but God himself speaks through David. In this case, that divine speech is pivotal to the Christological point Jesus is making to reveal his messianic, divine identity as Son of David and Son of God. As the religious leaders question his redemptive works and divine identity, Jesus turns to the Scriptures of Israel because there the divine author has spoken, and his messianic plan has been revealed in the person of his own Son.

Conclusion

In brief, this chapter has attempted to push the argument of this study one step further. Chapters 3 and 4 looked at the fulfilment theme to show that Jesus presupposes not only divine authorship but, on that basis, canonical unity, and sees himself as the Christological clamp (see chapter 1) that binds the testaments (covenants) together. With that foundation in place, this chapter has demonstrated that the way Jesus *fulfils* the Scriptures is through his covenant obedience *to* the Scriptures. To reiterate, in the Gospels Jesus is on a mission as the obedient Adamic Son to fulfil all right-eousness and attain redemption for God's covenant people, but that mission is successful only if he is obedient to the Scriptures. Examining his covenant obedience proves fruitful for the argument of this study because some of Jesus' most direct affirmations of Scripture's inspiration and authority are instilled within the redemptive mission he came to accomplish. But the point we cannot afford to miss is this: the covenant obedience of the Son to the Scriptures also says volumes about the Scriptures themselves. Living by every word from the mouth of God, Jesus reveals the Scriptures to be the very word from God.

6

The Word became flesh: from Christology to canon

If Jesus claims to be the fulfilment of the Scriptures, and if Jesus claims that the authority inherent in his own teaching is on par with the Scriptures, then the next logical question that begs to be answered is *Who is Jesus to claim such authority?*

That was the question Jesus' religious opposition posed repeatedly whenever he performed a miracle or claimed messianic or divine status (e.g. Mark 2:10; Luke 5:24). 'By what authority are you doing these things, and who gave you this authority?', asked the elders of Israel and the chief priests (Matt. 21:23). The masses, characterized by less scepticism at times, posed a similar question, or more of an exclamation. With wonder, they asked, 'What is this? A new teaching with authority! He commands even the unclean spirits, and they obey him' (Mark 1:27).

The question of authority colours Jesus' ministry from start to finish. On many occasions he underscores that he has not spoken on his own authority but speaks what his Father has sent him to say (John 12:49; cf. 17:2). But that only raises another question: Who is Jesus that he has such access to the Father? That is a question Jesus intends to raise. In the end, it is answered by an empty tomb. Raised on the third day, Jesus prepares to ascend to the right hand of his Father, but not before he commissions his disciples, saying, 'All authority in heaven and on earth has been given to me' (Matt. 28:18). Those who had an ear to hear would have anticipated such a climactic ending (John 8:28). The point is, whether it is Jesus or his nemeses, *authority* is the issue.

The connection between Jesus' identity and the authority he possesses is not insignificant for what he claims the Scriptures to be. As seen in previous chapters, not only does Jesus believe the Scriptures to originate from his Father, but he believes those same Scriptures speak of him from beginning to end:

The Word that 'was in the beginning' and is incarnate as Jesus (John 1:1–14) is the very Word that 'came to' the prophets (e.g. Ezek. 1:3), is offered back to God in the Psalms, and moves Israel's history (Isa. 55:11).[1]

That claim has little credibility, however, unless Jesus is who he says he is: the Son of God and the Messiah. Should he be sent from the Father to fulfil the Scriptures, then what he thinks the Scriptures to be and how he thinks they are to be interpreted cannot be mere opinion; he is not merely another rabbi. The incarnate Son speaks with the very authority of God himself because he is, says the author of Hebrews, the 'exact imprint of his nature' (Heb. 1:3). *Therefore, one of the most substantial proofs for the divine origin of Scripture is the testimony of Jesus Christ because his words carry divine authority due to his divine identity.*[2] His attestation to their divine origin goes a long way to confirm their inspiration since he carries a divine authority like none other as the eternal, only begotten Son of God.

Up to this point in this study much attention has been given to how the *words* of Christ reveal God, what Vos calls Christ's 'speech-revelation', but in what follows attention must also be given to how the *person* of Christ reveals God, what Vos labels 'character-revelation'.[3] The present chapter is not by any means disconnected to all that has preceded it. Nor can it be excused as an exercise in systematics, as if irrelevant to biblical theology. Instead, biblical theology now reaches its natural, *theological* outcome, one rooted in the *Trinitarian* Christology of the Gospel narratives themselves. If Jesus is right that the Scriptures are characterized by a canonical unity and can be read as a single narrative because they are breathed out by his Father and carry his Father's authorial intent throughout, and if Jesus is right that his Father's intent throughout that single narrative is to prefigure his Son predictively and typologically, then the proof of such a belief hinges on one single reality: whether Jesus truly is the eternal Son of God. In short, *scriptural authority comes unhinged if not rooted in biblical Trinitarian*

---

[1] Jenson 2010: 22.

[2] To clarify, I am not saying the OT Scriptures were not inspired until Jesus said so, as if they are mere expressions of human religious experience until Jesus adopts and gives them an inspired functionality. Rather, the Scriptures were inspired the minute they were breathed out by God. Nevertheless, the incarnation of the Son plays an important role because his divine authority serves to *confirm* and *verify* that these Scriptures are truly from God.

[3] Vos 1948: 346.

Christology. 'Indeed, our view of the canon will overwhelmingly be shaped by our view of Jesus,' says Bartholomew.[4]

The inherent connection between canon and Christology guards against those who would introduce a disconnect between what Christ *says* and who Christ *is*. On the one hand, should Christ's words prove to be false, misguided or wishful thinking, then no little harm is done to his person. On the other hand, should Christ's claim about his messianic and divine identity prove to be blasphemous and ill conceived, no little harm is done to his message, a message that depends entirely on the Scriptures and their fulfilment. For this reason, Jesus never allows his opponents to set his words and self-revealing works over against one another; neither should we.

Additionally, this inseparable tie between Christology and bibliology affects the way Jesus interprets the Old Testament and with what *authority* he interprets the Old Testament. If he is who he says he is, then he can interpret the Scriptures with unprecedented authority because (1) those Old Testament Scriptures speak of him and (2) he is their original author, as the Word who was with God and was God in the beginning (John 1:1). As Robert Jenson explains, '*If Christ interpreted the old Scripture "with authority," as if he were the author, it was because, in the final ontological analysis, that is what he is.*'[5]

What follows, then, is an exploration of Jesus' self-understanding and self-consciousness, his Christological identity, as portrayed by the Gospel writers, with an eye to how that identity reinforces and solidifies not only the Scriptures but his own teaching as well, which he considers equal in authority to the Scriptures.[6] It is the penultimate step in this study yet perhaps the most important step to establishing the reliability of Jesus' position on Scripture, *but in the light of who he is and what authority he claims to possess.*

While it is fruitful to explore each of the Gospels and the diverse ways they bear witness to Christ, this chapter will focus primarily on John's Gospel, though with a complementary treatment of the Synoptics towards the end. As will be argued, it is often overlooked what a substantial case for Christ's divine, Trinitarian identity the Synoptics present. Their presentation of Jesus' divinity is different from John's and we will see why. Nevertheless, in John we see a portrait of Jesus that directly reveals who

---

[4] Bartholomew 2015: 258.
[5] Jenson 2010: 22. Emphasis added.
[6] See Vos 1953.

Jesus is and what implications his identity has for what he says about the Scriptures. Only John, says Augustine, is

> like one who has drunk in the secret of His divinity more richly and somehow more familiarly than others, as if he drew it from the very bosom of his Lord on which it was his wont to recline when He sat at meat.[7]

Therefore, John will occupy the majority of this chapter.

As we begin, one qualification needs noting. As much as this chapter explores the self-consciousness of Jesus, one should not think it leaves behind the scriptural fulfilment and typology so central to the argument of previous chapters. Just the opposite. John reveals the former through the latter. As John introduces his readers to the divine, Trinitarian identity of the Son, he does so through a typological lens encrusted with scriptural metaphors that Israel would have identified. As hinted at before, while Matthew directly identifies Christological fulfilment with scriptural quotations, John loves to paint a picture with his words, and uses the many typological colours of the Old Testament on his Christological canvas.

The Johannine witness

The Word was God: John 1 and the Son's Trinitarian origin

The start of Mark's Gospel reads, 'The beginning of the gospel of Jesus Christ, the Son of God' (1:1). Mark echoes Genesis to take his readers to the beginning of the life of Christ. John may have been well aware of Mark's opening, but chooses to go back further: to the start of it all, the creation of the world and eternity itself. Like Mark, Jesus Christ, the Son of God, is present in John's opening words, but in contrast to Mark, John speaks more directly to this Son's eternal origin.[8] In the beginning the Son of God already was; never was there a time when the Son was not with the Father.[9]

Except, John chooses not to start with messianic ('Christ') or sonship language as Mark does, though he will get there soon enough. Instead, he

---

[7] Augustine 2012a: 1.3.5–6. Also see Aquinas 2010a: 1.23 (p. 12).
[8] See chapter 5.
[9] On the parallel between John and Mark, see Carson 1991: 114.

calls Jesus the *Word* (*logos*) in John 1:1, establishing the Son's Trinitarian origin:

> *En archē ēn ho logos, kai ho logos ēn pros ton theon, kai theos ēn ho logos.*

> In the beginning was the Word, and the Word was with God, and the Word was God.

As seen in chapter 4, such a title will unfold in meaning as John continues his narrative, but it is clear from the start that Jesus is the eternal Word, and therefore he is the revelation of the Father. He is not just another revelation but the supreme, definitive self-revelation of God.

Yet that can be true only if the Word is, as John says, not only the one who was *with* God but the one who *was* God. As to the former, John does not mean to convey that the Word started to exist at creation, for instance, but that this Word is eternal in origin, 'always united to God, before the world existed', says Calvin.[10] As to the latter, John means to say that this eternal Word must be none other than God himself; as John's Gospel progresses, the reader learns this Word is, more specifically, the *Son* of God himself, eternally begotten from the Father's nature, and therefore distinct in personhood yet equal in divinity.[11] Capturing both of John's titles – Word and Son – Aquinas says, 'We call him "Son" to show that he is of the same nature as the Father' and ' "Word" to show that he is begotten in an immaterial manner.'[12]

Some deny that *theos ēn ho logos* is John's way of ascribing equality with God to the Word since no article is included. Carson, however, gives two reasons why that is a mistaken assumption. First, to argue that John 1:1 conveys Jesus as divine but not God is to forget that the Greek language had a word for 'divine', namely *theios*, but John does not use it here. John cannot be saying, then, that Jesus is merely characterized by certain divine

---

[10] Calvin 2005a: 27.

[11] Here is the grammar of trinitarianism, that God is three *hypostases* (persons), each a subsistence of the one divine essence, the Son eternally begotten from the Father, and the Spirit eternally spirated from the Father and the Son. See Calvin's (ibid. 28–29) reflections on the use of vocabulary by the Fathers.

[12] Aquinas 2010a: 1.42 (p. 21). Space will not allow us also to explore the doctrine of eternal generation at length and how it too supports Christ's divinity, but see Carson 2017: 79–97, as well as John 5 to follow.

virtues or qualities; John is saying far more, ascribing to Jesus the very essence of God.[13] True God of true God, he is begotten from the Father.

Second, the New Testament abounds with instances where the article is absent. 'It has been shown', says Carson, 'that it is common for a definite predicate noun in this construction, placed before the verb, to be anarthrous.'[14] Carson argues that John's omission of the article is a way of emphasizing the Godness of Jesus, 'as if John were saying, "and the word was *God*!"'.[15] At the start of his Gospel, John is preparing his readers for the hostility of Jesus' opponents, who will charge him with blasphemy for his claims of equality with God.[16]

It is this metaphysical, ontological introduction that then serves as the foundation on which John moves from *who* this Word is to *what* this Word does, though of course never leaving the former behind to articulate the latter. If the Word truly was God, then he was with God in the beginning (1:1–2), and the personal agent of creation (1:3). He can only be said to perform God's creation work if he is, undoubtedly, God himself. 'Having affirmed that *the Speech is God*, and having asserted his eternal essence,' says Calvin, 'he now proves his Divinity from his works,' and the work of creation is John's starting point.[17] No 'sooner was the world created than *the Speech* of God came forth into external operation; for having formerly been incomprehensible in his essence, he then became publicly known by the effect of his power'.[18]

Here John peels back yet another layer, defining what it means for Jesus to be the Word. That the Father creates the world through the Son demonstrates that he must be the Father's *Word*. For as Genesis reveals, the universe is brought into being out of nothing when God *speaks*: 'And *God said*, "Let there be light", and there was light' (Gen. 1:3; emphasis added). That connection is clear in John's mind: 'All things were made *through him*' (John 1:3; emphasis added). Creation, then, is a trinitarian work that is from the Father through the Son by the Spirit. But since John's emphasis is on the Son in John 1, it is John's identification of the Word as the agent

---

[13] Carson 1991: 117.
[14] Carson (ibid.) gives the examples of John: 1:49; 8:39; 17:17. Also see Rom. 14:17; Gal. 4:25; Rev. 1:20.
[15] Carson 1991: 117.
[16] Added to this are the times when John strategically ascribes to Jesus the title *theos*: John 1:1, 18; 20:28; cf. Rom. 9:5; Titus 2:13; 2 Peter 1:1; Heb. 1:8. For a treatment of this title, see Wellum 2016: 201–208; Harris 1992.
[17] Calvin 2005a: 29. Emphasis original.
[18] Ibid. 30. Emphasis original.

of creation that clues the reader into his equality with God.[19] 'For to be the principle of all the things that are made', comments Aquinas, 'is proper to the great omnipotent God' (cf. Ps. 134:6), and therefore, the 'Word, through whom all things were made, is God, great and coequal to the Father'.[20] Being coeternal with the Father, the Word must also be consubstantial with the Father.

All this is further confirmed in the second half of John 1 when John not only says this Word 'was made flesh, and dwelt among us', but 'we beheld his glory, the glory as of the only begotten of the Father', who is 'full of grace and truth' (John 1:14).[21] How can this be? In the Old Testament, seeing the glory of God was an impossibility, as Moses himself learned at Sinai (Exod. 33:18–23). 'You cannot see my face, for man shall not see me and live,' he told Moses (Exod. 33:20). However, when the 'only Son from the Father' – the eternal Word begotten by the Father – 'became flesh' there is a sense in which John could then say, 'we have seen his glory'. Here the title 'Word' comes into full view: 'No one has ever seen God; the only God, who is at the Father's side, he has made him known' (John 1:18). Not only has John attributed full deity to the Son, but on that basis he has also drawn the conclusion that it is through the Son, the Word, that the Father has been manifested to humankind. He is the Word who reveals the Father because he is the 'only God', who sits 'at the Father's side'. Jesus, in other words, is the revelation of God, the Word made flesh; to see him, therefore, is to see the incarnate glory of God (cf. John 14:9).[22] As we will see next, John's appeal to Jesus' sonship will find a place on the lips of Jesus himself.

Equality with God as the Son of God and the Son from God: John 5, the divinity of the Son and eternal generation

A second text where Jesus' divinity shines through is John 5. With the feast of the Jews at hand, Jesus travels to Jerusalem and approaches the pool at Bethesda. Around the pool innumerable invalids swarm, each hoping to enter the pool first so that the stirring waters will heal them.

---

[19] For this reason, Augustine (2012b: I.11 [p. 100]) argues that the Word cannot be made since 'God by the Word made all things' and if 'the Word of God was itself also made, by what other Word was *it* made?' Emphasis original.

[20] Aquinas 2010a: 1.69, 71 (p. 31).

[21] KJV translation. 'Begotten' fits the context. See Irons (2017): 98–116. Or in Paul: 'He was manifested in the flesh' (1 Tim. 3:16; probably a quotation from an early hymn).

[22] Hence Jesus can say to Philip in John 14:9, 'Whoever has seen me has seen the Father.'

One man has been an invalid for thirty-eight years. Unfortunately, he has no one to help him into the pool. Yet at the command of Jesus to take up his bed and walk, the man who cannot walk is instantly healed (5:9). Certain Jews, however, miss the significance of the miracle as well as the identity of the miracle worker, instead fixating on the mat this healed man is carrying. 'It is the Sabbath, and it is not lawful for you to take up your bed' (5:10). The Mishnah prohibited thirty-nine types of work on the Sabbath and carrying one's mat was one of them.[23] The man healed by Jesus does not know who has healed him (5:13). He blames his breaking of the Sabbath on the one who healed him and told him to carry his mat (5:11). When the Jews press this man as to who it is that told him to carry his mat, the man healed is clueless since Jesus slipped away immediately (5:12–13). Afterward, Jesus reappears and instructs this man to sin no more lest something worse occur (5:14). Later, in John 9:1–2, Jesus will warn against assuming an illness is the result of one's sin (or the sin of one's parents), but in this case it appears this man's illness is, in one way or another, a consequence of a sin (or sins) this man committed.[24]

Fearing the Jews more than Jesus, the man reports to the Jews that it is Jesus who healed him (5:15). John then adds his explanatory comment 'And this was why the Jews were persecuting Jesus, because he was doing these things on the Sabbath' (5:16). These Jews first charged the healed man with breaking the Sabbath, but now lob the same charge at Jesus not only for telling this man to carry his mat but also perhaps for healing the man in the first place. This pericope only extends the continuing opposition to Jesus due to the works he does on the Sabbath day.[25]

Yet it is the response of Jesus to these Jews that proves most unacceptable: 'My Father is working until now, and I am working' (5:17). In Jewish tradition God rested on the seventh day of creation after creating for six days; nevertheless, even on the seventh day he continued to sustain the world that he had made. God 'consecrated' the seventh day, and yet, says Calvin, he

---

[23] Carson 1991: 244.

[24] On the variety of interpretations, see ibid. 245–246.

[25] Nor will it stop here. In John 7 this Sabbath conflict appears again, yet this time Jesus takes a different approach to expose the contradictory logic of the Jews and their adherence to the law: 'Moses gave you circumcision (not that it is from Moses, but from the fathers), and you circumcise a man on the Sabbath. If on the Sabbath a man receives circumcision, so that the law of Moses may not be broken, are you angry with me because on the Sabbath I made a man's whole body well? Do not judge by appearances, but judge with right judgment' (7:22–24).

did not cease to sustain by this power the world which he had made, to govern it by his wisdom, to support it by his goodness, and to regulate all things according to his pleasure, both in heaven and on earth.[26]

Creation may have been finished in six days, but God continued to govern his creation every day that followed.[27] Hence the present tense 'My Father is working until now' (5:17), which communicates a continuing and continuous work by God.[28]

Jesus can 'break' the Sabbath because he, just like his Father, is at work, and not only to sustain and govern creation but to *restore* and *renew* creation to what it was meant to be, as demonstrated in the healing of this lame man. He has the same prerogatives on the Sabbath as his Father. Why? Because he shares the same divine identity, being equal with the Father in divinity.[29] And, within the broader context of John 1:1, he was with the Father from the beginning, so that Jesus speaks not only *for* the Creator but *as* the Creator. Augustine paraphrases Jesus; it is as if Jesus says:

Why do ye expect that I should not work on the Sabbath? The Sabbath-day was ordained for you for a sign of me. You observe the works of God: *I was there when they were made, by me were they all made; I know them.*[30]

There may be a deeper echo of Genesis and the creation narrative at play here as well, or at least a theological implication. Just as God spoke creation into existence with but a word (Gen. 1:3), so too by the power of his word does Jesus speak healing into this man's paralysed and weak bones. The Word through whom the cosmos was spoken into existence now speaks again so that this man can walk. He really is the one through whom 'all things were made', and 'without him was not any thing made that was made' (John 1:3). Therefore, just as his Father can continue to work on the seventh day by sustaining the cosmos he made, so too can his Son work on

---

[26] Calvin 2005a: 196.

[27] Ibid.

[28] Aquinas 2010a: 5.739 (p. 268).

[29] Hebrews makes this same connection between the Son's divine identity and the works of creation and providence: 'He is the radiance of the glory of God and the exact imprint of his nature, and he upholds the universe by the word of his power' (1:3).

[30] Augustine 2012b: 116 (Tractate XVI, 15). Emphasis original.

the seventh day to restore creation from its fallen state. In this strict adherence to the Mishnah's prescriptions, these Jews miss the big picture: the new creation is being renewed by him through whom all things were made. The Word of the Creator has become incarnate to restore his creation order so that his image bearers may enjoy an eternal Sabbath rest. Just as the temple pointed to Jesus, the new temple, so too does the Sabbath typologically anticipate him who is its definitive rest.[31] All those who trust in Jesus will find a rest for their souls that brings to a culmination what the Sabbath day pictured but in part. Although John does not tell us Old Testament specifics, perhaps this is insinuated in Jesus' concluding claim that Moses 'wrote of me' (5:46).

All that to say, not only does John 5:17 imply Jesus' pre-existence as the Son, the type John asserts at the opening of his Gospel (i.e. the Word was with God; John 1:1), but it also assumes his co-equality with the Father. That Jesus meant to convey such divine equality with the Father is confirmed by the vehement response of the Jews: 'This was why the Jews were seeking all the more to kill him, because not only was he breaking the Sabbath, but he *was even calling God his own Father, making himself equal with God*' (5:18; emphasis added).

What the Jews may have in mind by 'equal with God' is not what John or Jesus have in mind. As becomes plain in John 5:19–47, Jesus does not mean that he is a second God, undermining the fabric of monotheism. 'Jesus is not equal with God as *another* God or as a *competing* God,' Carson qualifies.[32] In the forthcoming discourse Jesus will define monotheism in trinitarian (Christian) categories but without compromising monotheism itself (a point we will return to later in our look at the Synoptics). Jesus reveals himself to be the Son of the Father who is equal to the Father in his divinity, yet still distinct from the Father as a person. He is 'equal with God' (5:18) yet is the one 'sent' by God (5:36), which is an emphasis unique to John's Gospel, as seen in both John 1:1 and John 3:16.

Jesus claims unprecedented ontological unity and equality with the Father (e.g. 5:19, 26), while at the same time distinguishing himself from the Father as insinuated in the distinct mission the Father has entrusted to him (see e.g. 5:19–47). In trinitarian terms the temporal mission of the Son stems from and reveals the eternal relations of origin, in this case eternal

---

[31] This typology is not lost on Aquinas (2010a: 5.738 [p. 268]), who calls it a 'foreshadowing'.
[32] Carson 2016: 250. Emphases original.

generation (see John 5:26).[33] It is because the Son is eternally begotten of the Father that he voluntarily takes on the mission the Father has given to him (which originates in the *pactum salutis*, the 'covenant of redemption') and is sent by the Father to accomplish redemption through his incarnation.[34] More on this below.

This both–and, as opposed to either–or, tension between unity and distinction continues in John 5:19 and following. On the one hand, Jesus defies ditheism (the fear of the religious leaders) by stressing his indivisibility from the Father: 'Truly, truly, I say to you, the Son can do nothing of his own accord, but only what he sees the Father doing' (5:19a). He is no independent, challenging deity to Jewish monotheism. On the other hand, Jesus then confirms his divine equality: 'For whatever the Father does, that the Son does likewise' (5:19b). The works of Jesus are coextensive with the works of his Father, and that is, as was seen in 5:17, nothing less than a claim to divine equality with the Father. With both of these in plain view, 'Jesus both repudiates and accepts the charge that he makes himself equal with God (5:18),' says Carson. Jesus

> repudiates it in that he strenuously avoids any suggestion that he is an independent God, a second God, or an alternative God, since all that he does is utterly dependent on the Father; and he accepts the charge that he makes himself equal with God in that whatever the Father does he also does, to the end that he should receive the same glory as the Father.[35]

Unfortunately, the religious leaders do not possess a trinitarian paradigm to make sense of such an audacious claim.

---

[33] To be extra clear, the temporal mission(s) do not create eternal relations in the Trinity, but merely manifest an eternal reality. 'The historic missions of the Son and the Spirit reveal what is true in eternity: they do not constitute or make God three persons.' Giles 2012: 224. Giles echoes Bruce Marshall: 'Working in terms of procession and mission gives us conceptual tools for explaining quite clearly how the distinctions among the divine persons do not arise from the economy of salvation, but are presupposed to it . . . Mission includes procession, but procession does not include mission; procession is necessary for mission, but mission is not necessary for procession.' Marshall 2010: 14–15.

[34] This is a point Augustine makes throughout *The Trinity* (e.g. 2.3–4; 4.28–32; 5.15, 47–48), and many other patristic and medieval exegetes follow suit. It should be clarified, being sent by no means implies inferiority or eternal subordination for the Son; see Köstenberger and Swain 2008: 121. Space does not permit an exploration of eternal generation, but the reader should note its extreme importance not only for orthodox trinitarianism but for the Christology of the incarnation, as well as proper biblical exegesis itself, as seen in a Gospel like John's. See Giles 2012; Sanders 2016; Carson 2017; Köstenberger and Swain 2008: 179–185: Sanders and Swain 2017.

[35] Carson 2017: 84–85.

Son of God as eternal sonship

In John 1:49 Nathanael exclaims that Jesus is the 'Son of God'. In chapter 3 we saw how that title refers to Jesus as the Messiah and Davidic king, though even there it may press beyond those historical boundaries to say something transcendent of this Son. This use of Son of God to refer to the Messiah and Davidic king is common in the Gospels and the rest of the New Testament. However, in John 1 and 5 we have also seen that this same title can be used to refer to Jesus as the *eternal Son begotten from the Father*. Remember, John says at the opening of his Gospel not only that this Word 'was made flesh, and dwelt among us', but 'we beheld his glory, the glory as of the *only begotten of the Father*', who is 'full of grace and truth' (John 1:14, KJV; emphasis added). In John 5 Jesus' prerogative to work on the Sabbath is grounded in his eternal origin from the Father. The Jews hear this and understand Jesus to be *'calling God his own Father, making himself equal with God'* (5:18; emphasis added). Examples could be multiplied across the New Testament (Matt. 11:27; Luke 10:22; John 14:9; 17:1–8; Col. 1:15–19; Heb. 1:2–3; 1 John 5:20).

All that to say, in such passages Jesus

> is not the Son of God by virtue of being the ultimate Israel, nor is he the Son of God by virtue of being the Messiah, the ultimate Davidic king, nor is he the Son of God by virtue of being a perfect human being.[36]

All of which we explored in prior chapters. 'Rather,' says Carson, 'he is the Son of God from eternity, simultaneously distinguishable from his heavenly Father yet one with him, the perfect Revealer of the living God.'[37] Notice, John and Jesus' use of Son language is not divorced from John's concept of the Logos. As the eternal Son from the Father, the one who is equal in divinity to the Father, this Son can become incarnate and in doing so become the 'perfect Revealer' of the Father, that is, the Word.

This point cannot be emphasized enough. Recognizing Jesus to be the eternal Son from the Father is the basis on which we can then affirm him to be the supreme revelation, the Word, of the Father, not vice versa. The Word did not become Son, as if divine sonship starts with the incarnation (this is

---

[36] Carson 2012: 41.
[37] Ibid.

no adoptionist Christology).[38] Instead, the eternal Son became incarnate to reveal the Father to the world. The ontological always grounds the functional in Christology. 'Sonship precedes messiahship and is in fact the ground for the messianic mission.'[39] Never was there a time when the Father was without his Word, and at the appointed time the Word was revealed to the world so that he might in turn reveal God to the world (John 1:18).

John 5:26 bears this out. Remember, in 5:17–19 Jesus both accepts and challenges the charge of the religious leaders. On the one hand, he is teaching no ditheism as they think; rather than a second, challenging and independent deity, Jesus is one who 'can do nothing of his own accord, but only what he sees the Father doing' (5:19a). On the other hand, that does not preclude his divine equality with the Father: 'For whatever the Father does, that the Son does likewise' (5:19b). His affirmation of both only continues as he draws out implications for salvation and judgment in 5:20–29. It reaches a climax in 5:26, where again both are seen: 'For as the Father has life in himself, so he has granted the Son also to have life in himself.' What might Jesus mean?

Life in himself refers to the divine attribute of aseity. As the self-existent, self-sufficient, infinite and eternal God, the Creator in no way depends on something or someone external to himself, such as his creation or his creatures. Put positively, he not only has but *is* life in and of himself.[40] To claim such aseity from the Father in 5:26 is just as bold a claim to deity as 5:17 ('My Father is working until now, and I am working'), though perhaps with an even greater sense of lucidity. In context, it is on this basis that Jesus can then claim to give eternal life to those whom the Father has given to him (5:25).

But notice, the life Jesus has in himself is given to him by the Father, who has life in himself: 'For as the Father has life in himself, so he has granted the Son also to have life in himself' (5:26). While that may appear to be a contradiction, it is not. Keep in mind, this is the *eternal* God in view. The granting of life is, says Augustine, an eternal, timeless reality. Building on Augustine, Carson labels it an 'eternal grant':

---

[38] 'It is not that this eternal Word *became* the Son by means of the incarnation, so that it is appropriate to speak of Father, Son, and Holy Spirit only *after* the incarnation, whereas *before* the incarnation it would be more appropriate to speak of the Father, the Word, and the Spirit. No . . . *the Son* is the one by whom God made the universe.' Ibid. 41. Emphases original.

[39] Ladd 1974: 167. Also see Wellum 2016: 158–165.

[40] See Barrett 2019: 55–69.

It is not as if there was a moment when God granted to the Son to have life in himself, before which the Son did not have life in himself. If such were the case, then whatever it was that the Son was granted could not have been divine, independent, self-existence life.

Carson concludes:

this grant does not establish a certain time in chronological sequence when the grant took place; rather, if it is an eternal grant, it establishes the nature of the Father–Son relationship. In short, this is a way of establishing the eternal generation of the Son.[41]

What Carson calls an eternal grant, the Fathers labelled an eternal generation, a concept presupposed throughout John's Gospel whenever Jesus or John speak of the Son's eternal origin from the Father.[42] While the Father is unbegotten, the Son is eternally begotten by the Father. In other words, the Son is generated from the Father in eternity. For that after all is what it means to be the *Son*. To put it theologically, the one divine essence eternally subsists in three persons so that each person of the Godhead is wholly divine. Yet the persons are distinct according to their eternal relations of origin: paternity (the Father is eternally unbegotten), filiation (the Son is eternally begotten) and procession (the Spirit is eternally spirated). This technical vocabulary by Nicene exegetes captures the same 'both–and' dynamic described in John 5, where Jesus asserts his divine equality while simultaneously confirming his distinct personhood (e.g. 5:17–19). He is, as Nicaea so famously said, 'true God from true God, begotten not made; of the same essence as the Father'.[43]

Why mention 5:26 and eternal generation? Not only does Jesus' statement balance monotheism while distinguishing between trinitarian persons, but this eternal grant or eternal generation is a strong testimony

---

[41] In this quotation, Carson (2017: 82) is expounding Augustine's view (*The Trinity* 1.5.26; 1.5.30) and that of other Fathers, and after examining John 5:26 Carson concludes (2017: 85) that Augustine's interpretation is correct. For a critique of alternative contemporary interpretations, see ibid. 80–82. Makin (2017: 252) puts forward an additional argument countering the objection that eternal generation violates aseity. Describing the 'Grounding Model', Makin clarifies that aseity precludes God's depending on anything *external* to himself. However, eternal generation is a 'dependence relation located entirely "inside" God' and so is consistent with divine aseity.

[42] See my forthcoming work on the Trinity: Barrett 2021. For a superb defence of 'only begotten' language in John's Gospel, consult Irons 2017: 98–116. Also see Giles 2012; Holmes 2012; Bird and Harrower 2019; Sanders and Swain 2017.

[43] Pelikan and Hotchkiss 2003: 153.

to the full, absolute deity of the Son. In short, Jesus is claiming not to have been made a Son at the incarnation, but to be the eternal Son from the Father, eternally receiving from the Father life in himself. Again, Nicaea says it best when it describes the Son as 'the Only-begotten from the Father, that is *from the substance of the Father*'.[44] What stronger indication could Jesus possibly give to his divine identity and eternal origin?[45]

Before Abraham was, I AM: John 8 and the word of truth

As seen in chapter 4, in John 4 and 6 Jesus appeals to metaphors like water and bread to convey his identity and mission. In John 8 Jesus returns to a metaphor that John himself used to open his Gospel: *light*. 'In him was life, and the life was the light of men. The light shines in the darkness, and the darkness has not overcome it' (1:4–5). Now the reader hears the metaphor from Jesus himself in one of his 'I am' sayings: 'I am the light of the world. Whoever follows me will not walk in darkness, but will have the light of life' (8:12). As Carson points out, the metaphor is rooted in the Old Testament. Israel was guided out of Egypt and through the wilderness by means of a cloud and pillar of fire. These were not only symbols of God's presence and glory, but designated God's role to protect his covenant people and lead them in the way of life. Throughout the Old Testament light is used to refer to the life and salvation Yahweh gives to his covenant people (Pss 27:1; 36:9; 119:105; Prov. 6:23; Hab. 3:3–4) as well as the nations (Isa. 49:6). Furthermore, the 'coming eschatological age would be a time when the Lord himself becomes light for his people (Isa. 60:19–22; cf. Rev. 21:23–24)'.[46] Given John's Jewish audience, it makes sense then why 8:12 (and 1:4–5) mixes two metaphors, light and life. To leave the darkness and enter the light is to leave death and enter life. Jesus is that light and in him is life eternal, as he has indicated throughout John 3.

Without fail, the Pharisees question the basis on which Jesus can make such a claim: 'You are bearing witness about yourself; your testimony is not true' (8:13). Already, in John 5, Jesus went to great lengths to explain that he does not 'bear witness' about himself, but there 'is another who

---

[44] Ibid. 159.

[45] The *how* of eternal generation is mysterious, and it should be if our triune God is eternal, infinite and incomprehensible. Nevertheless, we may attempt to define eternal generation in (1) causal, (2) grounding or (3) essential categories. To understand all three options, see Makin 2017: 243–259, who believes an essential dependence model is best.

[46] The last day is one continually lit up (cf. Zech. 14:5–7). Carson 1991: 338.

bears witness' about Jesus and his testimony is 'true' (5:31–32). The problem is, the Pharisees do not accept Jesus' claim that he is the Son sent by the Father. That does not change in John 8 either.

Like John 5, in John 8 Jesus' response says much about his identity. First, he clarifies, even if he does bear witness about himself, his testimony is true since he knows where he comes from, unlike the Pharisees who are clueless as to his origins (8:14). Second, he is not alone in his witness to himself, for the Father too bears witness to his Son. 'I am the one who bears witness about myself, and the Father who sent me bears witness about me' (8:18). The law's demand for two witnesses is met and the truthfulness of Jesus' word is established (8:17). It does not matter, however, for the Pharisees will never believe as long as they 'judge according to the flesh' (8:15). Jesus, by contrast, does not judge by fallen, human appearances but instead according to the one who has sent him (8:15–16).

At this point in the narrative, Jesus draws the connection between who sent him and who he is, and ultimately what he has been sent to accomplish. Announcing that he is 'going away' and that the Pharisees will die in their sin (8:21; cf. 7:33–34), Jesus contrasts their worldly identity with his heavenly identity:

> You are from below; I am from above. You are of this world; I am not of this world. I told you that you would die in your sins, for unless you believe that I am he you will die in your sins.
> (8:23–24)

It is their unbelief that he is from the Father that keeps them enslaved to their sins, unable and unwilling to perceive who Jesus truly is; consequently, they remain condemned rather than forgiven.

For our purposes, the importance of Jesus' self-identifying title *egō eimi* in verse 24 cannot be overlooked. An exploration into the various interpretations of this phrase cannot be accomplished here, but there is good reason to believe Isaiah 40 – 55 sits in the background.[47] For example, in Isaiah 43:10 Yahweh says:

> 'You are my witnesses,' declares the LORD,
>   'and my servant whom I have chosen,

---

[47] See ibid. 343.

that you may know and believe me
　　and understand that *I am he* [*egō eimi*; LXX].'

What does this name mean? The context, says Carson, 'demands that
"I am he" means "I am the same", "I am forever the same", and perhaps
even "I am Yahweh", with a direct allusion to Exodus 3:14 (*cf.* Is. 43:11–
13)'.[48] In Exodus 3:14 Yahweh reveals to Moses his divine name by which
Israel is to know him: 'I AM WHO I AM.' Put together, Jesus' use of *egō eimi*
in John 8:24 should be taken in the strongest, most absolute sense: it is a
claim to divinity itself, and if not true is blasphemy.

Hearing *egō eimi* motivates the Pharisees to ask, 'Who are you?' (8:25).
Jesus again returns to his origin from the Father: 'he who sent me is true,
and I declare to the world what I have heard from him' (8:26). John
comments that the Pharisees did not 'understand that he had been speaking
to them about the Father' (8:27). Yet Jesus gives further insight as to how
his eternal origin from the Father will lead to the fulfilment of his mission
from the Father. Once completed, the eyes of his oppressors will be opened
to his true identity:

When you have lifted up the Son of Man, then you will know that I
am he, and that I do nothing on my own authority, but speak just as
the Father taught me. And he who sent me is with me. He has not left
me alone, for I always do the things that are pleasing to him.
(8:28–29; cf. 3:14)

Despite the opposition Jesus faces, John says 'many believed in him'
(8:30). Turning to address those who believe, Jesus returns to the theme of
his 'word'. Those who listen to, believe and receive his word have believed
in the 'truth', and such truth has liberating power. 'If you abide in my word,
you are truly my disciples, and you will know the truth, and the truth will
set you free' (8:31–32). Given the purposes of the present study, such an
emphasis on truth cannot be stressed enough. For Jesus, truth itself is
inherently interconnected to the word he has been given by his Father, the
word he is speaking to Israel. Far from some abstract concept of truth, this
truth liberates those in bondage; that is the power of Jesus' gospel. To abide
by the word of Jesus is to enter this redemptive truth. Word and truth, in

---

[48] Ibid. 344.

the mind of Christ, cannot be severed, not least because Jesus himself is the Word. To divorce one from the other is to harm not only the message Jesus has spoken but the person of the Son himself, as if everything he represents is not true.

However, when they hear Jesus' reference to freedom, his listeners object, 'We are offspring of Abraham and have never been enslaved to anyone. How is it that you say, "You will become free"?' (8:33). They see not their own spiritual bondage, but Jesus exposes it for what it is: 'Truly, truly, I say to you, everyone who commits sin is a slave to sin' (8:34). On the other hand, if 'the Son sets you free' – the Son of God that is! – then slavery to sin has lost its grip entirely; in the Son 'you will be free indeed' (8:36).[49]

Despite their claim to Abraham's heritage, they have not Abraham as their father. Their true identity is evidenced by their rejection of Jesus. They seek to kill the very one who fulfils the promises God made to Abraham. Tragically, 'my word', concludes Jesus, 'finds no place in you' (8:37). The word of Christ liberates some, but in the case of others it condemns. Where the word of Christ is not found, and for those who abide not in his word, no freedom is found, but only a slavery that leads to death. Whether one is a true son of Abraham is determined, then, by whether one receives the word of Abraham's true son, and rightful heir, Jesus, the Christ.

Furthermore, those who do not have the word of Christ within are under an illusion as to who their real father is: it is not Abraham, as they think, but the devil himself (8:38–40). Although they are convinced Abraham, and therefore God himself, is their father (8:39, 41), that is an impossibility since they have rejected the word of his Son. 'If God were your Father,' as they claim in 8:41 in contrast to Jesus, whom they say is born of sexual immorality,

> you would love me, for I came from God and I am here. I came not of
> my own accord, but he sent me. Why do you not understand what
> I say? It is because you cannot bear to hear my word.
> (8:42–43)

When Jesus announces their true father – 'You are of your father the devil, and your will is to do your father's desires' (8:44) – he pinpoints a

---

[49] Jesus has also made it clear up to this point that as the Son of the Father, he has authority to set sinners free. On this point, see Carson 2016: 350.

Father–son correlation (i.e. like Father like son). Just as the devil lied and murdered in the beginning (he is the 'father of lies'; 8:44), having 'nothing to do with the truth, because there is no truth in him' (8:44), so too have Jesus' opponents refused the Word of truth:

> But because I tell the truth, you do not believe me . . . If I tell the truth, why do you not believe me? Whoever is of God hears the words of God. The reason why you do not hear them is that you are not of God. (8:46–47)

Having put his finger on the ultimate reason for their unbelief ('you are not of God'; 8:47), it follows that they will not hear the words of God that Christ himself speaks. Again, the inseparability between word and truth deserves accentuating. Christ has drawn a contrast between his Father and their father, the devil. The former has conveyed truth by the Word, his Son; the latter speaks lies, lies that result in disbelief towards the Word of the Father. In contrast to their father, Christ's word comes from the Father and therefore is defined by truth; such truth is the dividing line between those 'of God' and those 'of the devil'.

If Jesus has closely tied 'word' and 'truth', then his next rhetorical step is to link 'word' and 'life', though such a link is not absent from his discourse up to this point: 'Truly, truly, I say to you, if anyone keeps my word, he will never see death' (8:51; cf. 6:63, 68). The Jews once again fail to see how Jesus could be communicating anything other than a physical paradigm. 'Abraham died, as did the prophets . . . Are you greater than our father Abraham, who died? And the prophets died! Who do you make yourself out to be?' (8:52–53). The question is rhetorical, and they are not inquisitive so much as they are outraged: 'you have a demon!' (8:52; cf. 8:48).

> For Jesus to suggest that Jesus' word is superior to what Abraham and the prophets mediated to others, so that if someone keeps Jesus' word he or she will never taste death, is so preposterous that only a demonic illusion could account for it.[50]

'Who do you make yourself out to be?' (8:53) is a question masking itself as an accusation.

---

[50] Carson 1991: 355–356.

Yet the question itself does isolate the heart of the matter, for that is exactly what Jesus is claiming, namely that he is greater than Abraham and the prophets. As the Scriptures of Israel reveal, he is the one they pointed to as the Saviour of God's covenant people. As Jesus said back in John 5, the Jews 'search the Scriptures' because they believe that these Scriptures give eternal life, yet how ironic since 'it is they that bear witness' about Jesus (5:39). They appeal to Moses, but Moses accuses them for 'he wrote of me', says Jesus (5:46).

Like John 5, the response Jesus gives in John 8 is divinely oriented and yet simultaneously grounded in the history of Israel. First, Jesus situates his 'glory' not in himself, as if he seeks glory for himself apart from his Father, but in the one who glorifies him, namely his Father. 'If I glorify myself, my glory is nothing. It is my Father who glorifies me, of whom you say, "He is our God"' (8:54). The Jews claim God is their Father, but they have failed to see that the Father is concerned with glorifying his Son.[51] This only heightens their guilt; they do not know the Father as they think they do. Hence Jesus can say, 'But you have not known him' (8:55a). Jesus, on the other hand, does know the Father and he would be a liar to say otherwise, much like his persecutors (8:55b). That it is Jesus who truly knows the Father is plain: he keeps the Father's word (8:55); that cannot be said of these Jews.

Second, such a claim to know the Father and to be glorified by the Father is further substantiated by the history of Israel, which Jesus brings into the present day. 'Your father Abraham rejoiced that he would see my day. He saw it and was glad' (8:56).[52] Carson observes that the Jews would not have been offended by this statement if Jesus merely meant Abraham had special, God-given foreknowledge of the messianic era. Jesus is making a far more provocative claim about himself and his own day. Between these two options below, Jesus chooses the second one:

'Your father Abraham rejoiced to see the messianic age'.

'Your father Abraham rejoiced to see my day'.[53]

Jesus is reading backwards to read forwards (see chapter 1). Whether Jesus has in mind a specific encounter Abraham experienced or the overall

---

[51] Ibid. 356.

[52] As seen in chapter 4, Jesus says something similar in John 12:41. There the same language is used, but of Isaiah: 'Isaiah said these things because *he saw his glory and spoke of him*.' Emphasis added.

[53] This point is made by Carson (1991: 357).

pattern of Abraham's reliance on the covenant God cut with him and the salvific promises that covenant guaranteed to his offspring, Jesus sees Abraham as proof for his own claims, his own identity and his own mission.[54] Abraham trusted in the promises of God, promises Christ is bringing to fulfilment. 'Jesus identifies the ultimate fulfillment of all Abraham's hopes and joys with his own person and work.'[55]

But again, the Jews cannot see beyond the physical realm: 'You are not yet fifty years old, and have you seen Abraham?' (8:57). Their spiritual blindness leads Jesus not only to say that Abraham saw Jesus' day (8:56) but that Jesus himself existed before Abraham ever did, a claim that echoes back to John 1:1 ('the Word was with God, and the Word was God'). 'Truly, truly, I say to you, before Abraham was, I am' (8:58). Once again, Jesus uses *egō eimi* and powerfully communicates his eternal deity and consubstantiality with the Father. On the one hand, says Augustine, Jesus was made the promised seed of Abraham (Gal. 3:29), but here John teaches us that Abraham himself was made by this seed. 'I am', therefore, must refer to 'the Divine essence'.[56] And, as Aquinas adds, his claim to the divine essence by means of the divine title is one that has no before or after: he is God eternal.[57] Not even father Abraham precedes him.

Additionally, by attributing the divine name to himself, Jesus not only communicates equality with the Father, but by alluding to and applying the divine name of Isaiah 41:4 and 43:13, as well as Exodus 3:14, Jesus boldly asserts that he is the Creator and Redeemer of Israel, the one through whom salvation has been planned since the beginning.[58] As Calvin says, not only does Jesus echo Exodus 3:14 in his affirmation of his eternal divinity, but on that basis insinuates that he is the 'Redeemer of the world', the 'Mediator, by whom God was to be appeased'. The 'efficacy which belonged, in all ages, to the grace of the Mediator depended on his eternal Divinity; so that this saying of Christ contains a remarkable testimony of his Divine essence'.[59]

Despite the many times Jesus' hearers walk away shrouded in ambiguity, this claim to divinity the Jews understand and for this reason they pick up

---

[54] Aquinas (2010b: 8.1287 [pp. 153–154]) gives examples from Genesis that could be in view.
[55] Carson 1991: 357.
[56] Augustine 2012b: XLIII.17 (p. 244).
[57] Aquinas 2010b: 8.1290 (p. 154).
[58] Again, on the linguistic correlation between John 8:58 and these OT passages, see Carson 1991: 358.
[59] Calvin 2005a: 362–363.

stones to kill him (8:59). He has in their eyes spoken blasphemy and, according to Leviticus 24:16, a blasphemer must die.

'You, being a man, make yourself God': John 10 and the Scriptures that cannot be broken

This tension between Jesus and the religious leaders only continues as Jesus walks in the temple, in the colonnade of Solomon, during the Feast of Dedication in Jerusalem. But this time his Jewish opposition asks outright, 'If you are the Christ, tell us plainly' (10:24). Such a question, however, fails to see what Jesus has done and said up to this point. Turning his attention to his works, works they have seen themselves, Jesus says, 'I told you, and you do not believe. The works that I do in my Father's name bear witness about me, but you do not believe because you are not part of my flock' (10:25–26). As much as these Jews claim God as their Father, Jesus once again makes it clear, as he did in John 8:39–47, that they do not have God as their father and for that reason they do not believe that he is from God. On the other hand, those who do have God for their Father believe in his Son. They know the shepherd's voice. 'My sheep hear my voice, and I know them, and they follow me' (10:27).

It is the prerogative of Jesus, therefore, to grant them life everlasting, which no one, not even these Jews, can negate. 'I give them eternal life, and they will never perish, and no one will snatch them out of my hand' (10:28). Jesus has such a prerogative because he is the only begotten Son from the Father. 'My Father, who has given them to me, is greater than all, and no one is able to snatch them out of the Father's hand. I and the Father are one' (10:29–30). 'Jesus is not saying that he and the Father are a single person,' Bauckham clarifies, 'but that together they are one God. The statement should perhaps be understood as Jesus' understanding of the Shemá, corresponding to the allusion to the Shemá by "the Jews" in 8:41: "we have one Father, God" (cf. Mal. 2:10).'[60]

Moreover, the reason no one can snatch the believer out of the hands of Jesus is because he and the Father are one. In their essential unity rests the believer's confidence of salvific assurance. As Aquinas explains, this 'would not follow if his [the Son's] power were less than the power of the Father'. Only if they are 'one in nature, honor and power' can the sheep have confidence.[61]

---

[60] Bauckham 2008: 104. Likewise, see Hays 2016: 355.
[61] Aquinas 2010b: 10.1451 (p. 212).

Even first-century Jews mindful of the Messiah's coming and fulfilment of the Scriptures would have been shocked to hear such a statement of divine unity.[62]

In that sense, Jesus' statement works from but also adds to the presuppositions of Jewish monotheism to establish what will become a Christian Christology or a Christological monotheism. 'It is in the portrayal of this intra-divine relationship that John's Christology steps outside the categories of Jewish monotheistic definition of the unique identity of the one God.' Bauckham concludes:

> It does not at all deny or contradict any of these (especially since the Shemá asserts the uniqueness of God, not his lack of internal self-differentiation) but, from Jesus' relationship of sonship to God, it redefines the divine identity as one in which Father and Son are inseparably united in differentiation from each other.[63]

That the Jews understand Jesus' statement 'I and the Father are one' as nothing less than a claim to absolute divinity is obvious by their violent reaction to pick up stones to kill Jesus. In their anger they make it known that they want to stone Jesus 'not for a good work' he has done but instead 'for blasphemy, because you, being a man, make yourself God' (10:33). The incarnation of the eternal Son is inconceivable as they stare at Jesus, ready to strike. Jesus 'makes' himself God, they charge. Yet, according to John's Gospel, he has not 'made himself' God, says Carson, but 'He is himself the eternal Word, the Word that was with God and was God.' In other words:

> He is the unique Son, utterly obedient to his Father and doing everything the Father does (5:19ff.). As the Son, there has indeed been a change in his status, but one that is almost the reverse of what the Jews think: he has obediently and humbly accepted the incarnation. The Word became flesh (1:14), the Son became a man.[64]

Jesus has not made himself God: he is God, the eternal Son of God, who has become man (John 1:14).[65]

---

[62] Hays 2016: 320.

[63] Bauckham 2008: 106.

[64] Carson 1991: 396.

[65] Here I am not trying to spell out the exact dynamic of the hypostatic union, but merely trying to expose how this Jewish thinking is the reverse of what it should be. Should we use

How Jesus responds says volumes not only about his divine origin but also about the scriptural basis on which he makes his claims. Quoting and appealing to Psalm 82:6 (LXX), Jesus asks:

Is it not written in your Law, 'I said, you are gods'? If he called them gods to whom the word of God came – and Scripture cannot be broken – do you say of him whom the Father consecrated and sent into the world, 'You are blaspheming', because I said, 'I am the Son of God'? If I am not doing the works of my Father, then do not believe me; but if I do them, even though you do not believe me, believe the works, that you may know and understand that the Father is in me and I am in the Father.
(10:34–38)

Consider several key components to Jesus' argument.

1. Jesus' reference to 'your Law' is a reference to the Scriptures these Jews affirmed. Such an appeal is strategic because Jesus is claiming that their Law itself supports what he has done and who he is. Law is most likely not limited to the Pentateuch but is far more inclusive, incorporating all the Scriptures, the whole Jewish canon (or what today is labelled the Old Testament).[66] That much is clear when Jesus quotes Psalm 82:6.

2. There has been much discussion as to whom Psalm 82:6 has in view when it refers to 'gods' (ANE deities, judges of Israel, angels or Israel). Hays, for example, believes ANE deities are referenced since verse 1 opens the psalm, saying:

God has taken his place in the divine council;
    in the midst of the gods he holds judgment.

These gods, then, will be held accountable for judging unjustly (82:2). They will die 'like men' for their crimes against humanity (82:7). Although Hays is open to the possibility that these gods refer to the rulers of foreign nations, who suffer the same fate for their injustice. If Hays is right that

---

(note 65 *cont.*) more theological precision, it would be important to clarify that the divine nature is not 'made' (transformed into) a human nature, as Chalcedon clarifies. The person of the Son assumes a human nature, but the two natures remain distinct, and yet they are united in the one person of Christ.

[66] Carson 1991: 397.

ANE gods are referenced, then Jesus' appeal to Psalm 82:6 is not a 'proof of his actual divine identity' but instead a 'playful gambit that works as an argument *a minori ad maius* [from smaller to greater]'. In that case, Jesus would be saying, 'If even these pretentious pagan rulers or phony mythological beings can be addressed by God's (unimpeachably authoritative) word as "gods," how much more can I (who really am divine) legitimately call myself God's Son?'[67]

Yet other exegetes believe there are good reasons to conclude that the psalmist does have in view the people of Israel at Sinai.[68] They are 'gods' in the sense of being 'sons' of God. As chapter 2 alluded to, Israel is the 'firstborn son' of Yahweh (Exod. 4:22), and was liberated from Egypt at the price of Pharaoh's firstborn son (cf. 4:23), only to arrive at Sinai, where he would receive his Father's covenant word. Tragically, he turns out to be a rebellious son who will not listen to his Father, inviting the discipline of his Father until final, spiritual liberation comes from the true Son of God, Jesus Christ. In the New Testament, as seen in chapter 3, the language (and concept) of sonship for Israel is typological of Jesus himself. As Carson recognizes, Israel is 'called God's firstborn son (Ex. 4:21–22), generating a typology which Jesus has already claimed to have fulfilled (*cf.* notes on 8:31ff.)'.[69] He is, in other words, the true Son of God.

As hinted at in chapter 4, Son of God language in John's Gospel recognizes Jesus as the messianic Davidic king, but it also does more; for John, Son of God moves upward, identifying Jesus' heavenly origin as well.[70] In the 'Fourth Gospel "Son of God" is more than an exalted way of acclaiming Israel's expected Davidic king: it carries larger metaphysical implications about Jesus' identity'.[71] The Jews know this, as perceptible in their hostile response that Jesus claims equality with Yahweh himself (John 10:33). If his identification as Son of God was merely political, it would still have created strife with the Jews (perhaps), but only if Son of God carries notions of divinity does it invite the charge of blasphemy and the demand for crucifixion.[72]

3. The typology mentioned above sits in the background as Jesus quickly responds with scriptural support, Psalm 82:6, that chills the heated reaction

---

[67] Hays 2016: 331.
[68] For an extended discussion of these views, see Carson 1991: 397–398.
[69] Ibid. 398.
[70] See my previous treatment of John 5.
[71] Hays 2016: 324.
[72] Ibid. 330.

of the Jews. Carson summarizes what Jesus seeks to communicate by his appeal to Psalm 82:6 this way:

> This Scripture proves that the word 'god' is legitimately used to refer to others than God himself. If there are others whom God (the author of Scripture) can address as 'god' and 'sons of the Most High' (*i.e.* sons of God), on what biblical basis should anyone object when Jesus says, *I am God's Son*?[73]

Furthermore, Augustine, building on John's Logos imagery, conveys the irony within Jesus' point: 'If the word of God came to men, that they might be called gods, how can the very Word of God, who is with God, be otherwise than God?'[74]

Jesus does not intend to retreat from his self-proclaimed messianic and divine identity as the Son of God, and the reaction of the Jews suggests that they understand the divine claims Jesus is making. Yet Jesus more or less presupposes such claims, as he defuses their immediate call to arms by recalling how the use of sonship is not foreign to their own Scriptures, as seen in its application to their forefathers. Such an exegetical tactic also shows their hatred for what it is, namely a rage out of step with the logic of their own scriptural heritage. At the same time, Jesus exposes their erroneous assumption that he is claiming to be a second, competing deity rather than one who is one with the Father.[75] Begotten by the Father before all ages, he is simultaneously one with the Father yet distinct from him, but these Jews have no category for such a claim.

4. What, then, does Jesus mean by referring to the Scripture that cannot be broken (10:35)? Jesus is appealing to a pre-commitment the Jews could never deny. Jesus summons the Hebrew Scriptures in support of his Christological argument but does so by cornering them epistemologically, reminding them they cannot divert from their own presupposition: these Scriptures cannot be broken, falsified, annulled, altered, dismissed, relegated or excused. These are the Scriptures God himself has given to his covenant people, spoken by his own mouth, written by his own finger, fully authoritative and sufficient. This does not mean, Blomberg qualifies, that 'the Old Testament applies in every instance in the *same* way in the

---

[73] Carson 1991: 397. Emphasis original. Augustine 2012b: XLVIII.9 (p. 269).
[74] Augustine 2012b: XLVIII.9 (p. 269).
[75] Carson 1991: 399.

new covenant that Jesus is enacting as it did during the period of the Mosaic covenant'.[76] Yet it also does not mean that the Old Testament Scriptures can be dismissed as if they are without authority, relevance or application in the light of Christ's fulfilment. The Jews may dismiss Jesus, says Aquinas, but they cannot dismiss his appeal to the 'irrefutable truth of Scripture: "O Lord your word endures forever" (Ps 118:89)'.[77]

Appealing to the nature of the Scripture is to Jesus' advantage. 'Conceptually, it complements *your Law*: it is reprehensible to set aside the authority of Scripture, the Scripture whose authority you yourselves accept, just because the text I have cited seems inconvenient to you at the moment.'[78] The implications for Scripture itself are significant. 'Jesus here', says Hays, 'not only claims warrant from the law for his proclamation but also articulates a very high view of Israel's Scripture as unbreakable and unimpeachably true.'[79]

5. As much as Jesus uses Psalm 82:6 to diffuse their irrational anger, Jesus builds on such typology to say he is the Son whom the Father has consecrated (John 10:36–39). The Feast of Dedication was a feast of consecration, one in which the Jewish people gathered to remember how their temple had been defiled but also restored and made holy once more, set apart for God's service and his sacred presence. Typology is inherent in this feast and the temple it celebrates, for Jesus is the temple of God (John 2:19–22), holy and set apart, the incarnate Son manifesting the Father's presence to his people in a saving way. As Jesus says after cleansing the temple, 'Destroy this temple, and in three days I will raise it up' (John 2:19). He was, the disciples would learn after the resurrection, speaking of himself (2:22).

Unfortunately, the Jews of Jesus' day do not look through typological lenses to understand who Jesus is, namely the true temple of God through whom Israel may be consecrated by means of a new covenant. 'In this way', says Carson, 'Jesus outstrips and fulfils this Feast as he has the others.'[80] Hence Jesus can say he is the 'Son of God' his Father has 'consecrated and sent into the world' (10:36).

Such a consecration, however, is only possible if there is unity between Father and Son. The works of the Son testify that the 'Father is in me and

---

[76] Blomberg 2016: 690. Emphasis original.
[77] Aquinas 2010b: 1460 (p. 216).
[78] Carson 1991: 399. Emphasis original.
[79] Hays 2016: 299.
[80] Carson 1991: 399.

I am in the Father' (10:38). Jesus cannot claim such unity with the Father, however, unless he is equal to him in divinity, begotten of the Father's essence. As temples of God in whom the Spirit dwells, we 'can sometimes say, "We are in God, and God is in us"', Augustine explains; 'but can we say, I and God are one?'[81] Of course not. We would never say, as Jesus does, 'Whoever has seen me has seen the Father' (John 14:9). The type of unity Jesus claims in 10:38, therefore, is not that between the Creator (Lord) and the creature (servant), but instead refers to a trinitarian unity that transcends the created realm. 'Recognize the prerogative of the Lord, and the privilege of the servant,' warns Augustine. 'The prerogative of the Lord is equality with the Father; the privilege of the servant is fellowship with the Saviour.'[82]

Such ontological unity defines the eternal Trinity but was revealed in history when the Son's supernatural works were performed.[83] These works, as the man born blind understood so readily, come only from one who is from the Father. Our purpose here, though, is not to explore the intricacies of trinitarian thought but merely to observe that Jesus' divine status as the Son of the Father is not only confirmed by Jesus himself but is also verified by the typological imagery within the Scriptures of Israel.

'That they may believe you sent me': John 11:25

If John 10 places the Christological spotlight on Jesus as the good shepherd, that spotlight changes shades in John 11 as Jesus claims to be the resurrection and the life. Jesus is sent news from Mary and Martha that Lazarus, whom the reader is told Jesus loved, is seriously ill (11:3). The assumption in the message is that Jesus will come quickly; surely the hope is that Jesus will heal Lazarus from this life-threating illness, much as Jesus did countless times for others.

Jesus has no immediate intention to do so. Instead, he says with confidence, 'This illness does not lead to death. It is for the glory of God, so that the Son of God may be glorified through it' (11:4). As the story progressively reveals, Jesus does not mean that Lazarus will not die, but that his death will not be the last word. His impending death is orchestrated by God to bring glory to God. Calling himself the 'Son of God', a title that again reveals who Jesus is and why he is able to do what he does, Jesus indicates

[81] Augustine 2012b: XLVIII.10 (p. 269).
[82] Ibid.
[83] For more on this unity from both a biblical and theological perspective, see Köstenberger and Swain 2008.

that through Lazarus he will be magnified and exalted *as the Son of God*. His Christological identity may be intentionally veiled at points throughout his ministry, but this will not be one of them. What Jesus is about to do will unequivocally communicate his divine sonship and messianic identity; it is a miracle like none other.

With the purpose of such glorification in mind, Jesus does not go immediately but stays two days, guaranteeing Lazarus's death (11:6). By the time Jesus does arrive, Lazarus has been dead four days. Jesus is first confronted by Martha's regret: 'Lord, if you had been here, my brother would not have died' (11:21). Martha, however, is not without faith: 'But even now I know that whatever you ask from God, God will give you' (11:22). 'Your brother', says Jesus in response, 'will rise again' (11:23). Knowing the Scriptures, both the Law and the Prophets, Martha expresses faith once more but this time in the eschaton. 'I know that he will rise again in the resurrection on the last day' (11:24).

While Martha looks to the eschaton, Jesus turns her attention to the one who is in her presence now, the very one who will bring the resurrection life of the eschaton to fruition. What Martha awaits on the last day is a resurrection life after death but Jesus himself is the life she anticipates. 'I am the resurrection and the life' (11:25). The eschaton has broken into the present in the *person* of the Son. All those who trust in him, therefore, will live eternally even though their body falls prey to death here and now. 'Whoever believes in me, though he die, yet shall he live, and everyone who lives and believes in me shall never die' (11:25–26).

As much as Jesus guarantees that faith in him secures resurrection life one day, his statement seems to address the present as well: not only will those who die rise if they believe in him, but those who live and believe will not die. Eternal life, in other words, is not only to be anticipated but for those in Christ eternal life is theirs to be had now. The already-not-yet tension is felt in Jesus' statement, not only promising what is not yet experienced in full, but effecting what eternity brings to the present state of those who have trusted in Jesus. For those who believe in him who is life itself, life everlasting starts now, even if it will not reach its consummation until the age to come. The last days have arrived, eschatology has been partially realized, so that all who believe in Christ possess eternal life now even as it progresses and matures in the life to come.

When Jesus asks Martha if she believes, Martha responds, 'Yes, Lord; I believe that you are the Christ, the Son of God, who is coming into the world' (11:27). Martha's faith is genuine; but it is also Christologically rooted. She understands that Jesus can offer life because of who he is, namely the Messiah and Son of God. She not only believes her brother will one day rise but she believes in the very one who will raise her brother in the eschaton.[84] On the one hand, Jesus is the stone over which the Jews continually stumble in John 3 – 10, refusing to accept his messianic claims, no matter what miracles Jesus performs. On the other hand, Martha has not seen the miracle Jesus is about to perform and yet she believes.

Martha's authentic faith will be rewarded in what occurs next: the raising of Lazarus from the grave (11:38–44). Since Martha believes in *who* Jesus says he is, the 'raising of Lazarus becomes a paradigm, an acted parable of the life-giving power of Jesus'.[85] Before Jesus says those effectual, life-giving words 'Lazarus, come out' (11:43), he prays, 'Father, I thank you that you have heard me. I knew that you always hear me, but I said this on account of the people standing around, that they may believe that you sent me' (11:42). Jesus never misses an opportunity to convey his origin from the Father. He says this not for his benefit but for his listener's, making it as clear as possible that he is none other than the Son of the Father, and the miracle he is about to perform only confirms his divine origin. Along with Martha, many others that day believe Jesus to be the Christ, God's Son. Yet still others run to the Pharisees, who then plot against Jesus, prohibiting him from walking freely among the Jews (11:45–57).

From God, back to God, the way to God: John 13 – 14

With full confidence in the authority given to him by the Father (John 12:44–50), Jesus prepares for his betrayal and crucifixion. With the Feast of the Passover at hand, the 'Lamb of God, who takes away the sin of the world!' (1:29) knows that 'his hour had come to depart out of this world to the Father' (13:1). Sent from the Father, now the time is at hand for him to return to the Father. Jesus, John tells the reader, knew 'that the Father had given all things into his hands, and that he had come from God and was going back to God' (13:3). John started his Gospel declaring that the Word – the one who reveals the Father – 'was with God' and 'was God' (1:1); he was the 'true light' who 'was coming into the world' (1:9). Now that

---

[84] For a detailed analysis of Martha's faith as both *fiducia* (faith) and *assensus* (assent), see Carson 1991: 413.

[85] Ibid. 414.

the mission his Father gave to him is reaching its culmination, he will return to his Father, whose glory he shared in all its fullness in eternity.

His return to the Father, however, will be through the suffering of a cross. Such suffering is vicarious – Jesus' substituting himself on behalf of sinners to bear the full force of sin's penalty, the wrath of God. In the eyes of his executioners the cross is foolishness; however, in the Father's eyes this surrender to death in fulfilment of the Scriptures is glorious. As paradoxical as it sounds, the cross is a type of glorification itself. Jesus uses the title 'Son of Man' to convey this paradox: the combination of glory and suffering, or, to be more precise, glory *through* suffering.[86]

Additionally, this glorification is trinitarian in nature, involving the Father and the Son simultaneously. There is, in other words, a mutual glorification that occurs, the Father's glorifying the Son and the Son's glorifying the Father. In Jesus' own words, 'Now is the Son of Man glorified, and God is glorified in him. If God is glorified in him, God will also glorify him in himself, and glorify him at once' (13:31–32). On the one hand, the Father is glorified by his Son's covenant obedience to the Scriptures (see chapter 5), fulfilling the mission given to him to the bitter end. On the other hand, the Son is glorified because it is through his suffering that he will return to the glory he had with the Father in eternity, which is why Jesus can pray in John 17, 'And now, Father, glorify me in your own presence with the glory that I had with you before the world existed' (17:5).[87]

Even though Jesus reassures his disciples that he is going to prepare a place for them in his Father's house (14:2) and he will return for them so that they may be where he is (14:3), anxiety and confusion enter the minds of his disciples when he says, 'And you know the way to where I am going' (14:4). Perhaps speaking for all the disciples, Thomas responds, 'Lord, we do not know where you are going. How can we know the way?' (14:5). Thomas fails to see that the way to the Father is through the Son because the Son is from the Father and one with the Father. Hence Jesus' response that he is the way, the truth and the life, and no one comes to the Father except through him (14:6). Jesus exposes the disconnect in Thomas's thought when he then says, 'If you had known me, you would have known my Father also' (14:7a). Jesus follows that clarification with one of his strongest statements on the unity between him and his Father: 'From now

---

[86] Ibid. 482.
[87] For a more detailed explanation of this mutual glorification, see ibid: 482–483.

on you do know him and have seen him' (14:7b). 'This is true of the Son alone,' adds Aquinas, 'who has the same nature as the Father.'[88]

Apparently, Thomas is not the only disciple who struggles to see the connection between the Son and the Father. Philip too shows his lack of understanding when he demands an instant display of the Father: 'Lord, show us the Father, and it is enough for us' (14:8). Jesus repeats himself, but this time with bluntness only the spiritually blind can misconstrue:

> Have I been with you so long, and you still do not know me, Philip? Whoever has seen me has seen the Father. How can you say, 'Show us the Father'? Do you not believe that I am in the Father and the Father is in me?
> (14:9–10)

Jesus' statement is shocking: to see Jesus is to see the Father! Here John 1:1 comes to its zenith; the Son *reveals* the Father. 'I have *manifested* your name to the people whom you gave me out of the world,' Jesus prays to his Father, just before going to the cross (John 17:6; emphasis added).

Furthermore, Jesus grounds his ability to reveal the Father on the unity between him and the Father: 'How can you say, "*Show us* the Father"? Do you not believe that *I am in the Father and the Father is in me*?' (14:9–10; emphasis added). In other words, the fundamental reason the Son, as the Word, can reveal the Father directly – that is, to see the Son is to see the Father, says Jesus – is because there is an eternal, essential bond between the Son and the Father: they are one in essence. Jesus, as the Son, is not only from the Father but is in the Father and the Father is in him. Or as Aquinas interprets Jesus, 'the essence of the Father is in the Son, and the essence of the Son is in the Father' so that the 'Son is in the Father, and the Father in the Son'.[89] Hilary of Poitiers adds further insight: 'The Father is in the Son, for the Son is from Him; the Son is in the Father, because the Father is His sole Origin.' Assumed in such language, says Hilary, is the eternal generation of the Son. The 'Only-begotten is in the Unbegotten, because He is the Only-begotten from the Unbegotten.'[90] Could Jesus connect his identity any closer to the Father than by using the vocabulary of eternal generation?

---

88 Aquinas 2010c: 14.1879 (p. 59).

89 Ibid. 14.1891 (p. 63).

90 Hilary of Poitiers 2002: II.4 (p. 62).

Apart from this perichoretic unity of essence, the revelation of the Father through his Word, the Son, is impossible. The reason Jesus can offer eternal life and show his disciples the way to the Father is because he is one with the Father. One need not enter deep philosophical waters to see that Jesus can make such a trinitarian assertion only if he, the Son, is, in the words of Nicaea, 'true God of true God'. Unless he is one in essence with the Father, he cannot say to his disciples that he is the way to the Father, let alone that to see him is to see the Father.

Yet Jesus is not finished. It is his perichoretic, essential unity with the Father that further establishes the *authority of his words*, a point that gets to the very purpose of this final chapter.[91] If he truly is from the Father and one with the Father, then the *words* he speaks find their origin in the Father (again, see John 17:6):

> The *words* that I say to you I do not speak on my own authority, but the Father who dwells in me does his works. Believe me that I am in the Father and the Father is in me, or else believe on account of the works themselves.
> (14:10–11; emphasis added)

The words of the Son are the words of the Father because the Son *speaks* with the same authority of his Father; that is what sons do, they represent their fathers. We should expect nothing less from him who is, as John says, the *Word* made flesh; that is, the Word who was with God and who is God.[92] The connection between Jesus' *words* and his *person*, therefore, is indivisible.[93] To drive a wedge between who Jesus is and what he says is to fail to see how Jesus moves from Christology to canon. The reason his word is authoritative is because, in the final analysis, he is none other than the Son of God himself.

---

[91] Consult Köstenberger and Swain 2008 to understand this perichoretic dynamic in more depth.

[92] Since they do not believe, Jesus points them to his *works* as well. Space will not permit an exploration of John 7:16–28, but there the crowds question that Jesus could be the Christ. In similar fashion, Jesus points to his heavenly origin from the Father but the crowds do not believe, claiming that when the real Christ appears he will do more signs than Jesus.

[93] This inseparability between who Jesus is and what he says is also seen in what Jesus says next: 'If anyone loves *me*, he will keep my *word*, and my Father will love him, and we will come to him and make our home with him. Whoever does not love *me* does not keep my *words*. And the word that you hear is not mine but the Father's who sent me' (John 14:23–24; emphases added).

The future of Christ's new covenant word secured and delivered by the Helper: John 14 – 16

Does this inseparable connection between Jesus' word and his person continue once he is resurrected, ascended to the right hand of his Father, leaving behind his disciples? Yes, but in a way in which the disciples did not yet understand while Jesus was with them.

The absence of Christ's bodily presence is not the absence of his word. As he tells his disciples, who are troubled by his departure, he will send the Holy Spirit, who will take the word of Christ and implant it within their hearts and minds:

> These things I have spoken to you while I am still with you. But the Helper, the Holy Spirit, whom the Father will send in my name, he will teach you all things and bring to your remembrance all that I have said to you.
> (14:25–26)

The Spirit, therefore, is not merely a 'substitute' for Jesus: he is his 'emissary'.[94]

Furthermore, just as the Son can reveal the Father and show the way to the Father because he is eternally from the Father and one with the Father, so too can the Spirit be the Helper because he is not from himself but proceeds from the Father and the Son.[95] As the one who is from the Father and the Son, his mission is to illuminate the Word of the Father. 'But when the Helper comes,' says Jesus, 'whom I will send to you from the Father, the Spirit of truth, who proceeds from the Father, he will bear witness about me' (15:26). There is a type of trinitarian circularity in Jesus' statement, one that ensures the efficacy of his word in the future. The Spirit can implant the word of Christ within because he proceeds from the Father and is sent by the Son himself. Yet as the one who is sent, his mission is not to draw direct attention to his person, as is the case with Jesus during his incarnational ministry; instead he is sent to 'bear witness about me', Jesus clarifies.

---

[94] Carson 1991: 505.
[95] Debates over filioque need not retain us here, but see Augustine 2012b: XCIX (pp. 380–384).

One could object, however, that John 15:26 is about the *mission* of the Spirit and therefore it is illegitimate to interpret 15:26 with eternal categories in mind. It is true that John 15:26 has the *mission* of the Spirit in view, but for John the mission of the Spirit presupposes the eternal origin of the Spirit, much like the mission of the Son presupposes where the Son has come from (cf. John 5:18–46; 17:1–6). Otherwise, John would not begin his Gospel with ontological categories ('the Word was with God, and the Word was God'; John 1:1). The Spirit's mission in redemptive history is possible only because he eternally proceeds from the Father and the Son. While 15:26 'does not itself specify a certain ontological status', says Carson, it 'joins with the matrix of Johannine Christology and pneumatology to presuppose it'.[96]

In John 16 sorrow continues to fill the hearts of Jesus' disciples, but again Jesus turns to the Spirit, explaining that until he goes the Helper will not come, the Helper whom Jesus himself will send (16:7). Their sorrow due to Jesus' departure is to be met by confidence in this Helper's arrival. His disciples need not worry, because with the Helper comes the truth Jesus spoke to them, and truth he still intends to speak to them through the Spirit's descent:

> I still have many things to say to you, but you cannot bear them now. When the Spirit of truth comes, he will guide you into all the truth, for he will not speak on his own authority, but whatever he hears he will speak, and he will declare to you the things that are to come. He will glorify me, for he will take what is mine and declare it to you. All that the Father has is mine; therefore I said that he will take what is mine and declare it to you.
> (16:12–15)

Previously the focus was on the Father–Son dynamic in the delivery of the word, but here Jesus includes the Spirit in that dynamic, bringing a trinitarianism in its fullness to bear on the disciples' reception of his word.[97]

Notice, first, that the truth Jesus intends to convey will be given to the disciples by the Spirit, who is himself truth. As the Spirit of truth, he will

---

[96] Carson 1991: 529.
[97] For more on this trinitarianism, see Poythress 1994: 99–100.

guide them into all truth (16:13). Therefore, the Spirit ensures that the apostles will not stray from God's revelation of himself in Christ.

Second, the Spirit will guide the apostles into all truth because in his mission he does not 'speak on his own authority'. Just as the incarnate Son spoke what he heard from his Father, so too the Spirit: 'whatever he hears he will speak' (16:13). He will even 'declare to you the things that are to come' (16:13). Things to come refers not only to the death and resurrection still future at this point in John's narrative, but also to everything that Christ's death and resurrection give birth to in the church through the Spirit. What the Spirit declares to Jesus' apostles will not only be consistent with the revelation of God in Christ, the Word, but will bring that revelation into its fullness after Pentecost. God's supreme revelation of himself in and through his Word will reach its final consummation as the Spirit bears witness to Christ in and through his apostles to his church.[98]

Third, as the Spirit of the Son, his mission is to draw attention to the Son. Formerly Jesus revealed how his suffering would be the glorification of the Father in the Son and the glorification of the Son in the Father. Now the Spirit too shares in that trinitarian glorification. 'He will glorify me,' says Jesus, and he will do so as he takes that which the Son has given to him and communicates it to the disciples. As emphasized elsewhere, there is a trinitarian hand-off of truth underway, from the Father to the Son through the Holy Spirit.[99] At the same time, that trinitarian hand-off of truth occurs only in the trinitarian glorification between the three: Father, Son and Spirit. The Spirit who proceeds from the Father and the Son is also the one who glorifies the Son by taking what the Son says and delivering it to God's people, even implanting the word of the Son within God's people as prophets like Ezekiel promised (36:26–27).

The focus of this study has not been on the inspiration of the *New Testament*. Nevertheless, John 16, and this study as a whole, prepares the way. For Christ did not leave his people as empty-handed orphans; he did not cut the new covenant in his own blood only to leave his covenant people without a covenant treaty. Just as Yahweh redeemed Israel from Egypt and then gave them the book of the covenant, so too Christ redeems

---

[98] For this interpretation, see Carson 1991: 540. Calvin (2005b: 144) says something similar, arguing that Jesus does not refer to future prophecies that foretell what happens after the apostles pass away, but instead refers to the 'future condition of his spiritual kingdom, such as the apostles, soon after his resurrection, saw it to be, but were at that time utterly unable to comprehend'.

[99] Barrett 2016.

his people and then gives them a permanent covenant witness through his disciples.

This may not be stated in John 16, but is the natural entailment that follows in the book of Acts. Just as Jesus promised, the Holy Spirit does come to bear witness to Christ. The Spirit does so through the Scriptures of Israel; but taking into account all that Jesus has accomplished as Israel's Messiah, the Spirit also carries along the New Testament authors as he did the prophets to ensure that those Christ came to redeem are instructed in the way of the new covenant. *This book of the new covenant is not an illegitimate addition to the book of the old covenant but its necessary sequel, continuing the story of Israel now that the long-awaited Messiah promised in the old covenant has arrived. Apart from Christ's sending the Spirit to finish writing the story of redemptive history, the Old Testament remains incomplete and a tragic tale of false hope.*

The synoptic witness

Some assume that John's Christology is a foreign construct to the synoptic authors and their portrait of Jesus. After all, John 1 – 5 is material un-paralleled in the Synoptics: his Logos vocabulary and prologue are unique to his Gospel.

Certainly, the Synoptic Gospels each have inimitable emphases that not only differ from one another but from John. Nevertheless, it would be a mistake to think that the Synoptics knew nothing of the divine identity we have witnessed so explicitly in John's Gospel. Stuhlmacher warns readers not to 'consider the testimony of the Synoptic Gospels concerning the historically unique work of Jesus to be Christologically less significant than that of the Gospel of John or the apostolic letters'. Such an 'attitude fails to recognize that these very Synoptic Gospels invite us to think of God's work of salvation in and through Christ in a historically concrete way'.[100]

To exhibit Stuhlmacher's point, we will turn to the recent, and sometimes groundbreaking, proposals of three New Testament scholars: Simon Gathercole, Richard Bauckham and Richard Hays. The purpose in all this is to validate further that the Evangelists avowed the divinity of Jesus, a divinity that only serves to authorize the Scriptures of Israel as well as Christ's own revelatory message and identity.

---

[100] Stuhlmacher 1995: 17–18.

Pre-existence

In a substantial way the thesis of New Testament scholar Simon J. Gathercole – that is, *'the preexistence of Christ can be found in the Synoptic Gospels'* – serves to solidify Stuhlmacher's correction quoted above.[101] The 'ditch often assumed between the Synoptic Gospels and the Fourth Gospel is not as ugly as many think', Gathercole claims, with thinkers like J. D. G. Dunn in mind.[102] 'References to Jesus' coming have much the same sense in all four Gospels, although John does of course make explicit what is only implicit in the other three: it is a coming "down from heaven" "into the world".'[103]

Why then have so many scholars fallen into this ditch? Gathercole believes it is because they judge the Synoptics through a Johannine lens, so that if they do not articulate pre-existence in Johannine vocabulary then the concept itself must be unique to John. Scholars fail to 'recognize preexistence in Matthew, Mark, and Luke' because 'they have judged the Synoptics against Johannine standards of preexistence'.[104] The synoptic authors may come to the same Christological and theological conclusions as John, but they do so through their own literary devices and emphases. The Synoptics, says Hurtado, 'amount to considerably more than merely claiming royal-messianic status for Jesus'.[105] Pre-existence and divinity are present too.

The biblical support Gathercole enlists is not original to his study but its collective voice is powerful. It can be summarized under three major premises:

1 The Synoptics present a Christ who transcends (a) the *heaven–earth divide*, as seen in the transfiguration (Mark 9:2–8 [Matt. 17:1–8; Luke 9:28–36]), heavenly hierarchy (Mark 12:32 [Matt. 24:36]; heavenly council (Luke 10:18–21; 22:31–32; [Matt. 11:25–26]; identification by demons and spirits (Mark 1:24; 3:11) and (b) the

---

[101] Emphasis original. Gathercole (2006: 2) is countering modern scholars who deny such a claim. Interestingly, Gathercole points out that pre-modern thinkers never doubted his thesis. 'In the opinion of pre-modern, pre-critical interpreters of the Gospels, it was widely held that preexistence could be found in all four Gospels.'

[102] Ibid. 295. On Dunn, cf. ibid. 5–6; Dunn 1980; 1998.

[103] Gathercole 2006: 295.

[104] Ibid.

[105] Hurtado 1999: 38.

God–creation divide, as seen in his election (Mark 3:13 [Luke 6:13];
Mark 13:27 [Matt. 24:31]; Matt. 11:27 [Luke 10:22]); authority
to forgive sins (Mark 2:1–12 [Luke 7:49]); charge of committing
blasphemy (Mark 2:1–12; 14:63–64); supernatural authority in
nature miracles (Mark 4:35–41 [Matt. 8:23–27; Luke 8:22–25];
6:45–52 [Matt. 14:22–33]); claim to the divine name (Matt. 18:20;
28:19; cf. Mark 13:6 [Matt. 24:5; Luke 21:8]; Matt. 7:22; 12:21);
reception of worship (Matt. 2:11; 14:33; 28:17–18); supernatural
knowledge (Matt. 12:25; Luke 19:29–34); the one who sends his
disciples as prophets (Matt. 5:11–12; 23:34–36); participation in
Trinitarian order (Matt. 28:19); identification with God himself
and his divine names and attributes (Mark 10:17–22; Luke 5:1–11;
Matt. 1:22–23); and transcendence of space (Matt. 18:15–20).[106]

2 The Synoptics present the 'I have come' and other purpose formulas
to demonstrate Jesus' pre-existence to his earthly ministry (Mark
1:38 [Luke 4:43]; 2:17 [Matt. 9:13; Luke 5:32]; Matt. 5:17; 10:34 [Luke
12:51]; Luke 12:49; 10:35; cf. Mark 10:45; 20:28; Luke 19:10; also note
the confession of demons: Matt. 8:29; Mark 1:24 [Luke 4:34]).[107]

3 The Synoptics present Jesus as one who has been 'sent' on a mission,
as manifested in summary statements describing the goal of Jesus'
mission (Matt. 15:24; Luke 4:18, 43), references to the one who sends
Jesus (Matt. 10:40; Mark 9:37; Luke 9:48; 10:16) and indirect 'sent'
statements in Jesus' parables (Mark 12:6; Luke 14:17).[108]

Each of these is not meant to replace the strong emphasis in the Synoptics
on Jesus *as Messiah*. Nevertheless, his messianic identity should not lead
one to set his Jewish identity over against his pre-existent identity as the
eternal Son. The two complement one another and never is his messianic
role meant to preclude his divine pre-existence.

To be added to these are names and titles such as Messiah, Lord, Son of
Man and Son of God, titles that Jesus receives and claims and in a variety

---

[106] Gathercole 2006: 46–79. In order to summarize, I may or may not always use Gathercole's
exact language.

[107] Ibid. 83–176.

[108] Ibid. 177–189. Gathercole intends the 'sent' references to be coupled with the 'I have come'
references if one is to see why they support pre-existence (189). Also, Gathercole engages with
the debate over whether Jesus should be identified as pre-existent wisdom. Since that is a brief
and nuanced discussion, I have left it out of the above points. But readers should consult ibid.
192–193.

of ways point back to his pre-existence and in some cases strongly identify him with Yahweh himself. For example, while messianic references (8 times in Mark; 17 times in Matthew; 12 times in Luke) 'do not in themselves give evidence for or contribute to our understanding of preexistence', they 'do have connotations of heavenly secrecy'. Yet *anatolē* in Luke 1:78 does refer to Jesus as one who 'will visit from heaven' and therefore 'we have the strongest impression in the Synoptic Gospels of messiahship specifically associated with heavenly preexistence'.[109] When explicit references to Jesus' eternal, divine origin (Matt. 22:41–45; Mark 12:35–37; Luke 20:41–44) – references that either quote or echo Old Testament passages (like Ps. 110) – join this chorus, it is impossible to avoid the unified voice of the synoptic authors concerning Jesus' divine pre-existence.

Christological monotheism

Other New Testament contributions, such as Richard Bauckham's reflections on Jesus and monotheism, have only added support to a high Christology in the Synoptics. Inviting his guild to reconsider their approach to Jewish monotheism, Bauckham argues that

> high Christology was possible within a Jewish monotheistic context, *not by applying to Jesus a Jewish category of semi-divine intermediary status, but by identifying Jesus directly with the one God of Israel, including Jesus in the unique identity of this one God.*[110]

Bauckham's thesis only further corroborates what was just attested to in Gathercole's contribution. If Gathercole is right that the Synoptics present a Jesus who transcends the heaven–earth or God–creation divide, has 'come' and has been 'sent' and is attributed titles that were identified with Yahweh himself, then it is not unjustified for the New Testament to

> take up the well-known Jewish monotheistic ways of distinguishing the one God from all other reality and use these precisely as ways of including Jesus in the unique identity of the one God as commonly understood in Second Temple Judaism.[111]

---

[109] Ibid. 242. I am painting with a broad brush; however, Gathercole does provide a further nuance as to which of these titles he believes supports his thesis in ways stronger than others.
[110] Bauckham 2008: 3; emphasis added.
[111] Ibid. 4.

Whether it be divine titles applied to Jesus or divine works performed by Jesus, the result is what Bauckham calls a 'Christological monotheism', one 'which is fully continuous with early Jewish monotheism, but distinctive in the way it sees Jesus Christ himself as intrinsic to the identity of the unique God'.[112]

Bauckham's point is confirmed in a plethora of ways, but one that stands out is the Evangelists' repeated appropriation of Psalm 110:1 ('The LORD says to my Lord: / "Sit at my right hand, / until I make your enemies your footstool"') to Jesus. Out of its twenty-one uses in the New Testament, seven come from the Gospels. Despite what one might assume, none of these references to Psalm 110 come from John's Gospel. Instead, all seven can be found in the Synoptics (Matt. 22:44; 26:64; Mark 12:36; 14:62; 16:19; Luke 20:42–43; 22:69), which once again reiterates Stuhlmacher's point that a high Christology is not original to John.[113] That Psalm 110 is absent from Judaic literature but pervades the New Testament canon says something. This 'difference simply reflects the fact that early Christians used the text to say something about Jesus which Second Temple Jewish literature is not interested in saying about anyone: that he participates in the unique divine sovereignty over all things'.[114]

It is important to clarify that there is no divide between what Jesus does and who he is: functionality and ontology cannot be segregated from one another. The Gospels know of no such dichotomy, as seen in chapters 3–4. While functional and ontological Christology might be distinguished for logical purposes, no wedge can be driven between the two. That matters lest one try, as some have, to say that the works Jesus performs are not so bold as to identify him with Yahweh, as if 'Jesus exercises the "functions" of divine lordship without being regarded as "ontically" divine'.[115] Bauckham responds by returning to Jewish monotheism itself. The

> unique sovereignty of God was not a mere 'function' which God could delegate to someone else. It was one of the key identifying characteristics of the unique divine identity, which distinguished

---

[112] Ibid. 19.

[113] At other points Ps. 110 is accompanied by Ps. 8:6, 'You made him ruler over the works of your hands / and placed all things under his feet' (e.g. Matt. 22:44; Mark 12:36). Bauckham 2008: 22.

[114] Ibid. 22.

[115] Ibid. 30.

the one God from all other reality. The unique divine sovereignty is a matter of *who God is*.[116]

That same logic, according to the New Testament writers, is to be applied to Jesus.

> Jesus' participation in the unique divine sovereignty is, therefore, also not just a matter of what Jesus does, but of *who Jesus is* in relation to God . . . It includes Jesus in the identity of the one God. When extended to include Jesus in the creative activity of God, and therefore also in the eternal transcendence of God, it becomes un-equivocally a matter of regarding Jesus as *intrinsic to* the unique identity of God.[117]

Bauckham's argument has implications for our view of the Synoptics. It means that the Synoptics possess just as high a Christology as John. Though it seems not to be as explicit as John, one must remember that the Synoptics need not move into an excursus on the person of Jesus to present a high view of his divinity and pre-existence. By portraying, in narrative format, the *works* Jesus performs, the Synoptics teach Jesus' divine identity just as much as John.[118]

Not just the miracles of Jesus, but the cross of Jesus, ironically, demon-strates Bauckham's point. Whether it be the exaltation motif in John's Gospel (see chapter 4) or the ransom motif of the Son of Man in Mark's Gospel (see chapter 5), what appears to the world as foolishness and defeat, the height of human failure, the Gospel writers (and the rest of the NT) see as proof for the divine identity of Jesus.[119] Both John and the Synoptics understand Jesus' atoning work as essential to his messianic and divine identity.

Such a glorification through humiliation reveals, ultimately, the type of King Jesus is and the type of kingdom he brings. Lord and servant are

---

[116] Ibid. Emphasis original.

[117] Ibid. 31. Emphases original.

[118] Bauckham (ibid.) makes this point with regard to the entire NT more broadly. The same point can be made when comparing the Gospel writers with the patristics. It is not as if the Gospel writers are faithful to their Jewish roots by emphasizing the ministry of Jesus while the Fathers have sold out to some type of Hellenistic philosophy obsessed with ontology. Rather, the ontological discussions over Jesus' divinity can occur only because the Gospel writers first put forward Jesus' ontology via his incarnate works.

[119] Ibid. 48.

not antithetical to one another but complimentary; that is the mystery of the cross. Such a dialectic is seen progressively as Jesus moves closer to the cross:

> Jesus is the king in humility (at the entry into Jerusalem), the king in humiliation (before Pilate and on the cross) and the king in death (his royal burial) ... Just as he is exalted in his humiliation and glorified in his disgrace, so also he reigns in being the servant.[120]

What import does this have for his divinity? 'In this way he reveals who God is. What it means to be God in God's sovereignty and glory appears in the self-humiliation of the one who serves.'[121]

Therefore, as counter-intuitive as it seems, the divinity of Jesus and his identity with God are manifested in his humiliation at the cross: through humiliation comes glorification. While those standing at the foot of the cross cannot see this, the empty tomb brings this dialectic to life.

To conclude, Bauckham's argument would improve if he approached Christ in the Gospels with a far more Trinitarian (Nicene) hermeneutic, as original to the Gospel writers themselves with their focus on Trinitarian relations. Nevertheless, Bauckham's thesis is valuable, establishing continuity between monotheism and Christology, between Old and New Testaments.

Synoptic diversity, Christological (canonical) continuity

Besides Gathercole and Bauckham, the contribution of Richard Hays is relevant as well. Hays pushes against the conclusions of modern biblical scholarship by refusing to assume the Synoptics and John are presenting incongruent Christologies. Each Gospel is distinct: they are not uniform. Nevertheless, that does not mean continuity is absent. Rather than interpreting their diverse emphases as a sign of dissimilarity from one another, one should understand the 'four distinctive voices singing in polyphony'.[122]

For Hays, the differences between the four Gospels are manifested in how they utilize the Old Testament and in how they interpret Jesus and his

---

120 Ibid.
121 Ibid. 50.
122 Hays 2016: 349. Emphasis original.

works through Old Testament categories: Mark 'delights in veiled, indirect allusion', so that the Scriptures are a mystery (concerning the *kingdom* in particular) that reach their 'climactic, yet paradoxical, embodiment in the figure of Jesus'.[123] Matthew reveals how Jesus fulfils the Scriptures of Israel and 'transfigures' the Torah.[124] Luke tells the *'story of Israel's redemption'*, and in 'contrast to Matthew's prediction–fulfillment schema', Luke 'emphasizes *promise* and fulfillment' in his presentation of Christ.[125] John, however, chooses to picture Jesus as the *'refiguration of Israel's temple and worship'*; John turns to Old Testament symbols – many of which I have traced already (Temple, Passover lamb, Bread from heaven, Serpent in the wilderness, etc.) in chapter 4 – to demonstrate how they prefigure Jesus, whom John will reveal to be the eternal Logos.[126]

Yet that diversity does not lead Hays, as it has others, to abandon a sense of Christological continuity. There are at least two reasons why.

First, synoptic diversity does not preclude but buttresses Christ's divinity. Each Gospel writer, in other words, brings the divinity of Christ to the surface in a unique way. Mark, on the one hand, 'shows relatively little interest in Scripture as a repository of explicit predictions about the Messiah; rather, for Mark, Scripture provides a rich symbolic vocabulary that enables the Evangelist to adumbrate the astounding truth about Jesus' divinity'.[127] Matthew, on the other hand, 'overtly portrays Jesus as "God with us," the living presence of God who is to be worshiped as the holder of all authority' and his 'robust Christology of divine identity lays the groundwork for a deep confidence in God's continuing guidance and presence in the church's life'.[128] Meanwhile, Luke places emphasis on Jesus' works as not merely a man's works but as the works of God as well as works by God: 'Luke regards these saving acts as performed *by God*' (emphasis original). In that light, uses of *kyrios* take on new meaning. 'Luke subtly identifies Jesus as the *Kyrios*, the one who is "Lord of all," the one who fulfills Isaiah's expectation of God as the Redeemer of Israel' and so his 'narrative thereby creates in the character of Jesus a paradoxical *Verbindungsidentität* that produces a much

---

[123] Ibid. 349.
[124] Ibid. 351.
[125] Ibid. 352. Emphases original.
[126] Ibid. 354–355. Emphasis original.
[127] Ibid. 349. 'Mark's subtle indirection may allow many readers to miss the message of Jesus' divine identity – as indeed many New Testament critics in the modern era have done.' Ibid. 350.
[128] Ibid. 352.

richer Christology of divine identity than modern New Testament criticism has tended to perceive'.[129] All that to say, synoptic Christological diversity does not weaken but strengthens the case for divinity. If Jesus is to be identified with Yahweh himself, as Jesus himself says, then it should not surprise us as readers that it would take four Gospels to capture the innumerable ways that divinity can be adumbrated.

Second, where does Hays believe such Christological continuity is located? It is located, first of all, *in the Scriptures of Israel*, a point that this study has laboured to demonstrate throughout (especially see chapters 2–4). 'Despite these differences in emphasis, however, all four of the Evangelists are united in their insistent demonstration that the story of Jesus finds its wellspring in Israel's Scripture.'[130] Although they may have diverse methods and varying emphases, each Gospel writer presupposes the legitimacy of intertextuality and a figural interpretation of the Old Testament in view of the resurrected Christ. But ultimately, the reason four Gospels need not be antithetical with competing Christologies is because the Old Testament they all draw from is characterized by an intrinsic unity due to its one divine author, who is its primary agent and scriptwriter.[131] In the end, Hays sounds similar to Stuhlmacher:

> When we listen carefully to the way that all four Evangelists narrate the story of Jesus through echoes of the Old Testament, we come to understand that the Christologies of the Synoptic Gospels actually have a close affinity to John's Christology of divine identity, though the *poetics* of their articulations of Jesus' scripturally grounded identity differ in interesting ways.[132]

---

[129] Ibid. 353. These distinctions between the Synoptics must not be pushed too far so that they box each Gospel writer into a caricature. E.g. Mark may be far more reticent about explicit predictions from the OT, but in other ways his attestation to Jesus' divine identity can be just as forthright, as seen in his portrayal of Jesus' miracles or authority over nature. That said, while the above are helpful distinctions that create a well-rounded presentation of Christ's divine identity, there is overlap in a multitude of ways, whether it be works, titles or OT allusions all applied to Jesus.

[130] Ibid. 363.

[131] Ibid. 364–365.

[132] Ibid. Emphasis original. There is some ambiguity in that word 'interesting'. At times Hays moves beyond the diversity of the Gospels to criticize their authors. Although Hays is not likely to be as critical as those modern biblical scholars whose methodology he decries, nevertheless Hays is not without criticism himself, which makes one wonder whether he has truly freed himself from the methods he critiques. See e.g. his criticisms of Matthew (ibid. 352). There is tension here: How does Hays reconcile his criticisms with his strong assertions concerning the primacy of the divine author across the canon?

Not all that different from Gathercole or Bauckham, Hays too believes that while the Synoptics and John may have variant methodologies, nevertheless their Christology has the same foundation. This much is seen when Hays strikes back against Bart Ehrman, who claims that the 'high' Christology of John, a Christology that stresses his divinity, was John's creation, but it is foreign to the 'low' Christology of the Synoptics. In other words, the Jesus of divinity was an invention of Hellenism, which John's Gospel is indebted to, and cannot be original to the Jewish picture of Jesus in the Synoptics.[133]

In a vein similar to Bauckham, Hays counters by acknowledging just how foreign this historical dichotomy is to the Gospels. To begin with, such a notion fails to consider how the synoptic authors draw on the monotheism of the Old Testament to present an exalted picture of Jesus (i.e. as one who cannot be a mere man). Sounding a similar argument to Bauckham, Hays says, 'it is precisely through drawing on Old Testament images that all four Gospels, in ways both subtle and overt portray the identity of Jesus as mysteriously fused with the identity of God'.[134] The Synoptics may not state their affirmation of Jesus' divinity as explicitly, or in the same style or from the same angle, as John. Yet they draw the same Christological conclusions when they identify this Jewish teacher with Israel's Yahweh, either by means of what he says or by means of the works he performs.

The scholarship of Hays takes us back to the basic premise of the current study: *the way Jesus and the Gospel writers interpret the Old Testament Christologically is absurd if the Scriptures of Israel do not have Yahweh as their divine author.* Apart from Yahweh's primacy in authorship, the Scriptures of Israel carry no divine authorial intent and progress towards nothing in particular. While Israel's sacred texts may be of historical interest, Israel's history is meaningless.

Yet if Yahweh is the divine author, if his authorial intent is present throughout, then the Scriptures have purpose, building to a God-designed climax in the person and work of Jesus Christ. Only such a view can justify Jesus and the Gospel writers interpreting the Scriptures of Israel through a Christological lens, as if Yahweh's word of the covenant has finally been fulfilled in the one who is the Word. Hays captures what is at stake when he writes:

---

[133] Ehrman 2009: 249; cf. Ehrman 1993; 2009; Hays 2016: 363.
[134] Hays 2016: 363. Emphasis removed.

There is only one reason why the Evangelists' Christological interpretation of the Old Testament is not a matter of stealing or twisting Israel's sacred texts: the God to whom the Gospels bear witness, the God incarnate in Jesus, is the same as the God of Abraham, Isaac, and Jacob.[135]

Hays concludes:

> Either that is true, or it is not. If it is not, the Gospels are a delusional pernicious distortion of Israel's story. If it is true, then the figural literary unity of Scripture, Old Testament and New Testament together, is nothing other than the climactic fruition of that one God's self-revelation.[136]

Conclusion: the Christology of the canon and the canon of Christology

The Christian canon of Scripture consists first and foremost, to borrow Jesus' own framework, of Moses and the Prophets and the Psalms (Luke 24:44). On that foundation the apostles and the rest of the New Testament authors stand. The link between the two, however, is Jesus Christ, as represented in the Gospels: he is the Christological clamp. He claims that the Scriptures spoke of him and he claims to fulfil what the Scriptures promised in him, as seen in previous chapters. If mistaken, invalid or fraudulent, then his works and words mean the witness of Moses and the Prophets is antiquated, messianic anticipation at best, or empty promises built on faulty religious logic at worst. If true, however, then his works and words not only vindicate the promises of old and demonstrate their divine power and trustworthiness but justify the type of impetus that defines the otherwise outrageous zeal of the apostles to take the gospel to those unaware that God has come through on his covenantal word in Jesus Christ, the Word.

In that regard, the Gospels occupy a unique position in redemptive history and in the Christian canon of Scripture. They put forward the works and words of Christ as the historical and canonical link between the writings of God's prophets and apostles. For that reason it is not an

---

[135] Ibid. 365.
[136] Ibid. Emphasis removed.

exaggeration to say everything hinges on Christology. The works and words of Christ substantiate the claim that God's word through the Prophets is divine in origin (inspiration), trustworthy in nature (inerrancy), perspicuous in its saving message (clarity) and effective in its truth claims (sufficiency). To be even more accurate, the *person* of Christ – whether Christ is who he says he is – verifies that God's word through the Prophets does not return to him void.

If Christ himself is the historical, redemptive, covenantal and, especially, canonical link between prophet and apostle, then one would expect his own words to carry a hermeneutical authority that not only is on par with the Scriptures, but supersedes them in chronological and typological fulfilment. That does not mean his words carry a licence to contradict what has preceded him. Rather, his words carry a superlative authority only in the sense that they bring God's word to a culmination, fulfilled by one who is the Son of God himself. 'No rabbi was so important to rabbinic Judaism as Jesus was to Christianity,' says Jewish scholar J. Neusner. 'None prophesied as an independent authority. None left a category of I am-sayings, for none had the prestige to do so.'[137] Barnett, building on the work of Riesner, concludes that 'Jesus' Amen-sayings marked his speech out as divinely inspired and revealed him as having messianic authority.'[138]

The relevance of this observation is seen when one considers the continuity of the Christian canon as a whole. It is not only the works of Christ that the Gospel writers record and interpret for the early church but his *words*. Those words, in short, are inscripturated under the inspiration of the Holy Spirit; yet they are also inscripturated because they are the words of the incarnate Son of God. As much as the Christian canon consists of the writings of prophets and apostles, the claims of both lose merit if the words of Christ lack canonical weight. The promises and claims of the former prove empty if the latter is unbelievable. In the words of Vos:

> Jesus regarded the whole Old Testament movement as a divinely directed and inspired movement, as having arrived at its goal in Himself, so that He Himself in His historic appearance and work

---

[137] Neusner 1970: 190. Cf. Riesner 1997: 208; Barnett 1997: 140.
[138] Barnett 1997: 140; cf. Riesner 1997: 29.

being taken away, the Old Testament would lose its purpose and significance. This none other could say.[139]

Hence Jesus stands in a unique redemptive–historical position and makes a claim about his person and his words that is unprecedented. 'He was the confirmation and consummation of the Old Testament in His own Person, and this yielded the one substratum of His interpretation of Himself in the world of religion.'[140]

That does not mean the writings of the prophets are without inspiration until Christ, in some unique way, adopts them as his own. The writings of Moses and the prophets and the Psalms are canonical as soon as God breathes out such words through Moses, the prophets and the psalmists. The words of God depend not on man's determination or authorization but are the words of God because it is God himself who utters them. At the same time, those inspired texts show themselves to be credible and trustworthy, and are validated for what they are by nature, when the divine promises within them are brought to fulfilment in the person, work and words of Jesus Christ, the eternal Son of God. Their words find canonical confirmation in the Word, Christ Jesus.

In addition, if Jesus is who he says he is, then not only does he validate God's word by means of his own word, but he carries the authority to speak a word that is just as authoritative and God inspired. If God spoke in a concursive manner through Moses and the prophets to communicate his authoritative word to his covenant people, now the triune God has spoken in a unilateral and direct manner to his people in the person of his own Son, their faithful covenant mediator (Heb. 1:1–2). The Word of God became incarnate for the purpose of lisping the word of the covenant to the people of the covenant. What is so remarkable about a Gospel like John's is that the word the Son brings from his Father concerns himself; Jesus *is* the Word. Revelation has been incarnated: the Word has become flesh (John 1:14).[141]

---

[139] Vos 1948: 358.

[140] Ibid.

[141] 'Consequently,' says Wenham (1994: 58–59), 'not his words only but his person and life also come as a new revelation . . . To fail to comprehend him as constituting a divine disclosure is to fail utterly to understand him at all.' Dempster says something similar: 'In the teaching of Jesus himself – orally transmitted at first before being preserved in documents that finally evolved into the Gospels – there is a clear recognition of the authority of the ancient Scriptures as well as Jesus's own transcendent authority, which he contrasts with the Torah. He can speak about the importance of every iota of the Scriptures being accomplished and yet in the great Antitheses immediately elevate his own teaching to a place higher than the commands in the Torah.' Dempster 2016: 138.

7

Is our doctrine of Scripture Christological enough? The future of inerrancy and the necessity of dogmatics[1]

A surprisingly resilient challenge for an evangelical doctrine of inerrancy

An intelligentsia with no constitution for condemnation

The twentieth century proved to be a turbulent one for an evangelical doctrine of Scripture. The 'battle for the Bible', as Harold Lindsell called it, has not only proved perpetual but volatile, far more complicated than evangelicals ever could have imagined. Inerrantists within the neo-evangelical movement were met head on by certain 'infallibists' within their own ranks, who affirmed the infallibility of Scripture's message but denied its plenary and verbal inerrancy.[2] The intramural debate is well documented by George Marsden in his history of Fuller Seminary.[3] By the 1970s institutional denials of inerrancy were conspicuous and conspicuously popular.[4]

---

[1] I include this last chapter as an example of how one can move from the argument and thesis of a biblical theology project as seen in this book to systematic and dogmatic construction. What follows is not a full, dogmatic presentation but more of a proposal to fill a lacuna in order to change the theological conversation currently underway. This chapter was first presented in 2017 at the Evangelical Theological Society in the Inerrancy Session. It was subsequently published in *Presbyterion* 44.1 (2018: 25–41). It is included here with permission and with some adaptation.

[2] For an introduction to the movement, see Marsden 2006.

[3] Marsden 1987.

[4] Rogers 1977; McKim and Rogers 1979. For a response, see Woodbridge 1982.

Often acknowledged but rarely analysed is the way such 'infallibists' were influenced by the success of Karl Barth's doctrine of Scripture. That is not to say infallibists necessarily adopted Barth's position wholesale. To be fair, modifications were made. Nevertheless, Barth's breakout from his own liberal headquarters in the midst of a world war proved just as liberating for some neo-evangelicals who were just as opposed to Protestant liberalism but equally opposed to the biblicism of fundamentalism.

Barth had relocated God back to the centre, redeeming theology itself from the confines of liberalism's anthropological methodology.[5] Even many who were critical of Barth were appreciative of such an advance.[6] J. Gresham Machen, for example, judged Barth's doctrine of Scripture inadequate, both in biblical and historical merit. Nevertheless, Machen said Barth was at least 'bringing us to the Word of God'.[7] Despite Barth's affirmation of an errant text, Kenneth Kantzer believed Barth's overall exegesis presupposed a trustworthy text. In practice, Barth did not look all that different from an evangelical methodology.[8] G. W. Bromiley, despite his criticism of Barth's subjectivist doctrine of inspiration, celebrated Barth because he demanded 'the Bible be read on the basis of biblical presuppositions rather than historical-critical ones'.[9] 'As much as Barth's theology, especially his doctrine of Scripture, raised a host of problems for American evangelicals,' observes D. G. Hart, 'evangelicalism's intelligentsia did not have the constitution for condemnation. As such, the evangelical response to Barth from roughly 1960 on was in effect, "he may be wrong but we need to listen".'[10]

The redemption of dogmatics

In the middle of Barth's rebellion against liberalism and mixed but positive reception by many evangelicals, Barth did not hide the fact that he would never go so far as those American 'fundamentalists', as he liked to call them. They shackled God's revelation of himself to a written, human, and therefore fallible text, thereby subjecting divine freedom to human control.

---

[5] Consider Gary Dorrien's definition of liberalism: 'The essential idea of liberal theology is that all claims to truth, in theology as in other disciplines, must be made on the basis of reason and experience, not by appeal to external authority. Christian Scripture may be recognized as spiritually authoritative within Christian experience, but its word does not settle or establish truth claims about matters of fact.' Dorrien 2003: 1.

[6] My treatment of Machen, Kantzer and Bromiley draws from Hart 2011: 42–72.

[7] Machen 1991: 197–205; cf. Hart 2011: 53.

[8] Kantzer 1983: 11; cf. Hart 2011: 51.

[9] Hart 2011: 48; cf. Bromiley 1959: 10–16.

[10] Hart 2011: 49.

Barth's rationale sounded *Christian* in character: Christ alone is intrinsically the true Word of God. The Word is not a human text, but a living person. The human text may become God's Word but only when and if God chooses to utilize portions of that human record to bear witness to the Word, Christ Jesus. 'The Bible', says Barth, 'is God's Word to the extent that God causes it to be His Word, to the extent that He speaks through it.' Scripture, says Barth, 'is God's Word in so far as God lets it *be* His Word'.[11] There is a sense in which the Bible is in a process of becoming for Barth, a presupposition that not only motivated modern theology's doctrine of Scripture but stemmed from theology proper itself.

It seemed conspicuous to infallibists influenced by Barth that if liberalism had abandoned Christian theology in the traditional (supernatural) sense, fundamentalism had short-circuited theology by retreating to the caves of a literal hermeneutic. Barth's *Church Dogmatics* was evidence that one could still take supernatural revelation seriously without going so far as to imprison revelation within a human record.

The result was, in the eyes of many, pure genius: theology had been saved. It was still grounded upon divine authority (contra liberalism), but without the baggage of having to justify Scripture's every detail or assertion (contra fundamentalism). Theology, for Barthians, was not only saved but restored to its gospel-centred DNA, as seen in the way Barth's doctrine of revelation and Scripture was Christological in its core.

Whether mid- to late-twentieth-century infallibists imbibed Barth's doctrine of Scripture in all its detail is beside the point. Barth had provided a way to break free from liberalism's radical denial of supernatural revelation, yet without falling into the ditch of fundamentalism's biblicism. More relevant still, one could remain theological, even dogmatic, throughout the entire process. That is an understatement to be sure. To be more precise, dogmatics was not just the fruit from Barth's Christological vine: dogmatics was the very means by which Barth arrived at his rejection of liberalism and his formulation of a Christological doctrine of revelation.

To paint with a broad brush, evangelicals in Barth's day and evangelicals today more or less struggle to see the significance of this point, though there are exceptions. Hart could not be more on target when he says that Barthianism is 'a system of teaching that came in a form, namely, dogmatics', which was 'inherently repulsive to the average American

---

[11] Barth 1975: I/1, 109–110. Emphasis original.

Christian'.[12] Could this be the reason why, to this day, so few evangelicals present a defence of inerrancy that is as oriented and invested in dogmatics and Christology as Barth's?

A dogmatic proposal

The focus of this brief study is not to explore these historical eras along with their theologians, nor is it to provide a polemical response to Barth or the infallibists who followed him, as fruitful as that might be.[13] These points are raised, rather, as a foil to address a more systemic issue still nagging at the coat-tails of evangelicalism: Have we, as evangelicals, demonstrated that our doctrine of inerrancy is *theological* in nature?

Not only has Barth's *Church Dogmatics* left a formidable presence, but his disciples also continue to put forward a theological buffet to which Christians on both sides of the Atlantic rush for their epistemological nutrients (e.g. Hunsinger, McCormack, Webster).[14] Noticeable in the works of these authors is a recurring theme: they have, building upon their master, a *theological* case to make; to be more precise, they have an explicit *Christological* case to make for their doctrine of revelation and Scripture. On the other hand, they are all but convinced that fundamentalists and evangelicals alike do not, nor have they at any point in the past, provided a theological, let alone Christological, rationale for their doctrine of inerrancy.

Such a Barthian assessment is not entirely accurate. Carl F. H. Henry, for example, did provide a theological case for inerrancy in *God, Revelation, and Authority*, a colossal and intellectual magnum opus that should command respect from liberals and neo-orthodox alike.[15] Yet, to this day, one is hard pressed to see either of those camps engage with its arguments. Not offered a seat at the table, the popular assumption (and caricature) is that Barth's doctrine of Scripture was motivated by *Christology*, while evangelical treatments like Henry's were sidetracked by a *propositional agenda*. To our detriment, Henry is little known in many evangelical circles in America, and is also six feet under to those across the Atlantic from America.

Besides Henry, J. I. Packer, E. J. Young and John Frame have provided a theological defence of inerrancy, and the Chicago Statement on Inerrancy,

---

[12] Hart 2011: 54.
[13] For my critique of Barth, see Barrett 2016: 100–107.
[14] Hunsinger 2012; McCormack 2008; Webster 2000a; 2000b.
[15] Henry 1999.

though meant to be more of a statement than a defence, cannot be overlooked either.[16] Contemporary treatments follow suit as well. For instance, in D. A. Carson's *The Enduring Authority of the Christian Scriptures*, P. Jensen, Henri Blocher, Osvaldo Padilla, Kevin Vanhoozer and David Gibson all offer theological assessments on a variety of issues.[17] In 2016 the Evangelical Theological Society's (ETS) inerrancy session, led by Robert Yarbrough, Michael Thigpen and Gregg Allison, was devoted to the intersection of biblical inerrancy and the doctrine the Trinity.[18]

Still, the above assessment by Barthians is not without warrant. Few, if any, of these old or new publications address inerrancy's ties to Christology. If dogmatics is the task of determining how one doctrinal domain should influence another, the Christian faith being treated as an inseparable, cohesive whole, then assessing the intersection of bibliology and Christology is an imperative. Yet the last book-length treatment that came close to doing so was John Wenham's *Christ and the Bible* back in 1972, which is now almost half a century old.[19] Hence the imperative of this current project in the NSBT series, which has sought to situate Jesus' view of Scripture within its canonical and covenantal context to comprehend better the nature of Scripture in the vein of its Christological fulfilment.

Though peripheral to evangelical treatments, Christology is the hinge on which revelation and Scripture turn in the eyes of neo-orthodoxy. Its absence from evangelical treatments of Scripture leaves them convinced that we have yet to take seriously the dogmatic nature of the doctrine. While evangelicals may be known for their biblical scholarship, and while our systematic theologies may be known for asking how each doctrine conforms to the biblical witness, evangelicals are less known for their ability to weave one doctrinal domain within another, asking how the entailments of one might influence the other. Dogmatics has not been our *modus operandi*. That must change.

In 2017 the ETS session on inerrancy asked the question 'Is the recent spike in books supporting inerrancy a dying gasp or wave of the future?' Perhaps the question needs to be modified to get at the heart of the issue: Are we, as evangelicals, facing the wrong direction? Unless our publications

---

[16] Packer 1958; Young 1957; Frame 2010.

[17] Carson 2016.

[18] Notable as well is the resurgence of interest in the discipline of dogmatics. E.g. Vanhoozer 2005a; Allen and Swain 2016.

[19] Wenham 1994.

start treating dogmatics with the same seriousness as Barthian publications, the continuing flurry of evangelical books may only be a matter of patting ourselves on the back.

In that light, evangelicalism is overdue for a dogmatic diagnostic, and critical attention must be given to inerrancy. *Do we, as evangelicals, have a doctrine of inerrancy that is as informed by Christology as the Barthian one? And what might a dogmatic case, one that is at its heart oriented by Christology itself, look like for an evangelical doctrine of inerrancy?* In a future project, I will argue that the ultimate dogmatic location of Scripture is our doctrine of God. But that will not be the focus here. Nor will what follows be an apologetic against Barthianism: many distinguished critiques have already been made.[20] Instead, what follows is more of a proposal as to how we, as evangelicals, might think far more Christologically about inerrancy than we have in the past, given this project's findings.

The conclusion reached is both ironic and surprising: *though they often do not realize it to be the case, evangelicals possess superior Christological warrant for their bibliology to that of their critics.* Although it claims otherwise, Barthianism, as its evangelical critics argue, divorces the divine from the human – Christ, the divine and perfect Word, from the human, fallible Scriptures, which only become the Word if and when God chooses to appropriate them. But evangelicalism proposes a marriage, one in which Christ the Word affirms, establishes and creates an inscripturated Word through the human authors that reflects his own divine perfection. In short, I propose there is a Christological warrant for inerrancy, one that moves our defence of inerrancy away from shallow proof texting to a more organic, redemptive–historical approach that reflects Scripture's typological and Christological focus, fulfilment and finality.

As mentioned, technically Christology is not the *ultimate* basis and dogmatic location for inerrancy, which is why I have used the word 'warrant' instead of 'ground' to describe the support Christology gives to the doctrine of Scripture. As I have asserted elsewhere, our ultimate foundation for our doctrine of Scripture is our *doctrine of God*.[21] The Triune God is, after all, the primary author of the canon (i.e. inspiration), and that canon reflects his communicable attributes (truth, righteousness in

---

[20] See my forthcoming book, *The Trinity and the Mystery of Inspiration* (2022).
[21] Barrett 2016. And such a claim is not original to me either. See Bavinck 2003; Webster 2016: 9–46.

inerrancy).[22] As I have stressed already (see chapters 2, 6), there is a trinitarian hand-off of truth, so that the Spirit perfects that which the Father and the Son have entrusted to him. And yet, since it is the Son whom the Father sends to become incarnate as *the Word* (John 1:1), it is appropriate to draw attention to Christ as God's revelation in the flesh and the divine authority he brings to God's inscripturated speech-act as God's speech personified.

The Christological warrant for inerrancy

Inerrantists as Enlightenment rationalists?

The subtitle of Mark Galli's new biography of Karl Barth, 'An Introductory Biography for Evangelicals', arouses curiosity.[23] Galli invites evangelicals to learn from Barth, perhaps in unexpected ways. Galli rebukes the subjective reliance upon religious experience that permeates evangelical churches, observing how our 'worship experience', as it is often called, presupposes the values and methodology of Protestant liberalism. Barth, on the other hand, puts the objective gospel and the Scripture's witness to that gospel back at the centre. Galli has a point and evangelicals would benefit from Galli's critique.

Elsewhere, Galli's appropriation of Barth as a tool to critique evangelicalism is questionable. Having introduced Barth's rejection of inerrancy, Galli is reluctant to acknowledge that evangelicals still hold on to terms like inerrancy and infallibility. Nevertheless, he responds,

---

[22] I have intentionally chosen the word 'communicable'. Those sympathetic to Barth will argue that we should not imprison God in a text, compromising his freedom. To do so is to compromise the Creator–creature distinction. Bibliolatry is the result! So they argue. In response, that is a caricature of the evangelical position. But more to the point, such an argument fails to recognize that the attributes of God reflected in God's word are his *communicable* attributes, attributes like ethical holiness and truthfulness. So rather than confusing the Creator–creature distinction, the evangelical doctrine properly applies it, so that the human author (creature) says what the divine author (Creator) says in a way that reflects the righteous, holy and truthful character of the divine author himself, yet without pretending it does so in infinite measure (as if God and the text are ontologically the same). To deny that this is possible is to throw into question not only God's ability to be immanent and accommodate himself through his own words by means of concursive operation, but also the creature's identity as the *imago Dei* and God-infused design to express the image of his/her Creator through his/her words, especially under the influence of the Holy Spirit. As I will explain later, there is an irony here because, as it turns out, it is not the evangelical but the Barthian who has restricted God's freedom, his freedom to communicate his words through human words. For more on this issue, see Barrett 2022.

[23] Galli 2017.

'many evangelical theologians today are asking whether "inerrancy" brings with it more problems than it solves'. Galli then jumps to a startling accusation:

> It [inerrancy] is a word and idea grounded in Enlightenment rationalism and thus is an attempt to build confidence in the Bible on the basis of rationalism. That, as Barth and many others would argue, is a shaky foundation indeed.[24]

From a historical standpoint, such a claim is not only aggressive but inaccurate. An assessment of an evangelical doctrine of inerrancy will only expose such a claim as an unfair misrepresentation, a caricature to be sure. To accuse evangelicals of the heresy of rationalism in their attempt to establish what they believe the *text itself* says about its own identity is to ignore the motive behind an evangelical apologetic for revelation and Scripture: fidelity to the voice of Scripture and the authority therein (i.e. *sola Scriptura*).

Nevertheless, why is it that evangelicals give such an impression, even if it is a misguided one? In preparation to write *God's Word Alone: The Authority of Scripture* (2016), it was necessary for me to explore countless shelves of publications on Scripture. In retrospect, innumerable volumes from the 1970s to the present day give the impression, even if never stated, that inerrancy is a doctrine that must be *proven* by solving any and every Bible difficulty. Without a doubt, there is a place for rigorous exegetical analysis and historical investigation; after all, the criticisms of recent sceptics like Bart Ehrman, for example, often hinge upon specific exegetical and historical conundrums.

However, as pointed out in *God's Word Alone*, evangelicals must be careful lest we give the impression that our human reasoning is the foundation upon which inerrancy sits. To do so does assume a modernist methodology, as if one comes to the text neutral, an illegitimate hermeneutical assumption postmodernism has sniffed out for decades now. Instead, we must come to the text allowing its own voice to 'affirm *and* correct our preunderstanding of what Scripture is and how it should be read'.[25] As demonstrated at some length, evangelicals must be committed,

---

[24] Ibid. 115.
[25] Barrett 2016: 146. Emphasis original.

as were the Reformers before them, to the *self-authenticating* nature of Scripture, otherwise our starting point differs little from Enlightenment higher criticism, which turned to the 'neutral' methods of historical investigation as the decisive judge over Scripture; as a result *sola Scriptura* was compromised.[26] While external evidences provide ancillary testimony, the self-authenticating nature of Scripture, when equipped with the internal testimony of the Spirit, proves primary.

The economy of the gospel

More to the point, the misconception Galli and others share might be avoided from the start if evangelicals, having the self-authenticating nature of Scripture in the right hand and the internal testimony of the Spirit in the left, approached inerrancy through the economy of the gospel on a more consistent basis. Before one turns to external studies in historical investigation, why not allow the redemptive structure of divine revelation itself to situate our doctrine of inerrancy in the first place? What might this look like?

First, it means formulating inerrancy within the promise–fulfilment pattern of God's saving, covenantal speech-acts, as I have done in chapters 2–5. From start to finish, the tapestry of redemptive history is characterized by three divinely initiated movements: (1) God reveals and declares what he will accomplish through covenant promises. (2) God then accomplishes his word, fulfilling exactly what he said he would do in those covenant promises. (3) Man is not left to interpret God's covenantal acts, but God's actions are met with divine speech that interprets his covenantal acts and how his people are to respond as covenant recipients. God is his own interpreter.[27] His divine authorial intent is conveyed from start to finish (see chapter 1).

God's authoritative interpretation of his covenantal actions may be manifested in a variety of ways, but none of them are so permanent for the people of God as his inscripturated Word, the Scriptures. The Torah, for example, is not only labelled the 'old covenant' but 'the Book of the Covenant' (Exod. 24:7; 2 Chr. 34:14–31; 2 Cor. 3:14). Breathed out by God (2 Tim. 3:16–17; cf. 2 Peter 2:21), it is Yahweh's living, active, personal and binding authority for his people. As the constitution of the covenant, it

---

[26] For that reason, these recent works are commendable: Kruger 2012; Piper 2016.

[27] On these three, see Barrett 2016: 160–162, as well as chapter 2 of the present study.

typologically points ahead to the fulfilment of the gospel promised therein. Or, as Peter Jensen says:

> The covenant is a characteristic form of the word of God, culminating in the gospel, the word of promise and demand that centres on Jesus Christ. The function of the Scripture is to record, expound, and apply this authority of God. That is why it is called the Word of God, the oracles of God, and the Holy Scriptures.[28]

Within such a covenantal framework, divine speech proves its credibility by means of this promise–fulfilment pattern. Yet, no event could be more significant to that credibility than the incarnation of the Son. The life, death and resurrection of Christ not only spell the inauguration of the new covenant, but the advent of the Son of God himself is the greatest testimony that God comes through on his word (Luke 24:25–27; Rom. 1:1–6; 16:25–27; Heb. 1:1–4; 1 Peter 1:10–12). With every old covenant type and promise hanging in the balance, the Word made flesh is proof that what God says can be trusted, a point Jesus repeatedly stresses in his own ministry (e.g. Matt. 5:17–18).[29]

Barthians, for all their stress upon Christ as the Word, fail to grasp this most fundamental principle. The reliability of God's revelatory speech, whether spoken or inscripturated, cannot be separated from the person of Christ and his new covenant work. Person and propositions may be distinguished, but, in the context of covenantal history they never diverge. The incarnate Son is evidence that what God says he does.

The trinitarian self-disclosure and self-understanding of Jesus

However, the incarnation is not just the fulfilment of the book of the covenant: the Son himself as the *Word* of God is the ultimate, climactic and full revelation of the God of the covenant. If Christ is proof that God's covenantal word proves true, then it is not surprising that the Word he unveils possesses finality. As Peter announces in Acts 3:15–26, the prophet promised in Deuteronomy 18:5–18 has arrived and has spoken.[30]

---

[28] Jensen 2002: 82.
[29] For a litany of additional passages, see Barrett 2016: 206–211.
[30] See chapter 2 of this study.

Perhaps no Gospel is so central as John's in this regard.[31] John 1, echoing the language of Genesis 1, is so remarkable because God's Word is not only considered powerful, creative, revelatory and redemptive – all of which Israel experienced from creation to exile[32] – but now God's Word is said to be a *person*, a person who not only was with God but was God (John 1:1). The personhood of the Word is inseparable from the eternality of the Word, and the eternality of the Word cannot be segregated from the divinity of the Word.[33]

Applied to Christ, the title communicates that Jesus is the superlative self-expression, self-revelation, of God. The Father not only speaks *through* his Son, but the Father's speech *is* his Son. No greater revelation could be given to his covenant people. And with that is removed the accusation so often lobbed by Barthians that an evangelical doctrine of inerrancy is static. No final conflict exists between divine propositions and the person of Christ: *Christ now is the proposition*. The information and knowledge the triune God desires to communicate can convey life eternal because they come in the form of the Word made flesh (John 1:14), the one who is, according to John, life itself (John 1:4; 3:36; 1 John 5:11–12).

A pivotal question at this stage is whether Jesus himself possessed such a self-understanding, a question we explored in chapters 3–5 of the present study. Beginning in John 1:18 we read that 'the only God, who is at the Father's side, he has made him known'. Coupled with John 5 and 14, this revelation of the Father is a self-disclosure on the part of Jesus. Jesus does only what 'he sees the Father doing' (John 5:19); the Father 'loves the Son and shows him all that he himself is doing' (5:20); the word Jesus speaks 'is not mine', he says, 'but the Father's who sent me' (14:24; cf. v. 10). As the revelation from the Father, the Son incarnate is the medium through which the former speaks revelation, revelation propositional in every sense of the word. Yet Jesus does not merely descend as the medium who delivers the word; it is because he *is* the Word that he can reveal truth from the Father, showing his listeners the way to eternal life (John 5:21, 24). As a prophet, he is not only instrumental to the delivery of revelation, but is the final prophet who is revelation itself. There is, in other words, an intra-trinitarian pattern to the channel of revelation, and as Jesus reveals in

---

[31] See chapter 4 of this study.

[32] *Creation*: Gen. 1:3; Ps. 33:6; *revelation*: Isa. 9:8; Jer. 1:4; Ezek. 33:7; Amos 3:1, 8; *redemption*: Ps. 107:20; Isa. 55:1.

[33] See chapter 5 of this study.

John 14 – 16, the Spirit is not left out either but is sent from the Father and the Son to bear witness to the Son through a permanent, inscripturated word.

But could this intratrinitarian revelation be fallible? Jesus himself precludes such a possibility by appealing to the unity that the Father and Son share in the communication of this revelation. 'If I alone bear witness about myself, my testimony is not deemed true. There is another who bears witness about me, and I know that the testimony that he bears about me is true' (John 5:31–32). Or, consider John 8, where the truthfulness of Jesus' words is brought into question with great hostility. 'You seek to kill me', Jesus responded, 'because my word finds no place in you' (John 8:37). The reason his enemies do not understand his word, Jesus explains in John 8:43, is because 'you cannot bear to hear my word'. If there was ever a contrast between an errant word and an inerrant word, it is verse 44, where Jesus identifies his enemies with their father, the devil, who 'has nothing to do with the truth, because there is no truth in him. When he lies, he speaks out of his own character, for he is a liar and the father of lies.' Not so with Jesus. As the Word from the Father, 'I tell the truth' (8:45), he says without qualification. Indeed, Jesus not only tells the truth; he *is* truth (John 14:6).

Christ, the Spirit and the inscripturated Word

In the mind of Jesus the truthfulness of his self-disclosure is married to the veracity of his spoken word but it must also be tied to the written Scriptures in at least two ways.

First, as Jesus reveals himself, he operates with the assumption that his own teaching is equal to the Scriptures in authority. The assumption is that the Scriptures to which he compares his own teaching are just as authoritative and reliable. Not only does Jesus say, 'until heaven and earth pass away, not an iota, not a dot, will pass from the Law until all is accomplished' (Matt. 5:18), but he also says, 'Heaven and earth will pass away, but my words will not pass away' (24:35; cf. Mark 13:31; Luke 21:33). Not only does Jesus attest to the abiding truthfulness of the Scriptures he fulfils, but his own words are also elevated to carry the same level of authority and with it the same level of reliability. To cling to Jesus as the Word while rejecting the plenary and verbal inspiration and inerrancy of the Scriptures contradicts the way Jesus himself conditions his word upon the truthfulness of God's inscripturated speech. Such a dichotomy is foreign to the mind of Christ.

If this were a full defence of inerrancy, rather than a mere methodological proposal, it would be critical at this point to engage with the way Jesus believed the Old Testament Scriptures were both inspired and inerrant. Nevertheless, one might consult chapter 7 of *God's Word Alone* (2016) on inspiration, which explores the variegated ways that (1) Jesus attributes the Old Testament writings to the authorship of the Holy Spirit, (2) selects the vocabulary he uses to refer to the Old Testament as 'Scriptures' from God, (3) interchanges 'Scripture' and 'God' when referencing authorship, (4) grounds the New Testament's fulfilment of the Old on divine authorship, (5) never appears to be questioned by his Jewish (scribal) enemies for his belief in scriptural inspiration, and (6) submitted himself to the authority of such Scriptures. Inerrancy, being a corollary to inspiration, is then addressed in chapter 8 of *God's Word Alone*, which attains support from (1) Jesus' factual use of historical figures and events, (2) his treatment of the Old Testament as a unitary, comprehensive whole, (3) his reliance upon the unbreakable character of the Scriptures, and (4) his appeal to the Old Testament Scriptures as divinely authoritative.[34]

Second, to drive a wedge between Christ as the Word and the inscripturated text is to miss the unified trinitarian delivery of revelation not only from the Father to the Son but also from the Father and Son to the Spirit. The word of truth is communicated not only through the Son but, in its most permanent form, through the Spirit of truth (John 15:26). The God-breathed character of the Scriptures is the natural consequence not only of the Word's advent but also his ascent into the heavens. Again, I dare not trespass into a full outline here, but chapters 6–8 of *God's Word Alone* (2016) are pertinent.[35] There one will discover an exegetical survey of texts like John 15 and 16, texts that demonstrate Christ's intention from the start of his incarnation to leave his new covenant people with a Spirit who bears witness to the risen Saviour – not despite human authorship but through it. In John 16:15 there is a 'trinitarian hand-off of truth':

> It began with the Father who gave his words to his Son, only for the Son to give these words to the Spirit, who testified concerning the Son. Not only did the Father testify concerning his Son (5:32, 37;

---

[34] Barrett 2016: 233–263.

[35] Ibid. 201–301.

6:27; 8:18) and the Son testify concerning his Father (17:6), but the Spirit also testified about the Son (15:26).[36]

John 16:15 is but the genesis of what is to come in the book of Acts and the epistles, both of which manifest the variety of ways the apostles believed their own writings were inspired and inerrant, a belief consistent with the authority they were convinced was given to them by Christ himself.[37]

Substance without forms?

Given the compatibility between the person of Christ and the words of Christ, several points should follow, points that encourage an evangelical doctrine of inerrancy to be more, not less, Christologically motivated than its critics believe.

To begin with, taking the person of Christ seriously means taking the words of Christ seriously. John's Gospel is unambiguous in the way it ties the words of Christ to his identity as the Word. It is difficult to maintain the Barthian dipolar separation of the Word (Jesus) from the word (Scripture), as if such a title (Word) is not an intrinsic characteristic of the latter as is the former. Should we criticize the words of Christ, whether oral or written, we would run afoul to then move beyond his words in order to petition his person. As John Frame explains, there is no legitimacy in an 'appeal to the substance or content of Jesus's words, beyond the forms in which they are presented'.[38] Substance without the forms is to dissect that which was never meant for surgery. The apostles saw such a connection. For instance, Paul writes to Timothy, warning him to be on guard against anyone who 'teaches a different doctrine and does not agree with the sound words of our Lord Jesus Christ and the teaching that accords with godliness' (1 Tim. 6:3).

To resist such continuity between the person and words of Christ does leave one in dangerous territory. Is it possible, we might ask, to discover error in what Christ has spoken, words inscripturated under the inspiration of the Holy Spirit in the apostolic testimony? If so, what then does one make of Christ's person? Would not his divine identity as the Word be

---

36 Ibid. 217.
37 On inspiration, see Rom. 16:25–26; 14:37–38; 1 Cor. 2:7, 10, 13; Gal. 1:11–12; Eph. 3:4–6; 1 Thess. 2:13–14; 1 Tim. 5:17–18; Titus 1:1–3; 2 Peter 1:16–20; 3:2–7, 15–16. On inerrancy, see Luke 1:1–4; John 21:24. Also, consider the many ways Paul sees his writings as authoritative.
38 Frame 2013: 559. Similarly, see Carson 1991: 302, 453. I also emphasize these points throughout Barrett 2016.

emptied of its authority should it be discovered that his instruction, passed down from Christ to his apostles, be unreliable or even corruptible? Notice, to segregate the words of Christ, spoken and inscripturated, from the identity of Christ is to fumble the gospel's credibility and discount the gospel's origin. Should Christ's word be thrown into question, a subjective element enters the room (or, as Hart and Bromiley call it, a dangerous subjectivism[39]), leaving the interpreter of Christ's testimony uncertain as to where to turn. Is it not ironic that in the Barthian insistence on an errant text, proponents of that view will not submit to the testimony of Christ himself? There is a reason for that hesitancy.

N. B. Stonehouse once said that it is 'not his [Jesus'] words only but his person and life also come as a new revelation . . . To fail to comprehend him as constituting a divine disclosure is to fail utterly to understand him at all.'[40] But Stonehouse's point could be of value if reversed as well: It is not his person and life only but his words also that come as a new revelation. To fail to comprehend his words as constituting a divine disclosure is to fail utterly to understand his person at all.

We are justified to conclude that the *truthfulness of God's inscripturated and inspired Word is never more powerfully displayed than in the person and work of Jesus, the Word.* Inerrancy has no greater ally than Christology.

Impeccable Christ, inerrant word

Before we continue, it is necessary to indulge in an all-too-brief metaphysical digression, yet one relevant to the point just made. To tether the person of Christ to the words of Christ – form to substance – also means that the hypostatic union itself may have implications for inerrancy. To be extra clear, it is not recommended that one use the hypostatic union as an exact *analogy* or *metaphor*, let alone a *theory* for the way we understand Scripture's inspiration. Such an approach is avoided in this study as it tends to introduce more problems than solutions, both in terms of Christology itself and of the doctrine of Scripture.[41] Instead, I merely appeal to the hypostatic union – really just one aspect of it – to solidify further the

---

[39] Hart 2011: 48; cf. Bromiley 1959: 10–16.

[40] As quoted in Wenham 1994: 59.

[41] In my opinion, the most recent example of this fault line would be Enns 2015. There is a basic failure to understand the difference between *union* (one person and two natures) and *concursus* (three persons of the Godhead working in and through many human persons to produce an inspired text). I will come back to this point in what follows. But see Warfield (1948: 162), who warns against pushing the incarnation analogy too far.

inerrant nature of Christ's own verbal and inscripturated word, much as I might appeal to the truthfulness of God (a communicable attribute) to establish the truthfulness of his exhaled speech-acts through the human author(s).[42]

Standard Christological orthodoxy demands the sinlessness of Christ. To be incarnate requires the Son to assume to his person a human nature, though without the stain of original sin. Doing so entails consubstantiality in two directions. As Chalcedon put it, it demands that the Lord Jesus be 'the same perfect in divinity and perfect in humanity, the same truly God and truly man'. He is 'consubstantial with the Father as regards his divinity', yet simultaneously 'consubstantial with us as regards his humanity'. But then Chalcedon adds that all-too-important qualifier: 'like us in all respects except for sin'.[43]

If such sinlessness stems from the impeccable unity of the two natures in the one person of Christ, however mysterious that unity may be in its functionality in the face of temptation, then the words of Christ are no exception to that spotless perfection. As the book of James stresses, purity is a matter of the heart, yet the heart reveals its true colours most by way of the tongue. It is true for the children of Adam that the tongue, as James says, 'is a fire, a world of unrighteousness'. It sets 'on fire the entire course of life'; it is 'set on fire by hell' itself (Jas 3:6). Not so with Christ! As the God-man, 'like us in all things apart from sin', his speech alone establishes a world of righteousness. As seen in John's Gospel, Jesus counters the lies of his nemeses with the declaration 'I tell the truth' (John 8:45).

Whether it be Jesus' immediate teaching or his teaching inscripturated by the Spirit through the inspiration event itself, the truthfulness, perfection and purity of Christ's words stem from the holiness of his personhood.

The infinite (freely) intones: covenantal unity, incarnation and inspiration

It is only fitting to conclude by answering one of the strongest objections to inerrancy. One of Barth's most serious protests to inerrancy is the way he believes it forfeits the freedom of God. To describe the literal words of Scripture as the Word, and an inerrant Word at that, is to enslave the living God to a dead letter. God is not tied down to a written text: his Word is a

---

[42] For the latter, see Barrett 2016: 272–274.
[43] Pelikan and Hotchkiss 2003: 180–181.

person, not a page. To belittle God in such a way is nothing short of bibliolatry in Barth's estimation.

Such an objection ignores the covenantal framework of history that God himself has structured and revealed (see chapter 2).[44] On the one hand, God's freedom is primary. After the fall, he is not obligated to speak. He is justified to remain silent, and such a silence would have voiced a loud condemnation. Yet God did not remain silent: he spoke. His speech was a saving discourse, publicly binding himself to covenant promises he himself had initiated. Therefore, once he voluntarily speaks, he is not free not to deliver on his promises, at least if he is to remain a just God. He is not free not to come through on his word. That, however, is not an infringement upon his freedom, for a violation of his word is not an exercise in true freedom but injustice. And where there is injustice, freedom, not bondage, is to be found. In short, God's character is at stake in the truthfulness of his spoken, incarnate and inscripturated word. The truest expression of his freedom is to be found in the voluntary fulfilment of his covenantal word.

Moreover, if there ever was an indicator that inscripturation is not a liability to divine freedom, it is the incarnation. It is God himself who became a man (John 1:14). To be precise, the Son of God voluntarily assumed to his person a human nature with all its limitations and agonies, though by no means at the expense of his divinity or its functionality.[45] The point is, if the Son can take the form of a servant and be born in the likeness of men (Phil. 2:7), then breathing out his word through the medium of human speech is but a small matter by comparison. The maxim *finitum non capax infiniti* (the finite cannot contain the infinite) is appropriate in theology, even essential. Yet should one use it to preclude the incarnation of the Son and his ability to speak in human words in the flesh, then the maxim itself has been misused, undermining what the infinite Creator is freely capable of accomplishing through his created order. For the person of the Son to assume a human nature is all the proof one needs that the finite can at least receive the infinite, even if it can never contain it, and the infinite can communicate through the finite, even though the former can never be circumscribed by the latter.[46] This nuance

---

[44] The following points are made in Barrett 2016: 104–106, but rephrased here with some elaboration and adaptation for the purpose of this book.

[45] For a full treatment of this point, see Wellum 2016.

[46] The nuance here ensures the *extra Calvinisticum*. The above is not meant to unpack Chalcedon but merely point out that we cannot divorce Jesus' divine origin from his divinely inspired words. He is, after all, the eternal Word.

both respects who God is (incomprehensible, infinite deity) but also stays true to how he has made himself known (revelation; accommodation through incarnation): we finite creatures cannot know God *exhaustively* in his *essence* but we can know him *truly* according to his *revelatory works*. The incarnation is one of those revelatory works; no, it is the capstone of revelation itself.

That entails the metaphysics of a hypostatic union (in the vein of Chalcedon I would argue) but also the incarnate Christ himself opening his mouth to make known the mystery of God's grace and mercy (John 1:18; Heb. 1:1–3). To be blunt, the nail that slams the Barthian coffin shut is heard when the transcendent, infinite, incomprehensible deity not only is born as a babe in a manger but then opens his mouth and begins speaking divine truth in human language, communicating with words, words that the Spirit then planted within the biblical authors.[47] Any divide between Christ and the Scriptures is eviscerated. Telford Work makes this point: 'When Jesus opens his mouth and speaks Scripture, [Barth's] distinction evaporates.'[48] Or, as Vanhoozer poetically says, 'The line between divine and discourse is breached: the infinite intones.'[49]

The Barthian nerve is further exposed, however, once we recognize that inspiration, not inerrancy, is the real barrier, as hinted at already. Barth writes:

> Verbal inspiration does not mean the infallibility of the biblical word in its linguistic, historical, and theological character as a human word. It means that the fallible and faulty human word is as such used by God and has to be received and heard in spite of its human fallibility.[50]

But as long as we are using the categories of the incarnation, Barth's understanding of Scripture resembles an adoptionistic Christology, one in which the human, fallible written text is nothing more than just that until God arrives after the fact to decide whether he will adopt such a text into his service. 'To say that Scripture only becomes God's word when God in his freedom makes use of it', Vanhoozer comments, 'is to return to the

---

47 Vanhoozer 2009: 54; Barrett 2016: 104–105.
48 Work 2002: 85.
49 Vanhoozer 2009: 54.
50 Barth 1975: I/2, 533; cf. Gibson 2016: 284.

Christological heresies, what *adoptionists* said about the Logos taking on humanity.'[51]

An adoptionist doctrine of Scripture is inadequate because, as David Gibson points out, '*concurses*, not union, is the language for inscripturation that emerges most naturally from the biblical data',[52] data, as we have seen, that originate from Jesus himself. Barth's view not only fails to align the inseparable tie between incarnation and inspiration, but it is also not the position Jesus himself embodied in his use of the Old Testament Scriptures. Ironic as it may be, Barthianism is not Christological enough. It cannot accept the biblical notion that 'what Scripture says, God says, and God's speech does not falter or fall short, especially in the inscripturated speech acts of his own Son'.[53]

Evangelical dogmatics and inerrancy

To conclude, it is time evangelicals stop letting others have all the dogmatic fun. It is also time to erase the myth that an evangelical doctrine of inerrancy is antithetical to Christology (i.e. without Christological warrant). For as it turns out, the evangelical doctrine of inerrancy has a Christological foundation that is far sturdier than that of its critics, for it not only solidifies itself in who Jesus is but also in what he has said.

---

[51] Vanhoozer 2009: 54. These points are made in Barrett 2016: 104–107 as well.
[52] Gibson 2016: 290. Emphasis original.
[53] Barrett 2016: 106–107.

Bibliography

Adam, A. K., S. E. Fowl, K. J. Vanhoozer and F. Watson (2006), *Reading Scripture with the Church: Toward a Hermeneutic for Theological Interpretation*, Grand Rapids: Baker Academic.

Albright, W. F., and C. S. Mann (1995), *The Anchor Bible Commentary*, vol. 26, *Matthew*, New Haven: Yale University Press.

Alexander, T. D. (2003), *The Servant King*, Vancouver: Regent College Publishing.

Allen, M., and S. Swain (2016), *Christian Dogmatics: Reformed Theology for the Church Catholic*, Grand Rapids: Baker Academic.

Allison, D. (2013), *The New Moses: A Matthean Typology*, Eugene: Wipf & Stock.

Allison Jr, D. C. (2012), *Studies in Matthew: Interpretation Past and Present*, Grand Rapids: Baker.

Alter, R. (1981), *The Art of Biblical Narrative*, New York: Basic.

—— (1987), 'Introduction to the Old Testament', in R. Alter and F. Kermode (eds.), *The Literary Guide to the Bible*, Cambridge, Mass.: Harvard University Press, 11–35.

Aquinas, T. (2010a), *Commentary on the Gospel of John, Chapters 1–5*, tr. F. Larcher and J. A. Weisheipl, ed. D. Keating and M. Levering, Washington, D.C.: The Catholic University of America Press.

—— (2010b), *Commentary on the Gospel of John, Chapters 6–12*, tr. F. Larcher and J. A. Weisheipl, ed. D. Keating and M. Levering, Washington, D.C.: The Catholic University of America Press.

—— (2010c), *Commentary on the Gospel of John, Chapters 13–21*, tr. F. Larcher and J. A. Weisheipl, ed. D. Keating and M. Levering, Washington, D.C.: The Catholic University of America Press.

Auerbach, E. (1968), *Mimesis*, Princeton: Princeton University Press.

—— (2013), *Mimesis: The Representation of Reality in Western Literature*, tr. W. R. Trask, Princeton: Princeton University Press.

—— (2014), 'Figura', in J. I. Paoter (ed.), *Time, History, and Literature: Selected Essays of Erich Auerbach*, tr. J. O. Newman, Princeton: Princeton University Press, 65–113.

Augustine (2001a), *Expositions of the Psalms, 1–32*, tr. M. Boulding, ed. J. E. Rotelle, *Works of St. Augustine* III/15, Hyde Park: New City.

—— (2001b), *Expositions of the Psalms, 51–72*, tr. M. Boulding, ed. J. E. Rotelle, *Works of St. Augustine* III/17, Hyde Park: New City.

—— (2005), *The Enchiridion on Faith, Hope, and Charity*, in *On Christian Belief*, I/8 of *The Works of Augustine*, ed. B. Ramsey, tr. M. O'Connell, New York: New City.

—— (2012a), *The Harmony of the Gospels*, in vol. 6, *First Series*, of *Nicene and Post-Nicene Fathers*, ed. P. Schaff, Peabody: Hendrickson.

—— (2012b), *Homilies on the Gospel of John, Homilies on the First Epistle of John, Soliloquies*, in vol. 7, *First Series* of *Nicene and Post-Nicene Fathers*, ed. P. Schaff, Peabody: Hendrickson.

Baker, D. L. (2010), *Two Testaments, One Bible: The Theological Relationship between the Old and New Testaments*, 3rd edn, Nottingham: Apollos; Downers Grove: InterVarsity Press.

Balla, P. (1997), *Challenges to New Testament Theology: An Attempt to Justify the Enterprise*, WUNT, Grand Rapids: Baker Academic.

Barker, K. L. (1982), 'False Dichotomies Between the Testaments', *JETS* 25: 3–16.

Barnett, P. W. (1997), *Jesus and the Logic of History*, NSBT, Downers Grove: InterVarsity Press.

Barr, J. (1976), 'Biblical Theology', in K. Crim and V. P. Furnish (eds.), *Interpreter's Dictionary of the Bible, Supplementary Volume*, New York: Abingdon, 104–111.

—— (1983), *Holy Scripture: Canon, Authority, Criticism*, Philadelphia: Westminster.

Barrett, C. K. (1947), 'The Old Testament in the Fourth Gospel', *JTS* 48: 155–169.

—— (1978), *The Gospel According to St. John*, 2nd edn, Philadelphia: Westminster.

Barrett, M. (2013), *Salvation by Grace: The Case for Effectual Calling and Regeneration*, Phillipsburg: P&R.

—— (2016), *God's Word Alone: The Authority of Scripture*, The Five Solas Series, Grand Rapids: Zondervan.

—— (2017), *40 Questions About Salvation*, Grand Rapids: Kregel Academic.

—— (2018), 'Is Our Doctrine of Inerrancy Christological Enough? The Future of Inerrancy and the Necessity of Dogmatics', *Presb* 44.1: 25–41.

—— (2019), *None Greater: The Undomesticated Attributes of God*, Grand Rapids: Baker Books.

—— (2021), *Simply Trinity: The Unmanipulated Father, Son, and Holy Spirit*, Grand Rapids: Baker.

— (2022), *The Trinity and the Mystery of Inspiration*, Grand Rapids: Baker Academic.

Barth, K. (1933), *The Epistle to the Romans*, 6th edn, tr. E. C. Hoskyns, London: Oxford University Press.

—— (1975), *Church Dogmatics*, 2nd edn, 14 vols., ed. G. W. Bromiley and T. F. Torrance, tr. G. W. Bromiley, New York: T&T Clark.

Bartholomew, C. G. (ed.) (2003), *Behind the Text: History and Biblical Interpretation*, Grand Rapids: Zondervan.

—— (2015), *Introducing Biblical Hermeneutics: A Comprehensive Framework for Hearing God in Scripture*, Grand Rapids: Baker Academic.

Bartholomew, C. G., and H. A. Thomas (eds.) (2016), *A Manifesto for Theological Interpretation*, Grand Rapids: Baker.

Barton, S. C. (2001), 'Many Gospels, One Jesus?', in M. Bockmuehl (ed.), *The Cambridge Companion to Jesus*, Cambridge: Cambridge University Press, 170–183.

Barton, S. C. (ed.) (2006), *The Cambridge Companion to the Gospels*, Cambridge: Cambridge University Press.

Bauckham, R. (1994), 'Jesus and the Wild Animals', in J. B. Green and M. Turner (eds.), *Jesus of Nazareth: Lord and Christ; Essays on the Historical Jesus and New Testament Christology*, Grand Rapids: Eerdmans, 3–21.

—— (2007), 'Jewish Messianism According to the Gospel of John', in *The Testimony of the Beloved Disciple: Narrative, History, and Theology in the Gospel of John*, Grand Rapids: Baker, 207–238.

—— (2008), *Jesus and the God of Israel: God Crucified and Other Studies on the New Testament's Christology of Divine Identity*, Grand Rapids: Eerdmans.

—— (2015), 'The Johannine Jesus and the Synoptic Jesus', in *Gospel of Glory: Major Themes in Johannine Theology*, Grand Rapids: Baker Academic, 185–200.

—— (2017), *Jesus and the Eyewitnesses: The Gospels as Eyewitness Testimony*, 2nd edn, Grand Rapids: Eerdmans.

Bavinck, H. (2003), *Reformed Dogmatics*, vol. 1, *Prolegomena*, Grand Rapids: Baker Academic.

—— (2018), *Philosophy of Revelation*, ed. N. Sutano and C. Brock, Peabody: Hendrickson.

Beale, G. K. (1994), 'Did Jesus and His Followers Preach the Right Doctrine from the Wrong Texts? An Examination of the Presuppositions of Jesus' and the Apostles' Exegetical Method', in G. K. Beale (ed.), *The Right Doctrine from the Wrong Texts: Essays on the Use of the Old Testament in the New*, Grand Rapids: Baker Academic, 387–404.

—— (2004), *The Temple and the Church's Mission: A Biblical Theology of the Dwelling Place of God*, NSBT, Downers Grove: InterVarsity Press.

—— (2011), *A New Testament Biblical Theology: The Unfolding of the Old Testament in the New*, Grand Rapids: Baker Academic.

—— (2012a), *Handbook on the New Testament Use of the Old Testament: Exegesis and Interpretation*, Grand Rapids: Baker Academic.

—— (2012b), 'The Use of Hosea 11:1 in Matthew 2:15: One More Time', *JETS* 55: 697–715.

Beale, G. K., and D. A. Carson (2007), 'Introduction', in G. K. Beale and D. A. Carson (eds.), *Commentary on the New Testament Use of the Old Testament*, Grand Rapids: Baker, xxiii–xxvi.

Beasley-Murray, G. R. (1999), *John*, 2nd edn, WBC 36, Waco: Word.

Beetham, C. A. (2008), *Echoes of Scripture in the Letter of Paul to the Colossians*, BIS, Leiden: Brill.

Berding, K., and J. Lunde (2008), *Three Views on the New Testament Use of the Old Testament*, Grand Rapids: Zondervan.

Bernard, J. H. (2000), *A Critical and Exegetical Commentary on the Gospel of John*, vols. 1–2, ICC, London: T&T Clark.

Biddle, M. E. (1996), 'Polyphony and Symphony in Prophetic Literature: Rereading Jeremiah 7–20', SOTI 2, Macon: Mercer University Press.

Billings, J. T. (2010), *The Word of God for the People of God: An Entryway to the Theological Interpretation of Scripture*, Grand Rapids: Eerdmans.

Bird, M. F. (2013), *Jesus Is the Christ: The Messianic Testimony of the Gospels*, Downers Grove: InterVarsity Press.

—— (2014), *The Gospel of the Lord: How the Early Church Wrote the Story of Jesus*, Grand Rapids: Eerdmans.

Bird, M. F., and S. Harrower (eds.) (2019), *Trinity Without Hierarchy: Reclaiming Nicene Orthodoxy in Evangelical Theology*, Grand Rapids: Kregel Academic.

Blocher, H. (2011), 'John 1: Preexistent Logos and God the Son', in R. M. Allen (ed.), *Theological Commentary: Evangelical Perspectives*, New York: T&T Clark, 115–128.

—— (2016), 'God and the Scripture Writers: The Question of Double Authorship', in D. A. Carson (ed.), *The Enduring Authority of the Christian Scriptures*, Grand Rapids: Eerdmans, 497–541.

Blomberg, C. L. (1992), *Matthew: An Exegetical and Theological Exposition of Holy Scripture*, NAC, Nashville: Holman.

—— (2007), *The Historical Reliability of the Gospels*. Downers Grove: IVP Academic.

—— (2009), *Jesus and the Gospels: An Introduction and Survey*, 2nd edn, Nashville: B&H.

—— (2016), 'Reflections on Jesus' View of the Old Testament', in D. A. Carson (ed.), *The Enduring Authority of the Christian Scriptures*, Grand Rapids: Eerdmans, 669–701.

—— (2018), *A New Testament Biblical Theology*, Waco: Baylor University Press.

Bock, D. L. (1994a), *Luke 1:1–9:50*, BECNT, Grand Rapids: Baker.

—— (1994b), *Luke 9:51–24:53*, BECNT, Grand Rapids: Baker.

—— (1999), 'Hermeneutics of Progressive Dispensationalism', in H. W. Bateman (ed.), *Three Central Issues in Contemporary Dispensationalism: A Comparison of Traditional and Progressive Views*, Grand Rapids: Kregel, 85–119.

—— (2002), *Studying the Historical Jesus: A Guide to Sources and Methods*, Grand Rapids: Baker.

—— (2006), *Interpreting the New Testament Text: Introduction to the Art and Science of Exegesis*, Wheaton: Crossway.

—— (2015), *Mark: New Cambridge Bible Commentary*, Cambridge: Cambridge University Press.

—— (2016), *Jesus the God-Man: The Unity and Diversity of the Gospel Portrayals*, Grand Rapids: Baker.

Bock, D. L., and B. I. Simpson (2017), *Jesus According to Scripture: Restoring the Portrait from the Gospels*, 2nd edn, Grand Rapids: Baker.

Bock, D. L., and R. L. Webb (eds.) (2010), *Key Events in the Life of the Historical Jesus: A Collaborative Exploration of Context and Coherence*, repr., Grand Rapids: Eerdmans.

Bockmuehl, M. (ed.) (2001), *The Cambridge Companion to Jesus*, Cambridge: Cambridge University Press.

Bolt, P. (2016), *The Cross from a Distance: Atonement in Mark*, NSBT, Downers Grove: InterVarsity Press.

Borchert, G. L. (1996), *John 1–11: An Exegetical and Theological Exposition of Holy Scripture*, NAC, Nashville: Holman.

—— (2002), *John 12–21: An Exegetical and Theological Exposition of Holy Scripture*, NAC, Nashville: Holman.

Bray, G. (1996), *Biblical Interpretation: Past & Present*, Downers Grove: InterVarsity Press.

Bromiley, G. W. (1959), 'Barth: A Contemporary Appraisal', *CT* 3: 10–16.

Brooks, J. A. (1991), *Mark: An Exegetical and Theological Exposition of Holy Scripture*, NAC, Nashville: Holman.

Brown, R. E. (1953), 'The History and Development of the Theory of a Sensus Plenior', *CBQ* 15: 141–162.

—— (1955), *The Sensus Plenior of Sacred Scripture*, Baltimore: St. Mary's University.

—— (1963), 'The *Sensus Plenior* in the Last Ten Years', *CBQ* 25: 262–285.

—— (1966), *The Anchor Bible Commentary: John 1–12*, New Haven: Yale University Press.

—— (1970), *The Anchor Bible Commentary: John 13–21*, New Haven: Yale University Press.

Bruce, F. F. (1968), *New Testament Development of Old Testament Theme*, Grand Rapids: Eerdmans.

—— (1983), *The Gospel of John*, Grand Rapids: Eerdmans.

Burge, G. M. (2000), *The Gospel of John*, NIVAC, Grand Rapids: Zondervan.

Burger, H. (2017), *Sola Scriptura: Biblical and Theological Perspectives on Scripture, Authority, and Hermeneutics*, Leiden: Brill.

Calvin, J. (1960), *Institutes of the Christian Religion*, ed. J. T. McNeill, tr. F. L. Battles, 2 vols., LCC 20, Louisville: Westminster John Knox.

—— (2005a), *Calvin's Commentaries: Volume XVII*, tr. W. Pringle, Grand Rapids: Baker.

—— (2005b), *Calvin's Commentaries: Volume XVIII*, tr. W. Pringle, Grand Rapids: Baker.

Cameron, N. M. de S. (1994), 'Scripture and Criticism: Evangelicals, Orthodoxy and the Continuing Problem of Conservatism', in P. E. Satterthwaite and D. F. Wright (eds.), *A Pathway into Holy Scripture*, Grand Rapids: Eerdmans, 237–256.

Campenhausen, H. von (1970), 'Die Entstehung des Neuen Testaments', in E. Käsemann (ed.), *Das Neue Testament als Kanon*, Göttingen: Vandenhoeck & Ruprecht, 109–123.

—— (1972), *The Formation of the Christian Bible*, Philadelphia: Fortress.

Caneday, A. B. (2010), 'Covenant Lineage Allegorically Prefigured: "Which Things Are Written Allegorically" (Galatians 4:21–31)', *SBJT* 14.3: 50–77.

—— (2019), 'Biblical Types: Revelation Concealed in Plain Sight to Be Disclosed – These Things Occurred Typologically to Them and Were Written Down for Our Admonition', in D. Burk, J. Hamilton and B. Vickers (eds.), *God's Glory Revealed in Christ: Essays on Biblical Theology in Honor of Thomas R. Schreiner*, Nashville: B&H Academic, 135–156.

Carson, D. A. (1980), 'Hermeneutics: A Brief Assessment of Some Recent Trends', *Them* 5: 11–20.

—— (1984), *Matthew*, in T. Longman III and D. E. Garland (eds.), *EBC*, Grand Rapids: Zondervan, 8: 3–602.

— (1991), *The Gospel According to John*, PNTC, Grand Rapids: Eerdmans; Leicester: Apollos.

— (1996), *The Gagging of God: Christianity Confronts Pluralism*, Grand Rapids: Zondervan.

—— (2000), 'Systematic Theology and Biblical Theology', in *NDBT*, 89–104.

—— (2004), 'Mystery and Fulfillment: Toward a More Comprehensive Paradigm of Paul's Understanding of the Old and the New', in D. A. Carson, P. T. O'Brien and M. A. Seifrid (eds.), *Justification and Variegated Nomism: The Paradoxes of Paul*, Grand Rapids: Baker Academic, 2: 393–436.

—— (2010), *Collected Writings on Scripture*, Wheaton: Crossway.

—— (2011), 'Theological Interpretation of Scripture: Yes, But . . .', in R. M. Allen (ed.), *Theological Commentary: Evangelical Perspectives*, New York: T&T Clark, 187–207.

—— (2012), *Jesus the Son of God: A Christological Title Often Overlooked, Sometimes Misunderstood, and Currently Disputed*, Wheaton: Crossway.

—— (ed.) (2016), *The Enduring Authority of the Christian Scriptures*, Grand Rapids: Eerdmans.

— (2017), 'John 5:26: *Crux Interpretum* for Eternal Generation', in *Retrieving Eternal Generation*, Grand Rapids: Zondervan, 79–97.

Carson, D. A., and J. D. Woodbridge (eds.) (1992), *Scripture and Truth*, Grand Rapids: Baker.

Carter, C. A. (2018), *Interpreting Scripture with the Great Tradition: Recovering the Genius of Premodern Exegesis*, Grand Rapids: Baker Academic.

Childs, B. S. (1964), 'Interpretation in Faith', *Int* 18: 437–438.

—— (1970), *Biblical Theology in Crisis*, Philadelphia: Westminster.

—— (1979), *Introduction to the Old Testament as Scripture*, Philadelphia: Fortress.

—— (1984), *The New Testament as Canon: An Introduction*, Philadelphia: Fortress.

—— (1992), *Biblical Theology of the Old Testaments: Theological Reflection on the Christian Bible*, Minneapolis: Fortress.

—— (1997), 'Toward Recovering Theological Exegesis', *ProEccl* 6: 26–45.

—— (2001), *Isaiah: A Commentary*, Louisville: Westminster John Knox.

—— (2004), *The Struggle to Understand Isaiah as Christian Scripture*, Grand Rapids: Eerdmans.

Clayton, C., and D. McCartney (1994), *Let the Reader Understand: A Guide to Interpreting and Applying the Bible*, Phillipsburg: P&R.

Cole, G. A. (2013), *The God Who Became Human: A Biblical Theology of the Incarnation*, Downers Grove: InterVarsity Press.

Collett, D. (2013), 'A Tale of Two Testaments: Childs, Old Testament Torah, and *Heilsgeschichte*', in C. R. Seitz and K. H. Richards (eds.), *The Bible as Christian Scripture: The Work of Brevard S. Childs*, Atlanta: SBL, 185–219.

Compton, J. M. (2008), 'Shared Intentions? Reflections on Inspiration and Interpretation in Light of Scripture's Dual Authorship', *Them* 33.3: 23–33.

Cranfield, C. (1977), *The Gospel According to St. Mark*, Cambridge: Cambridge University Press.

Crowe, B. D. (2017), *The Last Adam: A Theology of the Obedient Life of Jesus in the Gospels*, Grand Rapids: Baker Academic.

Crump, D. (2013), *Encountering Jesus, Encountering Scripture: Reading the Bible Critically in Faith*, Grand Rapids: Eerdmans.

Cullmann, O. (1967), *Salvation in History*, London: SCM.

Daley, B. E. (2003), 'Is Patristic Exegesis Still Usable?', in E. Davis and R. Hays (eds.), *The Art of Reading Scripture*, Grand Rapids: Eerdmans, 69–88.

Daley-Denton, M. (2000), *David in the Fourth Gospel: The Johannine Reception of the Psalms*, AGJU 47, Leiden: Brill.

—— (2004), 'The Psalms in John's Gospel', in S. Moyise and M. J. J. Menken (eds.), *The Psalms in the New Testament*, Bloomsbury: T&T Clark, 119–137.

Davidson, R. M. (1981), *Typology in Scripture: A Study of Hermeneutical Typos Structures*, AUSDDS 2, Berrien Springs: Andrews University Press.

Davies, P. R. (1995), *Whose Bible Is It Anyway?*, Sheffield: Sheffield Academic Press.

Davies, W. D. (1994), *The Gospel and the Land: Early Christianity and Jewish Territorial Doctrine*, BibSem 25, Sheffield: JSOT Press.

Davies, W. D., and D. C. Allison (1988), *A Critical and Exegetical Commentary on the Gospel of Matthew*, vols. 1–3, ICC, London: T&T Clark.

De Lubac, H. (2000), *Scripture in the Tradition*, tr. L. O'Neill, New York: Crossroad.

Dempster, S. G. (2000), 'The Prophetic Books', in *NDBT*, 122–126.

—— (2001), 'From Many Texts to One: The Formation of the Hebrew Bible', in M. Daviau and J. W. Weigl (eds.), *The World of the Arameans: Studies in Honour of Paul-Eugene Dion*, JSOTSup 324, Sheffield: Sheffield Academic Press, 19–56.

—— (2003), *Dominion and Dynasty: A Theology of the Hebrew Bible*, NSBT, Downers Grove: InterVarsity Press.

—— (2014), 'From Slight Peg to Cornerstone to Capstone: The Resurrection of Christ on "The Third Day" According to the Scriptures', *WTJ* 76: 373–375.

—— (2016), 'The Canon and Theological Interpretation', in C. G. Bartholomew and H. A. Thomas (eds.), *A Manifesto for Theological Interpretation*, Grand Rapids: Baker, 131–148.

—— (2018), 'The Tri-Partite Old Testament Canon and the Theology of the Prophetic Word', in A. Abernathy (ed.), *Interpreting the Old Testament Theologically: Essays in Honor of Willem A. VanGemeren*, Grand Rapids: Zondervan, 74–94.

Dennison, W. D. (2008), 'Reason, History, and Revelation: Biblical Theology and the Enlightenment', in L. G. Tipton and J. C. Waddington (eds.), *Resurrection and Eschatology: Theology in Service of the Church: Essays in Honor of Richard B. Gaffin Jr*, Phillipsburg: P&R, 340–360.

DeRouchie, J. S. (2018), 'Lifting the Veil: Reading and Preaching Jesus' Bible Through Christ and for Christ', *SBJT* 22.3: 157–179.

Dohmen, C., and T. Söding (eds.) (1995), *Eine Bibel – zwei Testamente: Positionen biblischer Theologie*, München: Paderborn.

Donaldson, T. L. (1985), *Jesus on the Mountain: A Study in Matthean Theology*, JSNTSup 8, Sheffield: JSOT.

Dorrien, G. (2003), *The Making of American Liberal Theology: Idealism, Realism, and Modernity, 1900–1950*, Louisville: Westminster John Knox.

Duby, S. (2019), *God in Himself: Scripture, Metaphysics, and the Task of Christian Theology*, Studies in Christian Doctrine and Scripture, Downers Grove: IVP Academic.

Dumbrell, W. J. (1981), 'The Logic of the Role of the Law in Matthew 5:1–20', *NovT* 23: 1–21.

—— (2013), *Covenant and Creation: An Old Testament Covenant Theology*, Milton Keynes: Paternoster.

Dunn, J. D. G. (1980), *Christology in the Making: An Inquiry into the Origins of the Doctrine of the Incarnation*, London: SCM.

—— (1998), *The Theology of Paul the Apostle*, Grand Rapids: Eerdmans; Edinburgh: T&T Clark.

Edwards, J. R. (2002), *The Gospel According to Mark*, PNTC, Grand Rapids: Eerdmans; Leicester: Apollos.

—— (2015), *The Gospel According to Luke*, PNTC, Grand Rapids: Eerdmans; Nottingham: Apollos.

Ehlen, A. J. (1964), 'Old Testament Theology as *Heilsgeschichte*', *CTM* 35.9: 517–544.

Ehrman, B. D. (1993), *The Orthodox Corruption of Scripture: The Effect of Early Christological Controversies on the Text of the New Testament*, New York: Oxford University Press.

—— (2009), *Jesus, Interrupted: Revealing the Hidden Contradictions in the Bible (and Why We Don't Know About Them)*, New York: HarperCollins.

—— (2014), *How Jesus Became God: The Exaltation of a Jewish Preacher from Galilee*, New York: HarperOne.

Enns, P. (2015), *Inspiration and Incarnation: Evangelicals and the Problem of the Old Testament*, Grand Rapids: Baker.

Enns, P., and J. J. Johnston (2018), *Searching the Scriptures*, London: T&T Clark.

Evans, C. A., and J. A. Sanders (1994), *Luke and Scripture: The Function of Sacred Tradition in Luke–Acts*, Minneapolis: Fortress.

—— (2015), *Mark 8:27–16:20*, WBC, Grand Rapids: Zondervan.

Evans, C. S. (1999), 'Methodological Naturalism in Historical Biblical Scholarship', in C. C. Newman (ed.), *Jesus and the Restoration of Israel: A Critical Assessment of N. T. Wright's Jesus and the Victory of God*, Downers Grove: InterVarsity Press, 180–205.

Farmer, C. S. (ed.) (2014), *John 1–12: Reformation Commentary on Scripture*, Downers Grove: IVP Academic.

Feinberg, J. S. (1988), 'Hermeneutics of Discontinuity', in J. S. Feinberg (ed.), *Continuity and Discontinuity: Perspectives on the Relationship Between the Old and New Testaments: Essays in Honor of S. Lewis Johnson Jr*, Wheaton: Crossway, 109–130.

—— (2018), *Light in a Dark Place: The Doctrine of Scripture*, Wheaton: Crossway.

Fesko, J.V. (2008), 'On the Antiquity of Biblical Theology', in L. G. Tipton and J. C. Waddington (eds.), *Resurrection and Eschatology: Theology in Service of the Church; Essays in Honor of Richard B. Gaffin Jr*, Phillipsburg: P&R, 443–477.

Fitzmyer, J. A. (1982), *The Anchor Bible Commentary: Luke 1–9*, New Haven: Yale University Press.

—— (1985), *The Anchor Bible Commentary: Luke 10–24*, New Haven: Yale University Press.

Frame, J. (1987), *The Doctrine of the Knowledge of God*, Phillipsburg: P&R.

—— (2010), *The Doctrine of the Word of God*, Phillipsburg: P&R.

—— (2013), *Systematic Theology: An Introduction to Christian Belief*, Phillipsburg: P&R.

France, R. T. (1971), *Jesus and the Old Testament: His Application of Old Testament Passages to Himself and His Mission*, London: Tyndale.

—— (1981), 'The Formula-Quotations of Matthew 2 and the Problem of Communication', *NTS* 27: 233–251.

—— (2002), *The Gospel of Mark*, NIGTC, Grand Rapids: Eerdmans.

—— (2007), *The Gospel of Matthew*, NICNT, Grand Rapids: Eerdmans.

—— (2008), *Matthew*, TNTC, Downers Grove: InterVarsity Press.

Frei, H. W. (1974), *The Eclipse of Biblical Narrative*, New Haven: Yale University Press.

Friedman, R. E. (1987), 'The Hiding of the Face: An Essay on the Literary Unity of Biblical Narrative', in J. Neusner, B. Levine and E. Freichs (eds.), *Judaic Perspectives on Ancient Israel*, Minneapolis: Fortress, 207–224.

Gabler, J. P. (1980), 'Oratio de justo discrimine theologiae biblicae et dogmaticae regundisque recte utriusque finibus', tr. and repr. J. Sandys-Wunsch and L. Eldredge, 'An Oration on the Proper Distinction Between Biblical and Dogmatic Theology', *SJT* 33: 134–144.

—— (1992), 'An Oration on the Proper Distinction Between Biblical and Dogmatic Theology and the Specific Objectives of Each', in B. C. Ollenburger, E. A. Martens and G. F. Hasel (eds.), *The Flowering of Old Testament Theology: A Reader in the Twentieth-Century Old Testament Theology, 1930–90*, Winona Lake: Eisenbrauns, 489–502.

Gaebelein, F. E. (ed.) (1984), *EBC*, vol. 8: *Matthew, Mark, and Luke*, Grand Rapids: Zondervan.

Gaffin Jr, R. B. (1988), 'The New Testament as Canon', in H. M. Conn (ed.), *Inerrancy and Hermeneutic: A Tradition, a Challenge, a Debate*, Grand Rapids: Baker, 165–183.

—— (2008), '"For Our Sakes Also": Christ in the Old Testament in the New Testament', in R. L. Penny (ed.), *The Hope Fulfilled: Essays in Honor of O. Palmer Robertson*, Phillipsburg: P&R, 61–81.

Galli, M. (2017), *Karl Barth: An Introductory Biography for Evangelicals*, Grand Rapids: Eerdmans.

Garland, D. E. (2001), *Reading Matthew: A Literary and Theological Commentary*, Macon: Smyth & Helwys.

—— (2008), *Matthew*, BECNT, Grand Rapids: Baker Academic.

—— (2011), *Luke*, ZECNT, Grand Rapids: Zondervan.

Gathercole, S. J. (2006), *The Pre-Existent Son: Recovering the Christologies of Matthew, Mark and Luke*, Grand Rapids: Eerdmans.

Geldenhuys, N. (1979), *The Gospel of Luke*, NICNT, Grand Rapids: Eerdmans.

Gentry, P. J., and S. J. Wellum (2012), *Kingdom Through Covenant: A Biblical-Theological Understanding of the Covenants*, Wheaton: Crossway.

George, T. (2011), *Reading Scripture with the Reformers*, Downers Grove: InterVarsity Press.

Gibson, D. (2016), 'The Answering Speech of Men: Karl Barth on Holy Scripture', in D. A. Carson (ed.), *The Enduring Authority of the Christian Scriptures*, Grand Rapids: Eerdmans, 266–291.

Gignilliat, M. S. (2012), *A Brief History of Old Testament Criticism: From Benedict Spinoza to Brevard Childs*, Grand Rapids: Zondervan.

Giles, K. N. (2012), *The Eternal Generation of the Son: Maintaining Orthodoxy in Trinitarian Theology*, Downers Grove: IVP Academic.

Glenny, W. E. (1995), 'The Divine Meaning of Scripture: Explanations and Limitations', *JETS* 38.4: 481–500.

Goldsworthy, G. (1986), '"Thus Says the Lord", the Dogmatic Basis of Biblical Theology', in P. T. O'Brien and D. G. Peterson (eds.), *A God Who Is Rich in Mercy: Essays Presented to Dr. D. B. Knox*, Sydney: Lancer, 25–40.

—— (2002), *According to Plan: The Unfolding Revelation of God in the Bible*, Downers Grove: IVP Academic.

—— (2012), *Christ-Centered Biblical Theology: Hermeneutical Foundations and Principles*, Downers Grove: IVP Academic.

Goppelt, L. (1982), *Typos: The Typological Interpretation of the Old Testament in the New*, tr. D. H. Madvig, Grand Rapids: Eerdmans.

Gould, E. P. (2000), *A Critical and Exegetical Commentary on the Gospel of Mark*, ICC, London: T&T Clark.

Gray, T. C. (2008), *The Temple in the Gospel of Mark: A Study of Its Narrative Role*, Grand Rapids: Baker.

Green, J. B. (1997), *The Gospel of Luke*, NICNT, Grand Rapids: Eerdmans.

—— (2010), *Hearing the New Testament: Strategies for Interpretation*, Grand Rapids: Eerdmans.

Green, J. B., and M. Turner (eds.) (1999), *Between Two Horizons: Spanning New Testament Studies and Systematic Theology*, Grand Rapids: Eerdmans.

Grenz, S., and R. Olson (1992), *20th Century Theology: God and the World in a Transitional Age*, Downers Grove: InterVarsity Press.

Guelich, R. A. (2015), *Mark 1–8:26*, WBC, Grand Rapids: Zondervan.

Gundry, R. (2002), *Jesus the Word According to John the Sectarian*, Grand Rapids: Eerdmans.

Gurtner, D. M., G. Macaskill and J. T. Pennington (eds.) (2016), *In the Fullness of Time: Essays on Christology, Creation, and Eschatology in Honor of Richard Bauckham*, Grand Rapids: Eerdmans.

Hägerland, T. (2018), *Jesus and the Scriptures: Problems, Passages, and Patterns*, London: T&T Clark.

Hagner, D. A. (1993), *Matthew 1–13*, WBC, Grand Rapids: Zondervan.

—— (1995), *Matthew 14–26*, WBC, Grand Rapids: Zondervan.

—— (2018), *How New Is the New Testament: First-Century Judaism and the Emergence of Christianity*, Grand Rapids: Baker.

Hamilton, J. (2010), *God's Glory in Salvation Through Judgment: A Biblical Theology*, Wheaton: Crossway.

Hamilton, V. P. (1990), *Genesis 1–17*, NICOT, Grand Rapids: Eerdmans.

—— (1995), *Genesis 18–50*, NICOT, Grand Rapids: Eerdmans.

Harris, M. J. (1992), *Jesus as God: The New Testament Use of* Theos *in Reference to Jesus*, Grand Rapids: Baker.

—— (2015), *John*, EGGNT, Nashville: B&H.

Harrisville, R., and W. Sundberg (2002), *The Bible in Modern Culture: Baruch Spinoza to Brevard Childs*, 2nd edn, Grand Rapids: Eerdmans.

Hart, D. G. (2011), 'Beyond the Battle for the Bible', in B. L. McCormack and C. B. Anderson (eds.), *Karl Barth and American Evangelicalism*, Grand Rapids: Eerdmans, 42–72.

Hauser, A. J., and D. F. Watson (eds.) (2017), *A History of Biblical Interpretation: The Enlightenment Through the Nineteenth Century*, vol. 3, Grand Rapids: Eerdmans.

Hays, R. B. (1989), *Echoes of Scripture in the Letter of Paul*, New Haven: Yale University Press.

—— (2006), 'The Canonical Matrix of the Gospels', in S. C. Barton (ed.), *The Cambridge Companion to the Gospels*, Cambridge: Cambridge University Press, 53–75.

—— (2014), *Reading Backwards: Figural Christology and the Fourfold Gospel Witness*, Waco: Baylor University Press.

—— (2015), *Reading the Bible Intertextually*, Waco: Baylor University Press.

—— (2016), *Echoes of Scripture in the Gospels*, Waco: Baylor University Press.

Henry, C. F. H. (1999), *God, Revelation, and Authority*, 2nd edn, 6 vols., Wheaton: Crossway.

Hill, C. (2010), *Who Chose the Gospels? Probing the Great Gospel Conspiracy*, Oxford: Oxford University Press.

Hoffmeier, J. K., and D. R. Magary (eds.) (2012), *Do Historical Matters Matter to Faith? A Critical Appraisal of Modern and Postmodern Approaches to Scripture*, Wheaton: Crossway.

Holmes, S. R. (2012), *The Quest for the Trinity: The Doctrine of God in Scripture, History and Modernity*, Downers Grove: IVP Academic.

Hooker, M. (1988), 'Mark', in D. A. Carson and H. G. M. Williamson (eds.), *It Is Written: Scripture Citing Scripture*, Cambridge: Cambridge University Press, 220–230.

House, P. R. (1990), *The Unity of the Twelve*, JSOTSup 77, Sheffield: Sheffield Academic Press.

House, P. R. (ed.) (1992), *Beyond Form Criticism: Essays in Old Testament Literary Criticism*, Winona Lake: Eisenbrauns.

—— (1998), *Old Testament Theology*, Downers Grove: IVP Academic.

Hunsinger, G. (ed.) (2012), *Thy Word Is Truth: Barth on Scripture*, Grand Rapids: Eerdmans.

Hurtado, L. W. (1999), 'Pre-70 CE Jewish Opposition to Christ-Devotion', *JTS* 50: 35–58.

Irons, C. L. (2017), 'A Lexical Defense of the Johannine "Only Begotten"', in F. Sanders and S. Swain (eds.), *Retrieving Eternal Generation*, Grand Rapids: Zondervan, 98–116.

Jensen, P. (2002), *The Revelation of God*, Downers Grove: InterVarsity Press.

Jenson, R. W. (2010), *Canon and Creed: Interpretation: Resources for the Use of Scripture in the Church*, Louisville: Westminster John Knox.

Jerome (2008), *Commentary on Matthew*, tr. T. P. Scheck, The Fathers of the Church, Washington, D.C.: Catholic University of America Press.

Johnson, D. E. (2015), *Walking with Jesus Through His Word: Discovering Christ in All the Scriptures*, Phillipsburg: P&R.

Kaiser Jr, W. C. (1985), *The Uses of the Old Testament in the New*, Chicago: Moody.

—— (1994), 'The Single Intent of Scripture', in G. K. Beale (ed.), *The Right Doctrine from the Wrong Texts? Essays on the Use of the Old Testament in the New*, Grand Rapids: Baker Academic, 55–69.

—— (2008), 'Single Meaning, Unified Referents: Accurate and Authoritative Citations of the Old Testament by the New Testament', in K. Berding and J. Lunde (eds.), *Three Views on the NT Use of the OT*, Grand Rapids: Zondervan, 45–89.

Kalimi, I. (2009), *The Retelling of Chronicles in Jewish Tradition and Literature: A Historical Journey*, Winona Lake: Eisenbrauns.

Kantzer, K. S. (1983), 'Biblical Authority: Where Both Fundamentalists and Neoevangelicals Are Right', *CT* 27: 10–13.

Käsemann, E. (1969), 'The Beginnings of Christian Theology', *JTC* 6: 17–46.

Keener, C. S. (2009), *The Historical Jesus of the Gospels*, Grand Rapids: Eerdmans.

—— (2011), *Matthew*, The IVP New Testament Commentary Series, Downers Grove: IVP Academic.

Keith, C., and L. W. Hurtado (eds.) (2011), *Jesus Among Friends and Enemies: A Historical and Literary Introduction to Jesus in the Gospels*, Grand Rapids: Baker.

Kirk, J. R. D. (2016), *A Man Attested by God: The Human Jesus of the Synoptic Gospels*, Grand Rapids: Eerdmans.

Kline, M. (1989), *The Structure of Biblical Authority*, 2nd edn, Eugene: Wipf & Stock, repr. 1997.

—— (2006), *Kingdom Prologue: Genesis Foundations for a Covenantal Worldview*, Eugene: Wipf & Stock.

Klink III, E. W., and D. R. Lockett (2012), *Understanding Biblical Theology: A Comparison of Theory and Practice*, Grand Rapids: Zondervan.

—— (2016), *John*, ZECNT, Grand Rapids: Zondervan.

Koester, C. (2018), *Portraits of Jesus in the Gospel of John*, London: T&T Clark.

Köstenberger, A. (2004), *John*, BECNT, Grand Rapids: Baker.

—— (2007), 'John', in G. K. Beale and D. A. Carson (eds.), *Commentary on the New Testament Use of the Old Testament*, Grand Rapids: Baker Academic, 415–512.

— (2009), *A Theology of John's Gospel and Letters: The Word, the Christ, the Son of God*, Grand Rapids: Zondervan.

Köstenberger, A., and S. R. Swain (2008), *Father, Son and Spirit: The Trinity and John's Gospel*, NSBT, Downers Grove: InterVarsity Press.

Köstenberger, A., and M. Kruger (2010), *The Heresy of Orthodoxy: How Contemporary Culture's Fascination with Diversity Has Reshaped Our Understanding of Early Christianity*, Wheaton: Crossway.

Krentz, E. (1975), *The Historical-Critical Method*, London: SPCK.

Kruger, M. J. (2012), *Canon Revisited: Establishing the Origins and Authority of the New Testament Books*, Wheaton: Crossway.

—— (2018), *Christianity at the Crossroads: How the Second Century Shaped the Future of the Church*, Downers Grove: InterVarsity Press.

Kruse, C. G. (2017), *John*, TNTC, Downers Grove: InterVarsity Press.

Kunjummen, R. D. (1986), 'The Single Intent of Scripture – Critical Examination of a Theological Construct', *GTJ* 7: 81–110.

Kvalbein, H. (1998), 'The Wonders of the End-Time: Metaphoric Language in 4Q521 and the Interpretation of Matthew 11.5 par.', *JSP* 18: 87–110.

Ladd, G. E. (1974), *A Theology of the New Testament*, Grand Rapids: Eerdmans.

Lampe, G. W. H., and K. J. Woolcombe (eds.) (1957), *Essay on Typology*, London: SCM.

Lane, W. L. (1974), *The Gospel of Mark*, NICNT, Grand Rapids: Eerdmans.

LaSor, W. S. (1978a), 'Prophecy, Inspiration, and Sensus Plenior', *TynBul* 29: 49–60.

—— (1978b), 'The *Sensus Plenior* and Biblical Interpretation', in W. W. Gasque and W. S. LaSor (eds.), *Scripture, Tradition, and Interpretation*, Grand Rapids: Eerdmans, 260–277.

Legaspi, M. C. (2010), *The Death of Scripture and the Rise of Biblical Studies*, Oxford: Oxford University Press.

Leithart, P. J. (2009), *Deep Exegesis: The Mystery of Reading Scripture*, Waco: Baylor University Press.

Lints, R. (1993), *The Fabric of Theology: A Prolegomenon to Evangelical Theology*, Grand Rapids: Eerdmans.

—— (2015), *Identity and Idolatry: The Image of God and Its Inversion*, NSBT, Downers Grove: InterVarsity Press.

Loader, W. (2017), *Jesus in John's Gospel: Structure and Issues in Johannine Christology*, Grand Rapids: Eerdmans.

Lohfink, N. (1965), *The Christian Meaning of the Old Testament*, Milwaukee: Bruce.

Long, V. P. (2016), '"Competing Histories, Competing Theologies?" Reflections on the Unity and Diversity of the Old Testament('s Readers)', in D. A. Carson (ed.), *The Enduring Authority of the Christian Scriptures*, Grand Rapids: Eerdmans, 369–389.

Longenecker, R. N. (1970), 'Can We Reproduce the Exegesis of the New Testament?', *TynBul* 21: 3–38.

Longman III, T. (1988), 'Storytellers and Poets in the Bible: Can Literary Artifice Be True?', in H. M. Conn (ed.), *Inerrancy and Hermeneutic: A Tradition, a Challenge, a Debate*, Grand Rapids: Baker, 137–149.

—— (1990), 'What I Mean by Historical-Grammatical Exegesis – Why I Am Not a Literalist', *GTJ* 11: 137–152.

Luther, M. (1960), 'Preface to the Old Testament', in E. T. Bachmann (ed.), *Luther's Works*, Philadelphia: Muhlenberg, 35: 235–236.

McCarthy, D. J. (1963), *Treaty and Covenant: A Study in Form in the Ancient Oriental Documents and in the Old Testament*, Rome: Biblical Institute Press.

McCartney, D. G. (1988), 'The New Testament's Use of the Old Testament', in H. M. Conn (ed.), *Inerrancy and Hermeneutic: A Tradition, a Challenge, a Debate*, Grand Rapids: Baker, 101–116.

McCormack, B. L. (2008), *Orthodox and Modern: Studies in the Theology of Karl Barth*, Grand Rapids: Baker Academic.

Macdonald, N. B. (2006), *Metaphysics and the God of Israel: Systematic Theology of the Old and New Testaments*, Grand Rapids: Baker.

McGrath, A. E. (1994), *The Making of Modern German Christology 1750–1990*, Grand Rapids: Zondervan.

Machen, J. G. (1991), 'Karl Barth and the "Theology of Crisis"', *WTJ* 53: 197–205.

McIntyre, J. (1966), *The Shape of Christology*, Philadelphia: Westminster.

McKim, D. K., and J. B. Rogers (1979), *The Authority and Interpretation of the Bible: An Historical Approach*, San Francisco: Harper & Row.

Makin, M. (2017), 'Philosophical Models of Eternal Generation', in F. Sanders and S. Swain (eds.), *Retrieving Eternal Generation*, Grand Rapids: Zondervan, 243–259.

Marcus, J. (2002a), *The Anchor Bible Commentary: Mark 1–8*, New Haven: Yale University Press.

—— (2002b), *The Anchor Bible Commentary: Mark 8–16*, New Haven: Yale University Press.

Marsden, G. (1987), *Reforming Fundamentalism: Fuller Seminary and the New Evangelicalism*, Grand Rapids: Eerdmans.

—— (2006), *Fundamentalism and American Culture*, 2nd edn, Oxford: Oxford University Press.

Marshall, B. (2010), 'The Unity of the Triune God: Reviving an Ancient Question', *Thomist* 74: 1–32.

Marshall, I. H. (1978), *The Gospel of Luke*, NIGTC, Grand Rapids: Eerdmans.

Mead, J. K. (2007), *Biblical Theology: Issues, Methods, and Themes*, Louisville: Westminster John Knox.

Meade, J. D., and E. L. Gallagher (2018), *The Biblical Canon Lists from Early Christianity: Texts and Analysis*, Oxford: Oxford University Press.

Merrill, E. (1994), *Deuteronomy*, NAC, Nashville: Holman.

Meyer, B. F. (1979), *The Aims of Jesus*, London: SCM.

Meyer, J. C. (2009), *The End of the Law: Mosaic Covenant in Pauline Theology*, Nashville: B&H.

Michaels, J. R. (2010), *The Gospel of John*, NICNT, Grand Rapids: Eerdmans.

Moberly, R. W. L. (1992), *The Old Testament of the Old Testament*, Minneapolis: Fortress.

—— (2001), 'The Christ of the Old and New Testaments', in M. Bockmuehl (ed.), *The Cambridge Companion to Jesus*, Cambridge: Cambridge University Press, 184–199.

Moloney, F. J. (1998), *The Gospel of John*, Collegeville: Liturgical Press.

Moo, D. (1984), 'Jesus and the Authority of the Mosaic Law', *JSNT* 20: 3–49.

—— (1986), 'The Problem of *Sensus Plenior*', in D. A. Carson and J. D. Woodbridge (eds.), *Hermeneutics, Authority and Canon*, Grand Rapids: Zondervan, 175–212.

Moo, D., and A. D. Naselli (2016), 'The Problem of the New Testament's Use of the Old Testament', in D. A. Carson (ed.), *The Enduring Authority of the Christian Scriptures*, Grand Rapids: Eerdmans, 702–746.

Morgan, R. (1995), 'On the Unity of Scripture', in J. Davies, G. Harvey and W. Watson (eds.), *Words Remembered, Texts Renewed: Essays in Honor of John F. A. Sawyer*, Sheffield: Sheffield Academic Press, 395–413.

Morris, L. (1992), *The Gospel According to Matthew*, PNTC, Grand Rapids: Eerdmans; Leicester: Apollos.

—— (1995), *The Gospel According to John*, rev. edn, NICNT, Grand Rapids: Eerdmans.

—— (2008), *Luke*, TNTC, Downers Grove: InterVarsity Press.

Motyer, J. A. (1993), *The Prophecy of Isaiah: An Introduction and Commentary*, Downers Grove: InterVarsity Press.

Moyise, S. (2011), *Jesus and Scripture: Studying the New Testament Use of the Old Testament*, Grand Rapids: Baker.

Murphy, R. E. (2000), 'Questions Concerning Biblical Theology', *BTB* 30: 81–89.

Neilson, C. (2009), 'St. Augustine on Text and Reality (and a Little Gadamerian Spice)', *HeyJ* 50: 98–108.

Neusner, J. (1970), *Development of a Legend: Studies on the Traditions Concerning Yohanan ben Zakkai*, SPB 16, Leiden: Brill.

Noland, J. (2005), *The Gospel of Matthew*, NIGTC, Grand Rapids: Eerdmans.

——— (2015a), *Luke 1–9:20*, WBC, Grand Rapids: Zondervan.

——— (2015b), *Luke 9:21–18:34*, WBC, Grand Rapids: Zondervan.

——— (2015c), *Luke 18:35–24:53*, WBC, Grand Rapids: Zondervan.

O'Collins, G. (1971), *Foundations of Theology*, Chicago: Loyola University Press.

O'Keefe, J. J., and R. R. Reno (2005), *Sanctified Vision: An Introduction to Early Christian Interpretation of the Bible*, Baltimore: Johns Hopkins University Press.

Olson, D. T. (1998), 'Biblical Theology as Provisional Monologization: A Dialogue with Childs, Brueggemann and Bakhtin', *BI* 6: 162–180.

Osborne, G. R. (2010), *Matthew*, ZECNT, Grand Rapids: Zondervan.

Oss, D. A. (1988), 'Canon as Context: The Function of Sensus Plenior in Evangelical Hermeneutics', *GTJ* 9: 105–127.

Packer, J. I. (1958), *'Fundamentalism' and the Word of God*, Grand Rapids: Eerdmans.

Parker, B. E. (2011), 'The Nature of Typology and Its Relationship to Competing Views of Scripture', paper presented at the annual meeting of the Evangelical Theological Society, San Francisco, Calif.

——— (2017), 'Typology and Allegory: Is There a Distinction? A Brief Examination of Figural Reading', *SBJT* 21.1: 57–83.

Pate, C. M. (2015), *40 Questions About the Historical Jesus*, Grand Rapids: Kregel.

Peckham, J. C. (2016), *Canonical Theology: The Biblical Canon, Sola Scriptura, and Theological Method*, Grand Rapids: Eerdmans.

Pelikan, J., and V. Hotchkiss (eds.) (2003), *Creeds & Confessions of Faith in the Christian Tradition*, vol. 1, New Haven: Yale University Press.

Pennington, J. T. (2009), *Heaven and Earth in the Gospel of Matthew*, Leiden: Brill.

——— (2012), *Reading the Gospels Wisely: A Narrative and Theological Introduction*, Grand Rapids: Baker.

—— (2016), 'Theological Commentary', in C. G. Bartholomew and
H. A. Thomas (eds.), *A Manifesto for Theological Interpretation*,
Grand Rapids: Baker, 237–256.

—— (2017), *The Sermon on the Mount and Human Flourishing:
A Theological Commentary*, Grand Rapids: Baker.

Piper, J. (2016), *A Peculiar Glory: How the Christian Scriptures Reveal
Their Complete Truthfulness*, Wheaton: Crossway.

Placher, W. C. (2008), 'How the Gospels Mean', in B. Gaventa and
R. Hays (eds.), *Seeking the Identity of Jesus: A Pilgrimage*, Grand
Rapids: Eerdmans, 27–42.

Plummer, A. (2000), *A Critical and Exegetical Commentary on the Gospel
of Luke*, ICC, London: T&T Clark.

Poitiers, Hilary of (2002), *On the Trinity*, in vol. 9, *Second Series* of *Nicene
and Post-Nicene Fathers*, ed. P. Schaff and H. Wace, Peabody:
Hendrickson.

—— (2012), *Commentary on Matthew*, tr. D. H. Williams, The Fathers
of the Church, Washington, D.C.: The Catholic University of America
Press.

Porter, S. E. (ed.) (2007), *Messiah in the Old and New Testaments*, Grand
Rapids: Eerdmans.

—— (2015), *John, His Gospel, and Jesus: In Pursuit of the Johannine
Voice*, Grand Rapids: Eerdmans.

—— (2016), *Sacred Tradition in the New Testament: Tracing Old
Testament Themes in the Gospels and Epistles*, Grand Rapids: Baker.

Power, E. B. (2003), *Jesus Reads Scripture: The Function of Jesus' Use
of Scripture in the Synoptic Gospels*, Leiden: Brill.

Poythress, V. S. (1986), 'Divine Meaning of Scripture', *WTJ* 48: 241–279.

—— (1987), *Understanding Dispensationalists*, Grand Rapids:
Zondervan.

—— (1988), 'Christ the Only Savior of Interpretation', *WTJ* 50: 305–321.

—— (1994), 'Divine Meaning of Scripture', in G. K. Beale (ed.), *Right
Doctrine from the Wrong Texts? Essays on the Use of the Old Testament
in the New*, Grand Rapids: Baker Academic, 82–113.

—— (1999), *God-Centered Biblical Interpretation*, Phillipsburg: P&R.

—— (2012), *Inerrancy and the Gospels: A God-Centered Approach to the
Challenges of Harmonization*, Wheaton: Crossway.

—— (2016), *Reading the Word of God in the Presence of God: A
Handbook for Biblical Interpretation*, Wheaton: Crossway.

Quarles, C. L. (2013), *A Theology of Matthew: Jesus Revealed as Deliverer, King, and Incarnate Creator*, Phillipsburg: P&R.

—— (2017), *Matthew*, EGGNT, Nashville: B&H.

Rad, G. von (1965), *Old Testament Theology*, 2 vols., New York: Harper & Row.

—— (1979), 'Typological Interpretation of the Old Testament', in C. Westermann (ed.), *Essays on Old Testament Hermeneutics*, Richmond: John Knox.

—— (2001), *Old Testament Theology: The Theology of Israel's Prophetic Traditions*, Louisville: Westminster John Knox.

Radmacher, E. D., and R. D. Preus (eds.) (1984), *Hermeneutics, Inerrancy, and the Bible: Papers from ICBI Summit II*, Grand Rapids: Eerdmans.

Rae, M. (2007), 'Texts in Context: Scripture in the Divine Economy', *JTI* 1: 23–45.

Rainbow, P. A. (2014), *Johannine Theology: The Gospel, The Epistles, and the Apocalypse*, Downers Grove: InterVarsity Press.

Räisänen, H. (1990), *Beyond New Testament Theology: A Story and a Programme*, London: SCM.

Rendtorff, R. (2005), *The Canonical Hebrew Bible: A Theology of the Old Testament*, Leiden: Deo.

Ridderbos, H. N. (1957), *When the Time Had Fully Come: Studies in New Testament Theology*, Grand Rapids: Eerdmans.

—— (1975), *Paul: An Outline of His Theology*, Grand Rapids: Eerdmans.

—— (1978), *Studies in Scripture and Its Authority*, Grand Rapids: Eerdmans.

—— (1988), *Redemptive History and the New Testament Scriptures*, Phillipsburg: P&R.

—— (1997), *The Gospel of John: A Theological Commentary*, Grand Rapids: Eerdmans.

Riesner, R. (1991), 'Jesus as Preacher and Teacher', in H. Wansbrough (ed.), *Jesus and the Oral Gospel Tradition*, Sheffield: JSOT, 185–210.

—— (1997), *Paul's Early Period: Chronology, Mission Strategy, Theology*, tr. D. W. Stott, Grand Rapids: Eerdmans.

Rogers, J. B. (ed.) (1977), *Biblical Authority*, Waco: Word.

Rogerson, J. W. (1984), *Old Testament Criticism in the Nineteenth Century: England and Germany*, London: SPCK.

Rosner, B. (2000), 'Biblical Theology', in *NDBT*, 3–11.

Sailhamer, J. (1999), *Introduction to Old Testament Theology: A Canonical Approach*, Grand Rapids: Zondervan.

—— (2001), 'The Messiah and the Hebrew Bible', *JETS* 44.1: 5–23.

Sanders, F. (2016), *The Triune God*, NSD, Grand Rapids: Zondervan Academic.

Sanders, F., and S. Swain (eds.) (2017), *Retrieving Eternal Generation*, Grand Rapids: Zondervan.

Sanders, J. A. (1972), *Torah and Canon*, Eugene: Wipf & Stock.

Schaff, P., and H. Wace (eds.) (2012a), *A Select Library of Nicene and Post-Nicene Fathers of the Christian Church: First Series: 7*, Peabody: Hendrickson.

—— (2012b), *A Select Library of Nicene and Post-Nicene Fathers of the Christian Church: First Series: 14*, Peabody: Hendrickson.

Schnabel, E. J. (2017), *Mark*, TNTC, Downers Grove: InterVarsity Press.

Schnackenburg, R. (1990), *The Gospel According to St. John*, 3 vols., New York: Crossroad.

Schneiders, S. (2006), 'The Gospels and the Reader', in S. C. Barton (ed.), *The Cambridge Companion to the Gospels*, Cambridge: Cambridge University Press, 97–120.

Schnelle, U. (2007), *Theologie des Neuen Testaments*, Göttingen: Vandenhoeck & Ruprecht.

—— (2009), *Theology of the New Testament*, Grand Rapids: Baker, 2009.

Scholder, K. (1990), *The Birth of Modern Critical Theology: Origins and Problems of Biblical Criticism in the Seventeenth Century*, London: SCM.

Schreiner, T. R. (1993), *The Law and Its Fulfillment: A Pauline Theology of the Law*, Grand Rapids: Baker.

—— (2008), *New Testament Theology*, Grand Rapids: Baker Academic.

Schrock, D. (2017), 'From Beelines to Plotlines: Typology That Follows the Covenantal Topography of Scripture', *SBJT* 21.1: 35–56.

Schwöbel, C. (1992), *God: Action and Revelation*, SPT 3, Kampen: Kok Pharos.

Scobie, C. H. H. (1991), 'The Challenge of Biblical Theology', *TynBul* 42.1: 31–61.

—— (2003), *The Ways of Our God: An Approach to Biblical Theology*, Grand Rapids: Eerdmans.

Seitz, C. R. (2001), *Figured Out: Typology and Providence in Christian Scripture*, Louisville: Westminster John Knox.

—— (2011), *The Character of Christian Scripture: The Significance of a Two-Testament Bible*, STI, Grand Rapids: Baker Academic.

Selms, A. van (1976), 'Telescoped Discussion as a Literary Device in Jeremiah', *VT* 26: 99–112.

Sequeira, A., and S. C. Emadi (2017), 'Biblical-Theological Exegesis and the Nature of Typology', *SBJT* 21.1: 11–34.

Shead, A. G. (2012), *A Mouth Full of Fire: The Word of God in the Words of Jeremiah*, NSBT, Downers Grove: InterVarsity Press.

Soulen, R. K. (2003), 'Protestantism and the Bible', in A. E. McGrath and D. C. Marks (eds.), *The Blackwell Companion to Protestantism*, London: Blackwell, 251–267.

Sparks, K. L. (2008), *God's Word in Human Words: An Evangelical Appropriation of Critical Biblical Scholarship*, Grand Rapids: Baker Academic.

Spellman, C. (2014), *Toward a Canon-Conscious Reading of the Bible: Exploring the History and Hermeneutics of the Canon*, Sheffield: Sheffield Phoenix.

Stanglin, K. D. (2018), *The Letter and Spirit of Biblical Interpretation: From the Early Church to Modern Practice*, Grand Rapids: Baker.

Stanton, G. (2002), *The Gospels and Jesus*, 2nd edn, Oxford: Oxford University Press.

Stein, R. H. (1993), *Luke: An Exegetical and Theological Exposition of Holy Scripture*, NAC, Nashville: Holman.

—— (1996), *Jesus the Messiah: A Survey of the Life of Christ*, Downers Grove: InterVarsity Press.

—— (2008), *Mark*, BECNT, Grand Rapids: Baker.

Steinmetz, D. C. (1980), 'The Superiority of Pre-Critical Exegesis', *ThTo* 37: 27–38.

Strauss, M. L. (2007), *Four Portraits, One Jesus: A Survey of Jesus and the Gospels*, Grand Rapids: Zondervan.

—— (2014), *Mark*, ZECNT, Grand Rapids: Zondervan.

Stuhlmacher, P. (1979), *Historical Criticism and Theological Interpretation of Scripture: Toward a Hermeneutic of Consent*, London: SPCK; Eugene: Wipf & Stock.

—— (1995), *How to Do Biblical Theology*, Eugene: Wipf & Stock.

—— (2018), *Biblical Theology of the New Testament*, Grand Rapids: Eerdmans.

Swain, S. (2011), *Trinity, Revelation, and Reading: A Theological Introduction to the Bible and Its Interpretation*, Bloomsbury: T&T Clark.

Sykes, A. H. (1979), *Paraphrasis des Briefes an die Hebräer*, tr. J. D. Semler, n.p.

Tan, K. H. (1997), *The Zion Traditions and the Aims of Jesus*, Cambridge: Cambridge University Press.

Tasker, R. V. G. (1953), *Our Lord's Use of the Old Testament*, Glasgow: Pickering & Inglis.

Thielman, F. (1994), *Paul and the Law: A Contextual Approach*, Downers Grove: InterVarsity Press.

Thiselton, A. C. (2000), *The First Epistle to the Corinthians: A Commentary on the Greek Text*, NIGTC, Grand Rapids: Eerdmans.

Thompson, A. J. (2017), *Luke*, EGGNT, Nashville: B&H.

Timmer, D. C. (2018), 'The Old Testament as Part of a Two-Testament Witness to Christ', in A. T. Abernethy (ed.), *Interpreting the Old Testament Theologically: Essays in Honor of Willem A. VanGemeren*, Grand Rapids: Zondervan, 95–108.

Tomson, P. J. (2001), 'Jesus and His Judaism', in M. Bockmuehl (ed.), *The Cambridge Companion to Jesus*, Cambridge: Cambridge University Press, 25–40.

Trier, D. J. (2005), 'Typology', in *DTIB*, 823–827.

Turner, D. L. (2008), *Matthew*, BECNT, Grand Rapids: Baker.

VanGemeren, W. (1996), *The Progress of Redemption: The Story of Salvation from Creation to the New Jerusalem*, Grand Rapids: Baker Academic.

Vanhoozer, K. J. (1998), *Is There a Meaning in This Text? The Bible, the Reader, and the Morality of Literary Knowledge*, Grand Rapids: Zondervan.

—— (2000), 'Exegesis and Hermeneutics', in *NDBT*, 52–64.

—— (2005a), *Dictionary for Theological Interpretation of the Bible*, Downers Grove: InterVarsity Press; Grand Rapids: Baker Academic.

—— (2005b), *The Drama of Doctrine: A Canonical-Linguistic Approach to Christian Theology*, Louisville: Westminster John Knox.

—— (2006), 'Imprisoned or Free? Text, Status, and Theological Interpretation in the Master/Slave Discourse of Philemon', in A. K. M. Adam, S. Fowl, K. Vanhoozer and F. Watson (eds.), *Reading Scripture with the Church: Toward a Hermeneutic for Theological Interpretation*, Grand Rapids: Baker Academic, 51–94.

—— (2009), 'Triune Discourse: Theological Reflections on the Claim That God Speaks (Part 1)', in D. Treier and D. Lauber (eds.), *Trinitarian Theology for the Church*, Downers Grove: IVP Academic, 25–49.

Vos, G. (1948), *Biblical Theology: Old and New Testaments*, Grand Rapids: Eerdmans; repr., Edinburgh: The Banner of Truth Trust, 2014.

—— (1953), *The Self-Disclosure of Jesus: The Modern Debate About the Messianic Consciousness*, 2nd edn, Phillipsburg: P&R.

—— (1980), 'The Idea of Biblical Theology as a Science and as a Theological Discipline', in R. B. Gaffin Jr (ed.), *Redemptive History and Biblical Interpretation: The Shorter Writings of Geerhardus Vos*, Phillipsburg: P&R, 3–24.

—— (2002), *The Self-Disclosure of Jesus: The Modern Debate About the Messianic Consciousness*, Phillipsburg: P&R.

Waltke, B. K. (2007), *An Old Testament Theology: An Exegetical, Canonical, and Thematic Approach*, Grand Rapids: Zondervan.

Warfield, B. B. (1932), *Biblical Doctrines*, New York: Oxford University Press; repr., Grand Rapids: Baker, 2003.

—— (1948), *The Inspiration and Authority of the Bible*, Philadelphia: P&R.

Watson, F. (2001), 'The Quest for the Real Jesus', in M. Bockmuehl (ed.), *The Cambridge Companion to Jesus*, Cambridge: Cambridge University Press, 156–169.

—— (2009), *Text and Truth: Redefining Biblical Theology*, Edinburgh: T&T Clark; Grand Rapids: Eerdmans.

—— (2016), *The Fourfold Gospel: A Theological Reading of the New Testament Portraits of Jesus*, Grand Rapids: Baker.

Watts, R. E. (2007), 'Mark', in G. K. Beale and D. A. Carson (eds.), *Commentary on the New Testament Use of the Old Testament*, Grand Rapids: Eerdmans, 111–250.

Webster, J. (2000a), *The Cambridge Companion to Karl Barth*, Cambridge: Cambridge University Press.

—— (2000b), *Karl Barth*, 2nd edn, New York: Continuum.

—— (2003), 'A Great and Meritorious Act of the Church? The Dogmatic Location of the Canon', in J. Barton and M. Wolter (eds.), *Die Einheit der Schrift und die Vielfalt des Kanons*, Berlin: de Gruyter, 95–126.

—— (2016), *Confessing God: Essays in Christian Dogmatics II*, Bloomsbury: T&T Clark.

Weinandy, T. (2018), *Jesus Becoming Jesus: A Theological Interpretation of the Synoptic Gospels*, Washington, D.C.: Catholic University of America Press.

Wellum, S. J. (2016), *God the Son Incarnate: The Doctrine of Christ*, Wheaton: Crossway.

Wenham, D. (2018), *From Good News to Gospels: Rediscovering the Oral Tradition About Jesus*, Grand Rapids: Eerdmans.

Wenham, J. (1994), *Christ and the Bible*, 3rd edn, Eugene: Wipf & Stock, repr. 2009.

Westermann, C. (ed.) (1969), *Essays on Old Testament Hermeneutics*, Richmond: John Knox.

Williams, R. (2004), 'Historical Criticism and Sacred Text', in D. F. Ford and G. Stanton (eds.), *Reading Texts, Seeking Wisdom: Scripture and Theology*, Grand Rapids: Eerdmans, 217–228.

Witherington III, B. (1995), *John's Wisdom*, Louisville: Westminster John Knox.

Woodbridge, J. D. (1982), *Biblical Authority: A Critique of the Rogers/McKim Proposal*, Grand Rapids: Zondervan.

—— (1986), 'Some Misconceptions of the Impact of the "Enlightenment" on the Doctrine of Scripture', in D. A. Carson and J. D. Woodbridge (eds.), *Hermeneutics, Authority, and Canon*, Grand Rapids: Zondervan, 237–270.

—— (2016), 'German Pietism and Scriptural Authority: The Question of Biblical Inerrancy', in D. A. Carson (ed.), *The Enduring Authority of the Christian Scriptures*, Grand Rapids: Eerdmans, 137–170.

Work, T. (2002), *Living and Active: Scripture in the Economy of Salvation*, Grand Rapids: Eerdmans.

Wright, N. T. (1992), *The Climax of the Covenant: Christ and the Law in Pauline Theology*, Minneapolis: Fortress.

—— (1997), *Jesus and the Victory of God*, 6th edn, Minneapolis: Fortress.

—— (2015), *The Challenge of Jesus: Rediscovering Who Jesus Was and Is*, Downers Grove: InterVarsity Press.

Wright IV, W. M., and F. Martin (2019), *Encountering the Living God in Scripture: Theological and Philosophical Principles for Interpretation*, Grand Rapids: Baker.

Young, E. J. (1957), *Thy Word Is Truth: Some Thoughts on the Biblical Doctrine of Inspiration*, Edinburgh: The Banner of Truth Trust.

—— (1985), *My Servants the Prophets*, Grand Rapids: Eerdmans.

Index of authors

Index of Scripture references

Index of Scripture references

Titles in this series:

An index of Scripture references for all the volumes may be found at
http://www.thegospelcoalition.org/resources/nsbt.